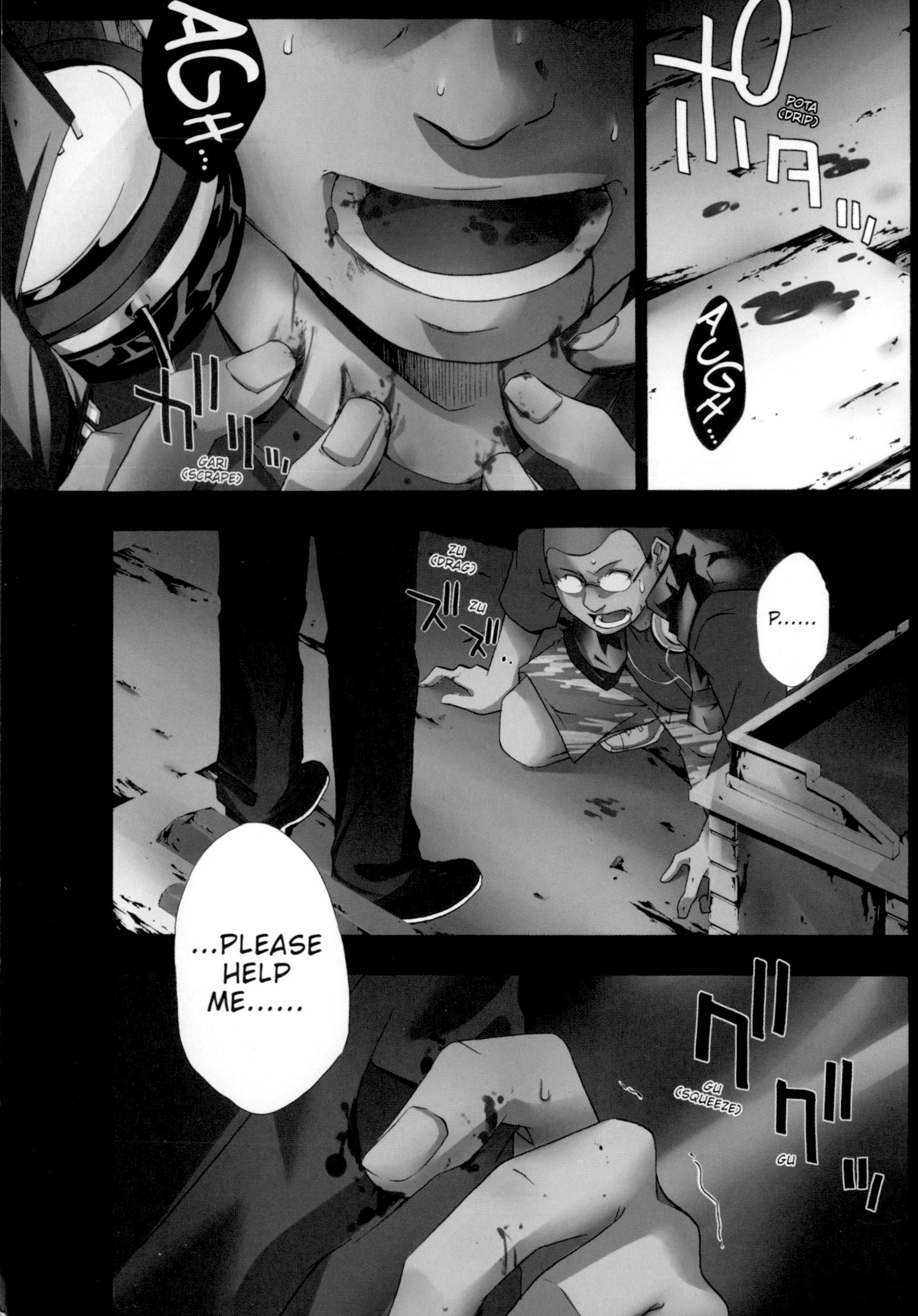
POTA
(DRIP)
AUGH...
AGH...
GARI
(SCRAPE)
P......
ZU
(DRAG)
ZU
...PLEASE HELP ME......
GU
(SQUEEZE)
GU

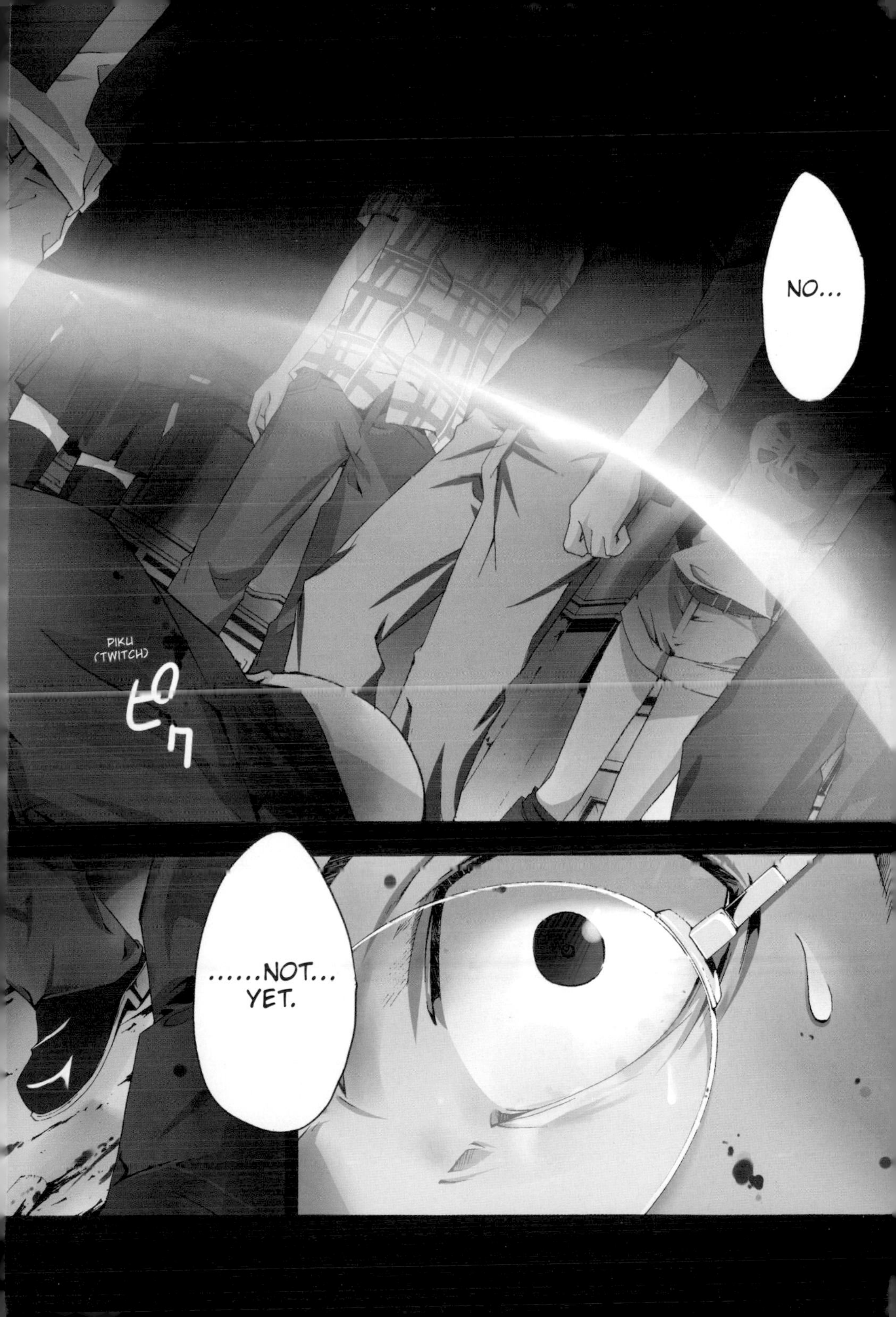
NO...
PIKU (TWITCH)
ピク
......NOT... YET.

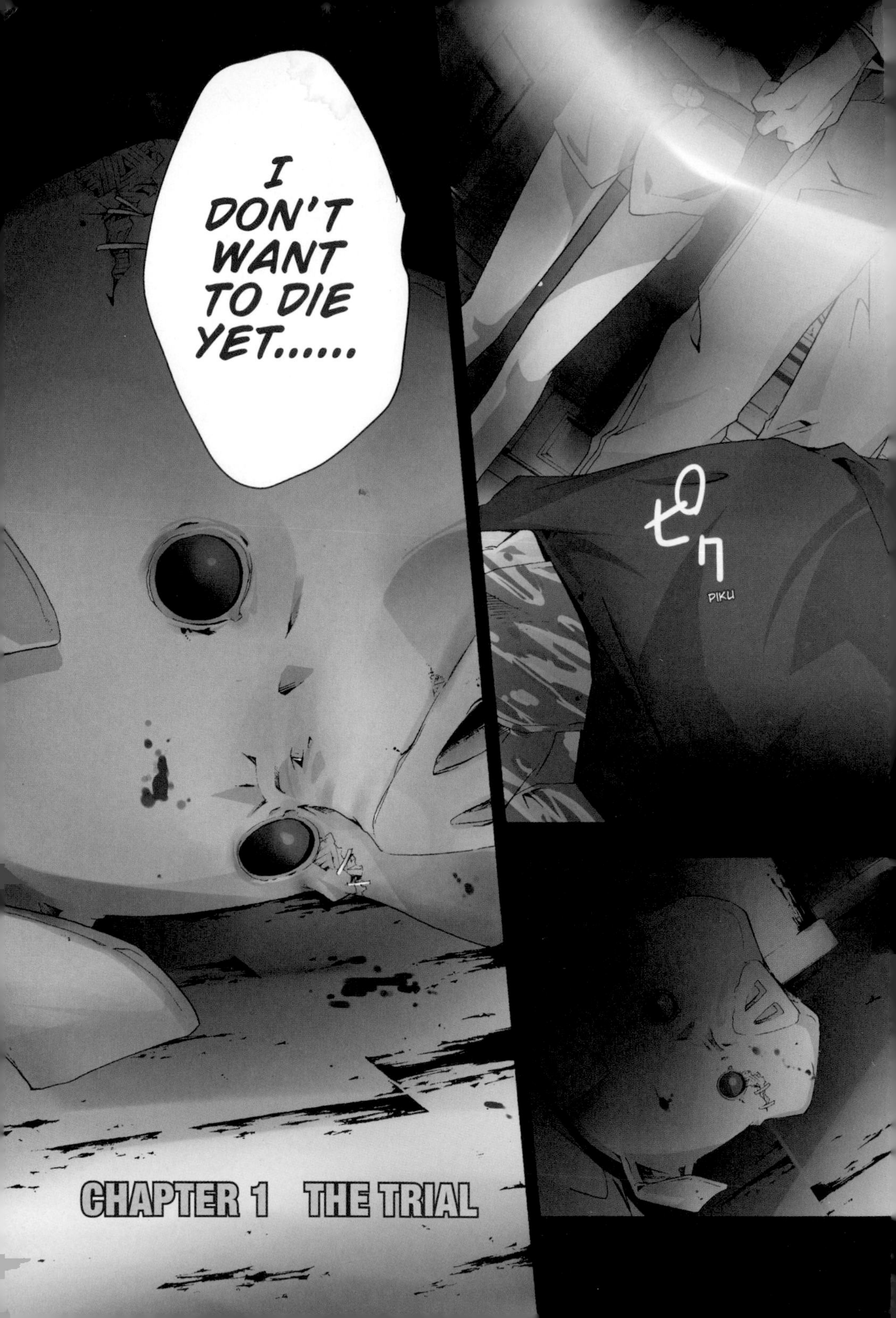
ピク
PIKU
I DON'T WANT TO DIE YET......
CHAPTER 1 THE TRIAL

JUDGE

YOSHIKI TONOGAI

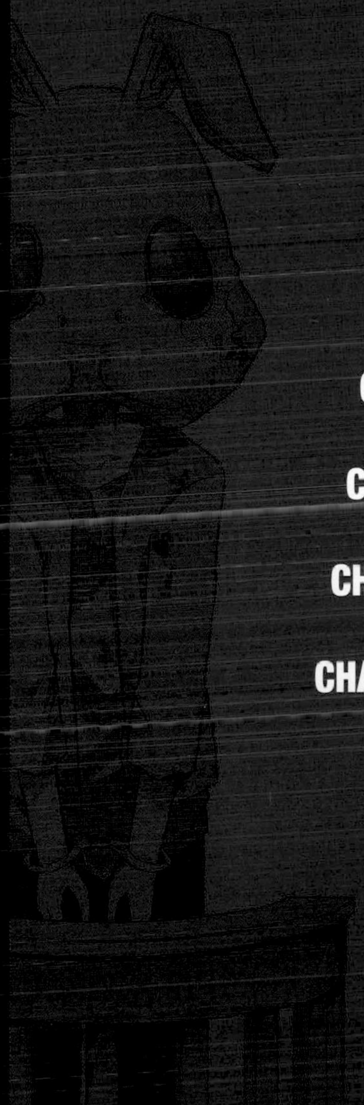

1

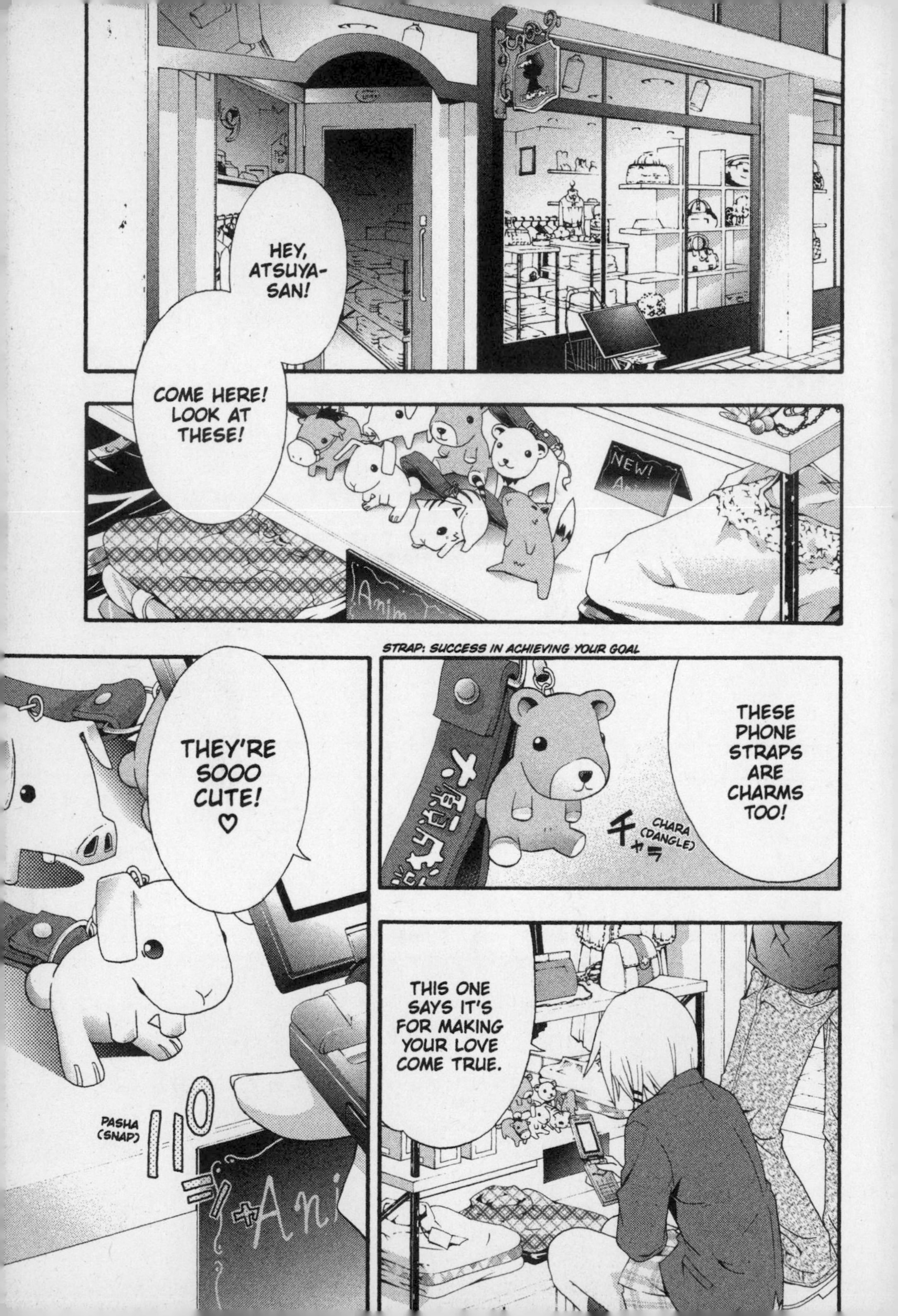
HEY, ATSUYA-SAN!
COME HERE! LOOK AT THESE!
STRAP: SUCCESS IN ACHIEVING YOUR GOAL
THESE PHONE STRAPS ARE CHARMS TOO!
チャラ
CHARA (DANGLE)
THIS ONE SAYS IT'S FOR MAKING YOUR LOVE COME TRUE.
THEY'RE SOOO CUTE! ♡
PASHA (SNAP)

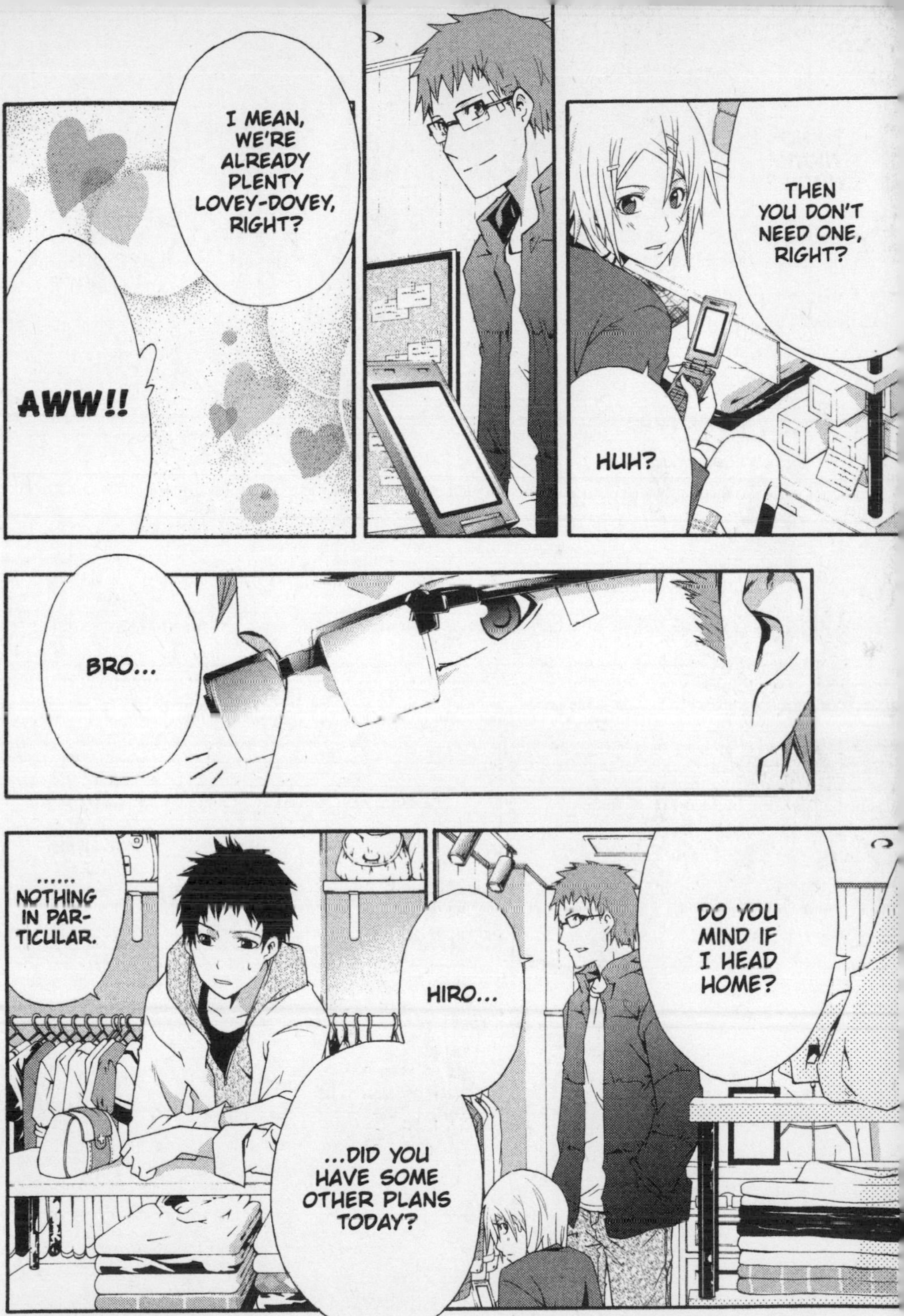
THEN YOU DON'T NEED ONE, RIGHT?
HUH?
I MEAN, WE'RE ALREADY PLENTY LOVEY-DOVEY, RIGHT?
AWW!!
BRO...
DO YOU MIND IF I HEAD HOME?
HIRO...
...DID YOU HAVE SOME OTHER PLANS TODAY?
...... NOTHING IN PAR-TICULAR.

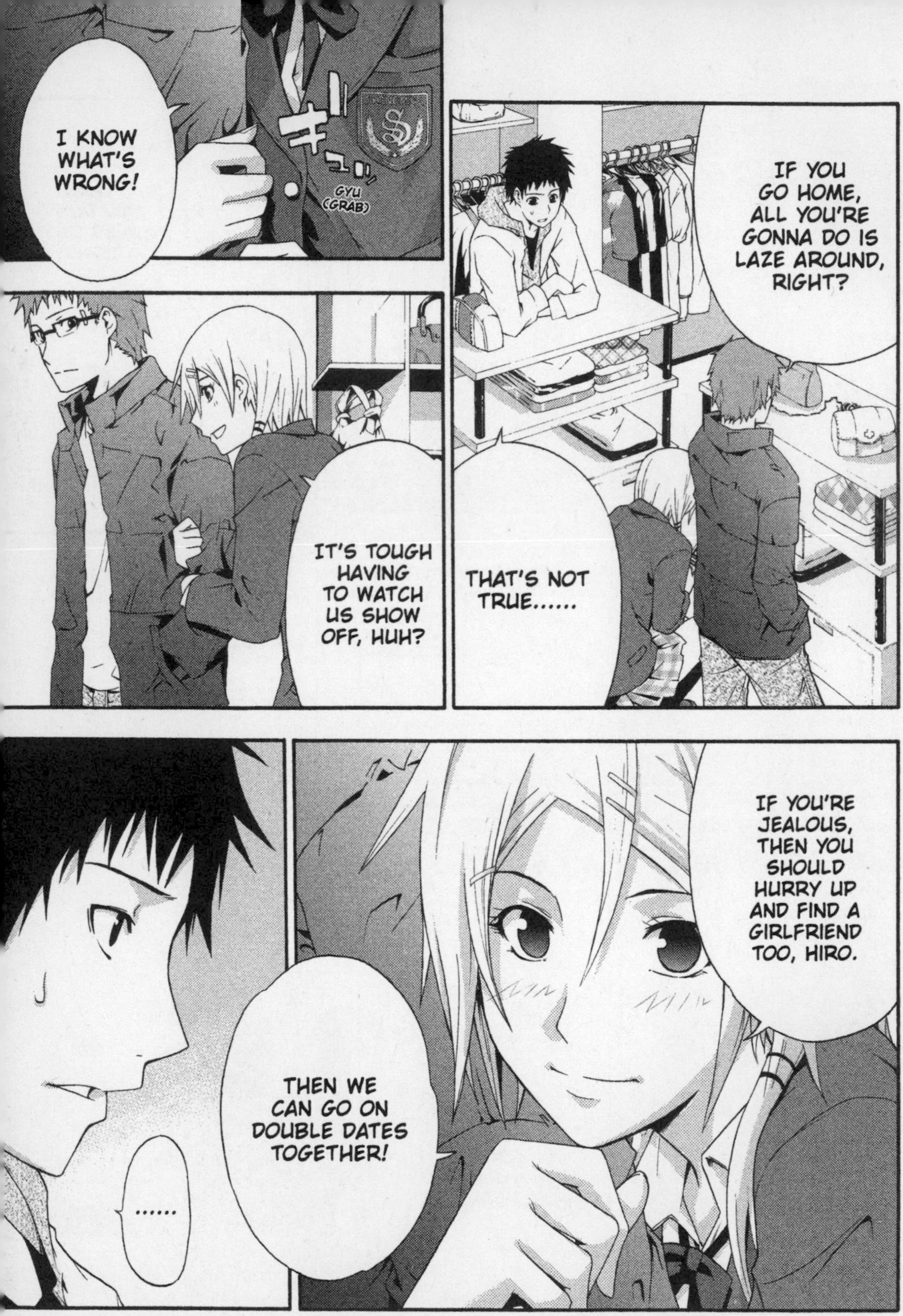
IF YOU GO HOME, ALL YOU'RE GONNA DO IS LAZE AROUND, RIGHT?
THAT'S NOT TRUE......
I KNOW WHAT'S WRONG!
GYU (GRAB)
IT'S TOUGH HAVING TO WATCH US SHOW OFF, HUH?
IF YOU'RE JEALOUS, THEN YOU SHOULD HURRY UP AND FIND A GIRLFRIEND TOO, HIRO.
THEN WE CAN GO ON DOUBLE DATES TOGETHER!
......

SIGN: ENTRANCE

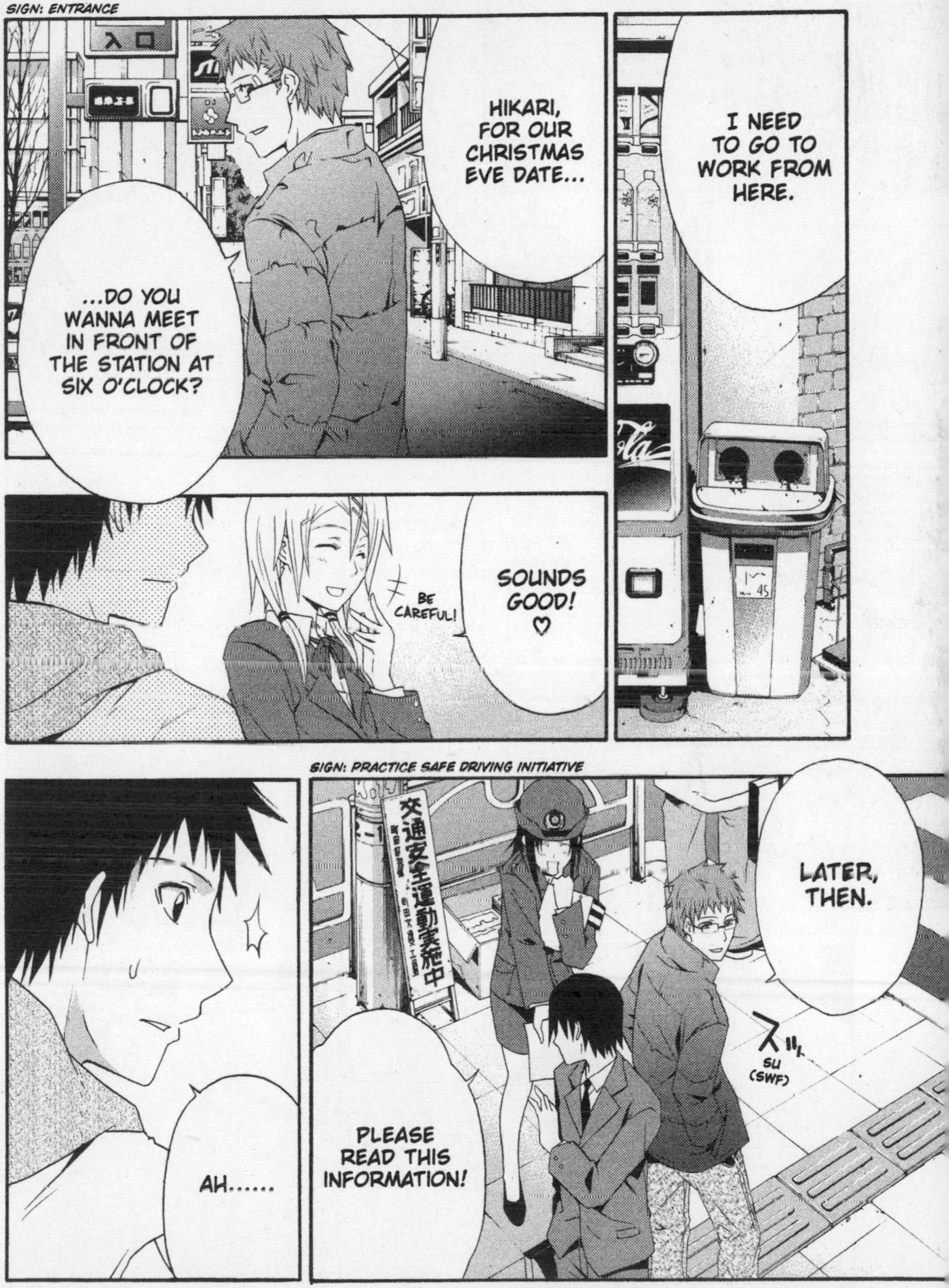
I NEED TO GO TO WORK FROM HERE.
HIKARI, FOR OUR CHRISTMAS EVE DATE...
...DO YOU WANNA MEET IN FRONT OF THE STATION AT SIX O'CLOCK?
SOUNDS GOOD! ♡
BE CAREFUL!
入口
交通安全運動実施中
LATER, THEN.
スッ
SU (SWF)
PLEASE READ THIS INFORMATION!
AH......

SIGN: PRACTICE SAFE DRIVING INITIATIVE

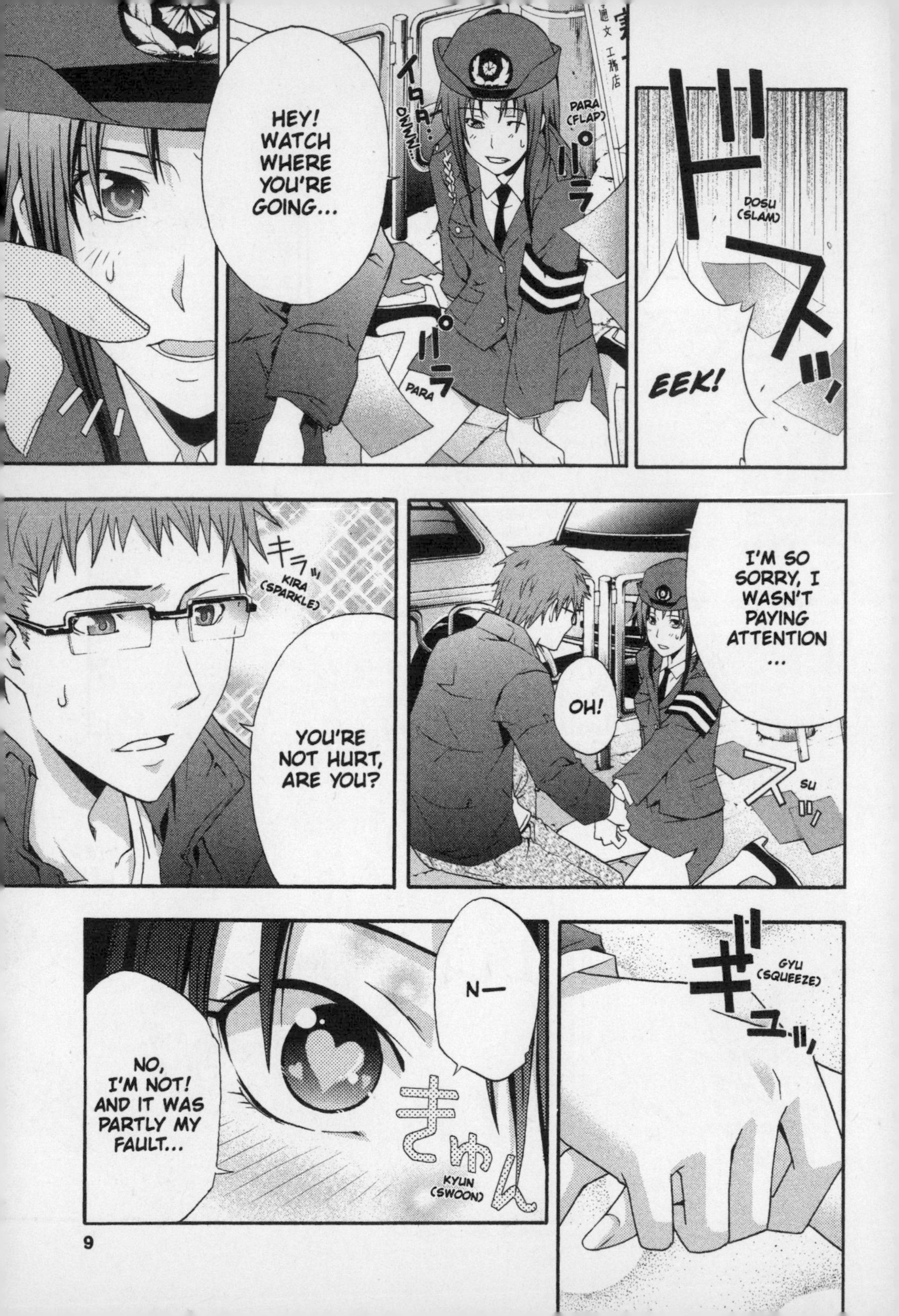
ドスッ
DOSU (SLAM)
EEK!
HEY! WATCH WHERE YOU'RE GOING...
イタタ…
OWWW...
パラ
PARA (FLAP)
パラ
PARA
I'M SO SORRY, I WASN'T PAYING ATTENTION ...
OH!
スッ
SU
キラッ
KIRA (SPARKLE)
YOU'RE NOT HURT, ARE YOU?
ギュッ
GYU (SQUEEZE)
N—
NO, I'M NOT! AND IT WAS PARTLY MY FAULT...
きゅん
KYUN (SWOON)

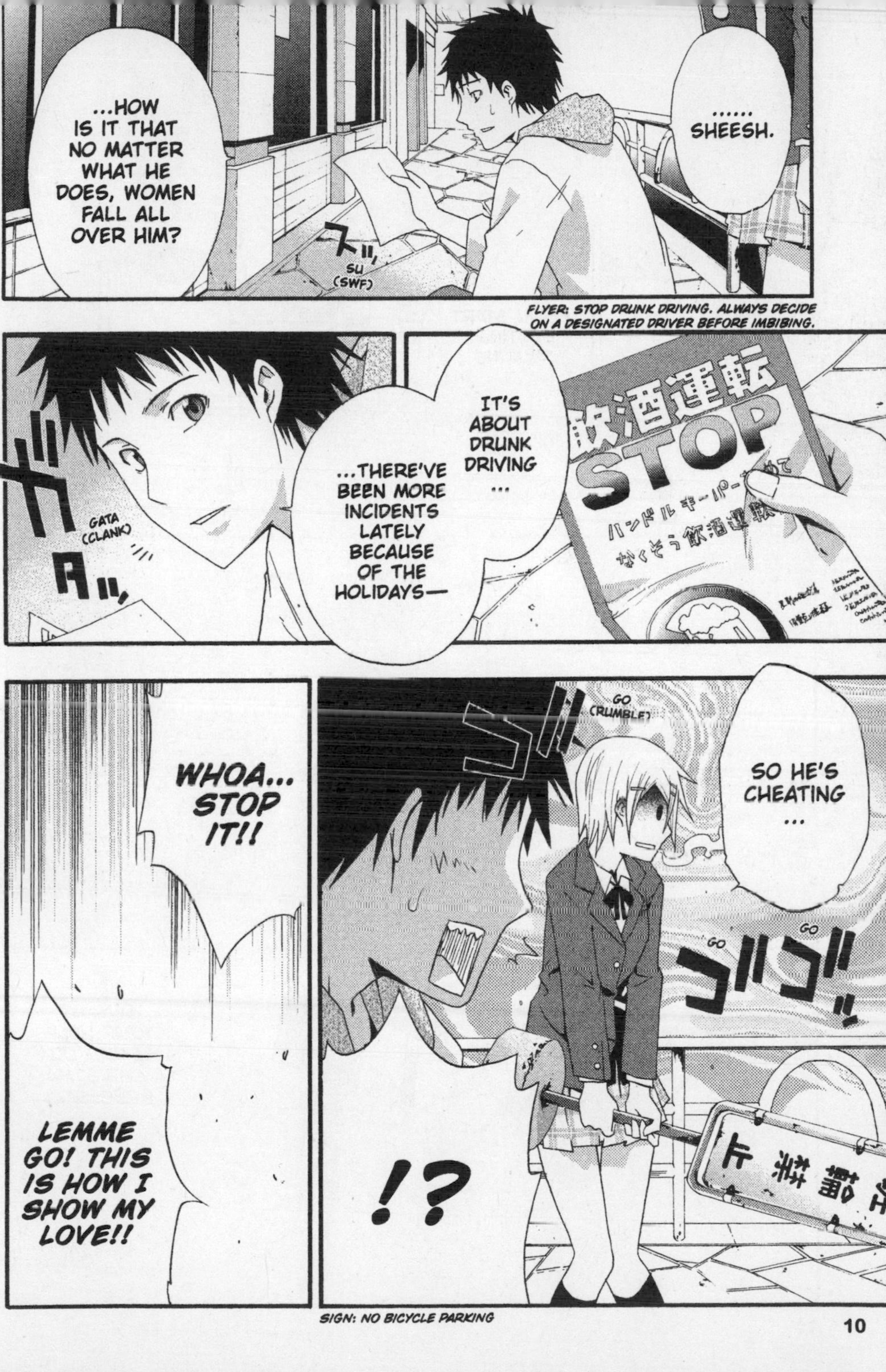

......
SHEESH.
...HOW IS IT THAT NO MATTER WHAT HE DOES, WOMEN FALL ALL OVER HIM?
SU (SWF)
飲酒運転
STOP
ハンドルキーパー決めて
なくそう飲酒運転
IT'S ABOUT DRUNK DRIVING...
...THERE'VE BEEN MORE INCIDENTS LATELY BECAUSE OF THE HOLIDAYS—
GATA (CLANK)
SO HE'S CHEATING...
GO (RUMBLE)
GO GO
!?
WHOA... STOP IT!!
LEMME GO! THIS IS HOW I SHOW MY LOVE!!

FLYER: STOP DRUNK DRIVING. ALWAYS DECIDE ON A DESIGNATED DRIVER BEFORE IMBIBING.

SIGN: NO BICYCLE PARKING

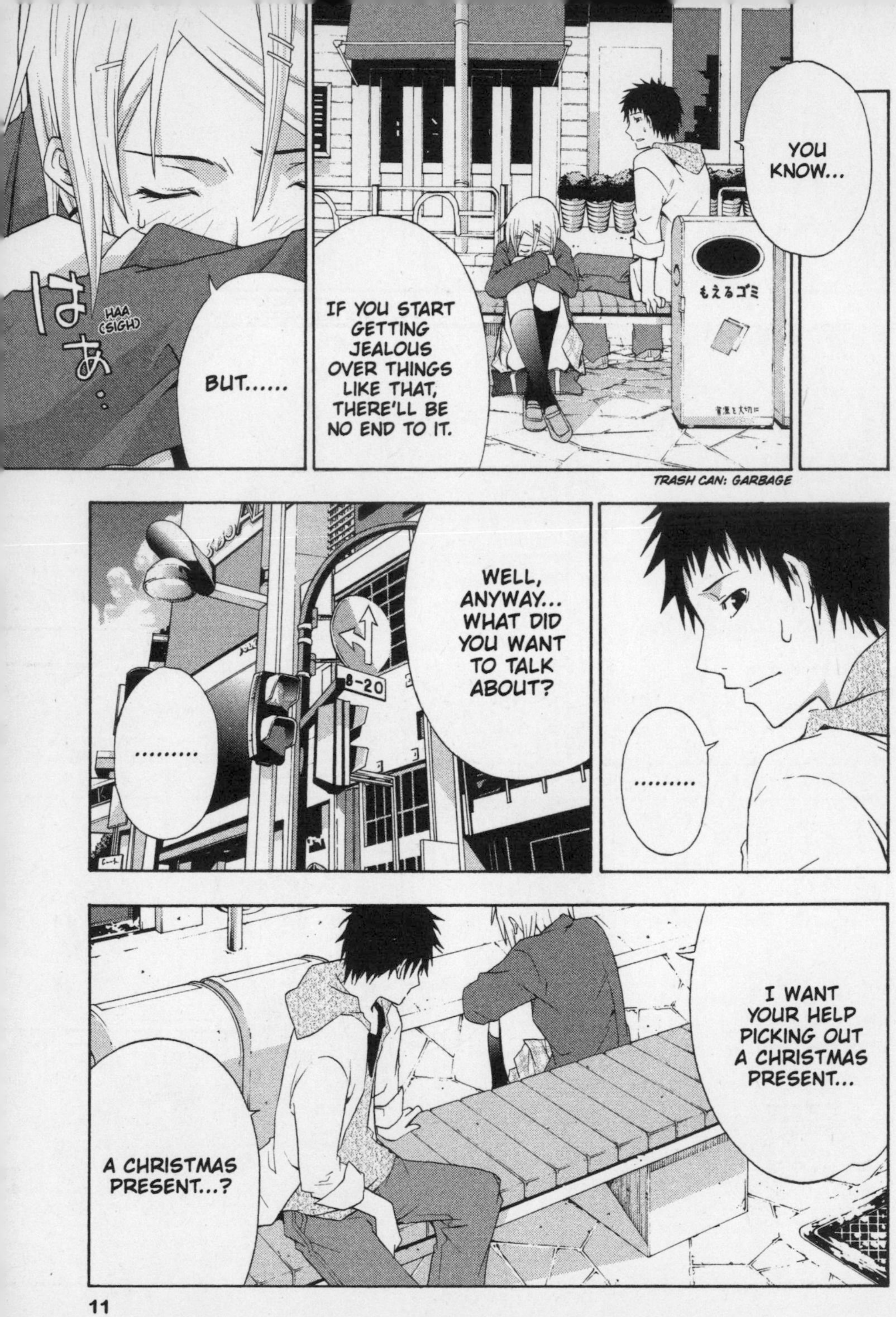
YOU KNOW...
IF YOU START GETTING JEALOUS OVER THINGS LIKE THAT, THERE'LL BE NO END TO IT.
もえるゴミ
TRASH CAN: GARBAGE
はぁ…
HAA (SIGH)
BUT......
....
WELL, ANYWAY... WHAT DID YOU WANT TO TALK ABOUT?
8-20
....
I WANT YOUR HELP PICKING OUT A CHRISTMAS PRESENT...
A CHRISTMAS PRESENT...?

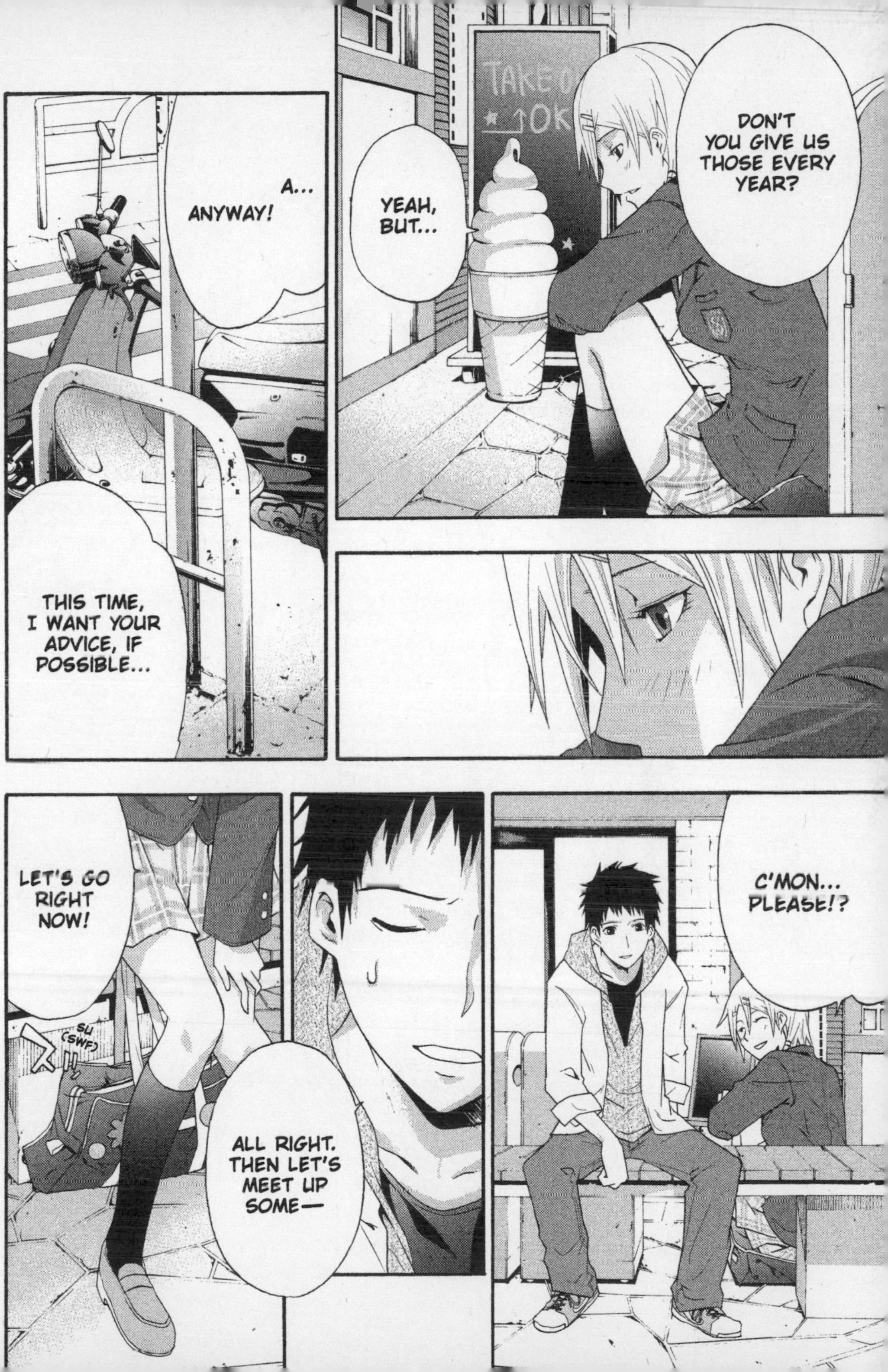
DON'T YOU GIVE US THOSE EVERY YEAR?
YEAH, BUT...
A... ANYWAY!
THIS TIME, I WANT YOUR ADVICE, IF POSSIBLE...
C'MON... PLEASE!?
ALL RIGHT. THEN LET'S MEET UP SOME—
LET'S GO RIGHT NOW!
SU (SWF)

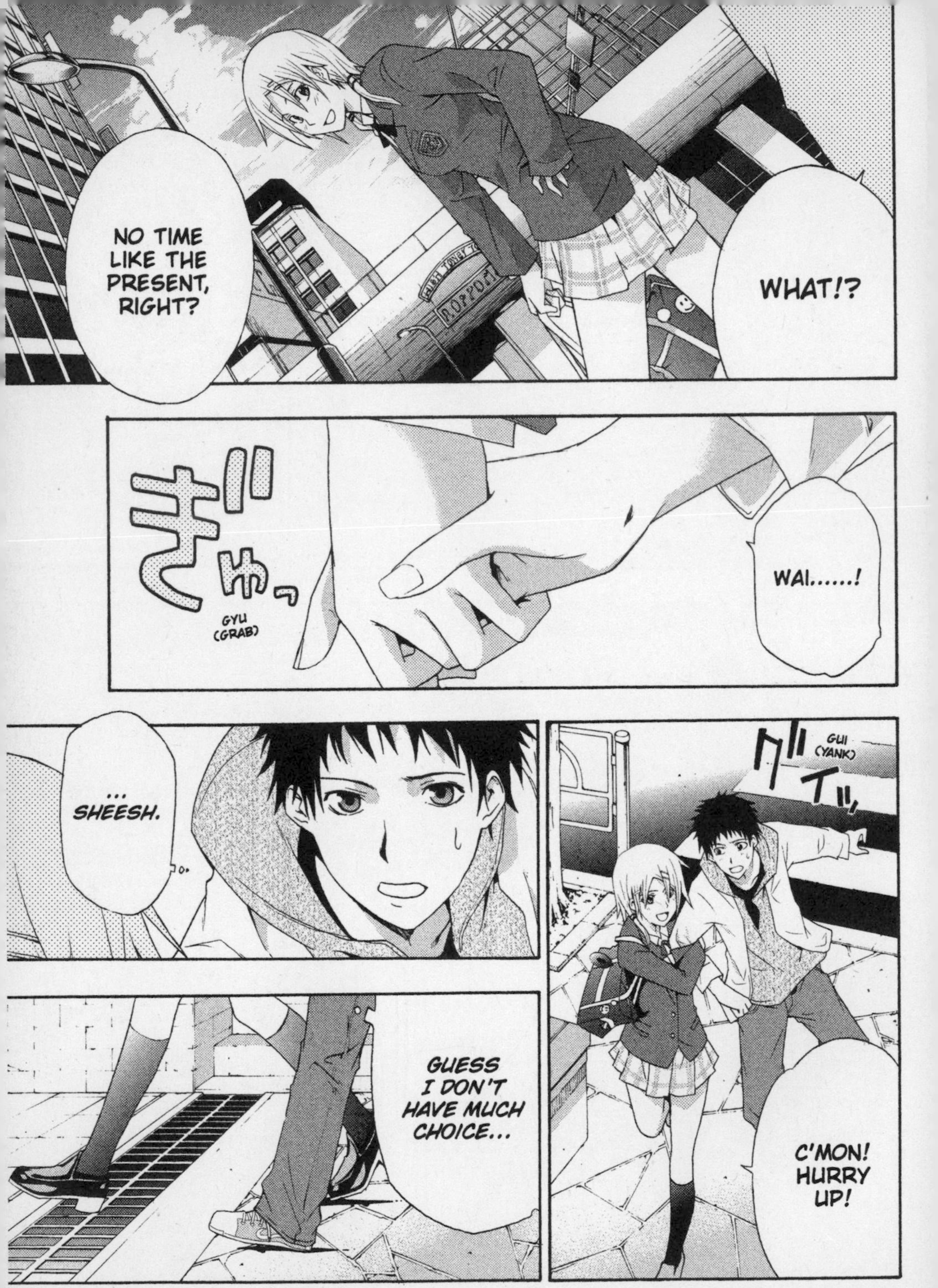
NO TIME LIKE THE PRESENT, RIGHT?
WHAT!?
WAI......!
ぎゅっ
GYU (GRAB)
グイッ
GUI (YANK)
C'MON! HURRY UP!
... SHEESH.
GUESS I DON'T HAVE MUCH CHOICE...

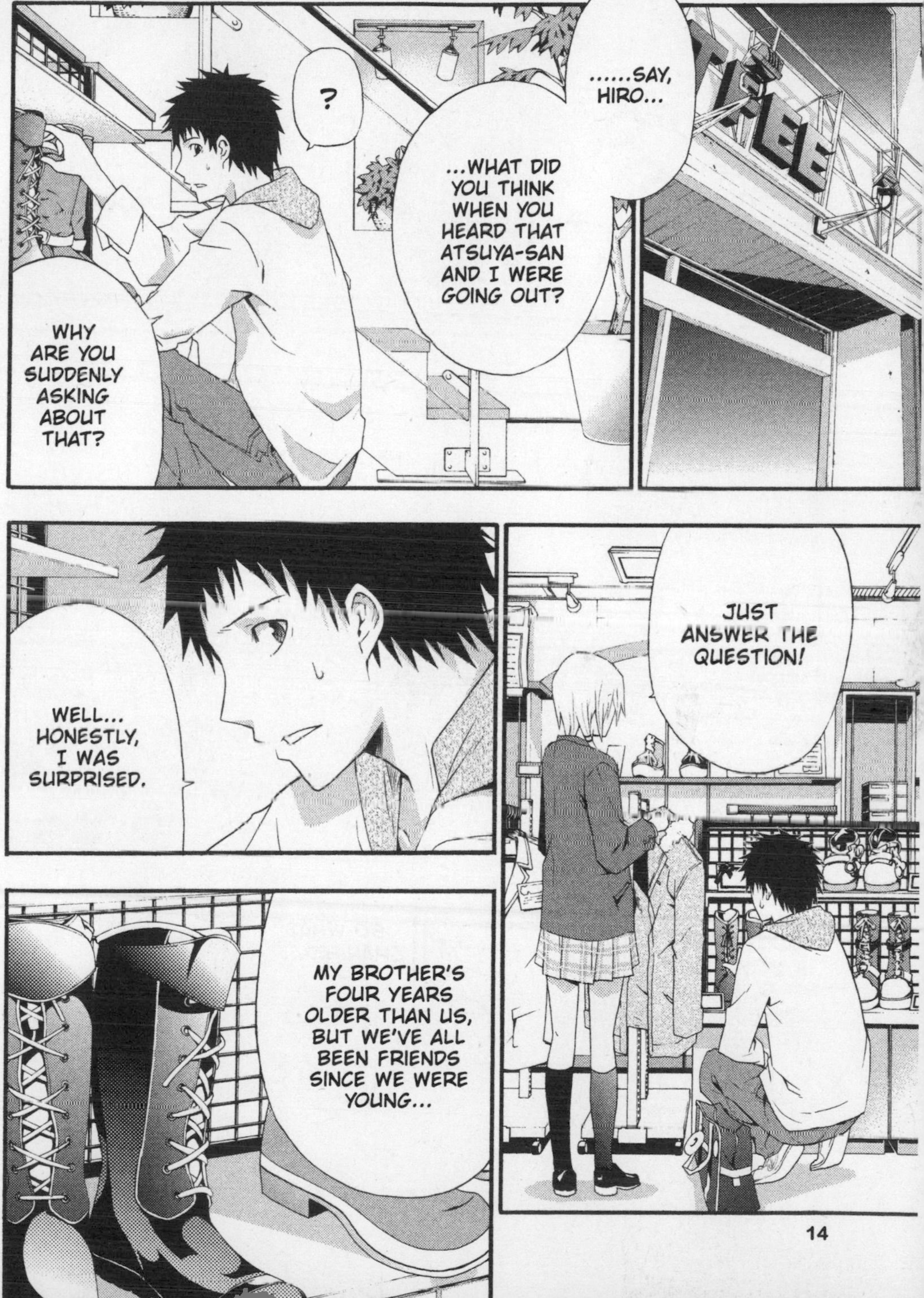
......SAY, HIRO...
...WHAT DID YOU THINK WHEN YOU HEARD THAT ATSUYA-SAN AND I WERE GOING OUT?
?
WHY ARE YOU SUDDENLY ASKING ABOUT THAT?
JUST ANSWER THE QUESTION!
WELL... HONESTLY, I WAS SURPRISED.
MY BROTHER'S FOUR YEARS OLDER THAN US, BUT WE'VE ALL BEEN FRIENDS SINCE WE WERE YOUNG...

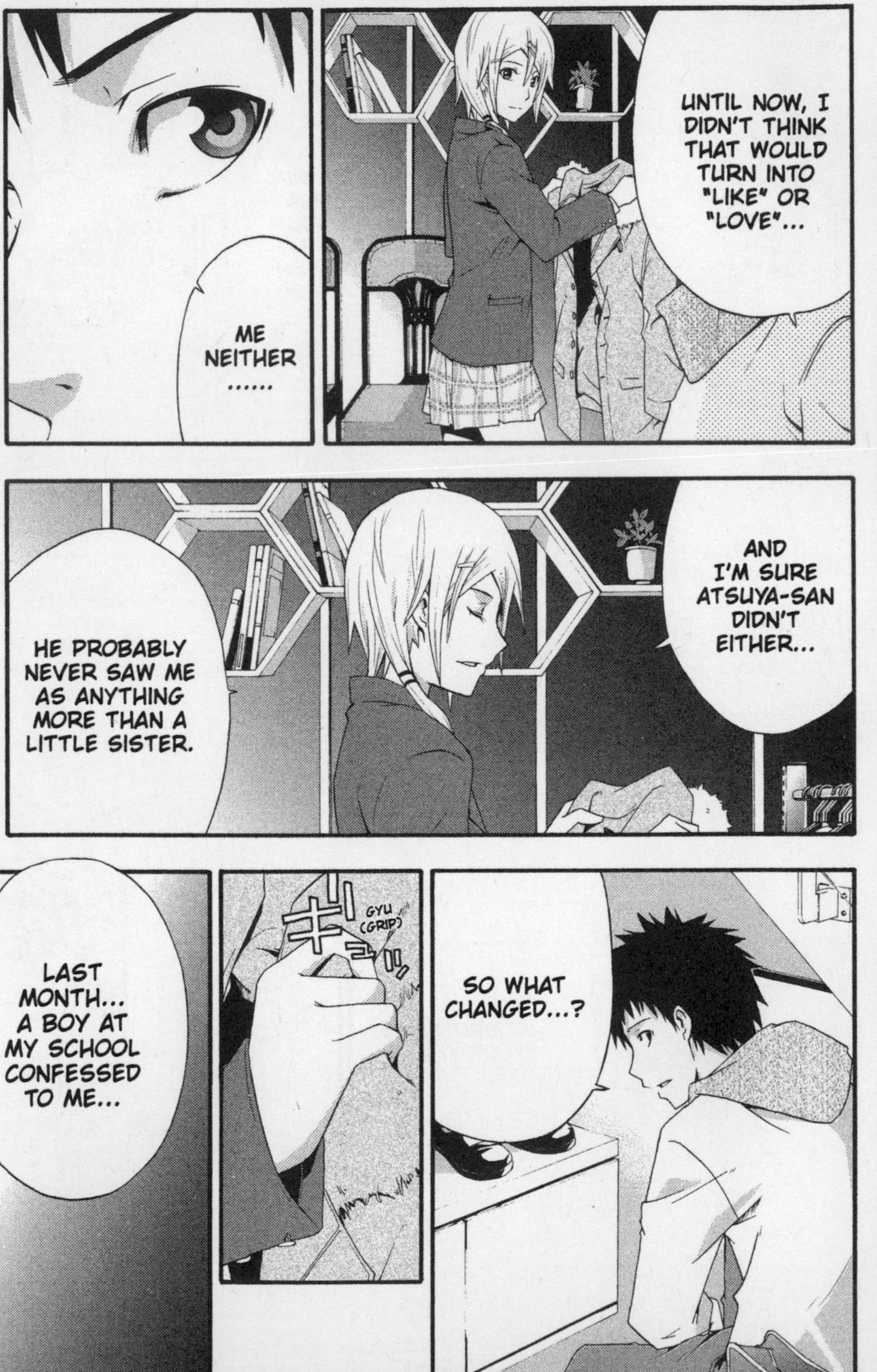
UNTIL NOW, I DIDN'T THINK THAT WOULD TURN INTO "LIKE" OR "LOVE"...
ME NEITHER ......
AND I'M SURE ATSUYA-SAN DIDN'T EITHER...
HE PROBABLY NEVER SAW ME AS ANYTHING MORE THAN A LITTLE SISTER.
SO WHAT CHANGED...?
GYU (GRIP)
LAST MONTH... A BOY AT MY SCHOOL CONFESSED TO ME...

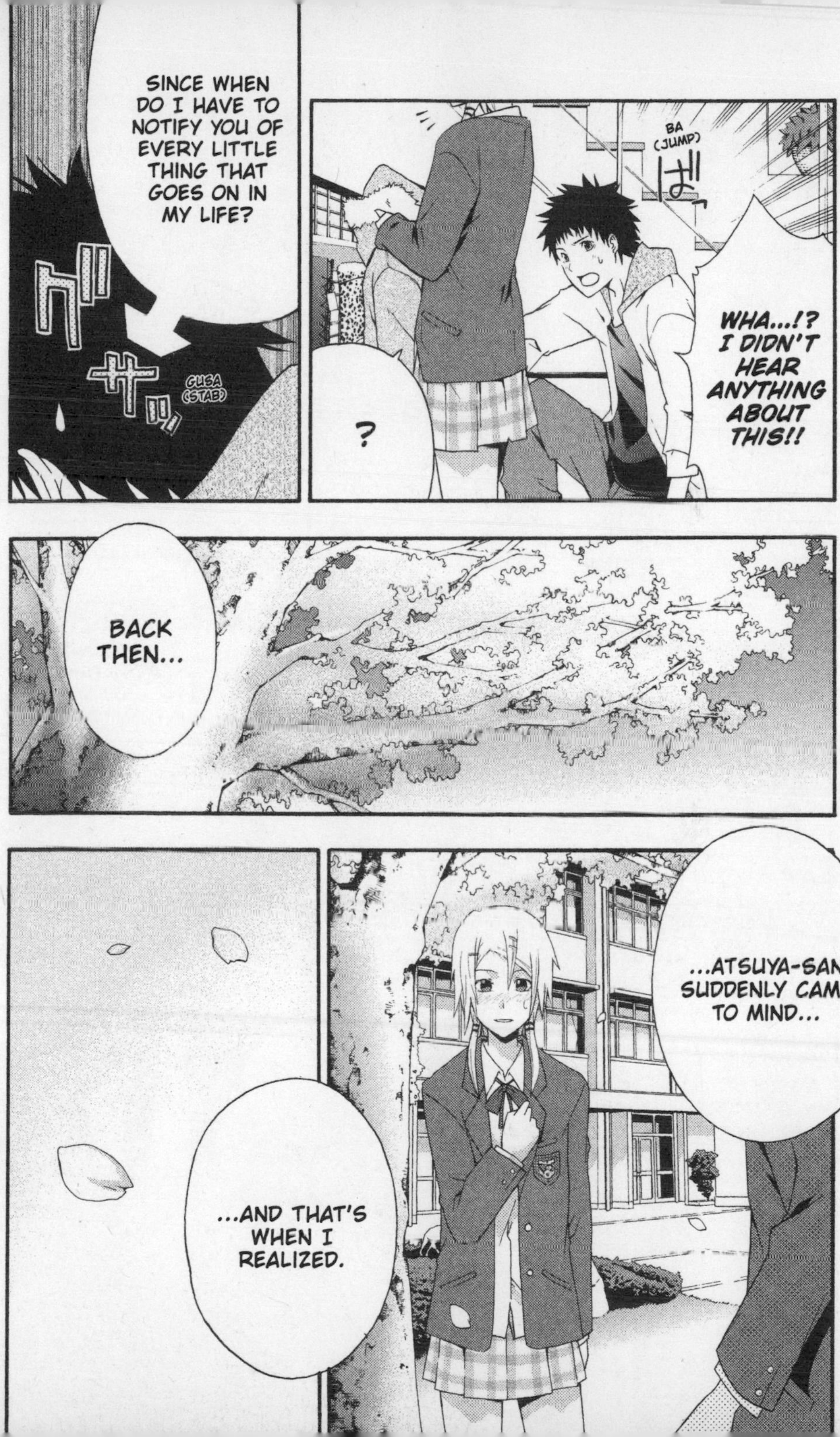
BA (JUMP)
ぱっ
WHA...!? I DIDN'T HEAR ANYTHING ABOUT THIS!!
?
SINCE WHEN DO I HAVE TO NOTIFY YOU OF EVERY LITTLE THING THAT GOES ON IN MY LIFE?
GUSA (STAB)
BACK THEN...
...ATSUYA-SAN SUDDENLY CAME TO MIND...
...AND THAT'S WHEN I REALIZED.

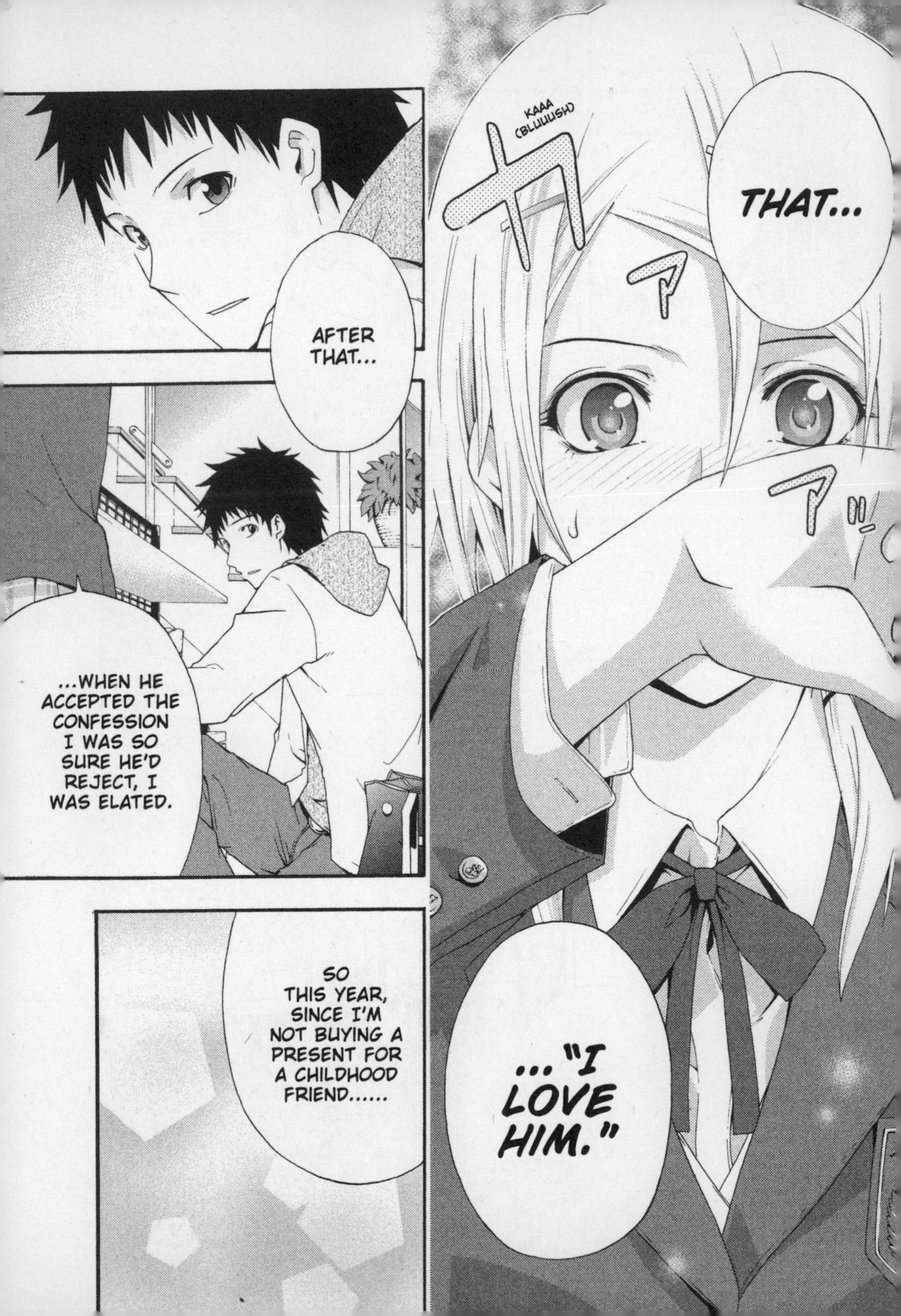
AFTER THAT...
...WHEN HE ACCEPTED THE CONFESSION I WAS SO SURE HE'D REJECT, I WAS ELATED.
SO THIS YEAR, SINCE I'M NOT BUYING A PRESENT FOR A CHILDHOOD FRIEND......
KAAA (BLUUUSH)
THAT...
..."I LOVE HIM."

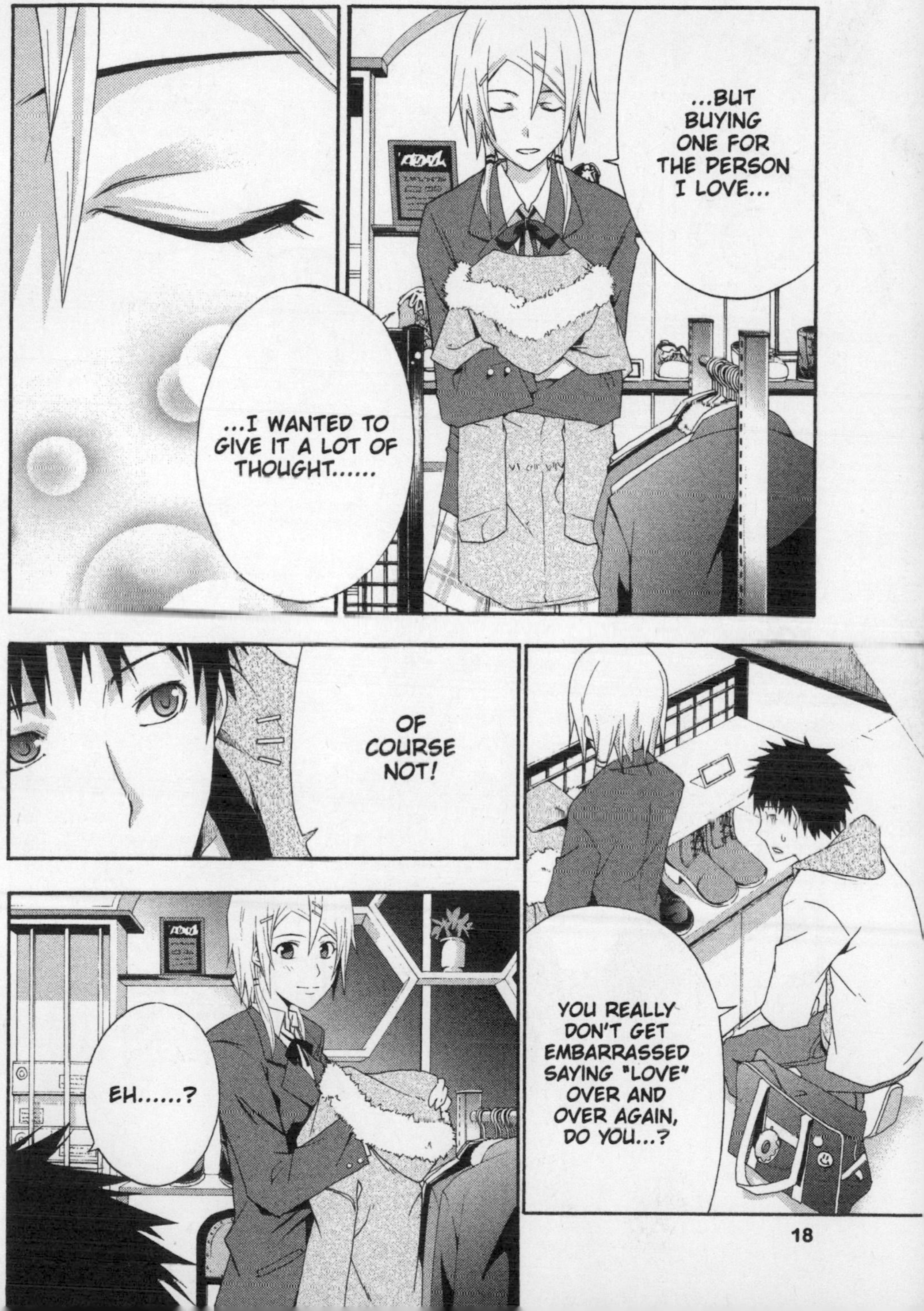
...BUT BUYING ONE FOR THE PERSON I LOVE...
...I WANTED TO GIVE IT A LOT OF THOUGHT......
YOU REALLY DON'T GET EMBARRASSED SAYING "LOVE" OVER AND OVER AGAIN, DO YOU...?
OF COURSE NOT!
EH......?

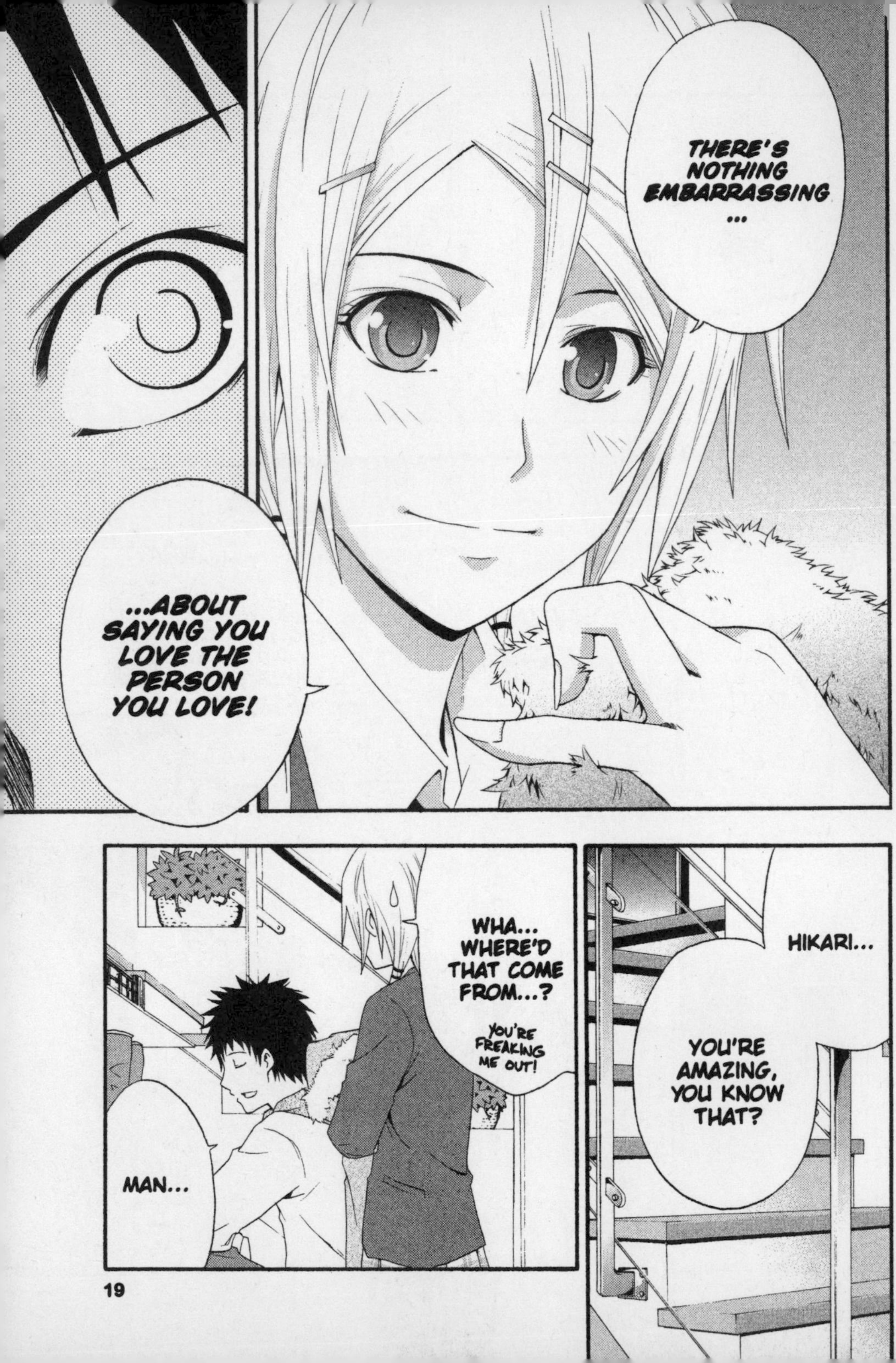
THERE'S NOTHING EMBARRASSING ...
...ABOUT SAYING YOU LOVE THE PERSON YOU LOVE!
HIKARI...
YOU'RE AMAZING, YOU KNOW THAT?
WHA... WHERE'D THAT COME FROM...?
YOU'RE FREAKING ME OUT!
MAN...

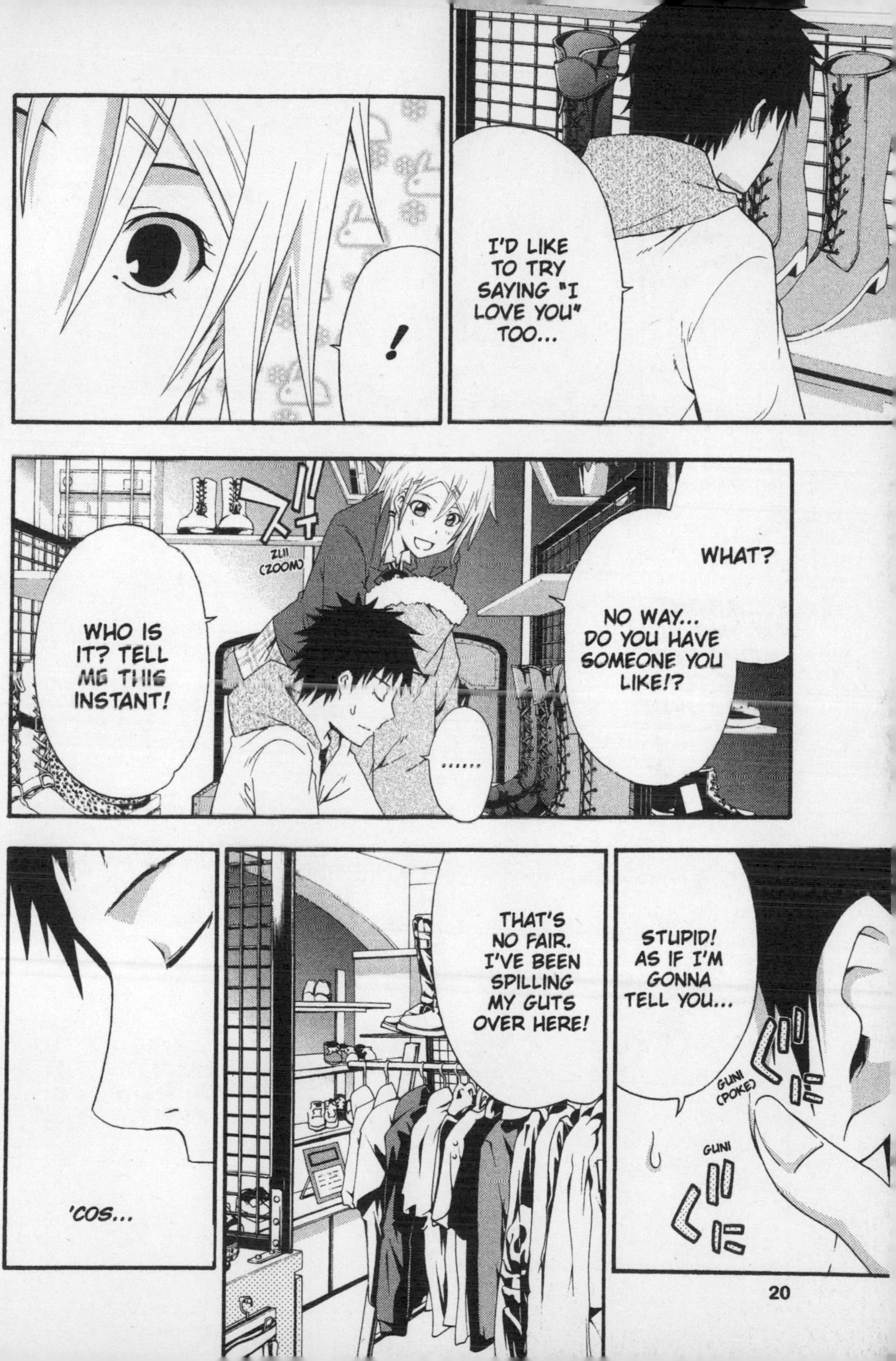
I'D LIKE TO TRY SAYING "I LOVE YOU" TOO...
!
WHAT?
NO WAY... DO YOU HAVE SOMEONE YOU LIKE!?
......
ZUI (ZOOM)
WHO IS IT? TELL ME THIS INSTANT!
STUPID! AS IF I'M GONNA TELL YOU...
GUNI (POKE)
GUNI
THAT'S NO FAIR. I'VE BEEN SPILLING MY GUTS OVER HERE!
'COS...

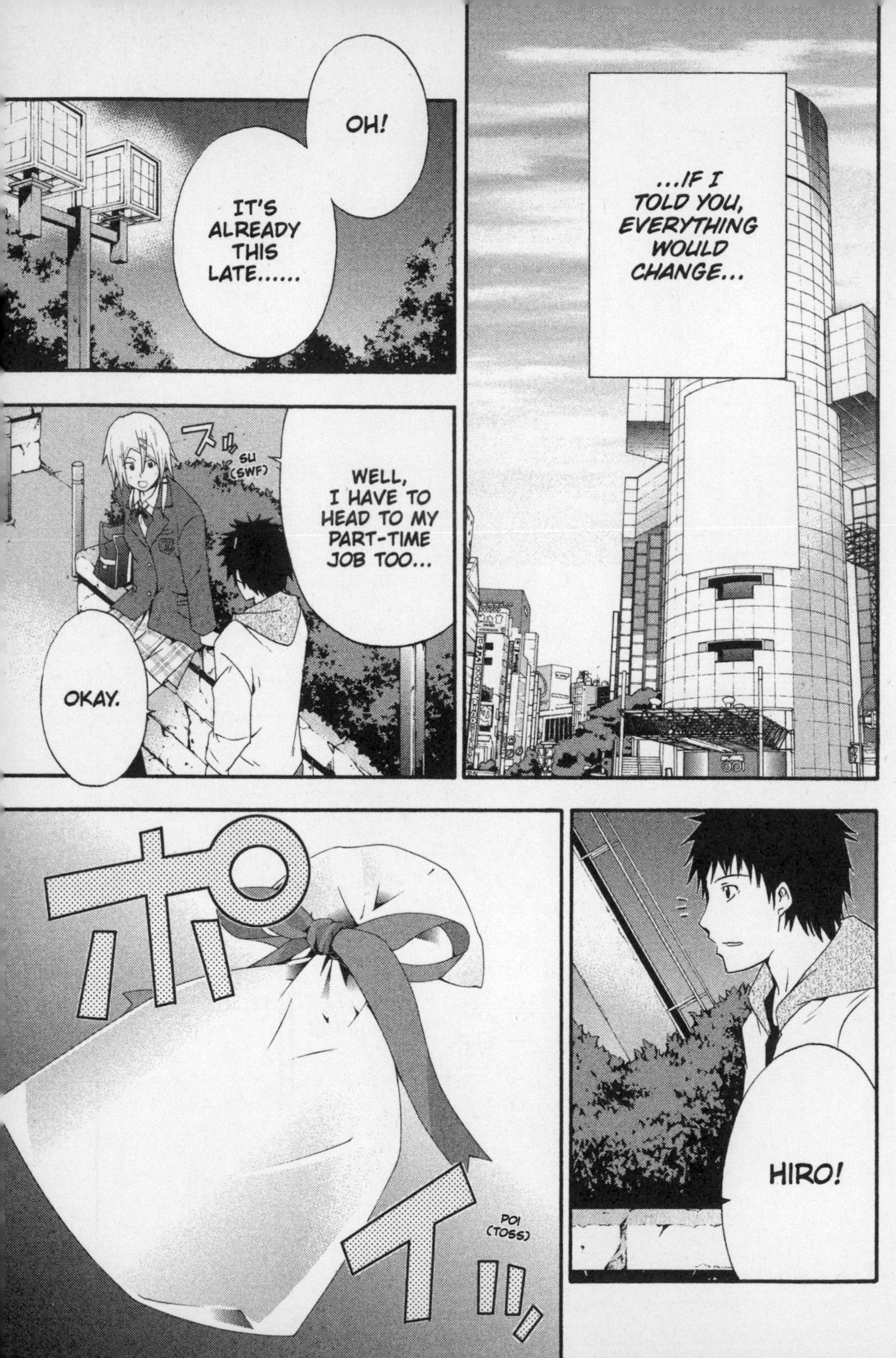
...IF I TOLD YOU, EVERYTHING WOULD CHANGE...
OH!
IT'S ALREADY THIS LATE......
SU (SWF)
WELL, I HAVE TO HEAD TO MY PART-TIME JOB TOO...
OKAY.
HIRO!
POI (TOSS)

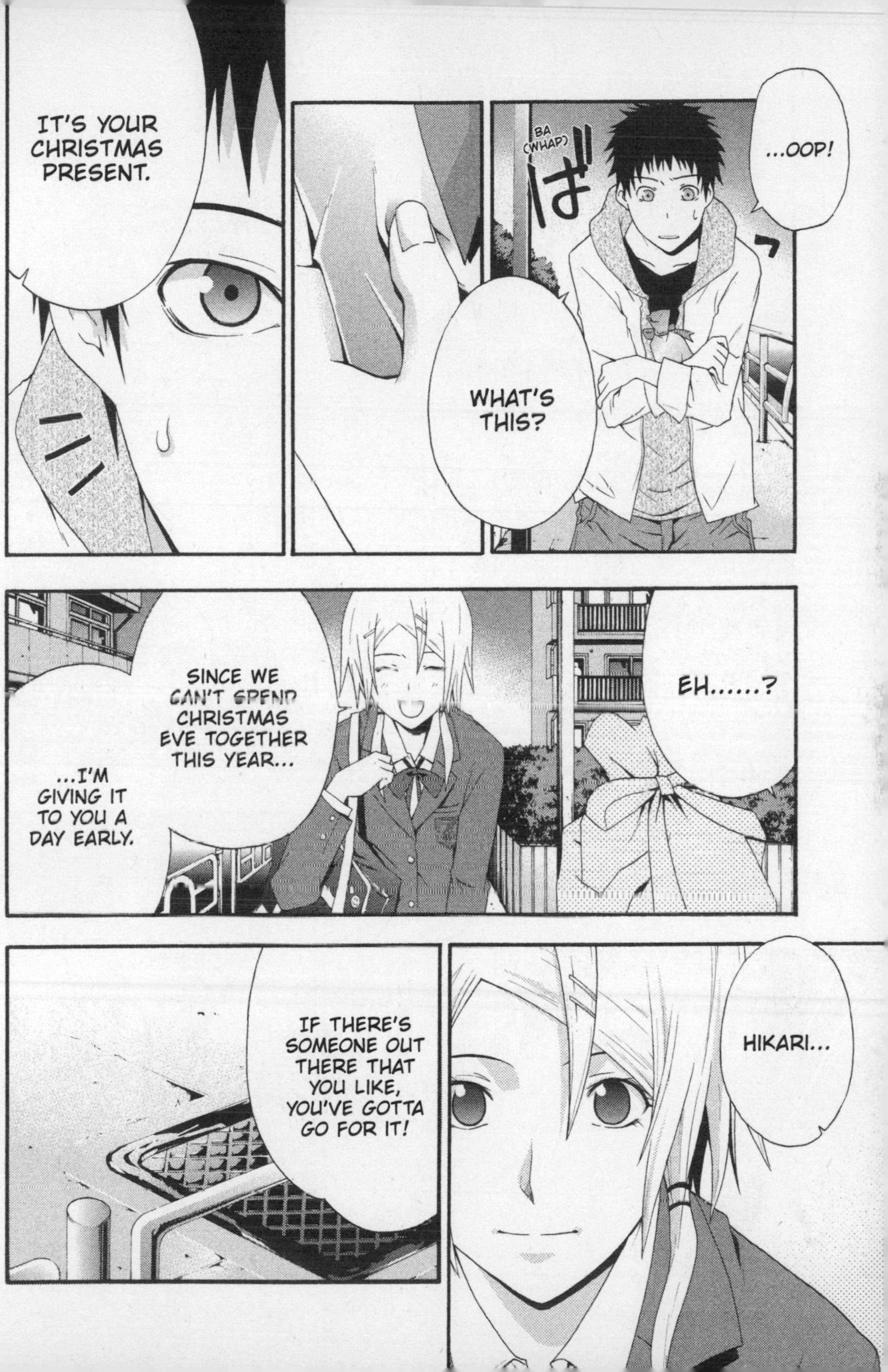
...OOP!
BA (WHAP)
ば
WHAT'S THIS?
IT'S YOUR CHRISTMAS PRESENT.
EH......?
SINCE WE CAN'T SPEND CHRISTMAS EVE TOGETHER THIS YEAR...
...I'M GIVING IT TO YOU A DAY EARLY.
HIKARI...
IF THERE'S SOMEONE OUT THERE THAT YOU LIKE, YOU'VE GOTTA GO FOR IT!

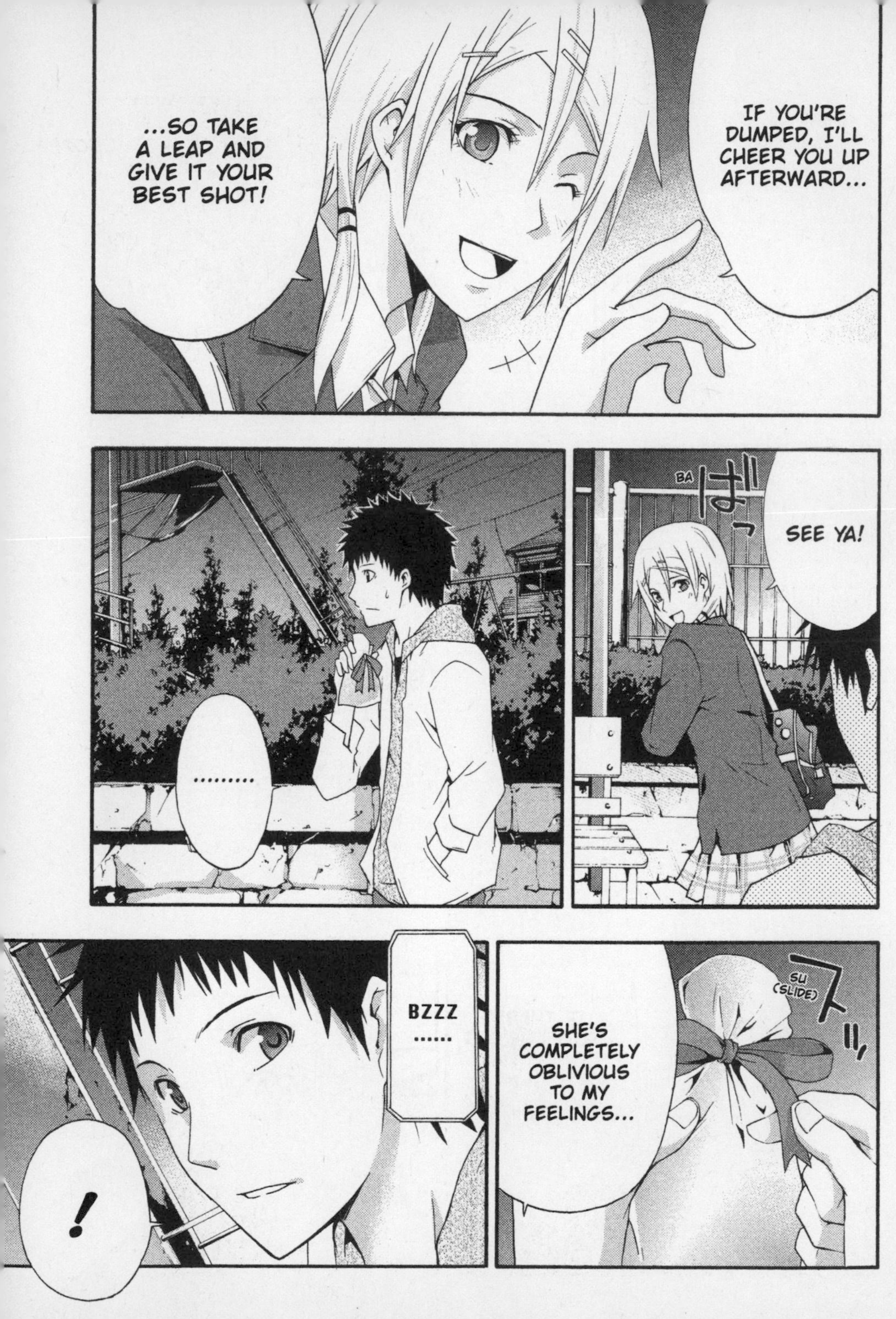
IF YOU'RE DUMPED, I'LL CHEER YOU UP AFTERWARD...
...SO TAKE A LEAP AND GIVE IT YOUR BEST SHOT!
BA ばっ
SEE YA!
....
SU (SLIDE) ス
SHE'S COMPLETELY OBLIVIOUS TO MY FEELINGS...
BZZZ ......
!

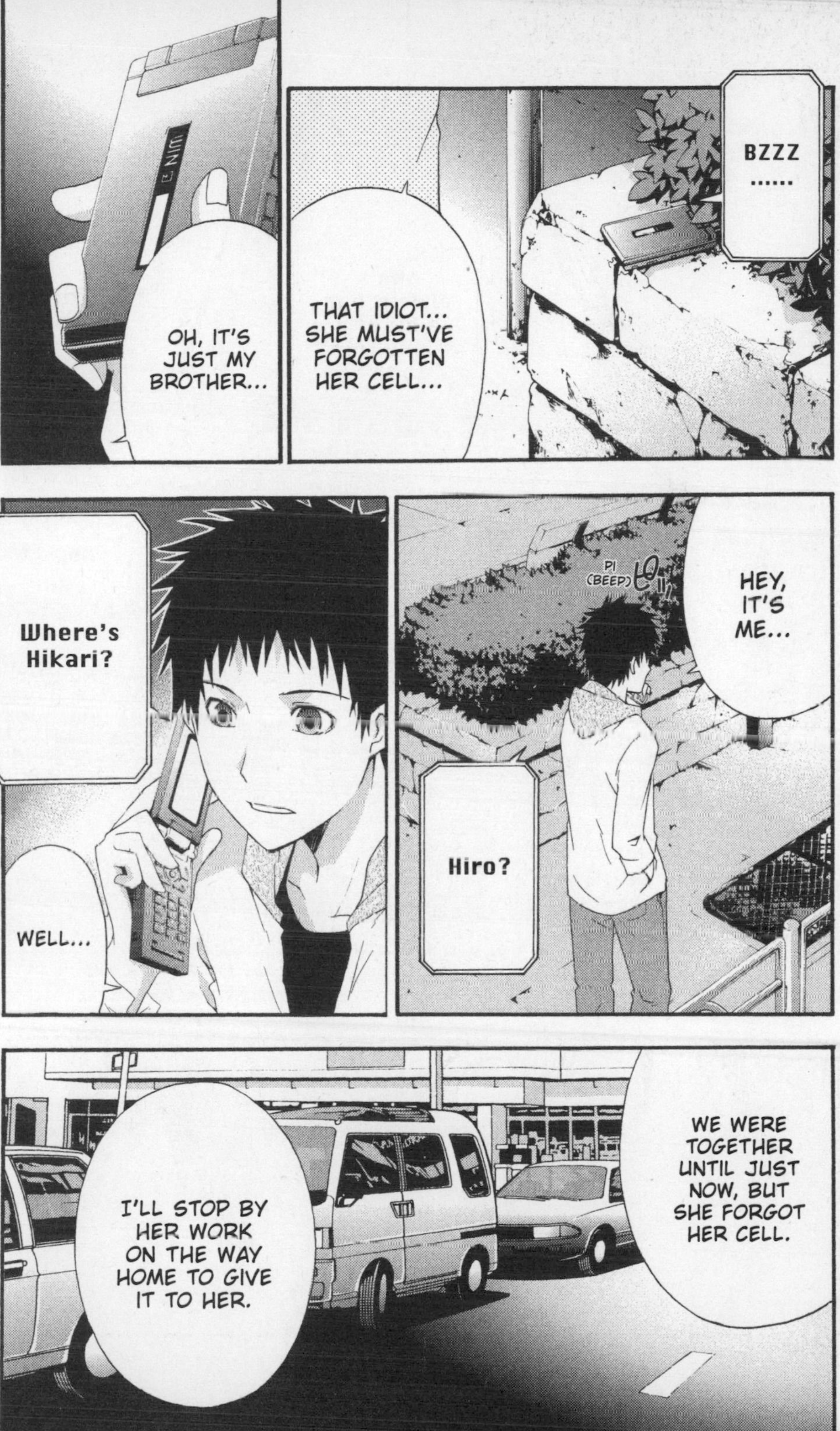
BZZZ ......
THAT IDIOT... SHE MUST'VE FORGOTTEN HER CELL...
OH, IT'S JUST MY BROTHER...
PI (BEEP)
HEY, IT'S ME...
Hiro?
Where's Hikari?
WELL...
WE WERE TOGETHER UNTIL JUST NOW, BUT SHE FORGOT HER CELL.
I'LL STOP BY HER WORK ON THE WAY HOME TO GIVE IT TO HER.

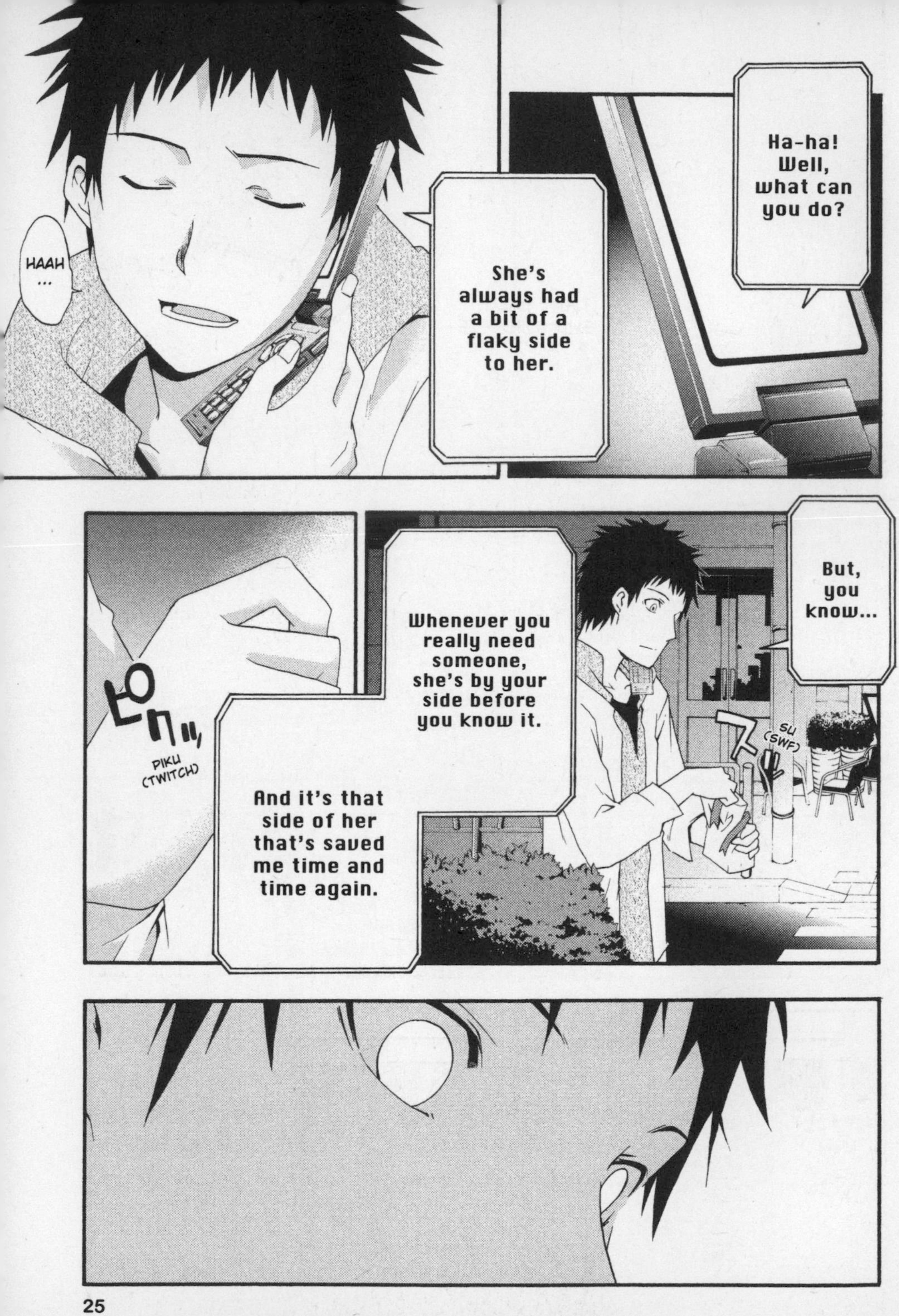
Ha-ha! Well, what can you do?
She's always had a bit of a flaky side to her.
HAAH ...
But, you know...
Whenever you really need someone, she's by your side before you know it.
And it's that side of her that's saved me time and time again.
SU (SWF)
PIKU (TWITCH)

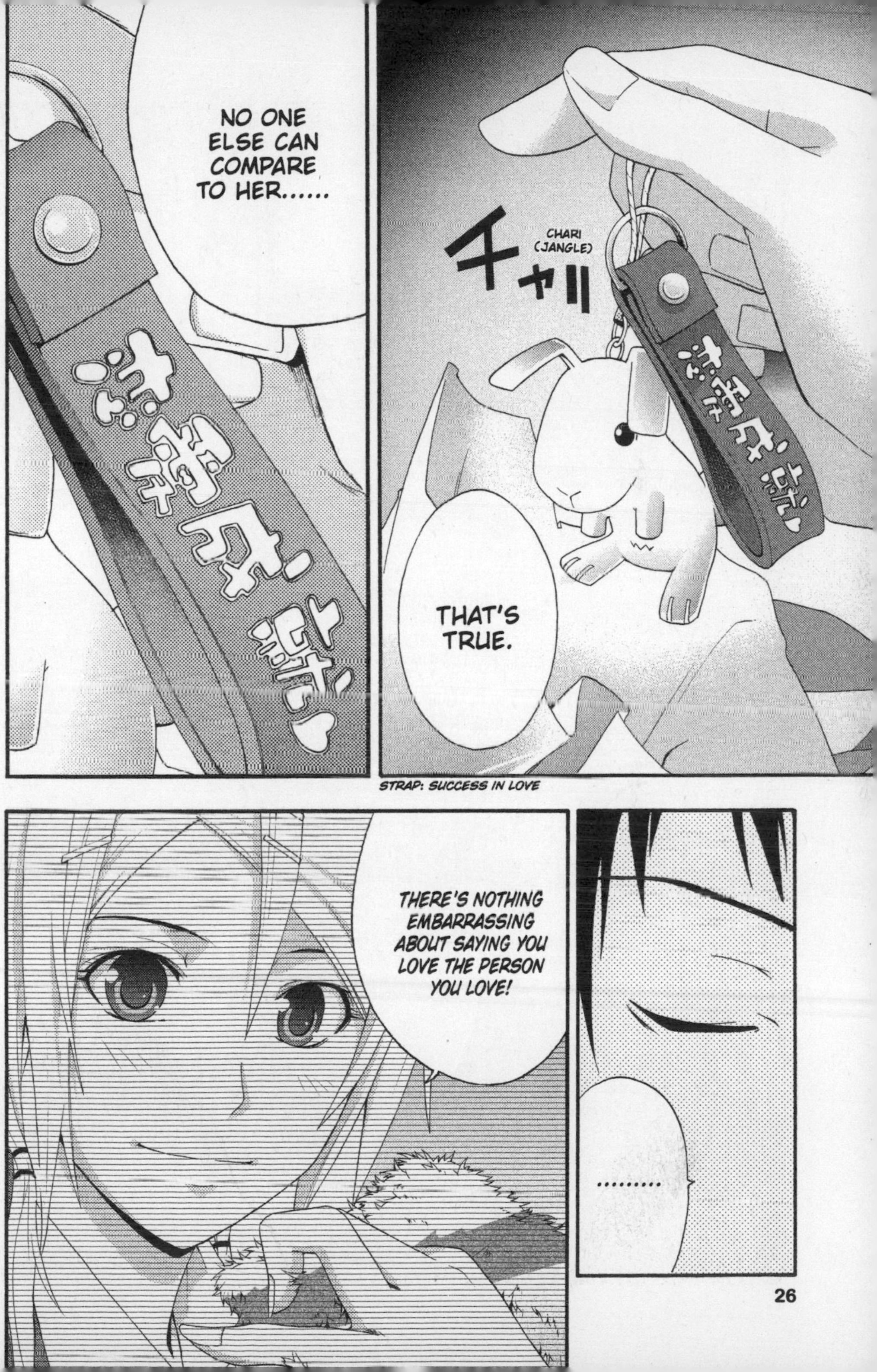

CHARI (JANGLE)
チャリ
THAT'S TRUE.
NO ONE ELSE CAN COMPARE TO HER......
....
THERE'S NOTHING EMBARRASSING ABOUT SAYING YOU LOVE THE PERSON YOU LOVE!

STRAP: SUCCESS IN LOVE

WHEN HIKARI LEFT EARLIER, SHE ASKED ME TO GIVE YOU A MESSAGE.

Hmm?

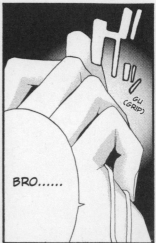
GU (GRIP)

BRO......

SHE WANTED TO CHANGE THE MEETING TIME FOR YOUR CHRISTMAS EVE DATE...

...TO AN HOUR LATER THAN PLANNED......

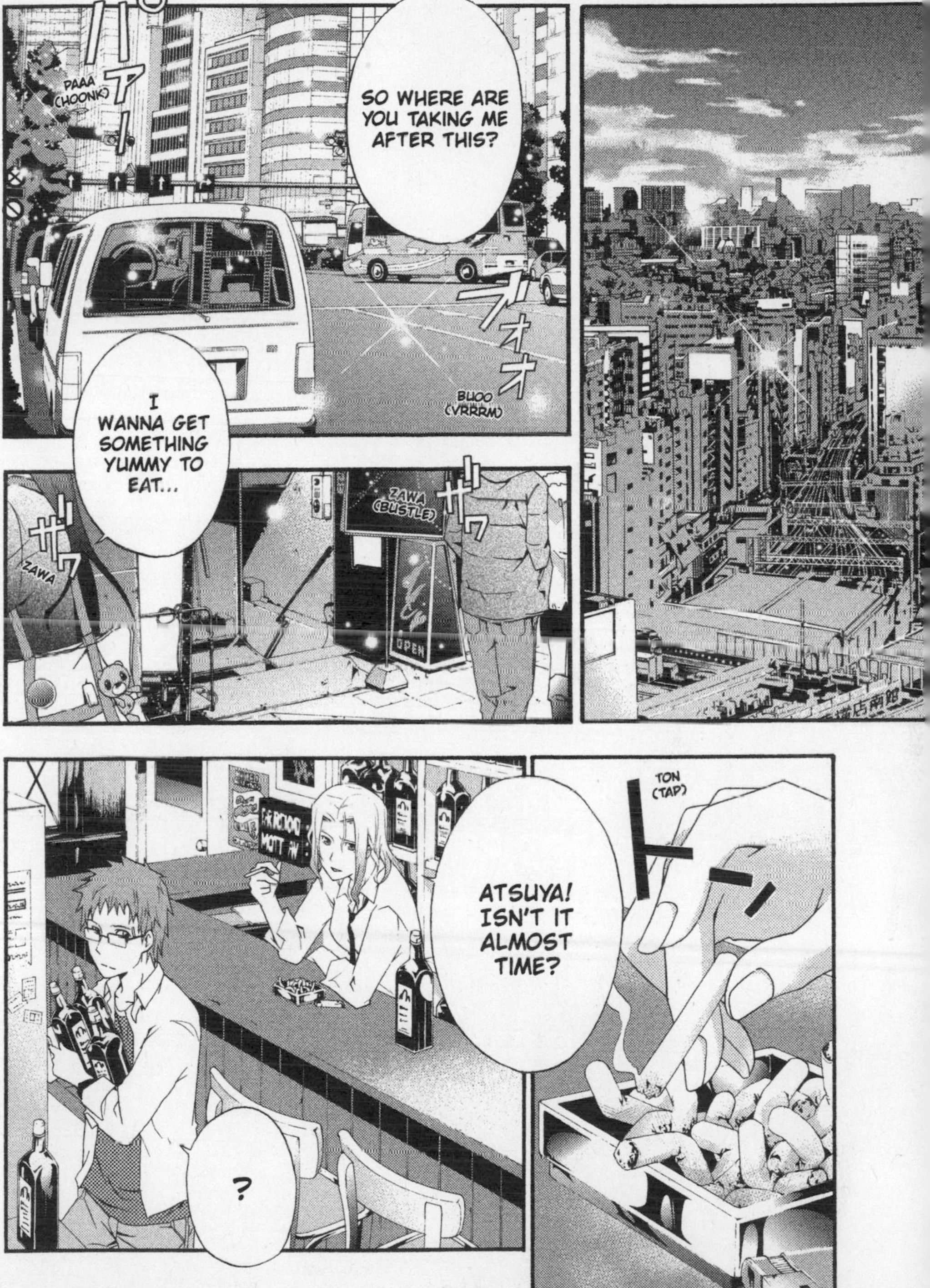
SO WHERE ARE YOU TAKING ME AFTER THIS?
PAAA (HOONK)
BUOO (VRRRM)
I WANNA GET SOMETHING YUMMY TO EAT...
ZAWA (BUSTLE)
ZAWA
TON (TAP)
ATSUYA! ISN'T IT ALMOST TIME?
?

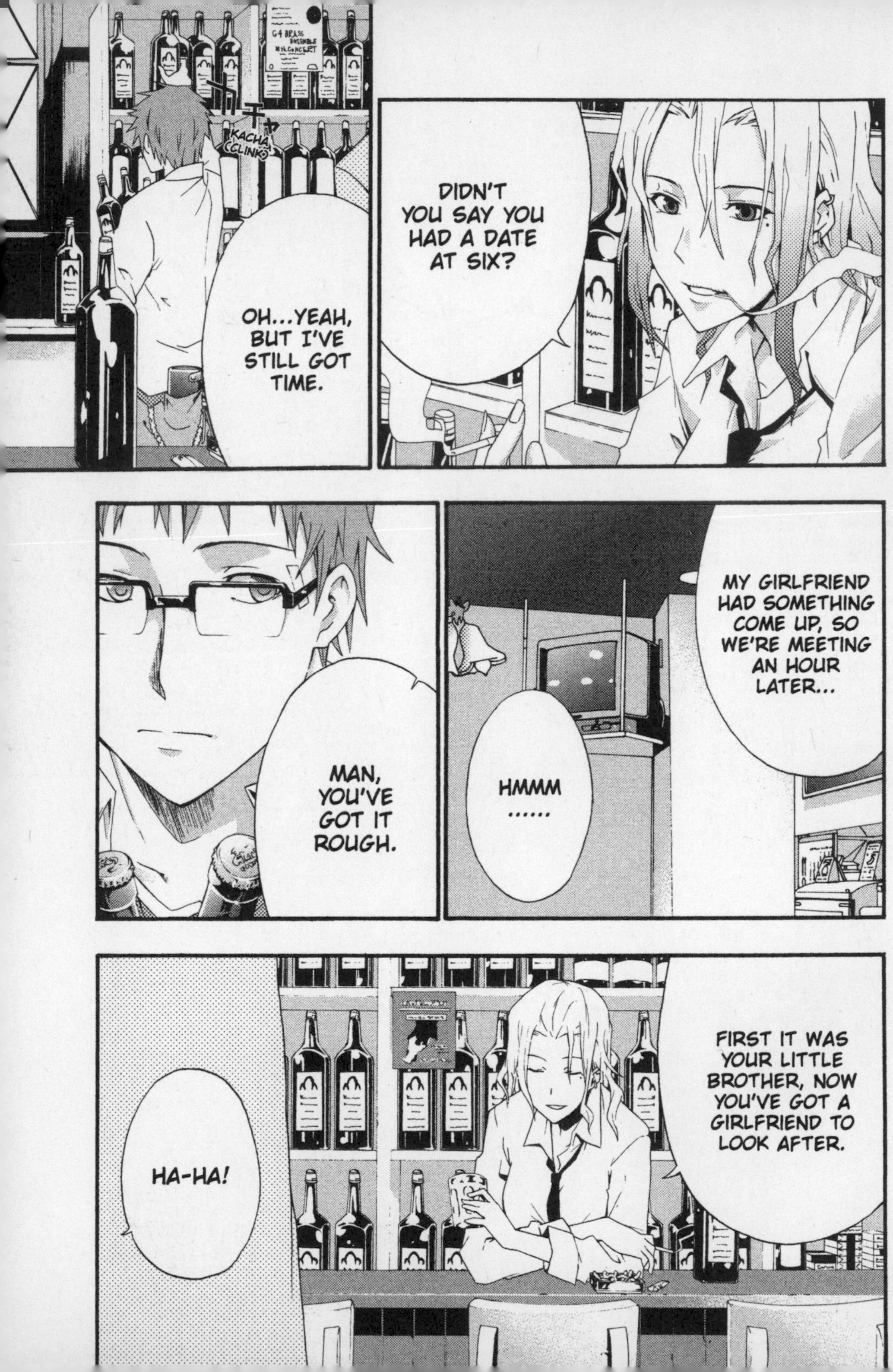

DIDN'T YOU SAY YOU HAD A DATE AT SIX?
KACHA (CLINK)
OH...YEAH, BUT I'VE STILL GOT TIME.
MY GIRLFRIEND HAD SOMETHING COME UP, SO WE'RE MEETING AN HOUR LATER...
HMMM ......
MAN, YOU'VE GOT IT ROUGH.
FIRST IT WAS YOUR LITTLE BROTHER, NOW YOU'VE GOT A GIRLFRIEND TO LOOK AFTER.
HA-HA!

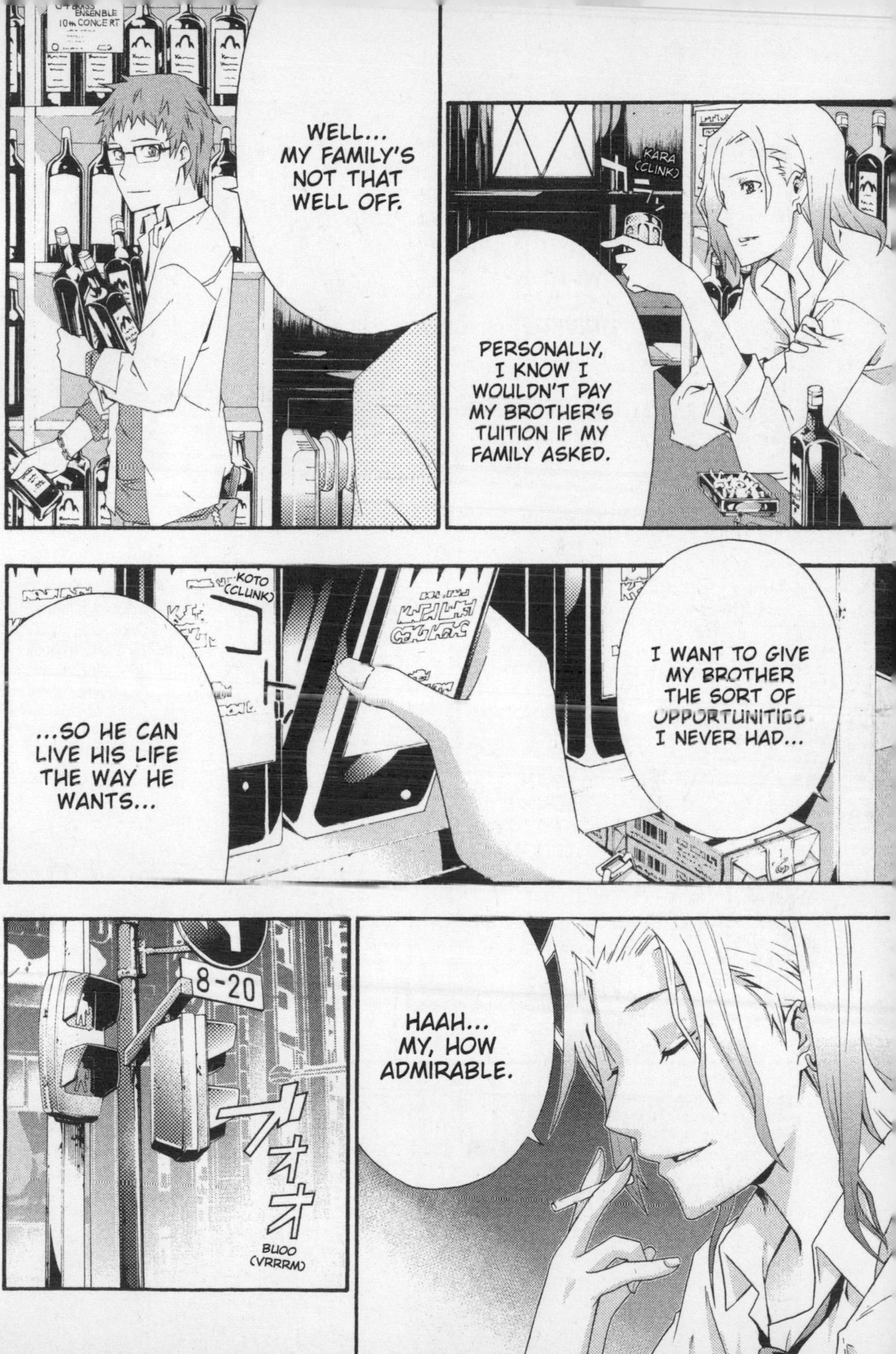
KARA (CLINK)
PERSONALLY, I KNOW I WOULDN'T PAY MY BROTHER'S TUITION IF MY FAMILY ASKED.
ENSEMBLE 10th CONCERT
WELL... MY FAMILY'S NOT THAT WELL OFF.
I WANT TO GIVE MY BROTHER THE SORT OF OPPORTUNITIES I NEVER HAD...
KOTO (CLINK)
...SO HE CAN LIVE HIS LIFE THE WAY HE WANTS...
HAAH... MY, HOW ADMIRABLE.
8-20
BUOO (VRRRM)

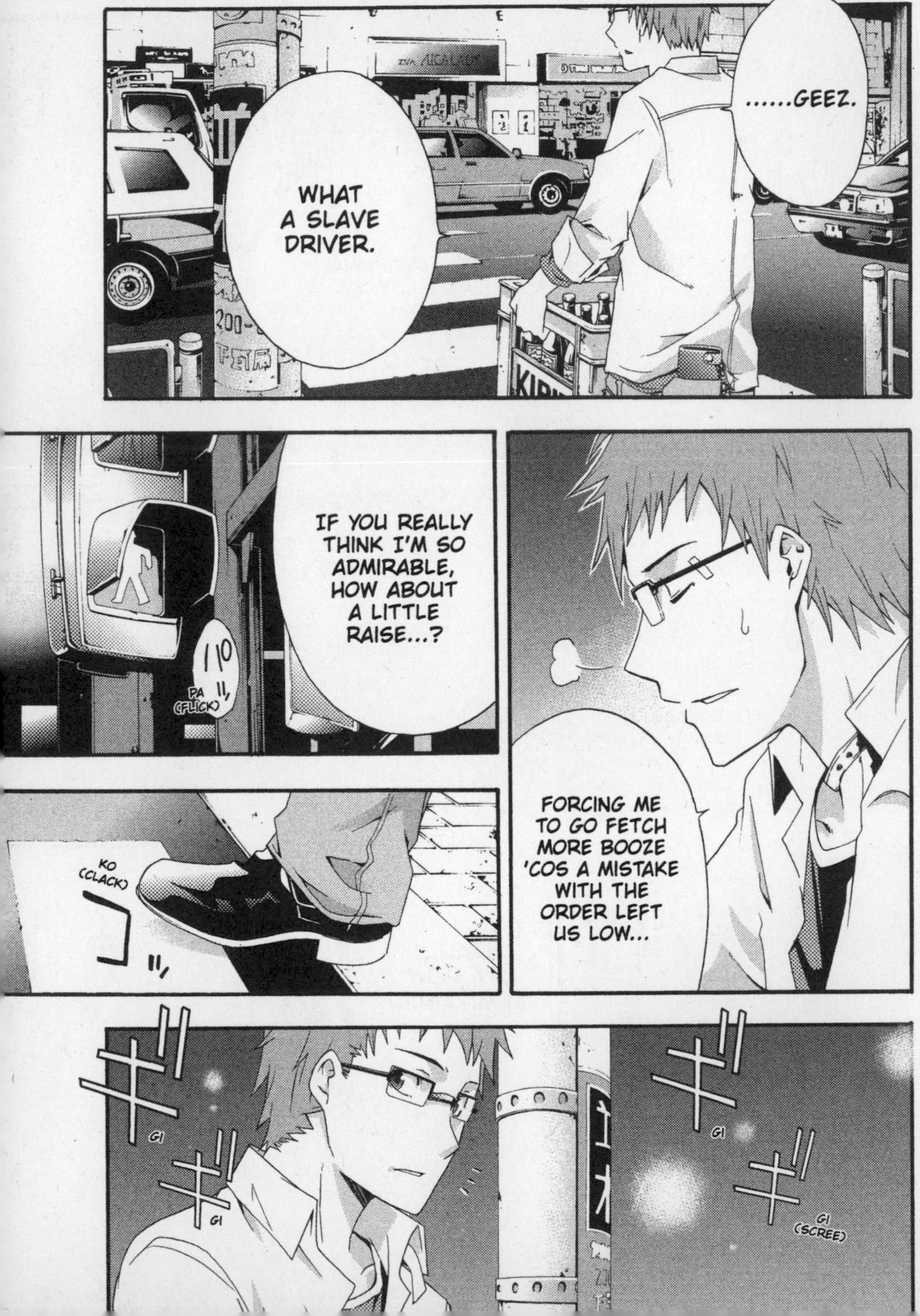
......GEEZ.
WHAT A SLAVE DRIVER.
FORCING ME TO GO FETCH MORE BOOZE 'COS A MISTAKE WITH THE ORDER LEFT US LOW...
IF YOU REALLY THINK I'M SO ADMIRABLE, HOW ABOUT A LITTLE RAISE...?
PA (FLICK)
KO (CLACK)
GI
GI
GI
GI (SCREE)

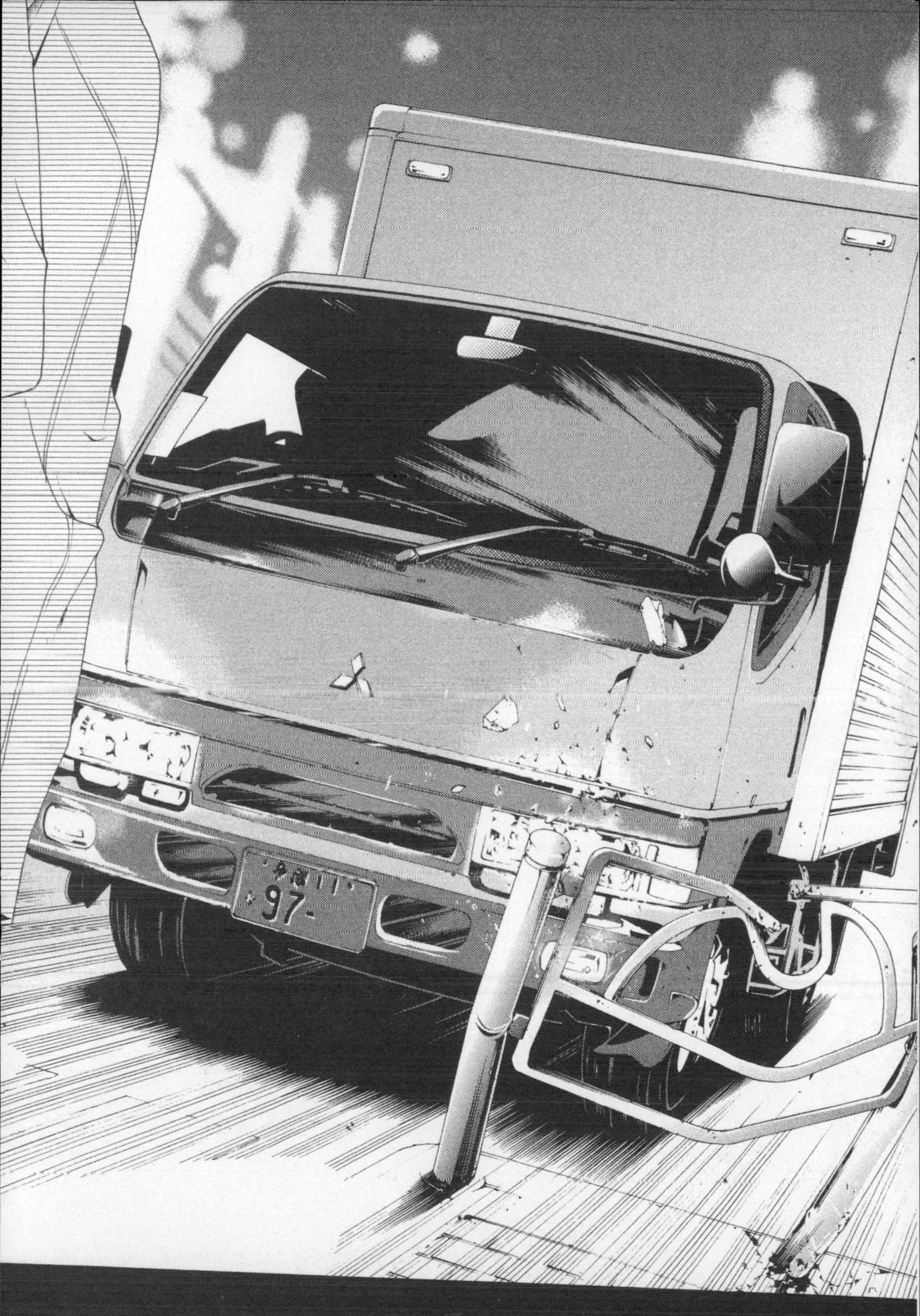
97-

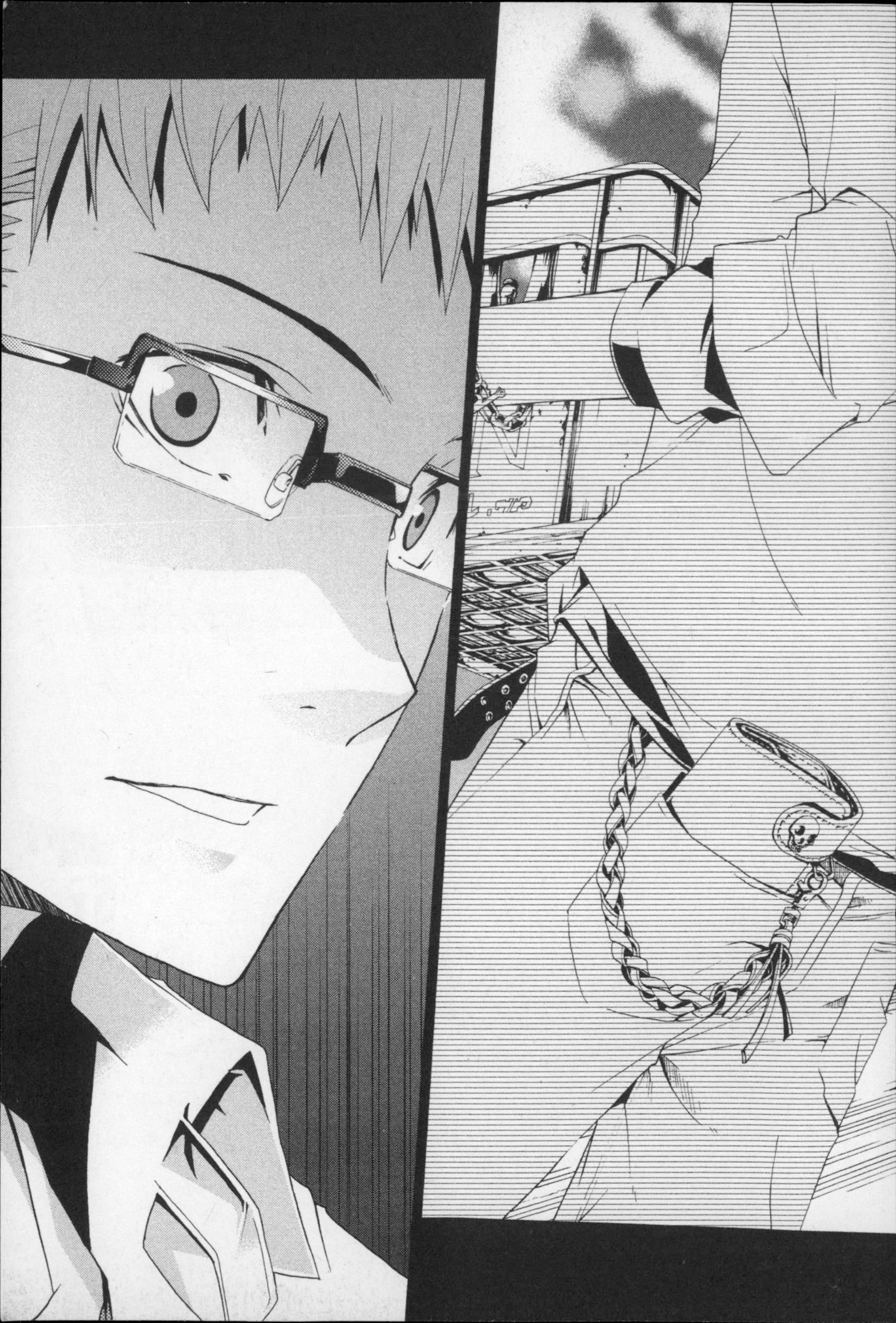

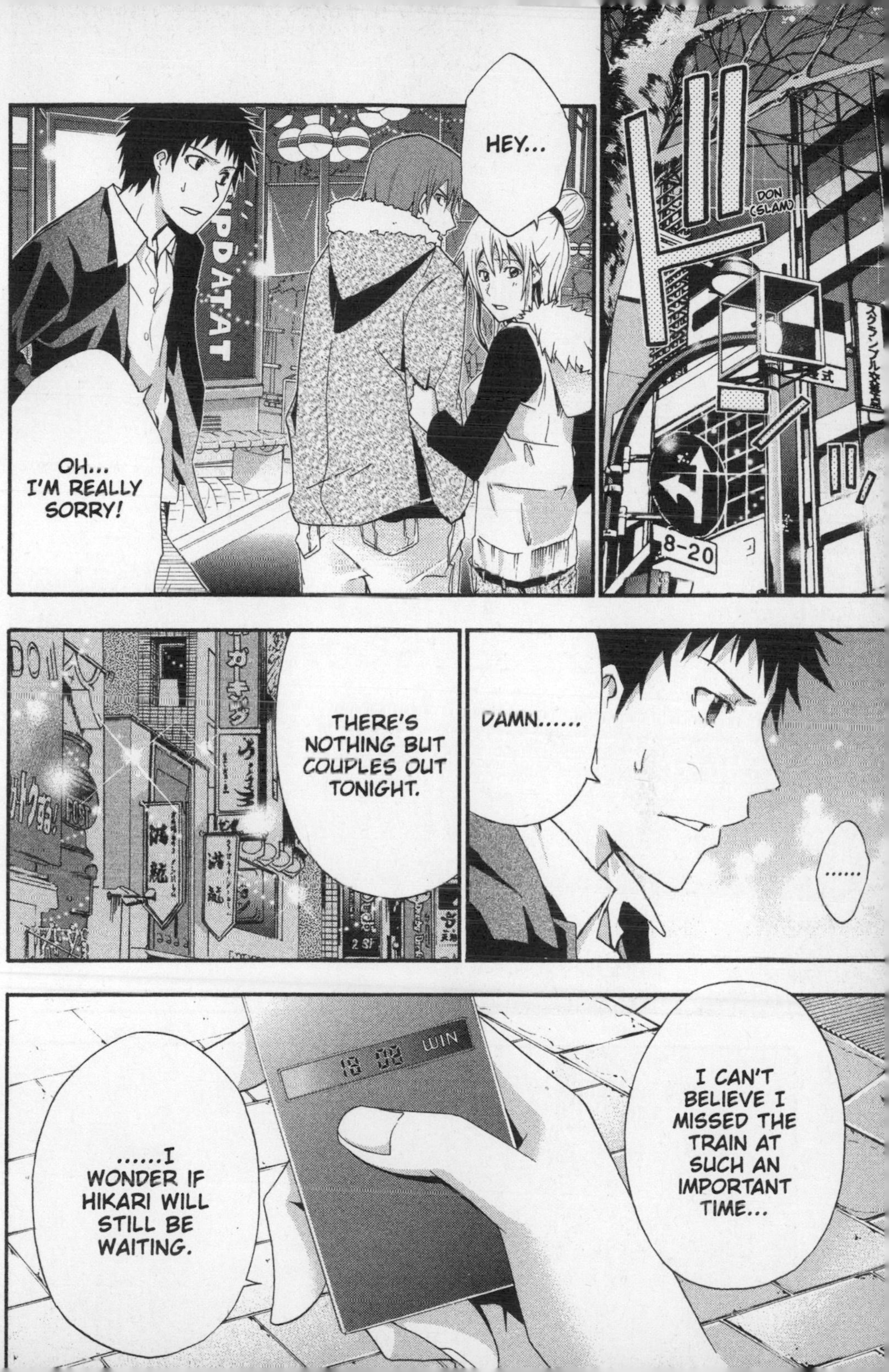
DON (SLAM)
HEY...
OH... I'M REALLY SORRY!
DAMN......
......
THERE'S NOTHING BUT COUPLES OUT TONIGHT.
I CAN'T BELIEVE I MISSED THE TRAIN AT SUCH AN IMPORTANT TIME...
......I WONDER IF HIKARI WILL STILL BE WAITING.

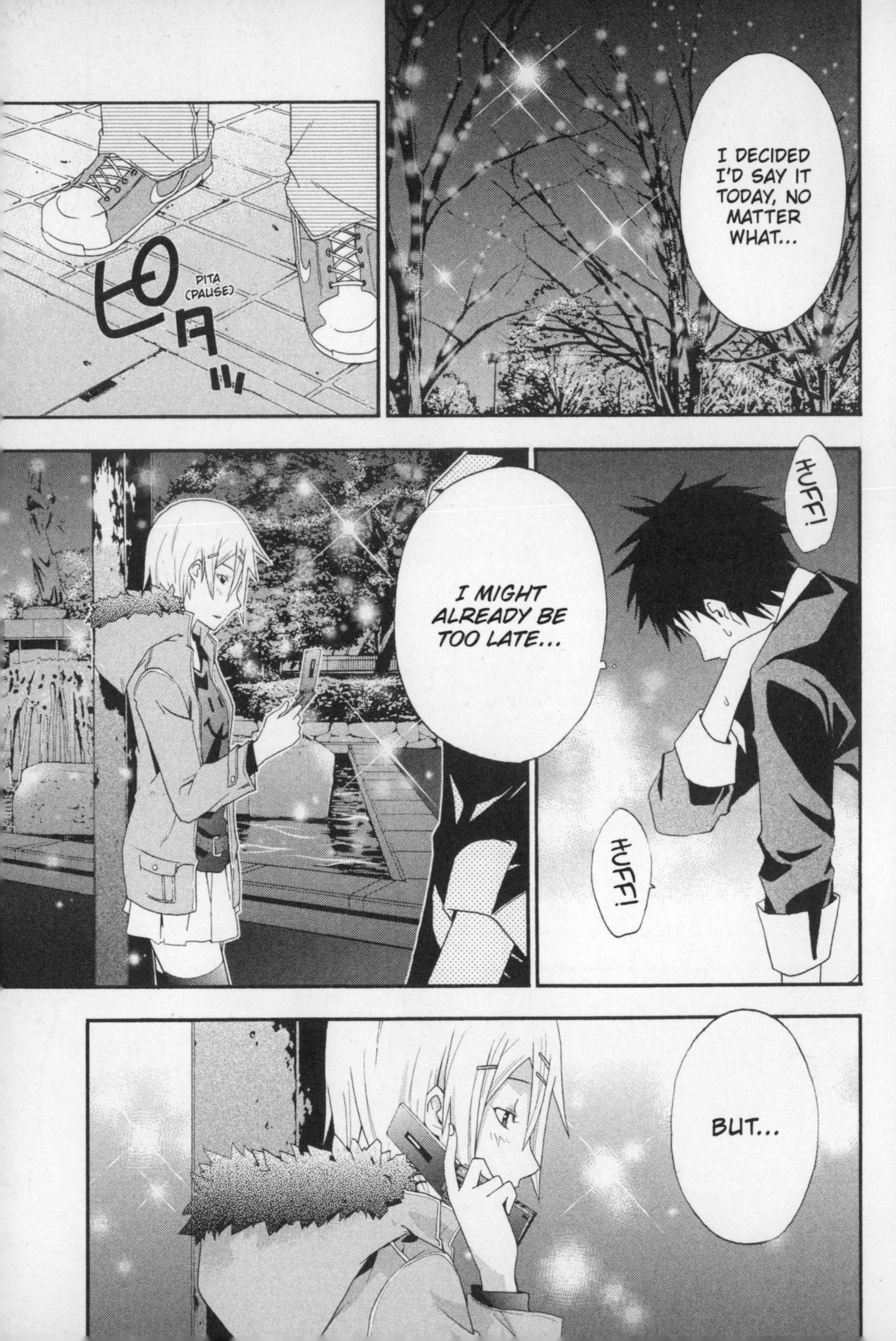
I DECIDED I'D SAY IT TODAY, NO MATTER WHAT...
ピタッ
PITA (PAUSE)
HUFF!
HUFF!
I MIGHT ALREADY BE TOO LATE...
BUT...

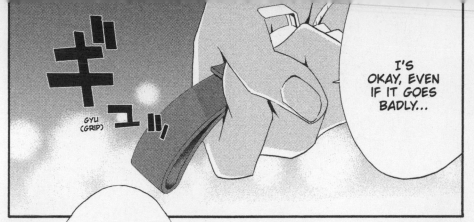

ギュッ
GYU
(GRIP)

I'S OKAY, EVEN IF IT GOES BADLY...

...I DECIDED I'D TELL HER HOW I FEEL!

ザワ
ZAWA

ザワ
ZAWA
(BUSTLE)

HI......

HIKARI!!

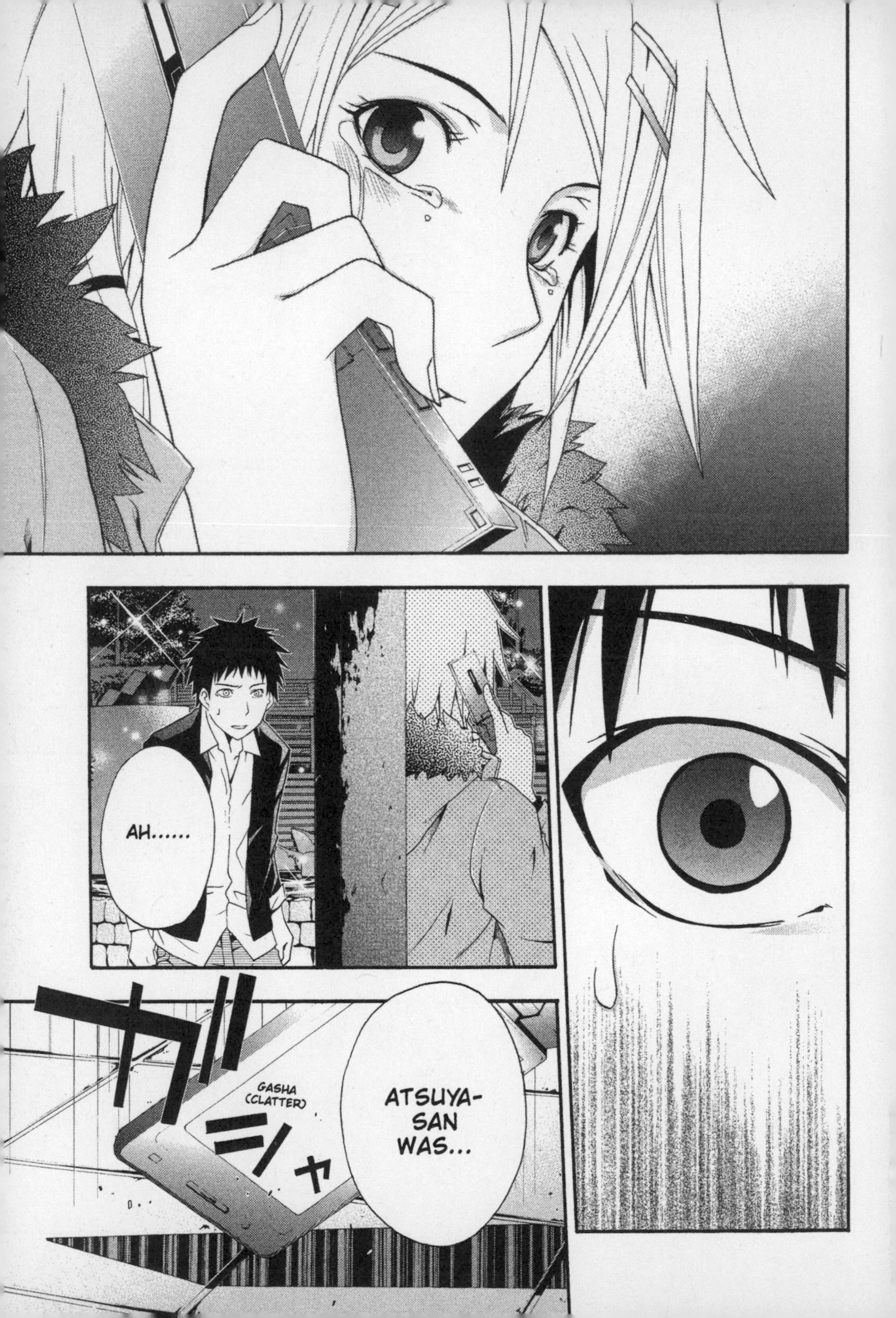
AH......
ATSUYA-SAN WAS...
GASHA (CLATTER)

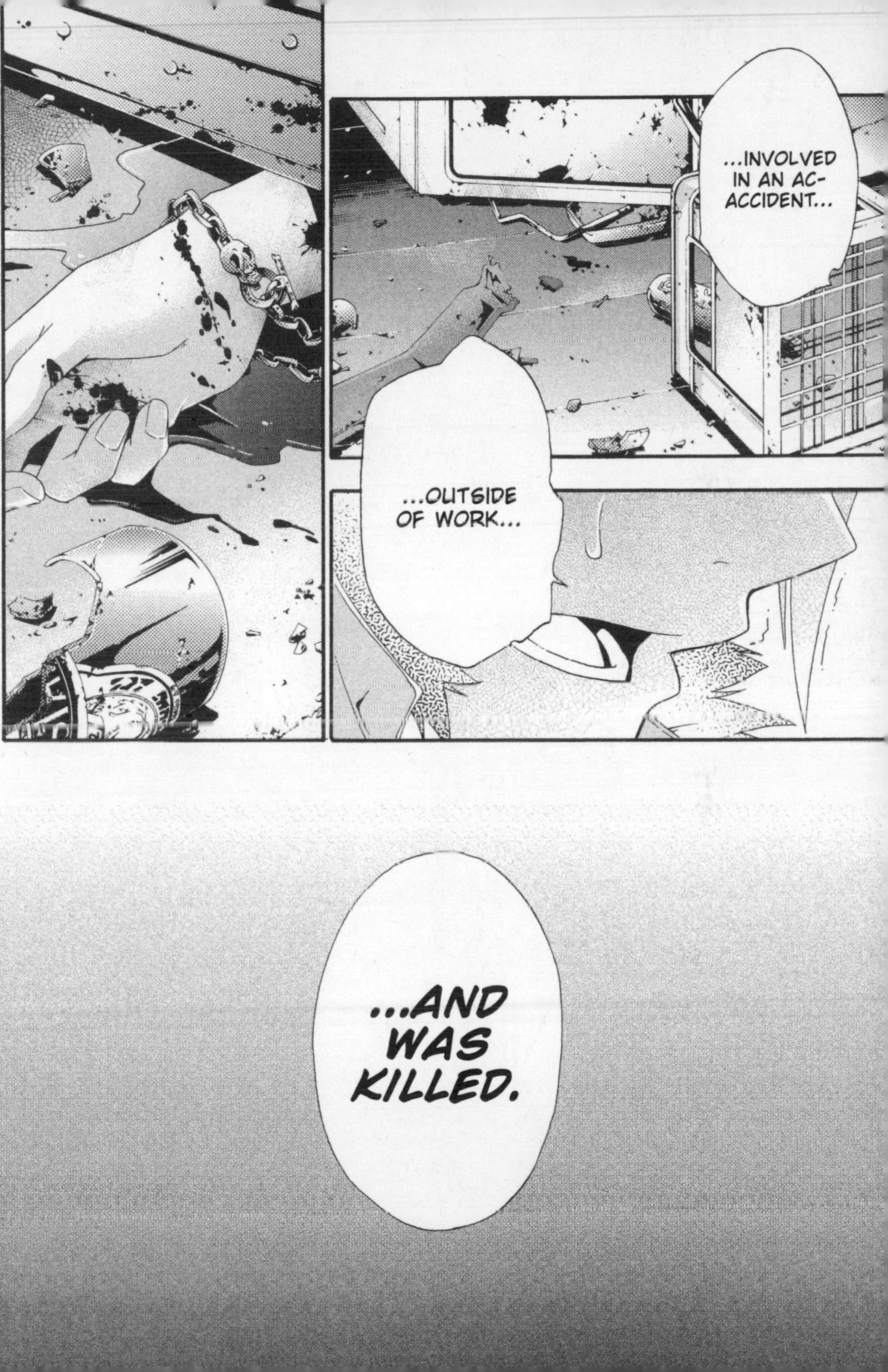
...INVOLVED IN AN AC-ACCIDENT...
...OUTSIDE OF WORK...
...AND WAS KILLED.

DOSA
(FWUMP)

HEY...

HOW COME ......?

GYU
(GRIP)

......HUH?

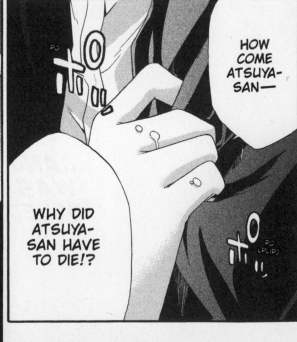

PO

HOW COME ATSUYA-SAN—

WHY DID ATSUYA-SAN HAVE TO DIE!?

PO
(PLIP)

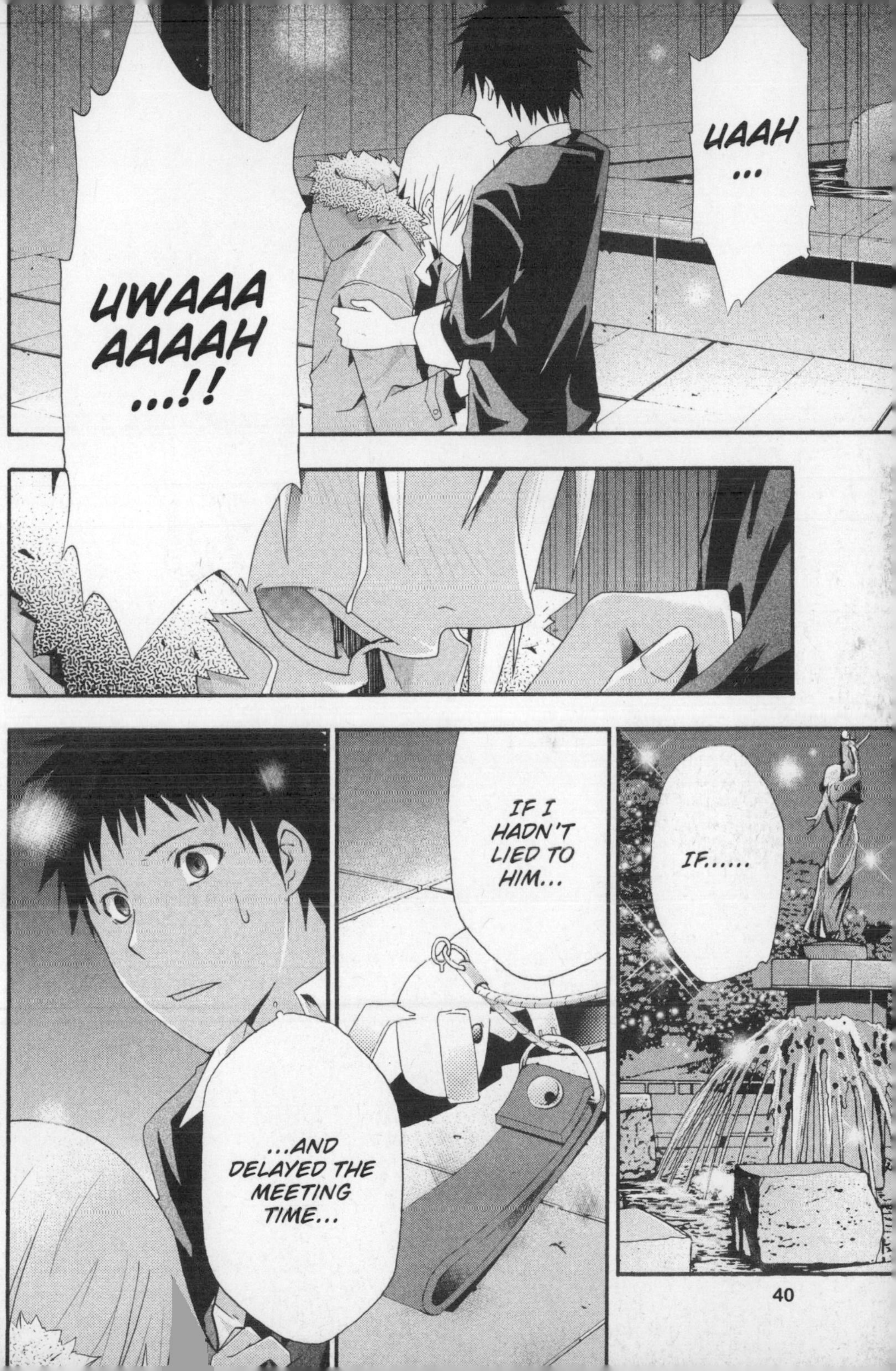
UAAH ...
UWAAA AAAAH ...!!
IF......
IF I HADN'T LIED TO HIM...
...AND DELAYED THE MEETING TIME...

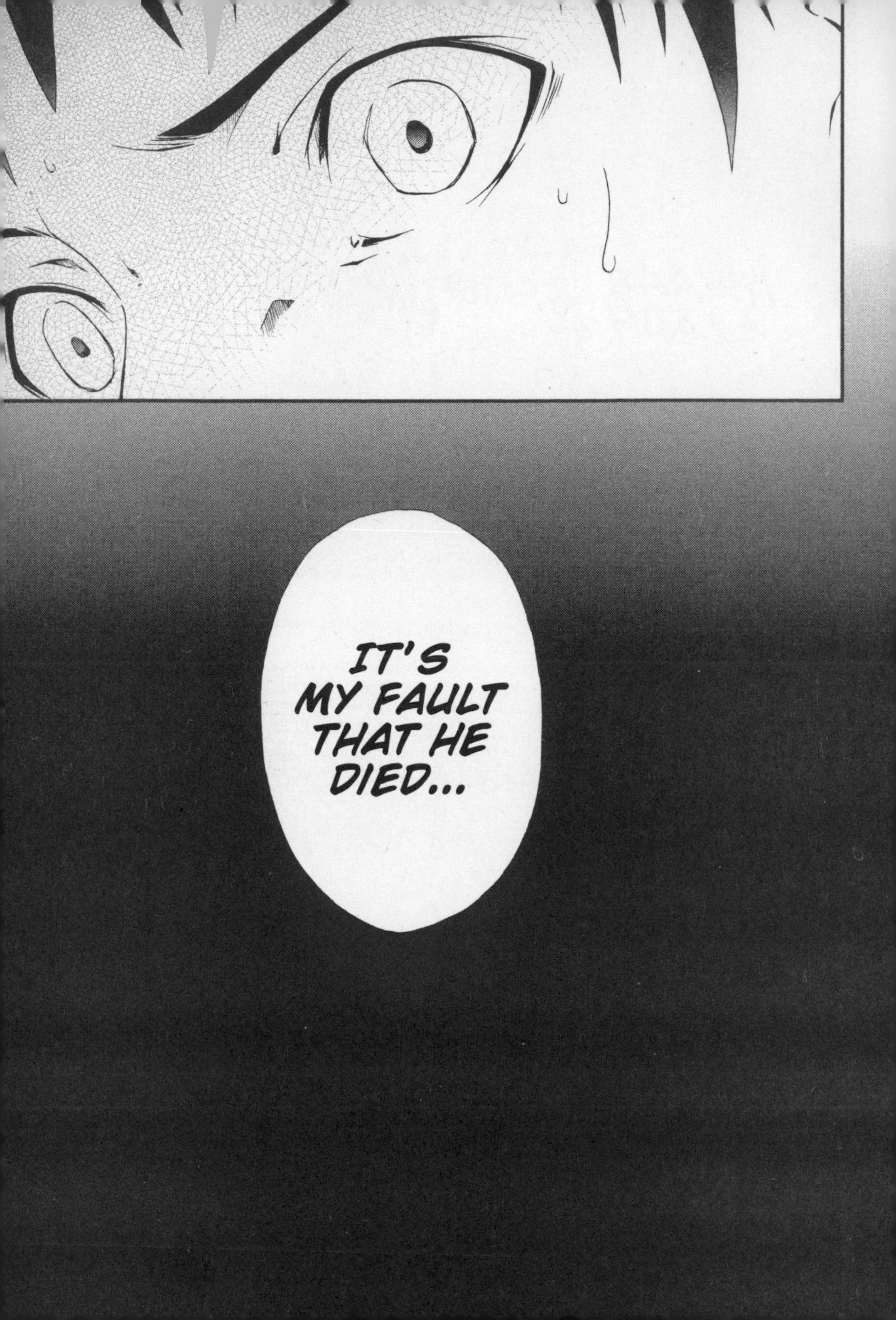
IT'S MY FAULT THAT HE DIED...

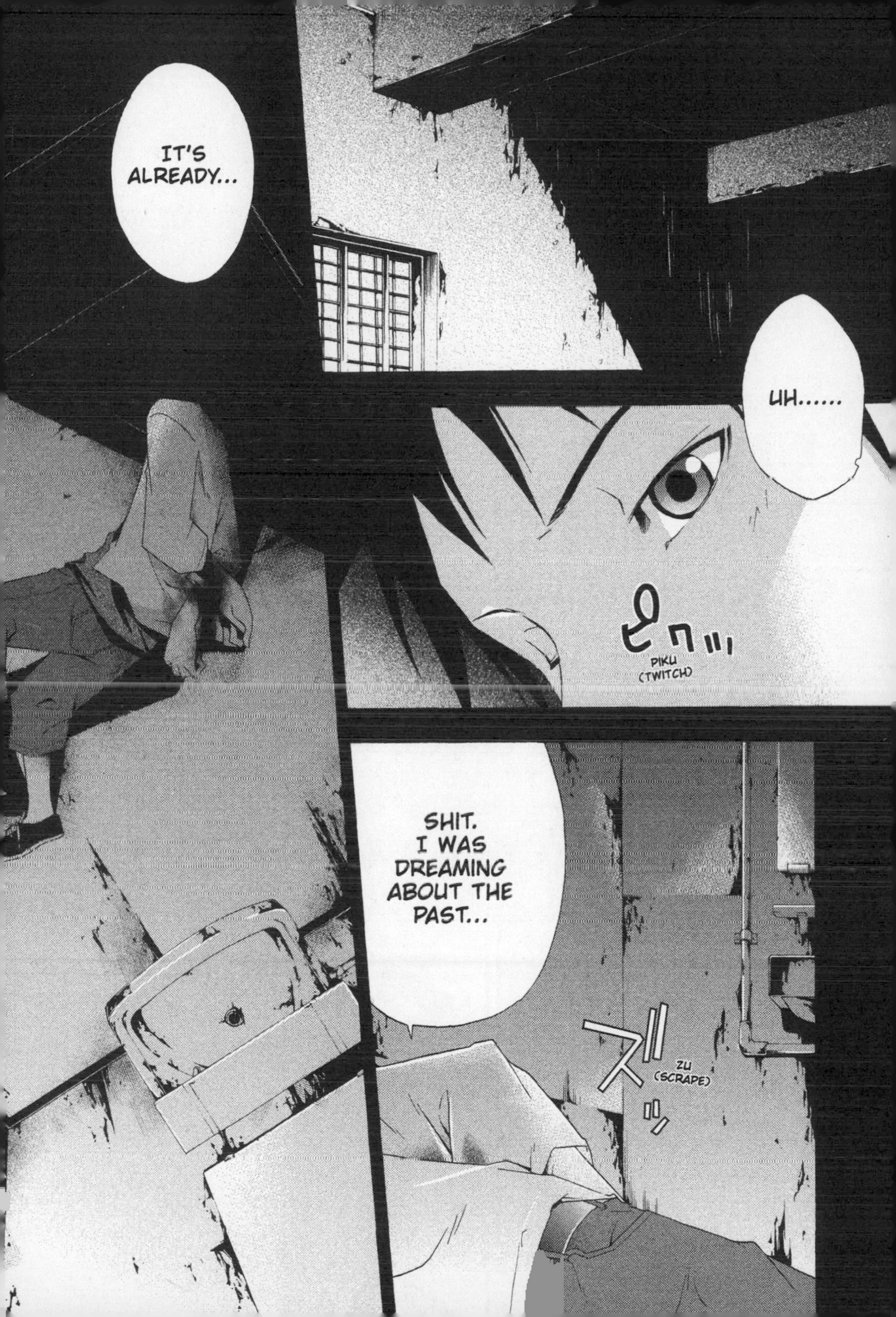
IT'S ALREADY...
UH......
ピクッ
PIKU (TWITCH)
SHIT. I WAS DREAMING ABOUT THE PAST...
ズッ
ZU (SCRAPE)

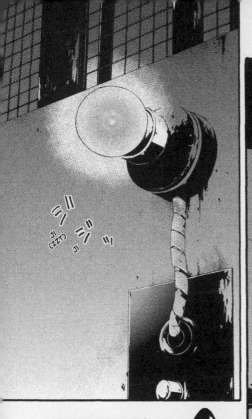

...BEEN TWO
YEARS SINCE
THEN...

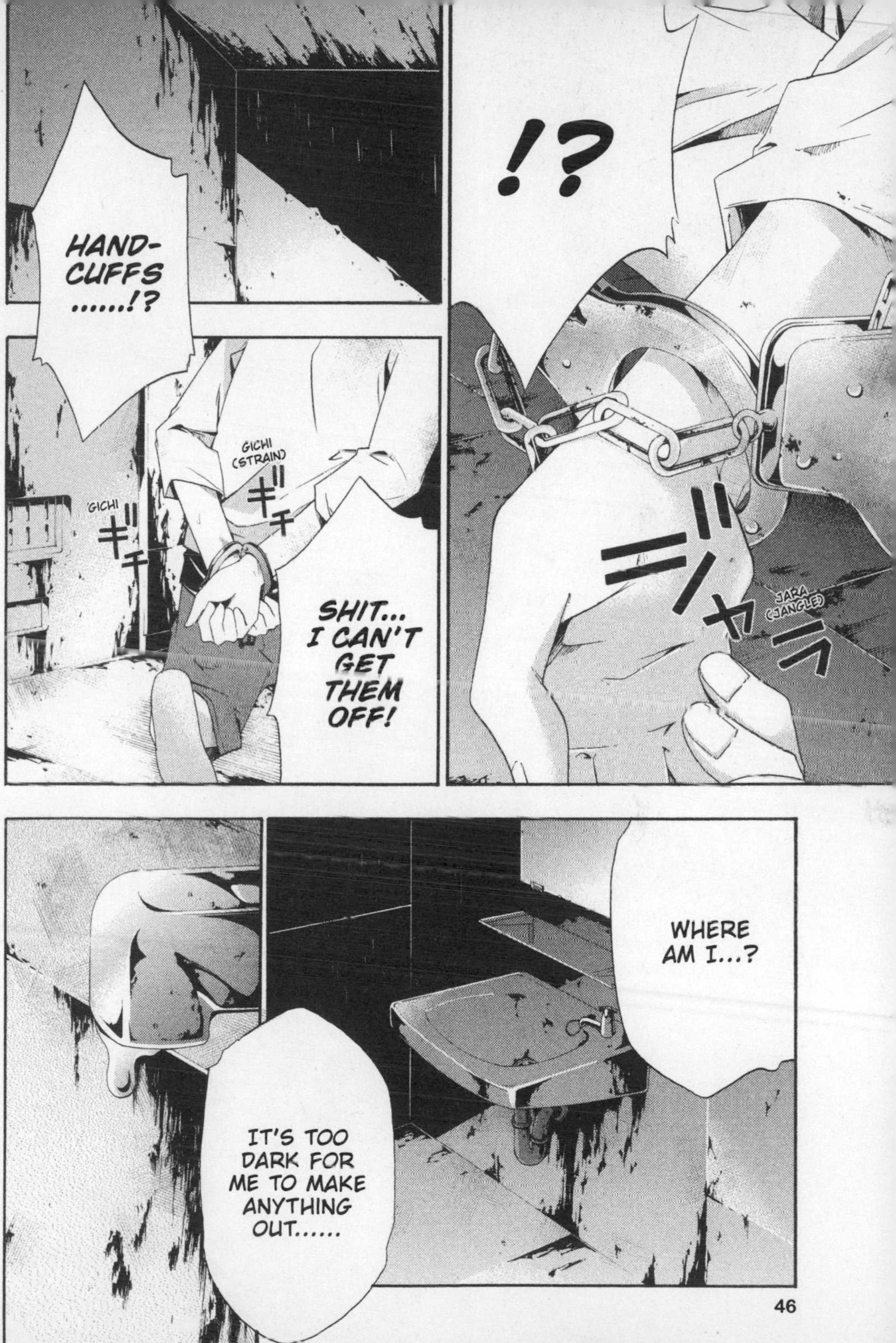
!?
ジャラ
JARA (JANGLE)
HAND-CUFFS ......!?
ギチ
GICHI (STRAIN)
ギチ
GICHI
SHIT... I CAN'T GET THEM OFF!
WHERE AM I...?
IT'S TOO DARK FOR ME TO MAKE ANYTHING OUT......

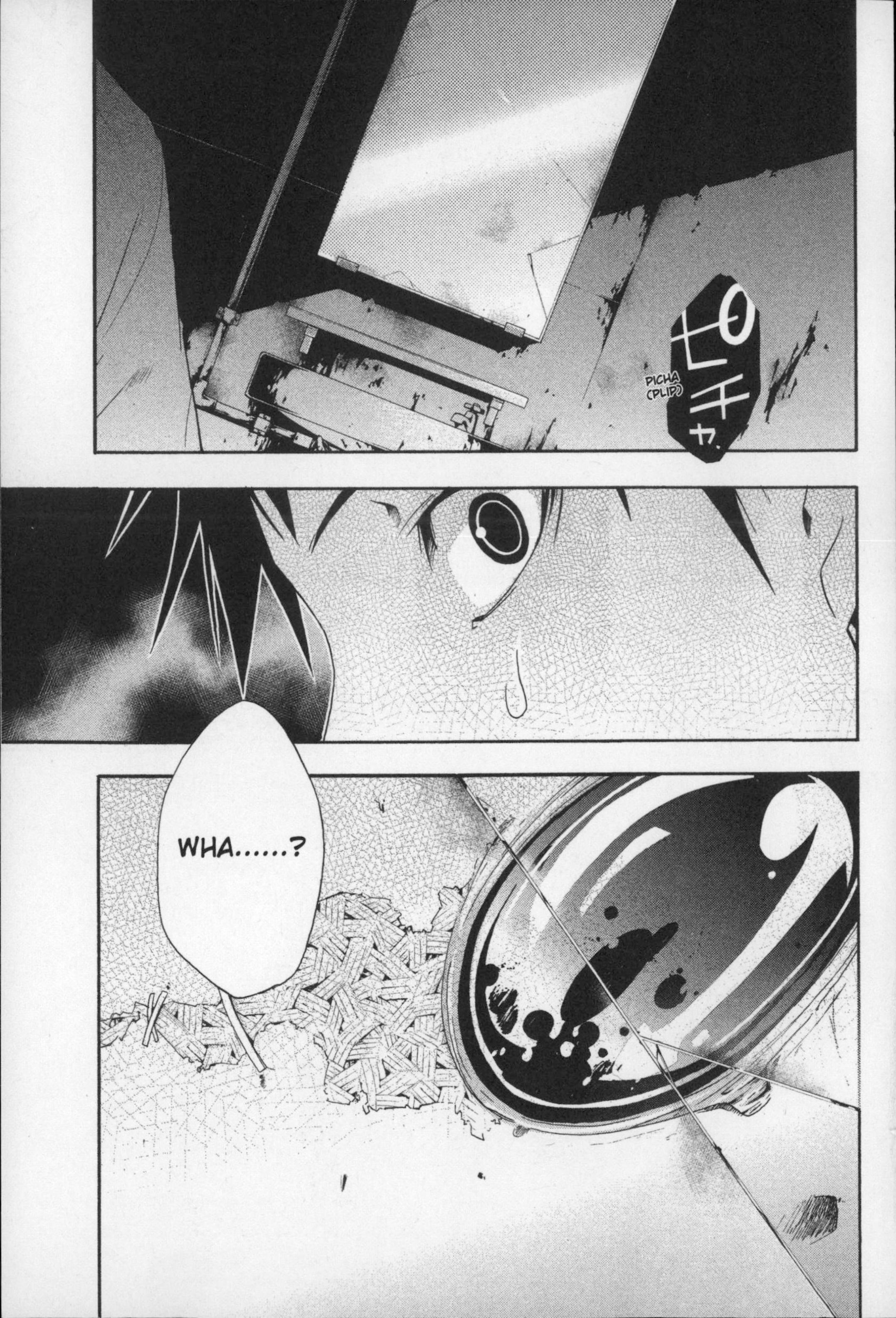
ピチャ
PICHA (PLIP)
WHA......?

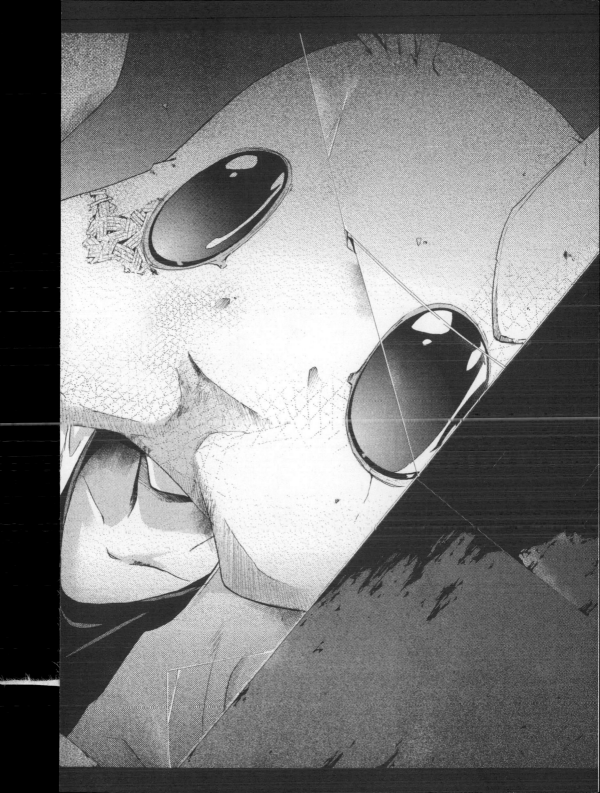

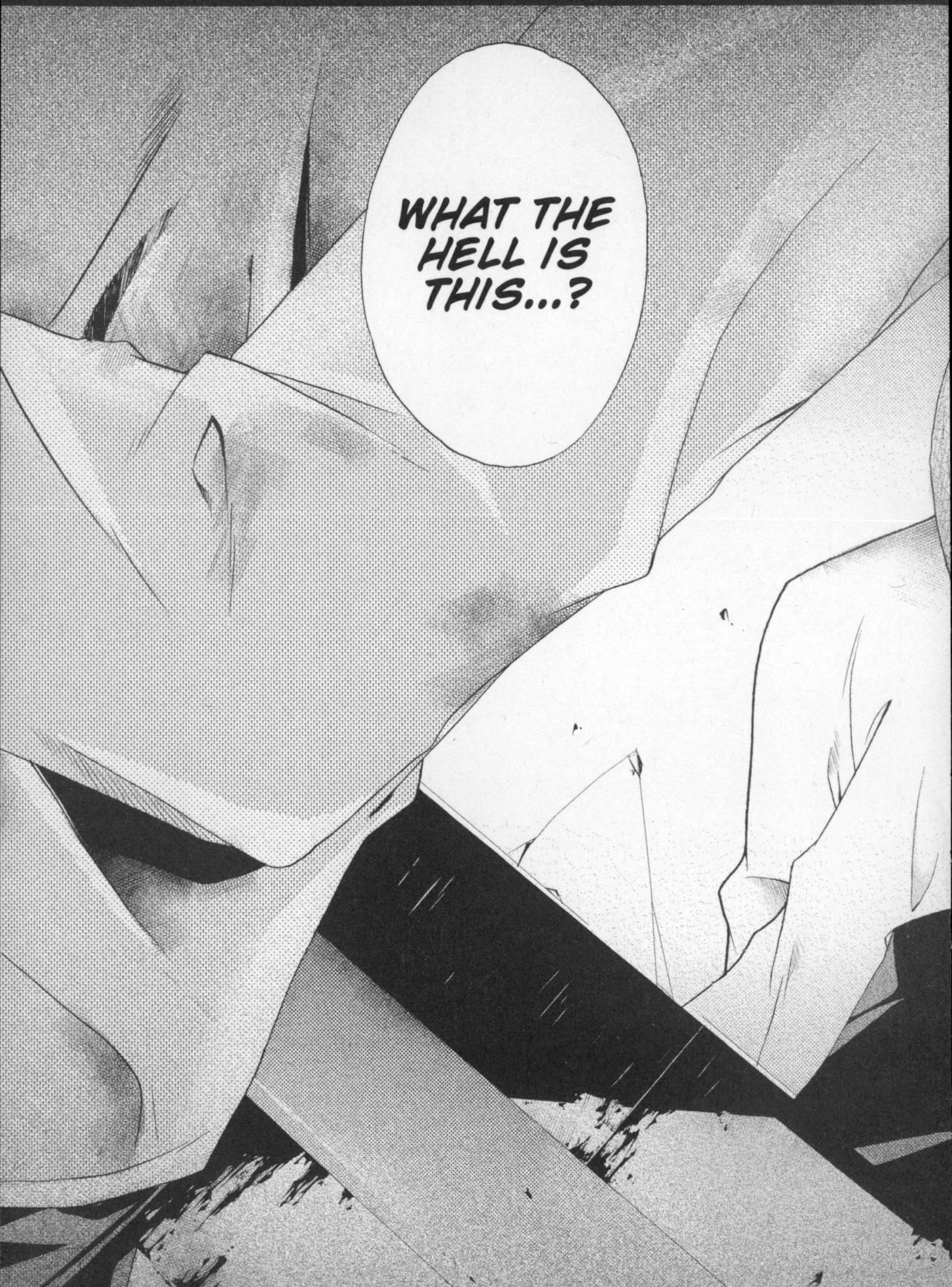
WHAT THE HELL IS THIS...?

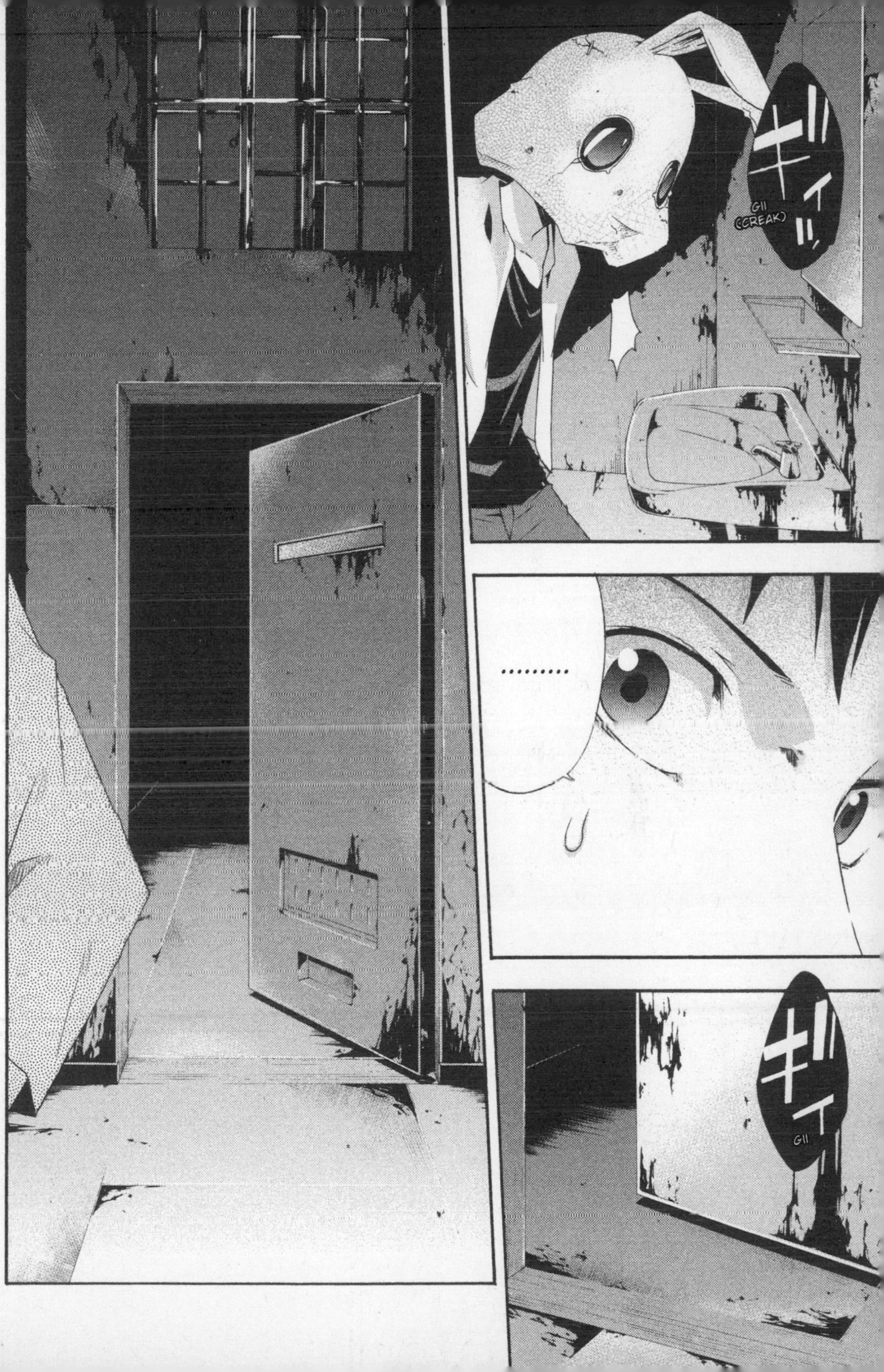
GII
(CREAK)
....
GII

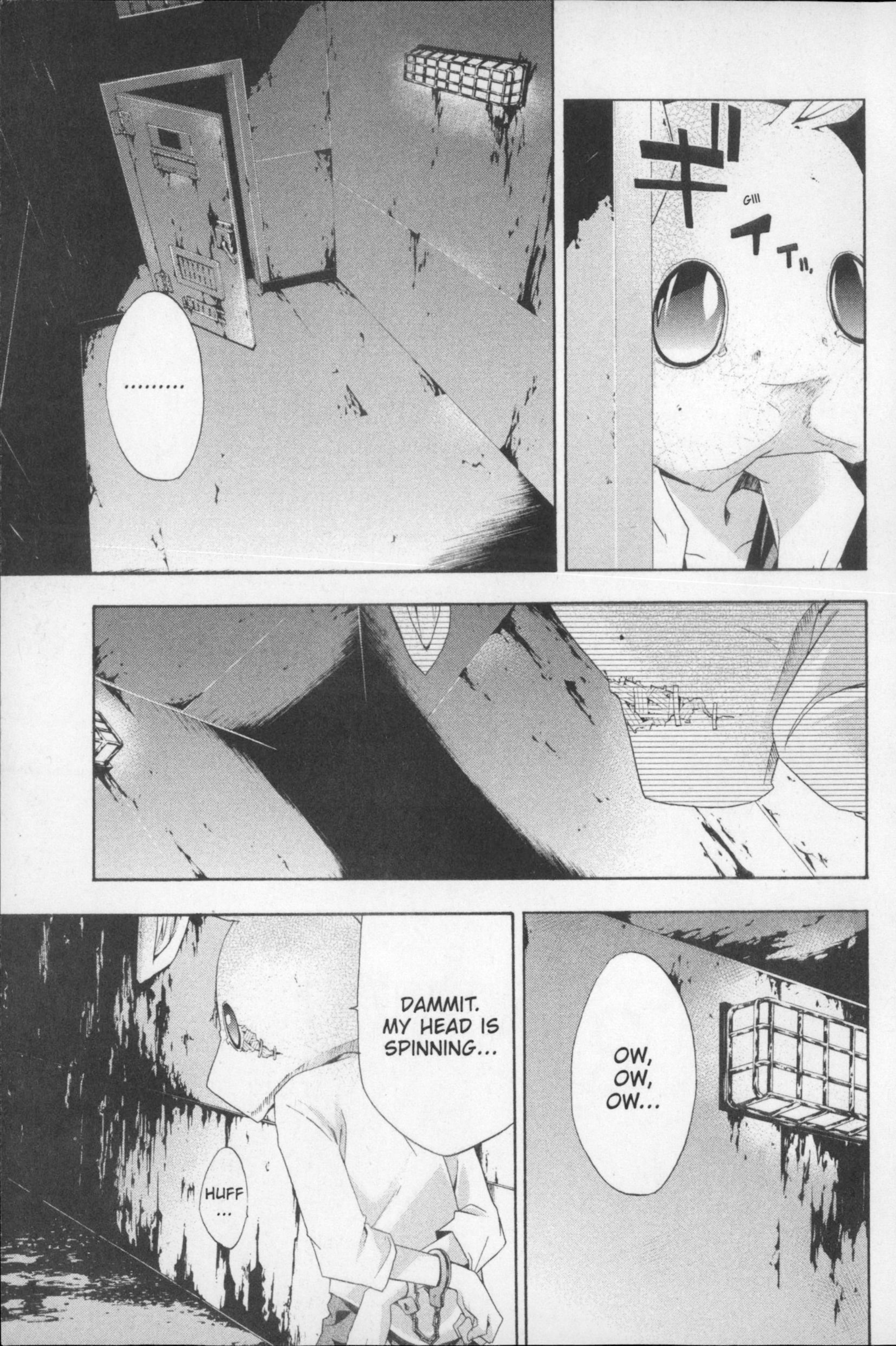
GIII
....
OW, OW, OW...
DAMMIT. MY HEAD IS SPINNING...
HUFF ...

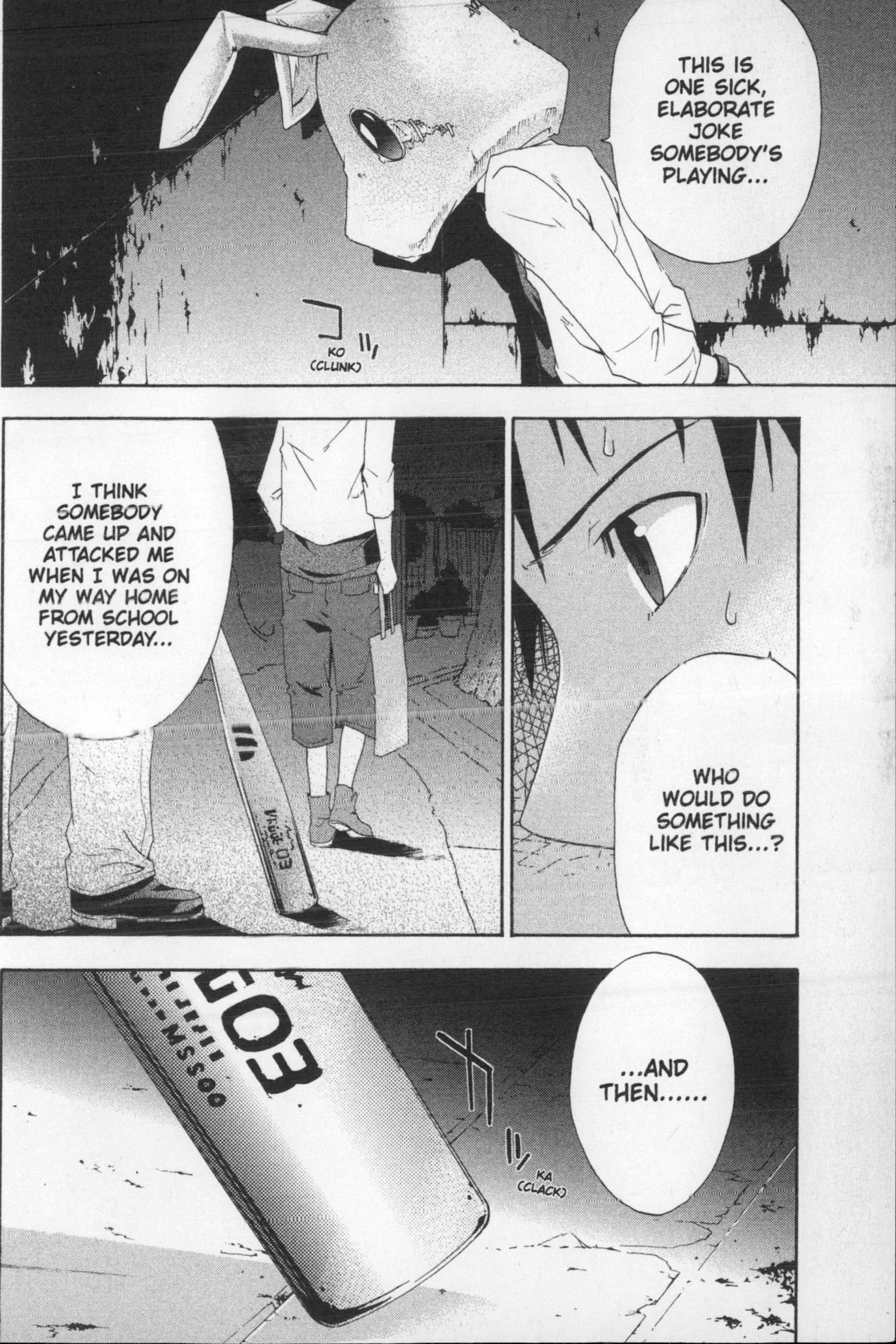
THIS IS ONE SICK, ELABORATE JOKE SOMEBODY'S PLAYING...
KO (CLUNK)
WHO WOULD DO SOMETHING LIKE THIS...?
I THINK SOMEBODY CAME UP AND ATTACKED ME WHEN I WAS ON MY WAY HOME FROM SCHOOL YESTERDAY...
...AND THEN......
KA (CLACK)

VOICES
...!!

IS......

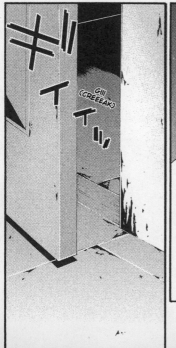

GIII
(CREEEAK)

KA

IS ANYBODY THERE!?

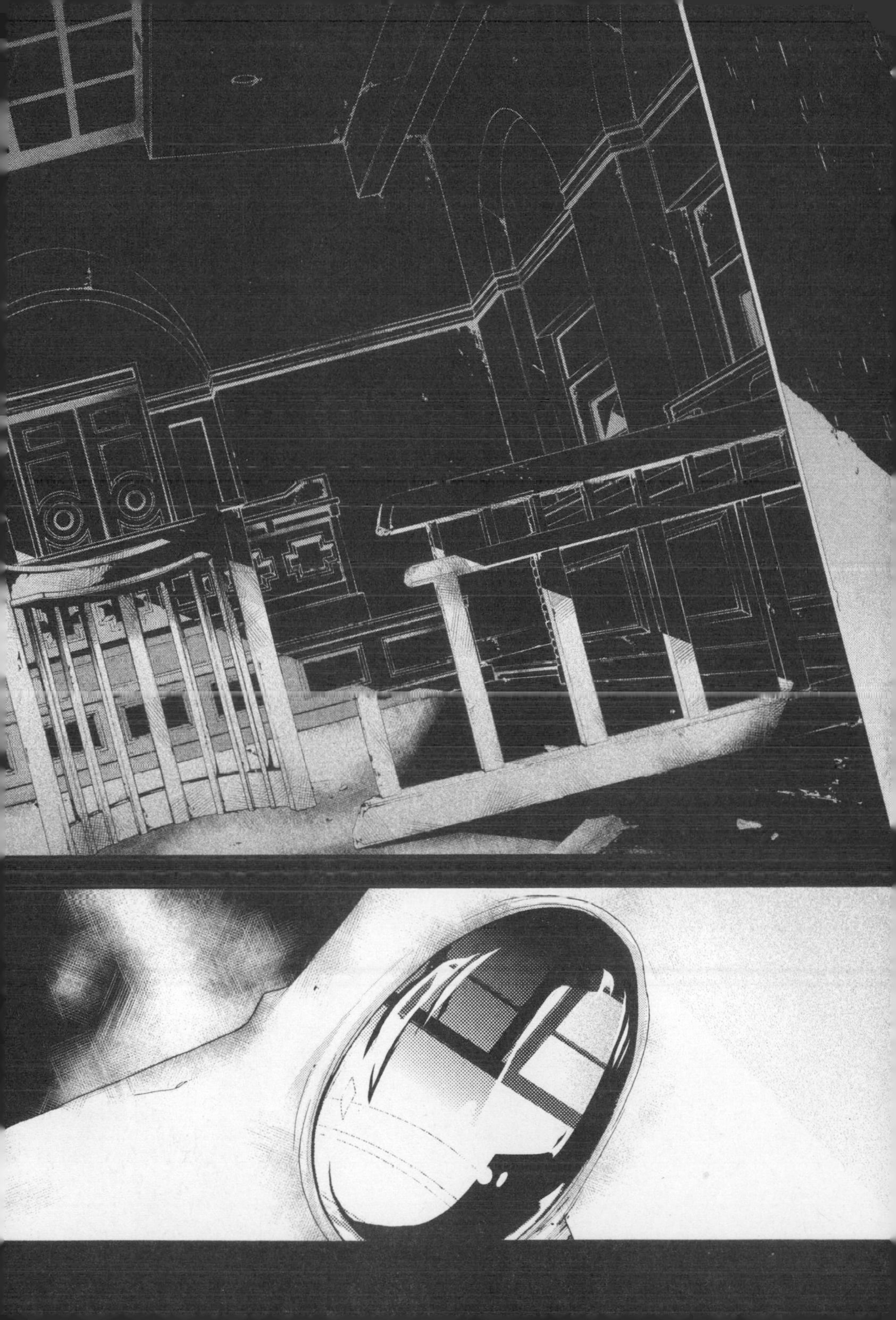

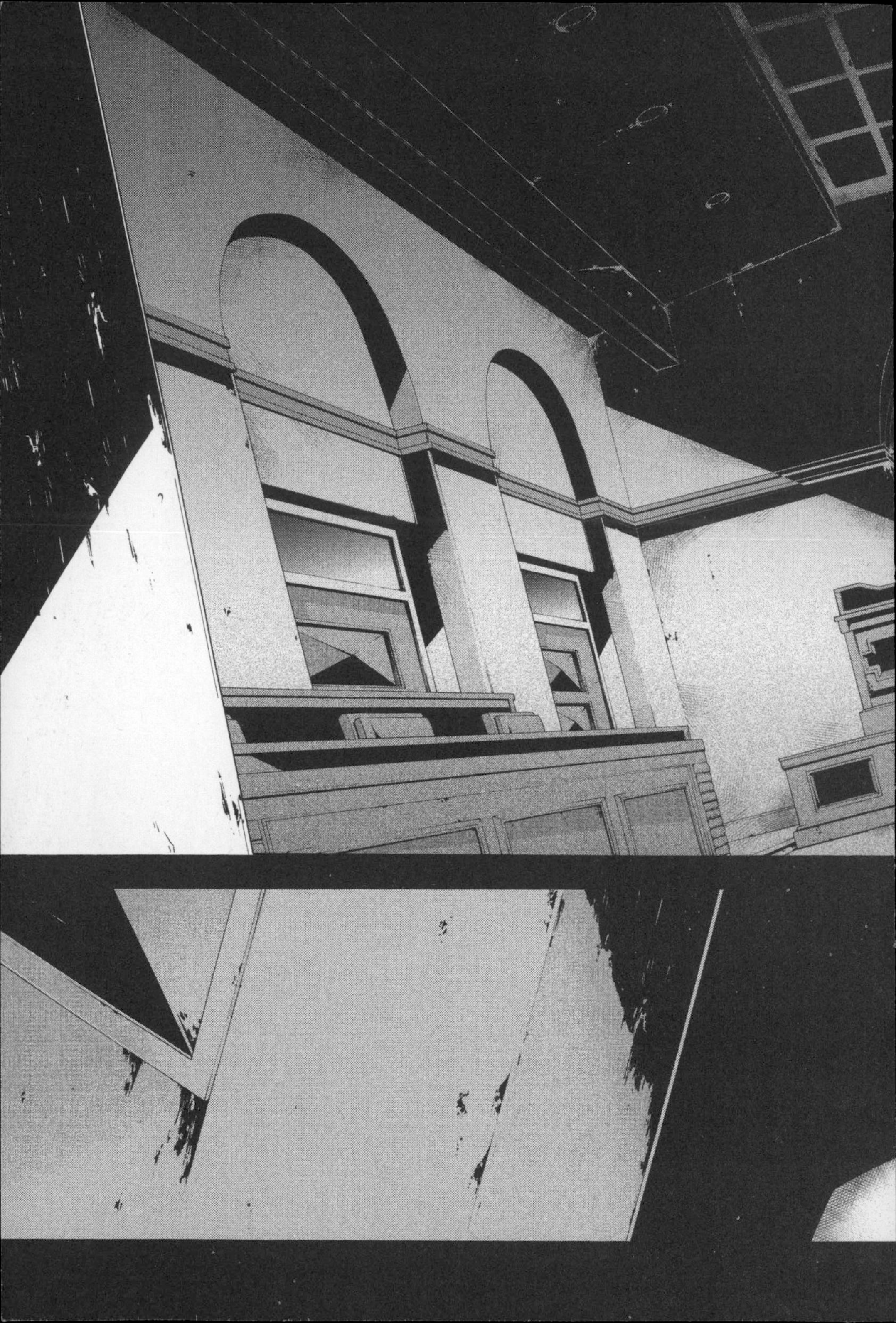

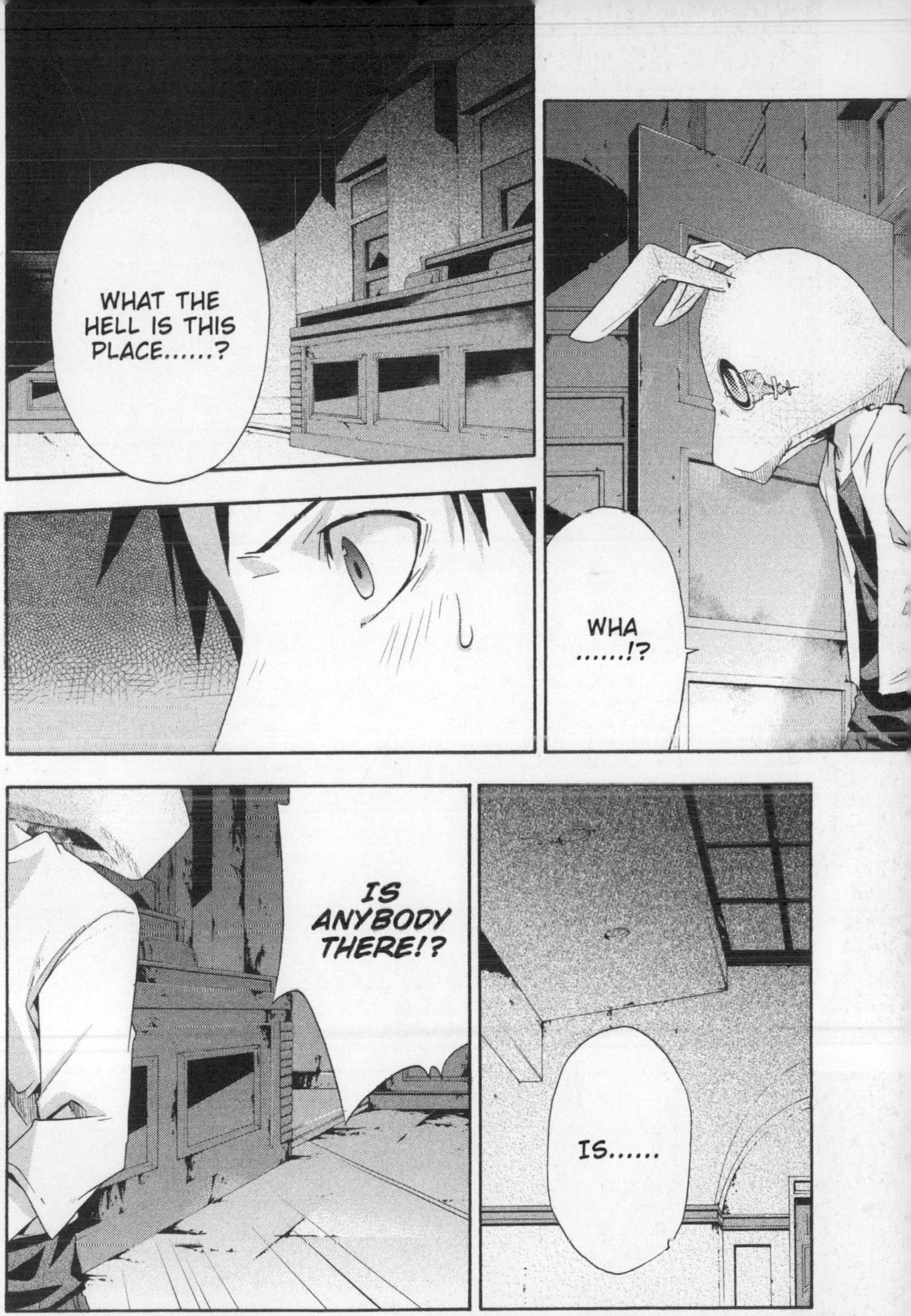
WHA ......!?
WHAT THE HELL IS THIS PLACE......?
IS......
IS ANYBODY THERE!?

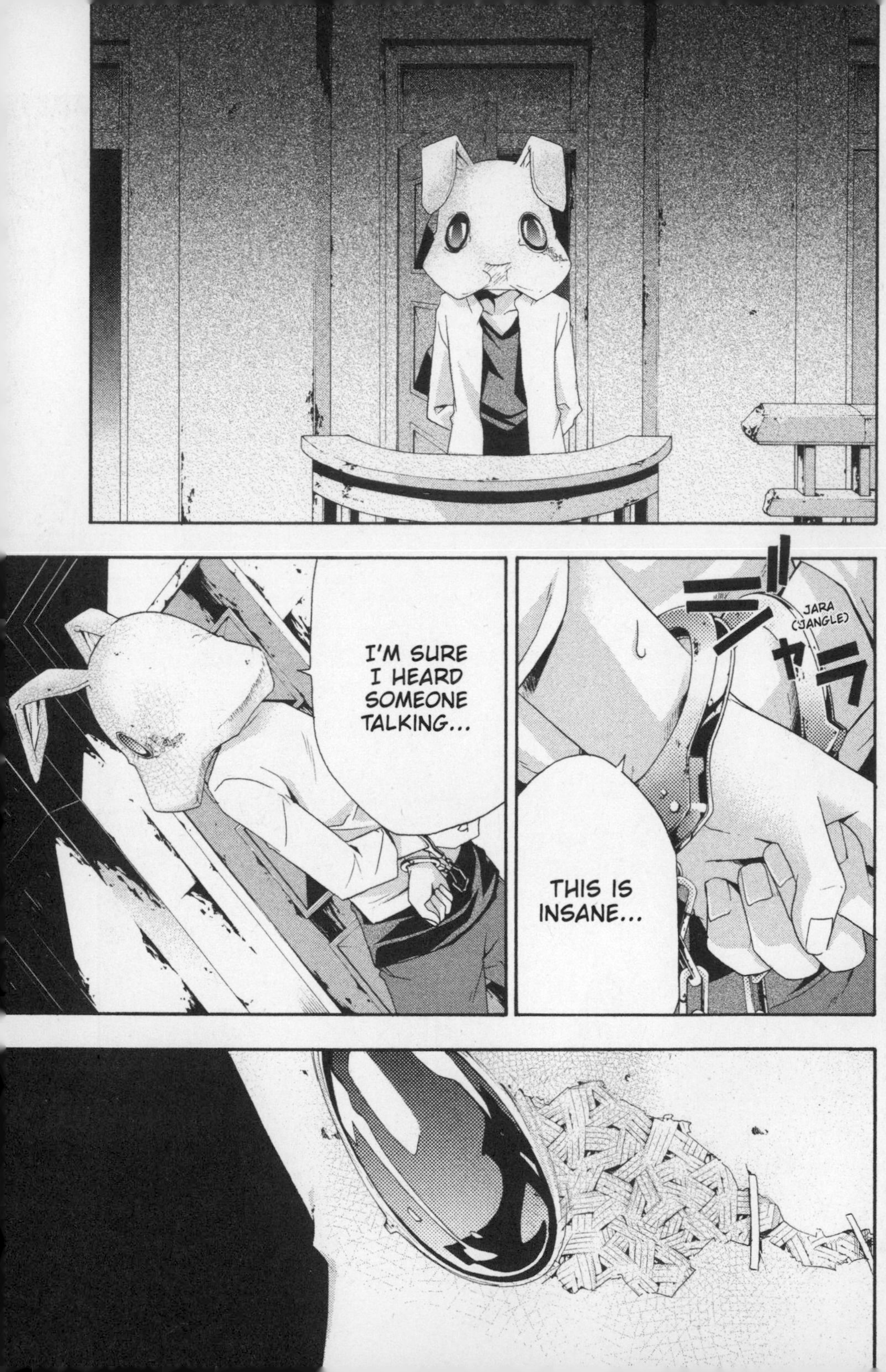
ジャラ
JARA (JANGLE)
THIS IS INSANE...
I'M SURE I HEARD SOMEONE TALKING...

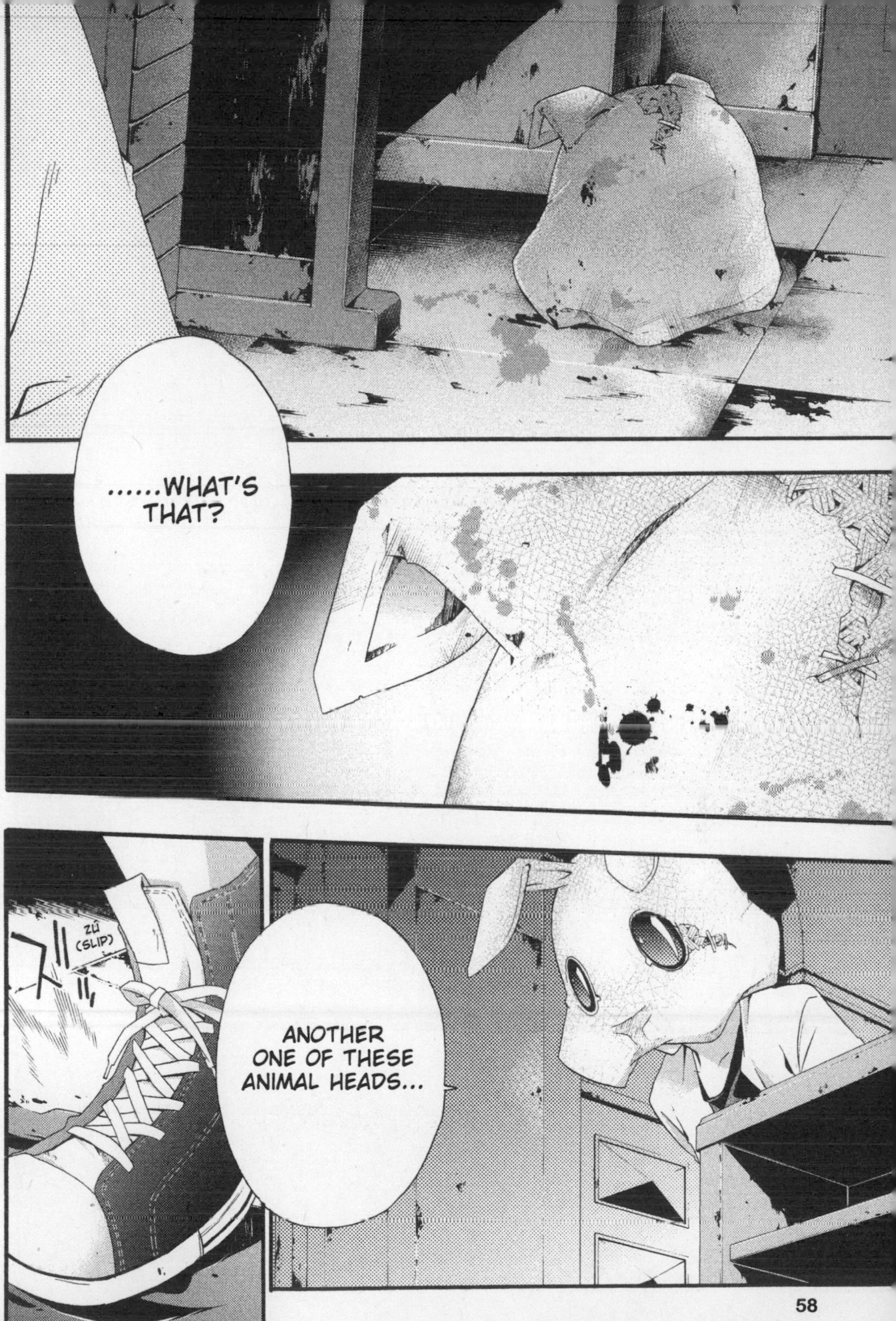
......WHAT'S THAT?
ANOTHER ONE OF THESE ANIMAL HEADS...
ZU (SLIP)

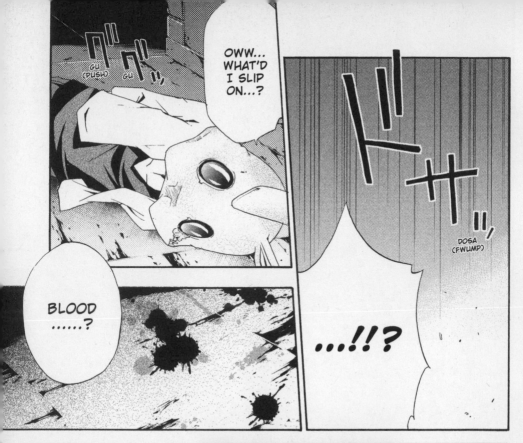

OWW... WHAT'D I SLIP ON...?

GU (PUSH)

GU

DOSA (FWUMP)

BLOOD ......?

...!!?

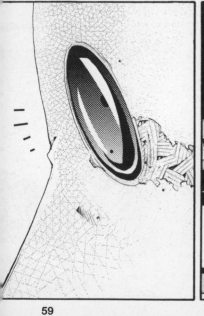

WHA—!? WHERE DID THAT COME FROM......?

ZURU (SLLUMP)

59

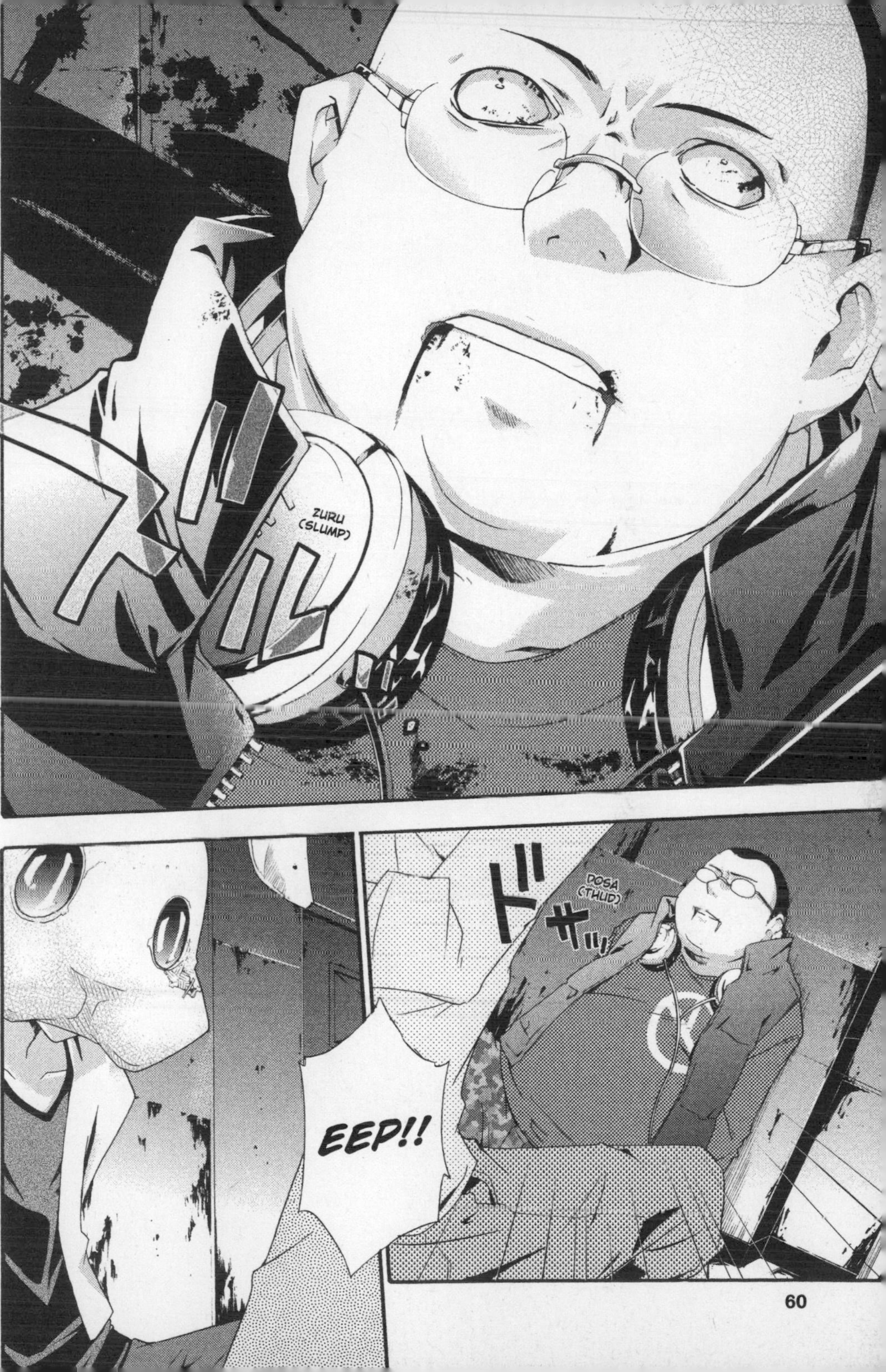
ZURU (SLUMP)
DOSA (THUD)
EEP!!

HE......
HE'S
DEAD!?

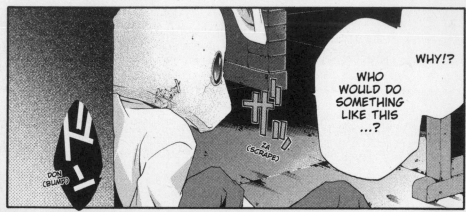

WHY!?

WHO
WOULD DO
SOMETHING
LIKE THIS
...?

DON
(BUMP)

ZA
(SCRAPE)

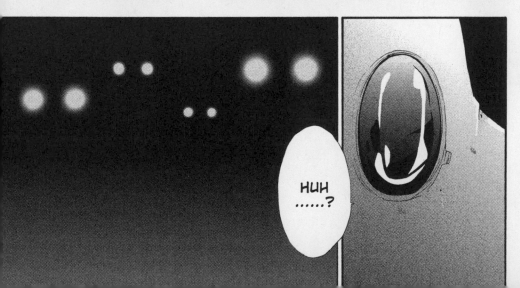

HUH
......?

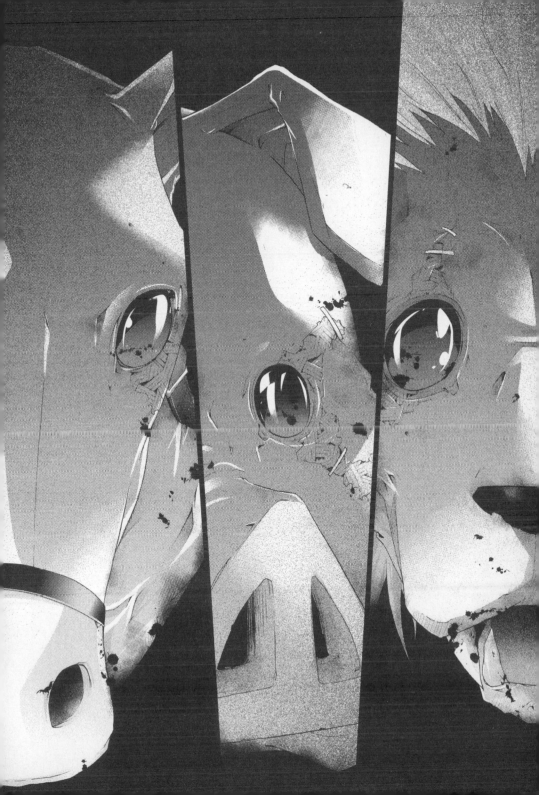

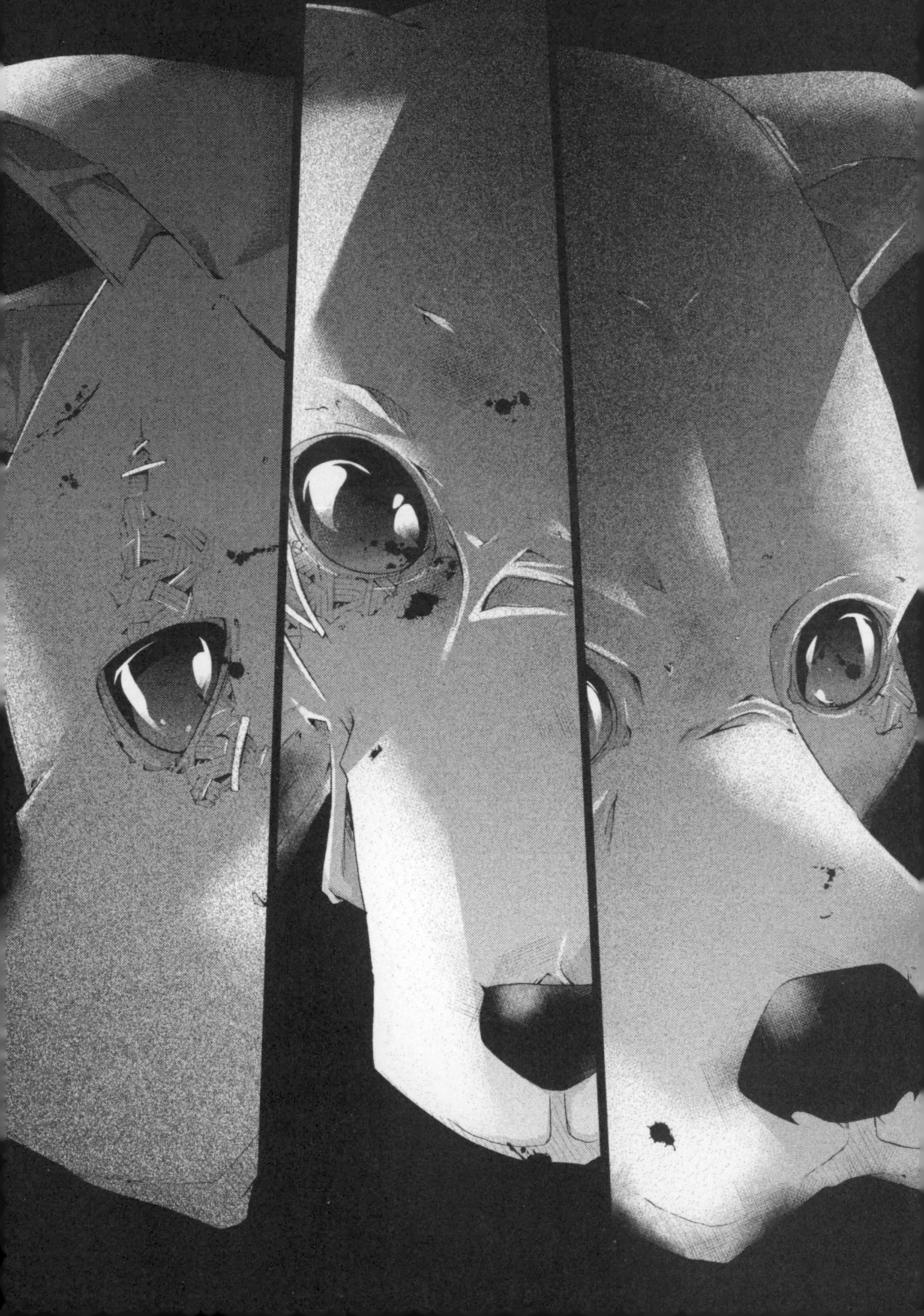

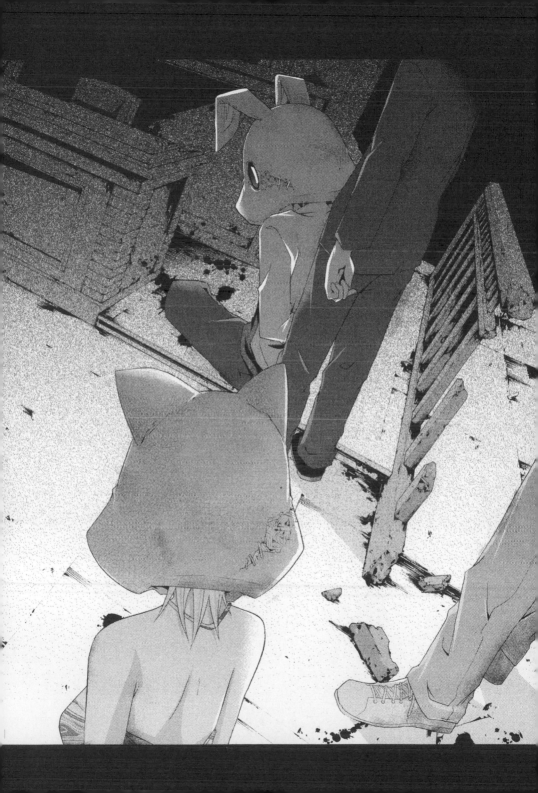

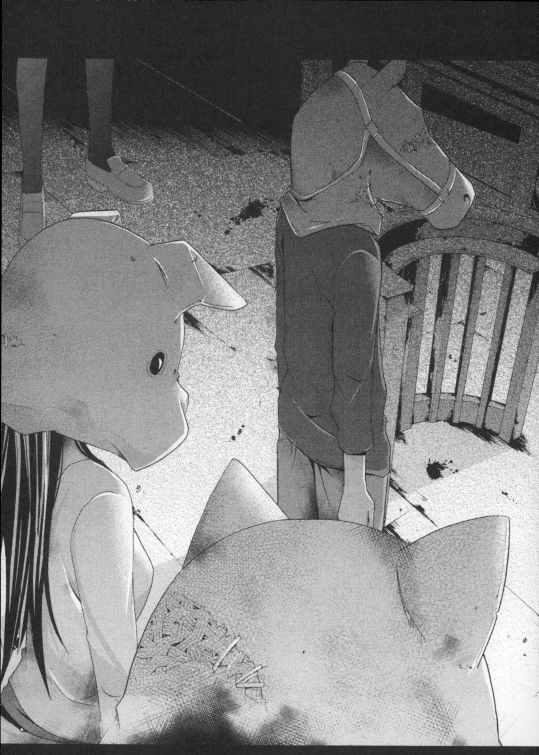

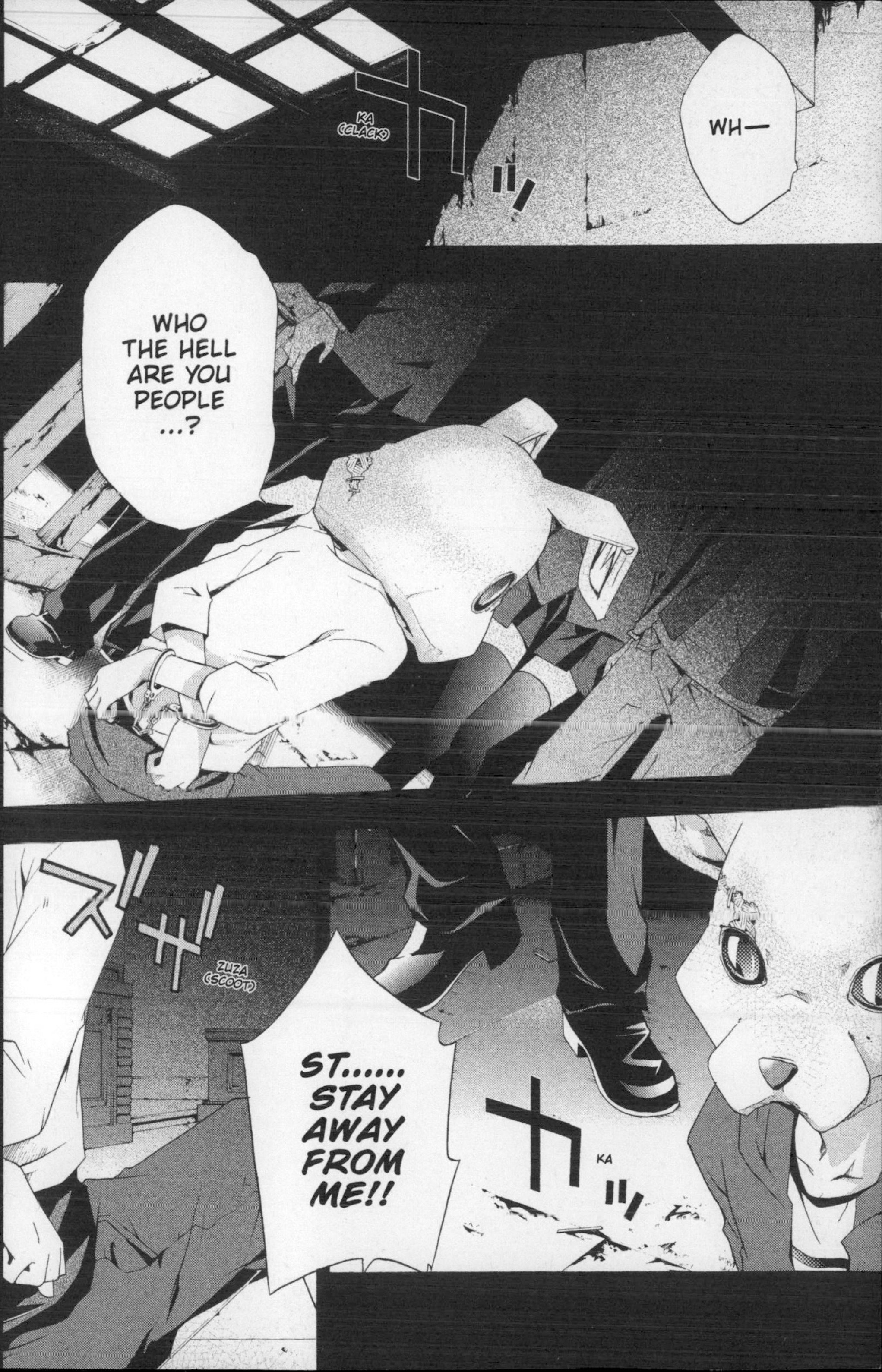
WH—
KA (CLACK)
WHO THE HELL ARE YOU PEOPLE ...?
KA
ST...... STAY AWAY FROM ME!!
ZUZA (SCOOT)

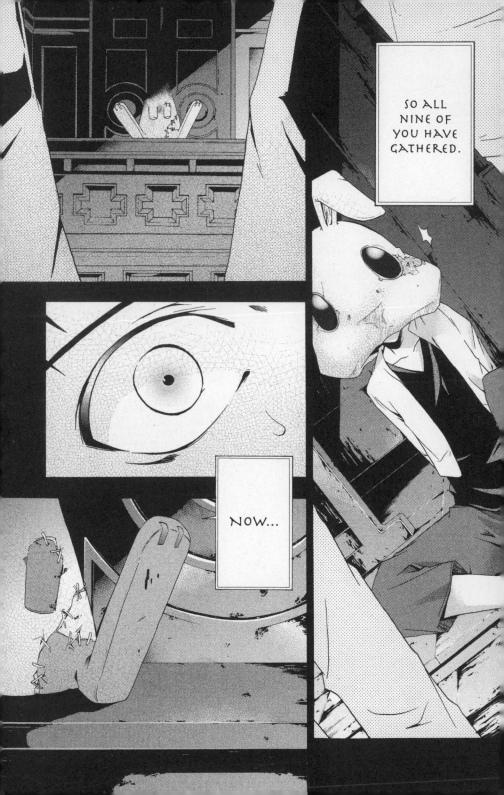

SO ALL
NINE OF
YOU HAVE
GATHERED.

NOW...

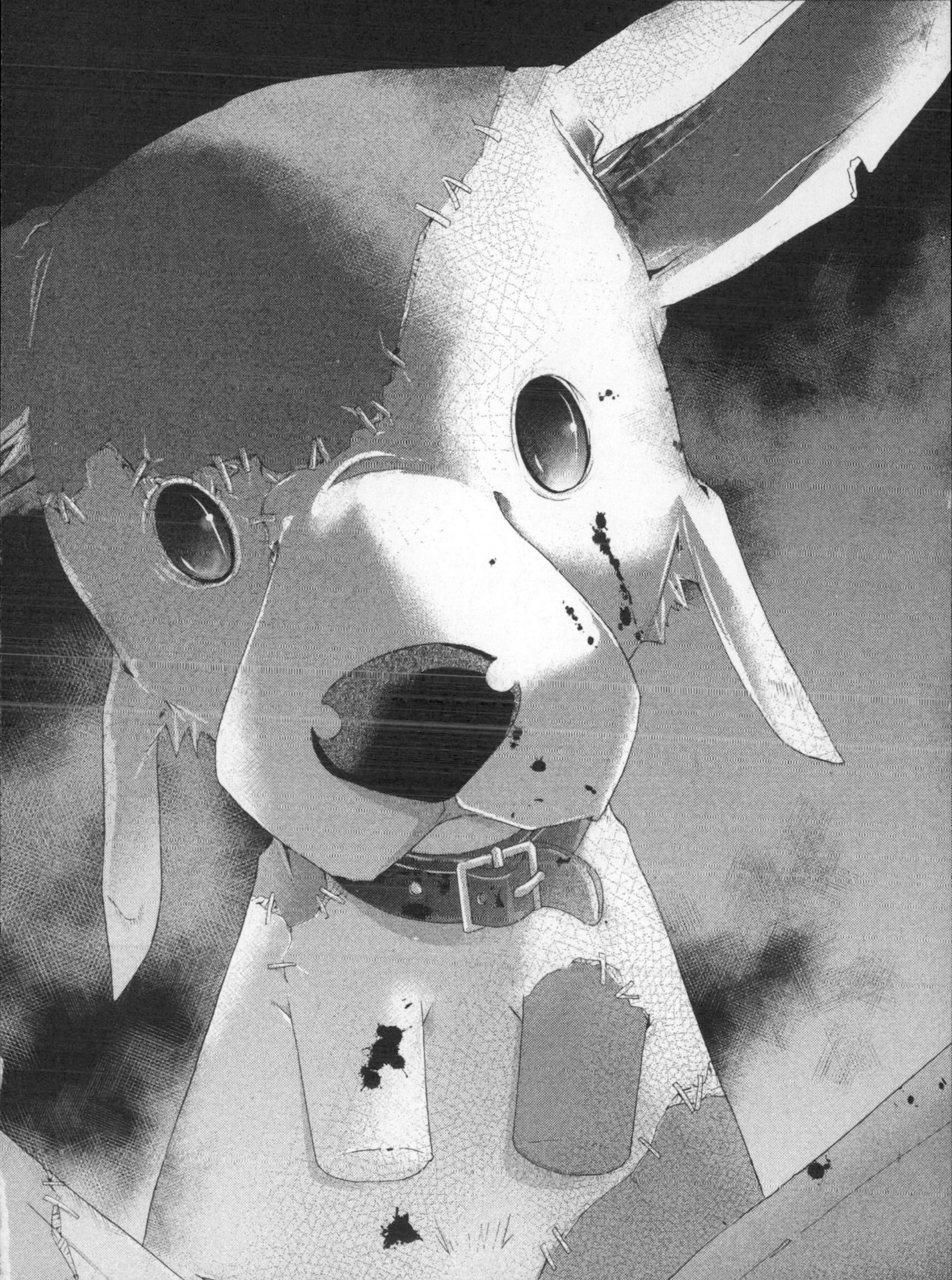

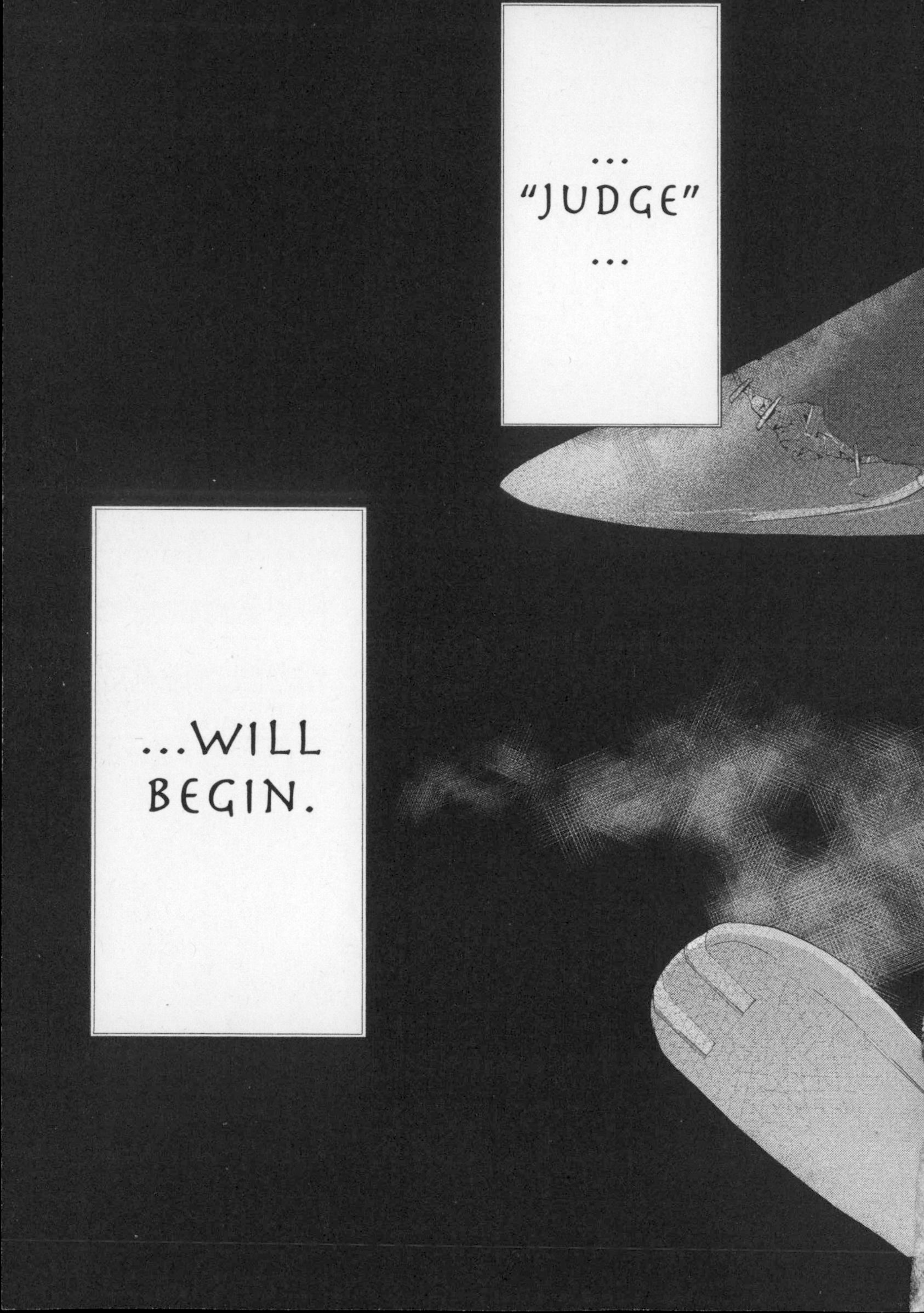
...
"JUDGE"
...
...WILL BEGIN.

Envy

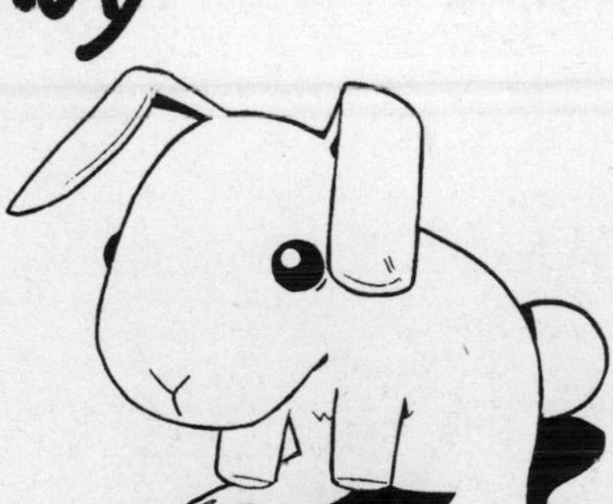

CHAPTER 2   UNLOCKED

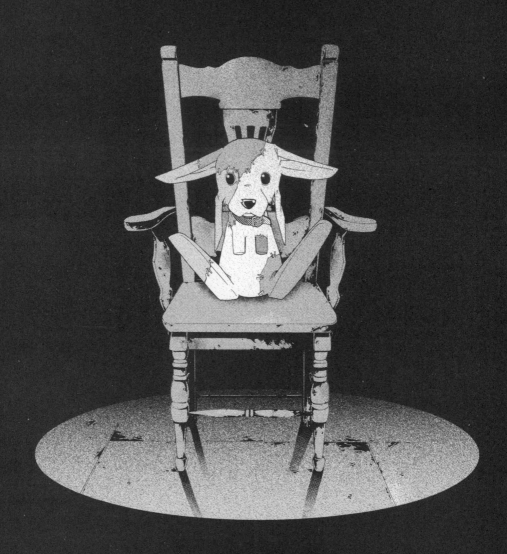

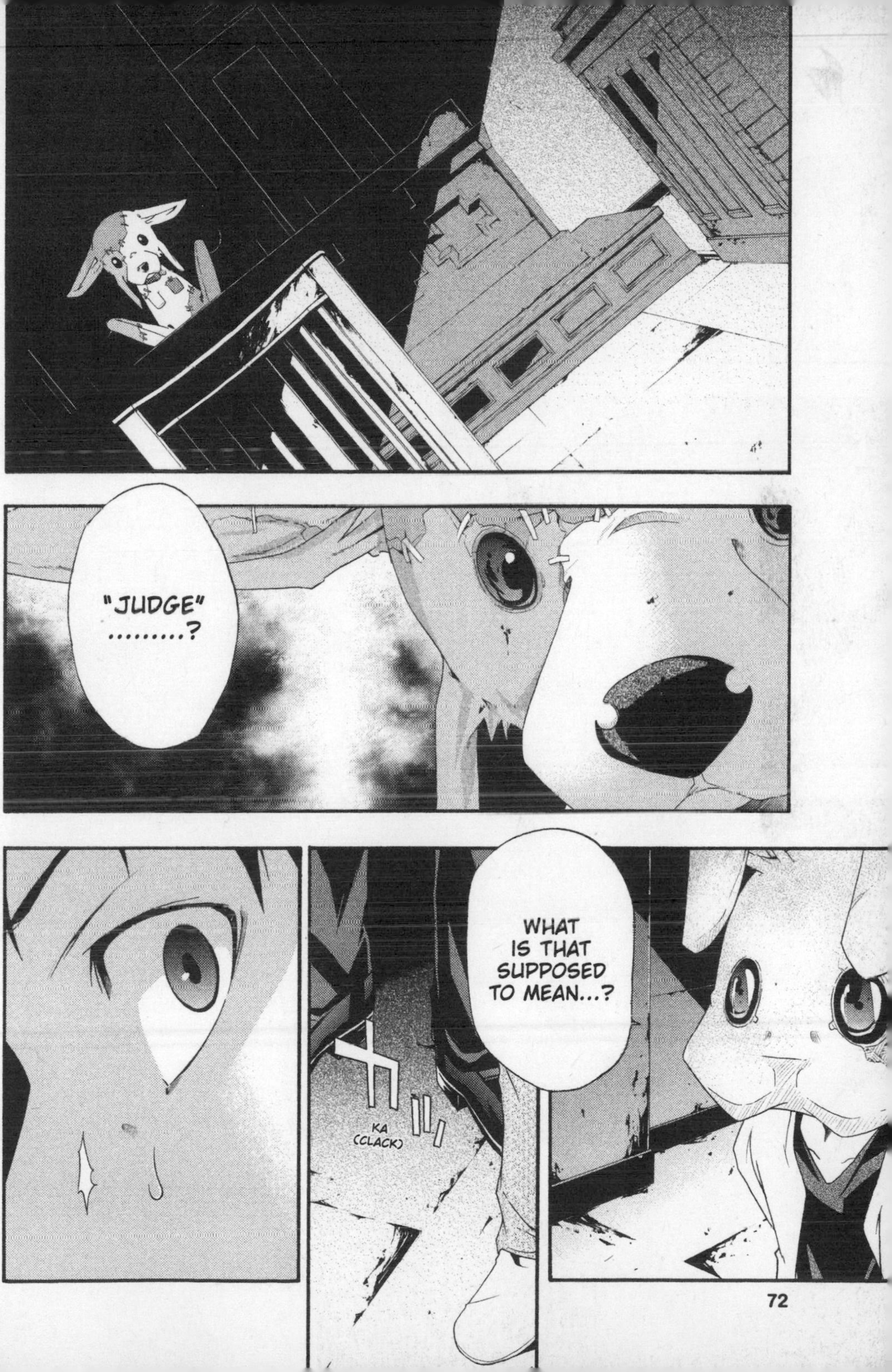
"JUDGE" ....?
WHAT IS THAT SUPPOSED TO MEAN...?
KA (CLACK)

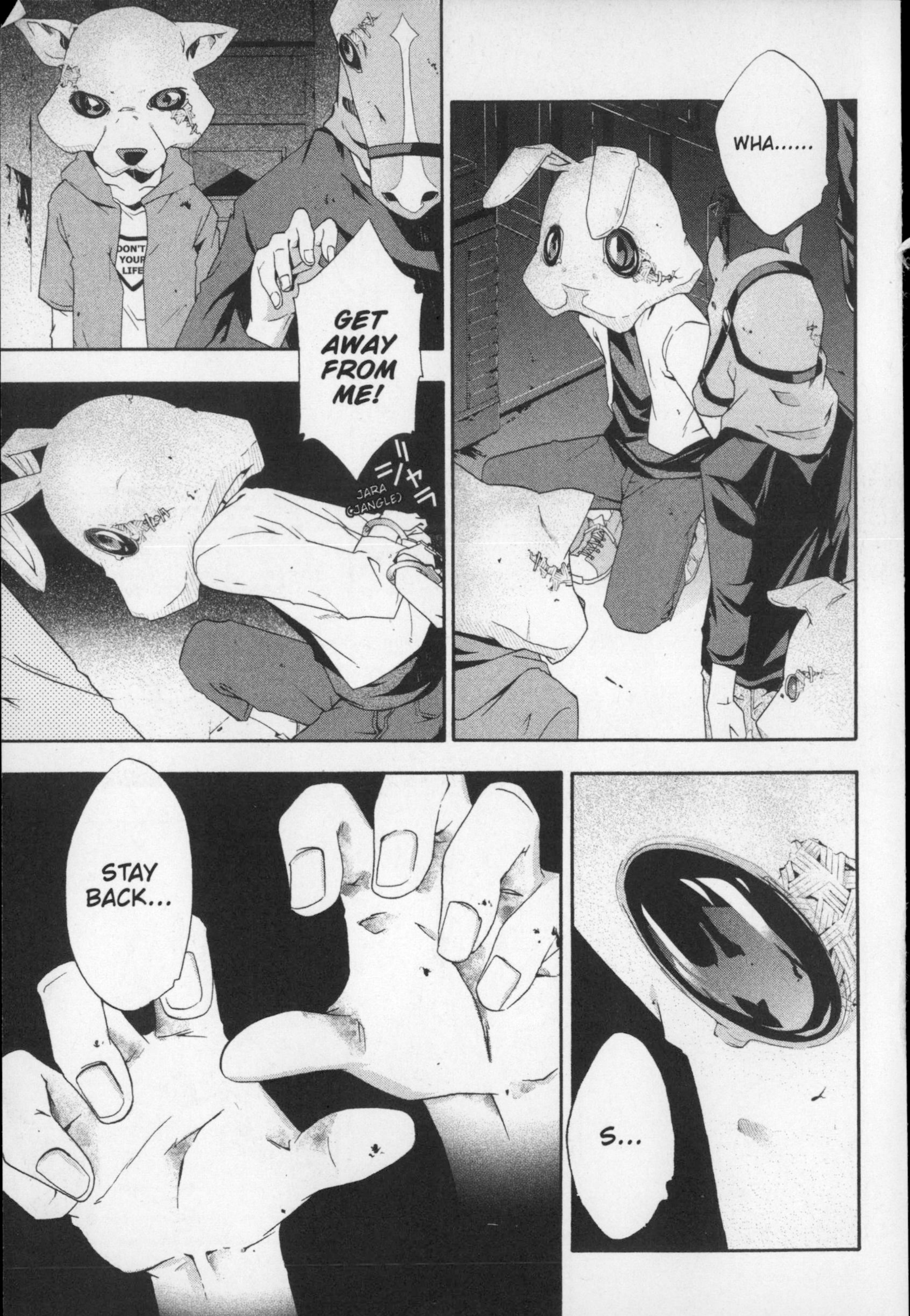
WHA......
DON'T YOUR LIFE
GET AWAY FROM ME!
ジャラ
JARA (JANGLE)
S...
STAY BACK...

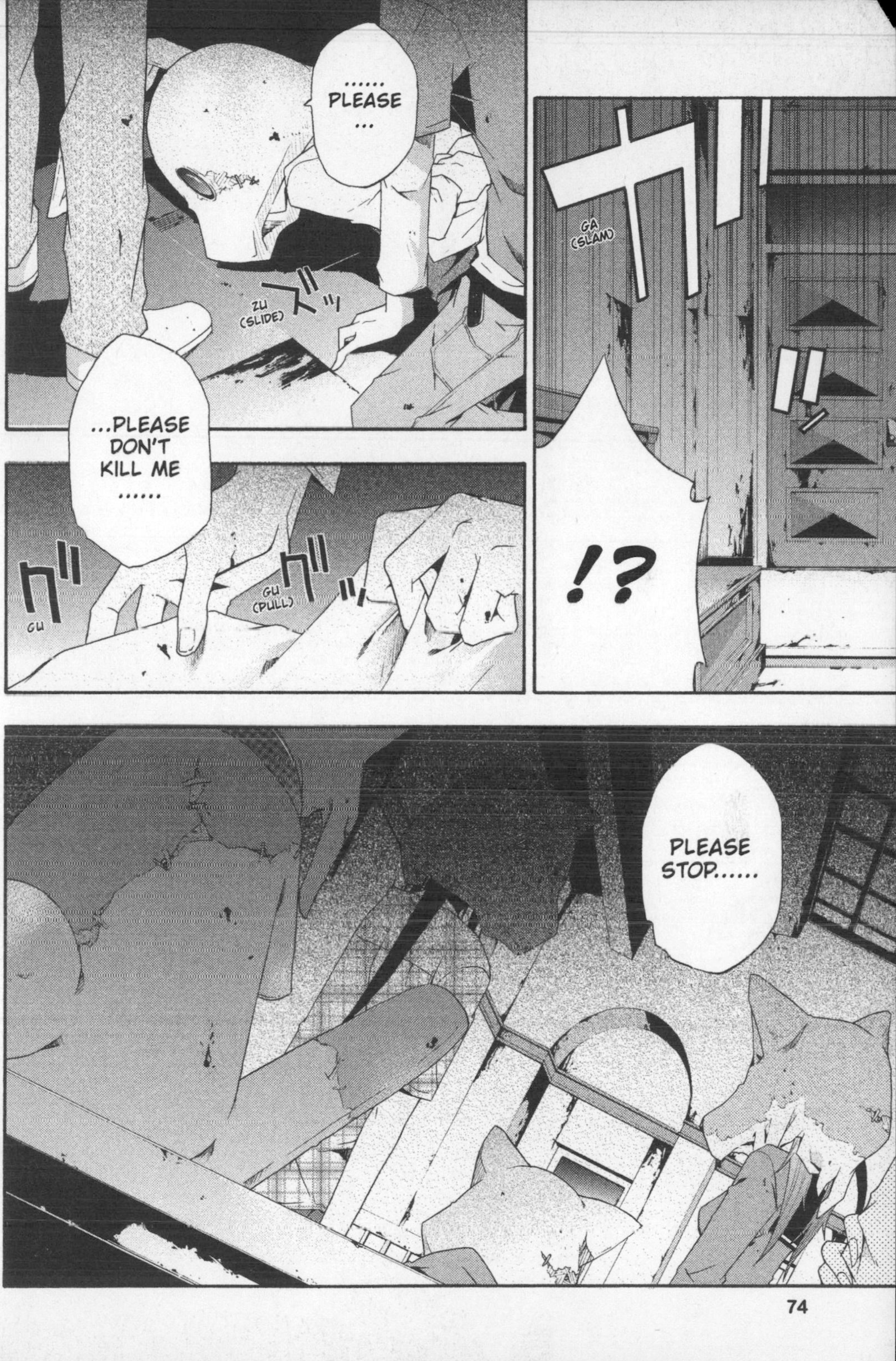
GA (SLAM)
!?
......PLEASE...
ZU (SLIDE)
...PLEASE DON'T KILL ME......
GU (PULL)
GU
PLEASE STOP......

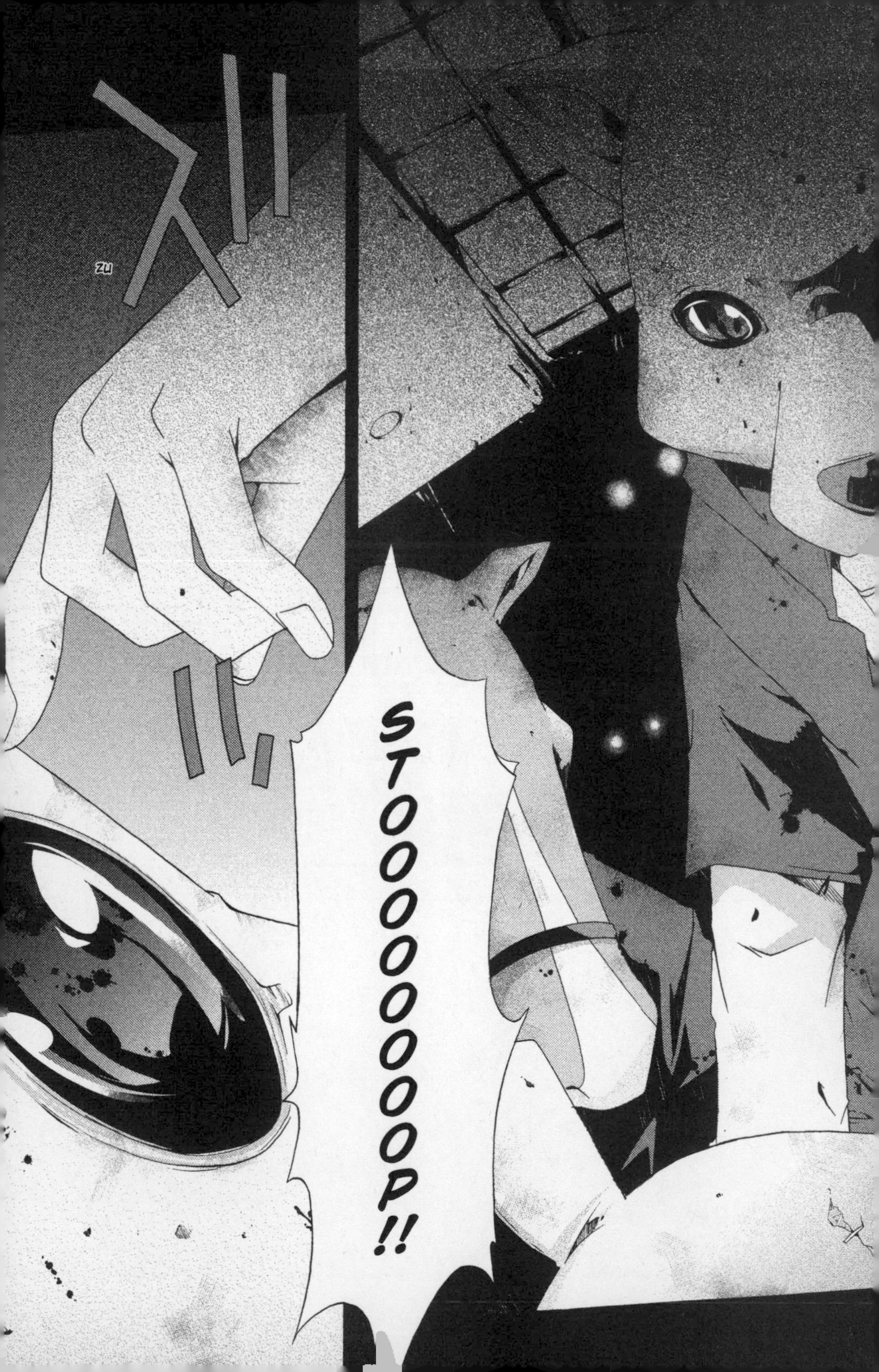
ZU
STOOOOOOOOOOP!!

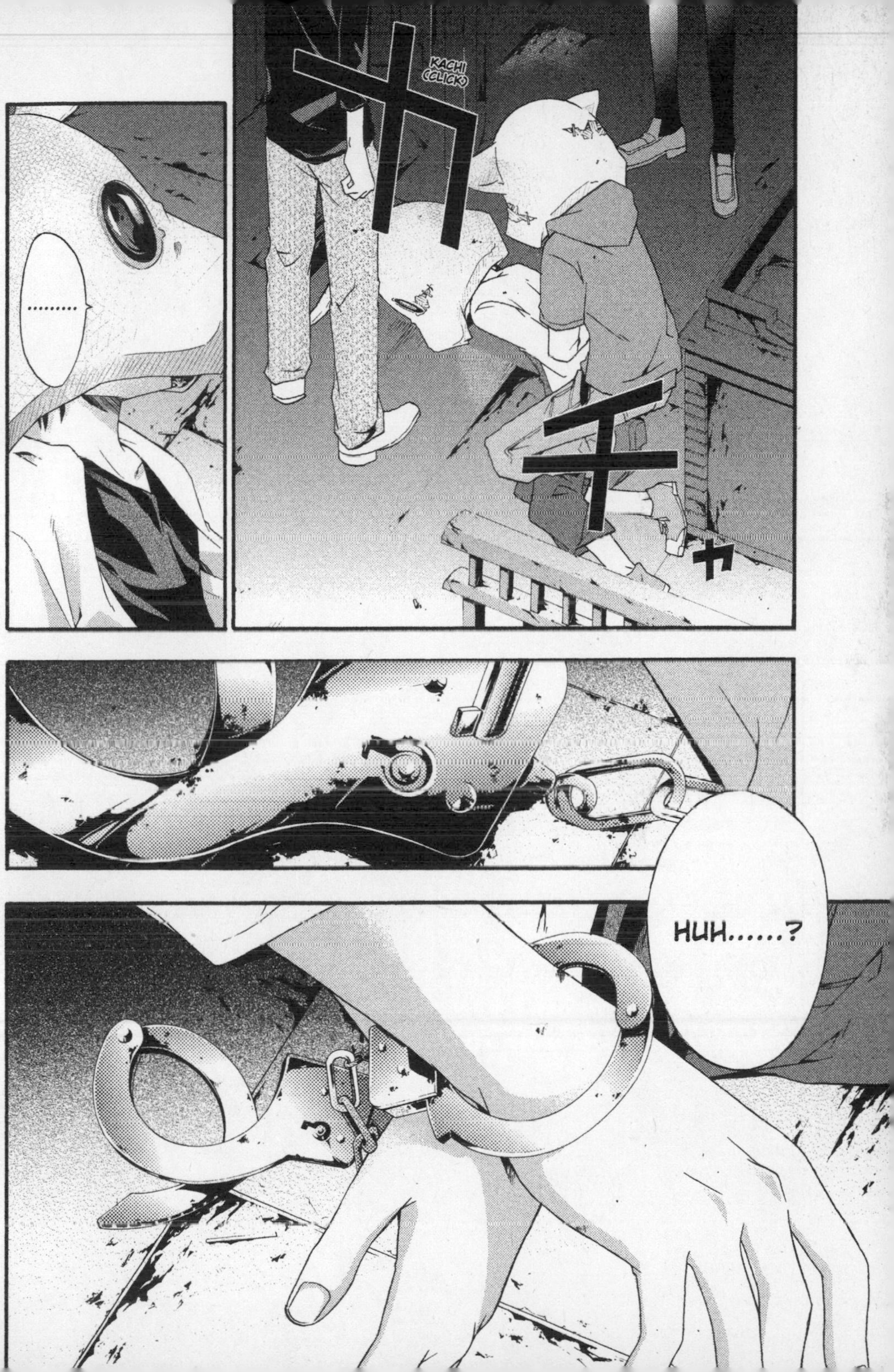
カチッ
KACHI (CLICK)
....
HUH......?

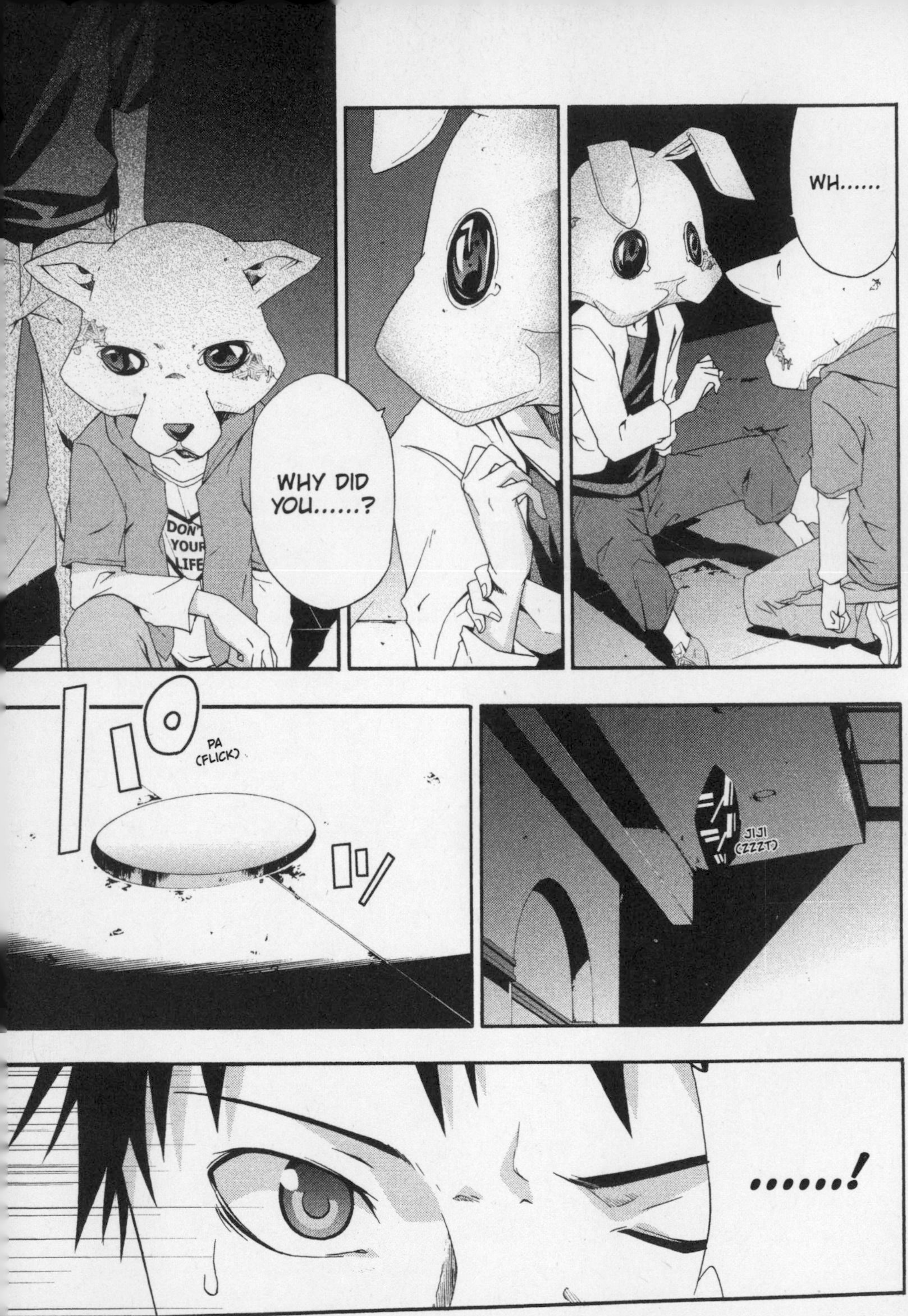
WH......
WHY DID YOU......?
JIJI (ZZZT)
PA (FLICK)
......!

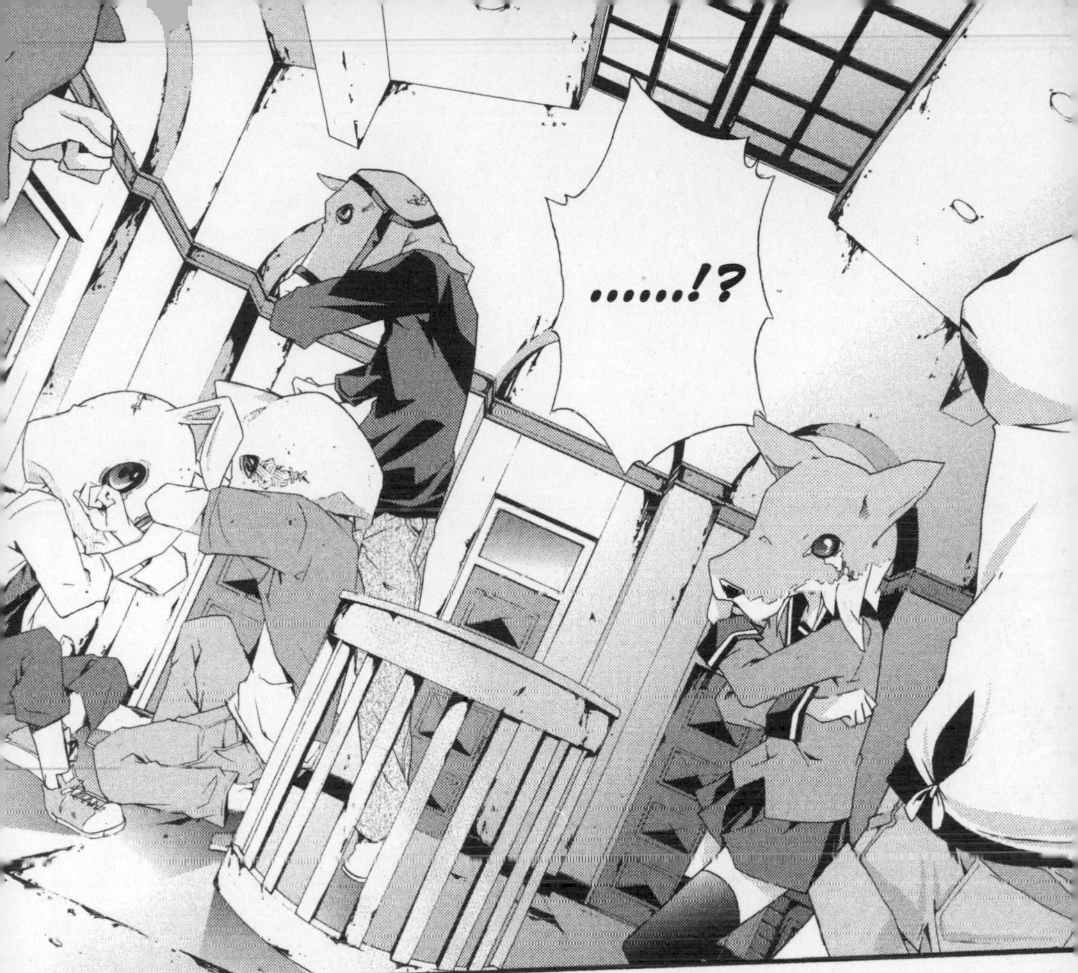
......!?

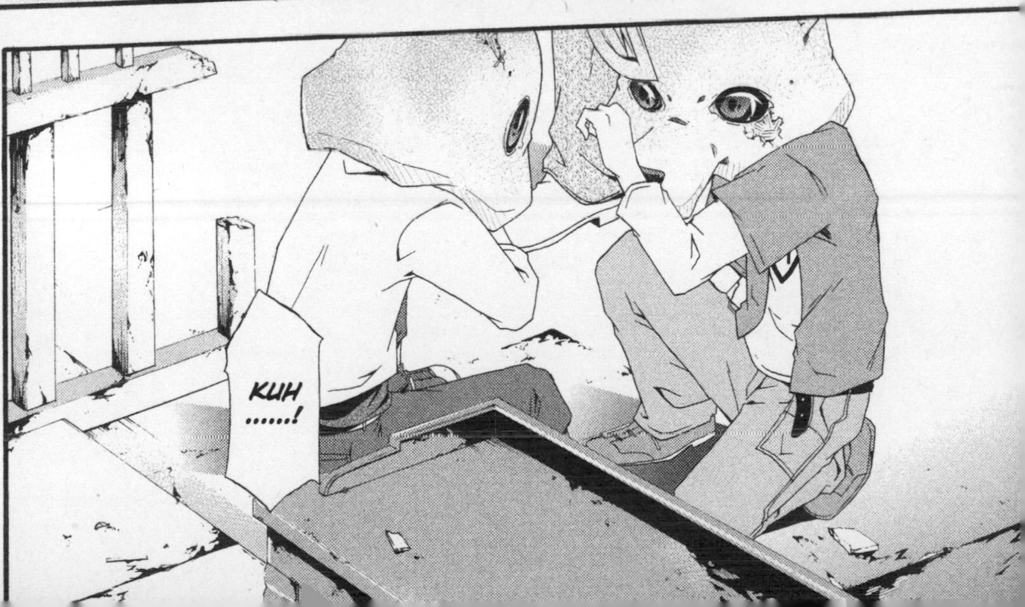
KUH ......!

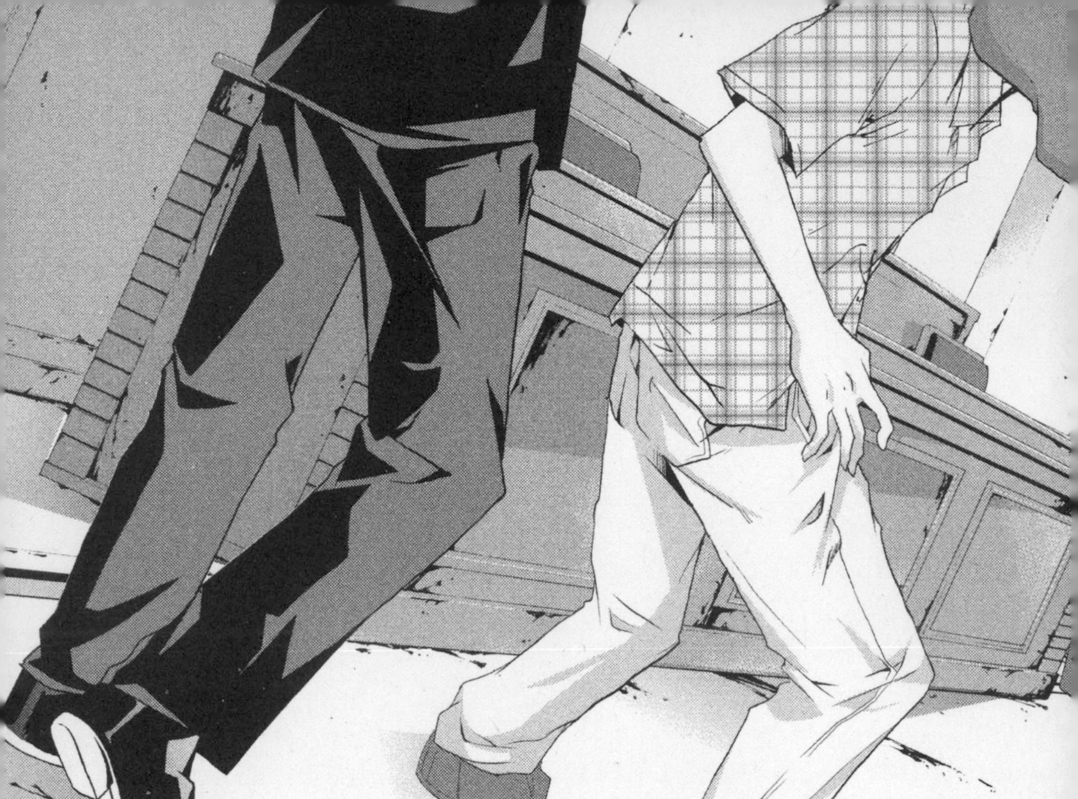

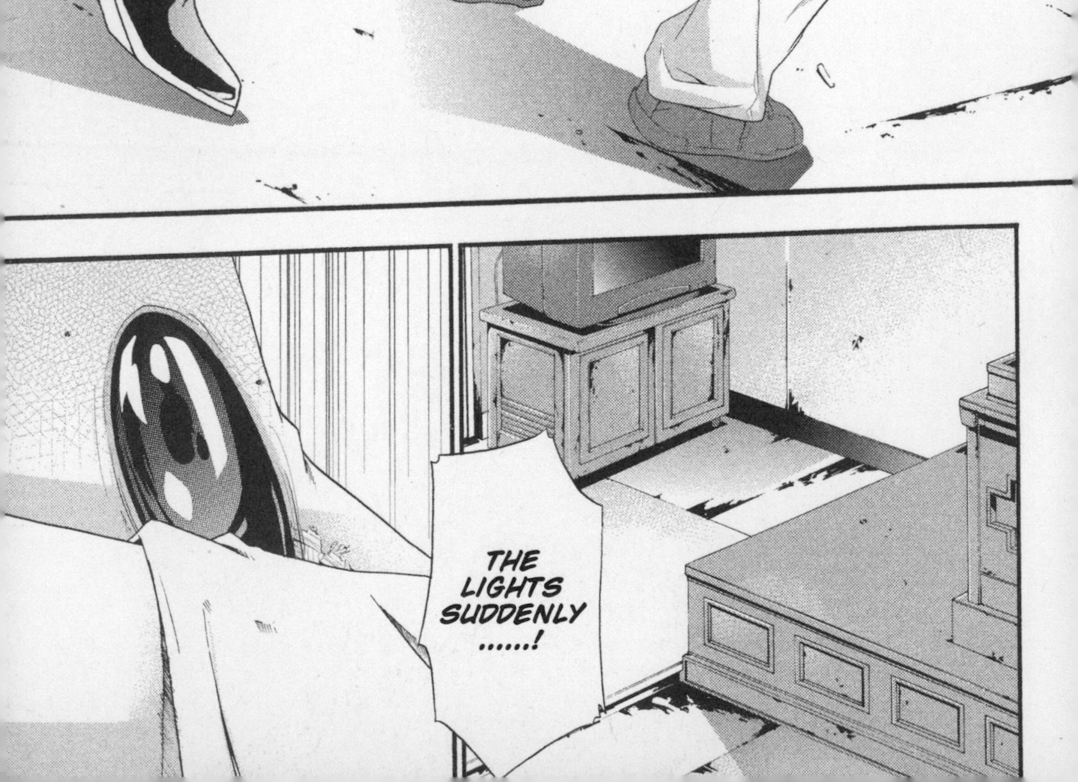
THE LIGHTS SUDDENLY ......!

?

DAMN.

MY EYES HAD GOTTEN SO USED TO THE DARKNESS THAT IT'S PAINFUL...

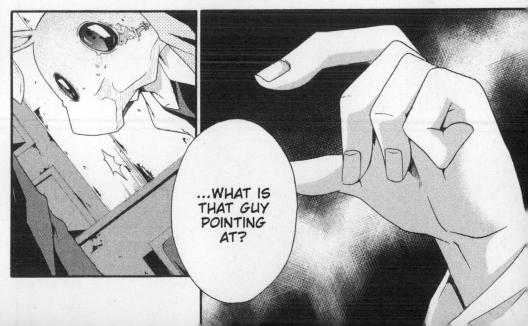

...WHAT IS THAT GUY POINTING AT?

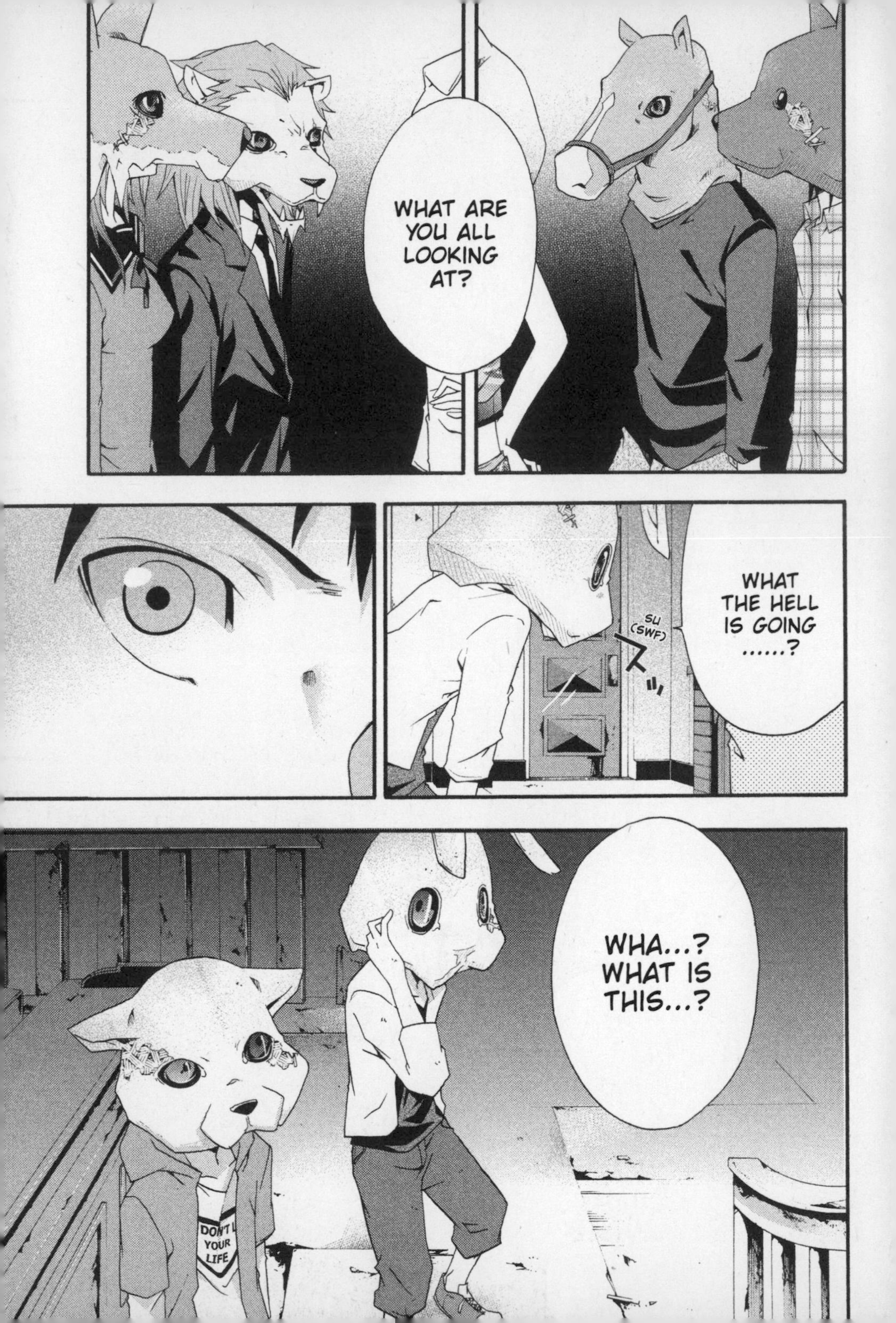
WHAT ARE YOU ALL LOOKING AT?
WHAT THE HELL IS GOING ......?
SU (SWF)
WHA...? WHAT IS THIS...?
DON'T
YOUR LIFE

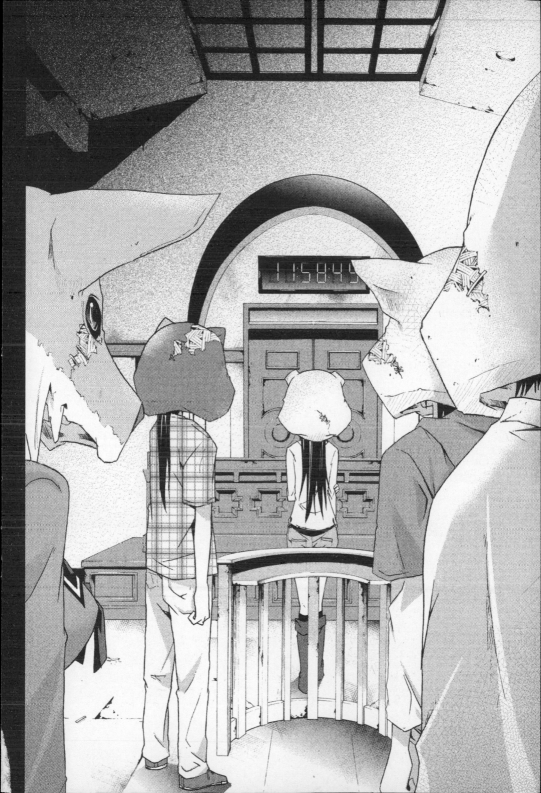

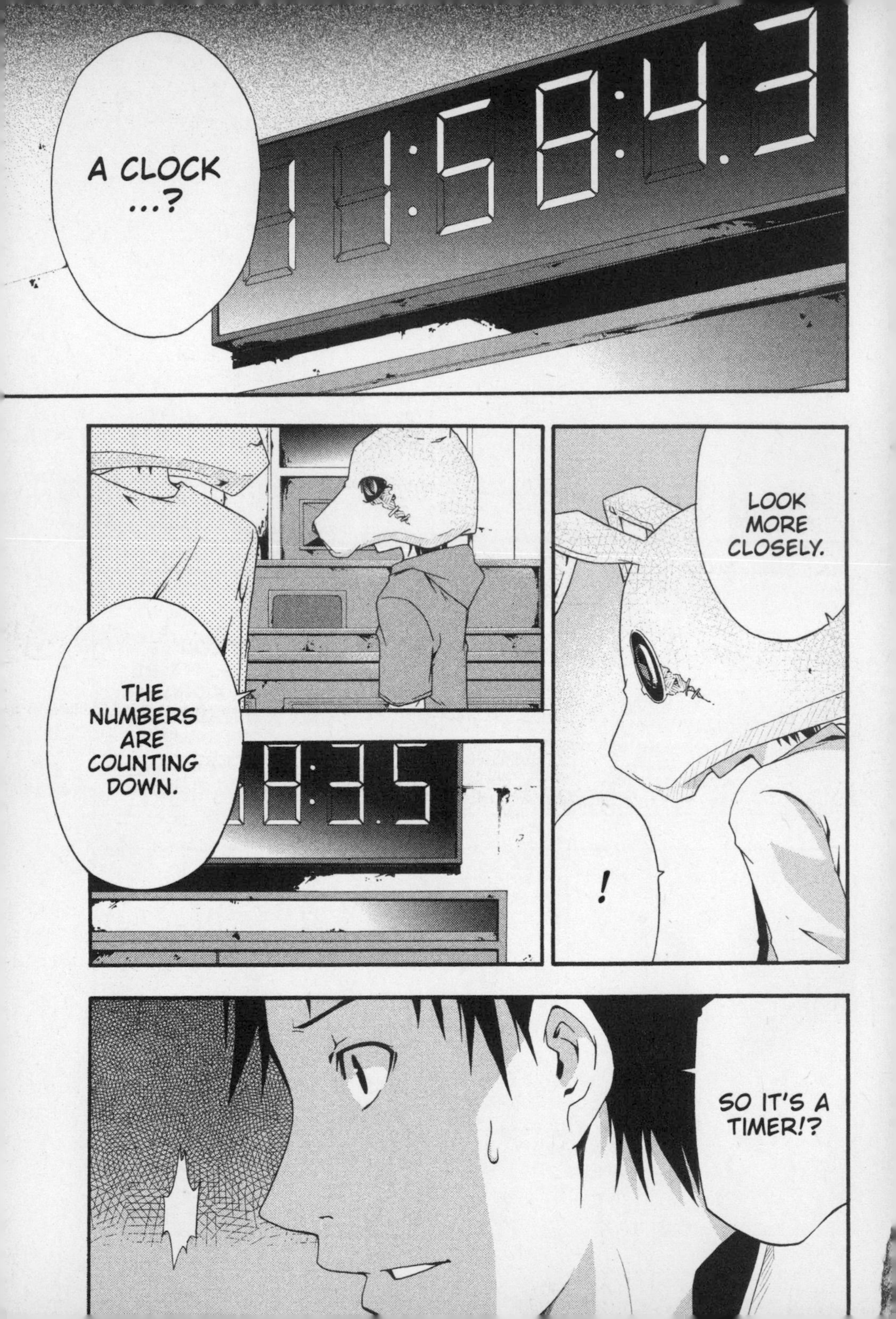
A CLOCK ...?
LOOK MORE CLOSELY.
!
THE NUMBERS ARE COUNTING DOWN.
SO IT'S A TIMER!?

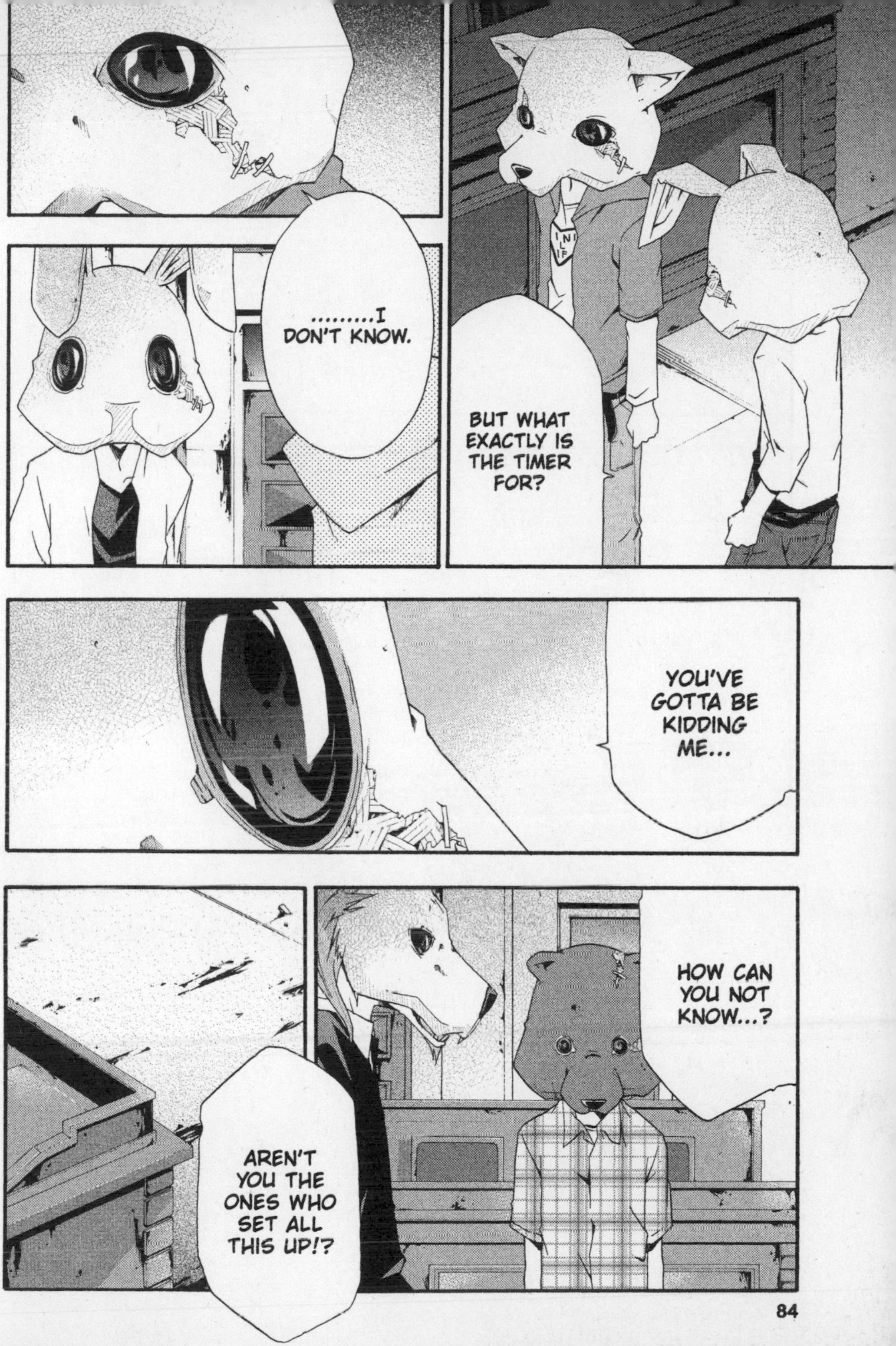
BUT WHAT EXACTLY IS THE TIMER FOR?
.........I DON'T KNOW.
YOU'VE GOTTA BE KIDDING ME...
HOW CAN YOU NOT KNOW...?
AREN'T YOU THE ONES WHO SET ALL THIS UP!?

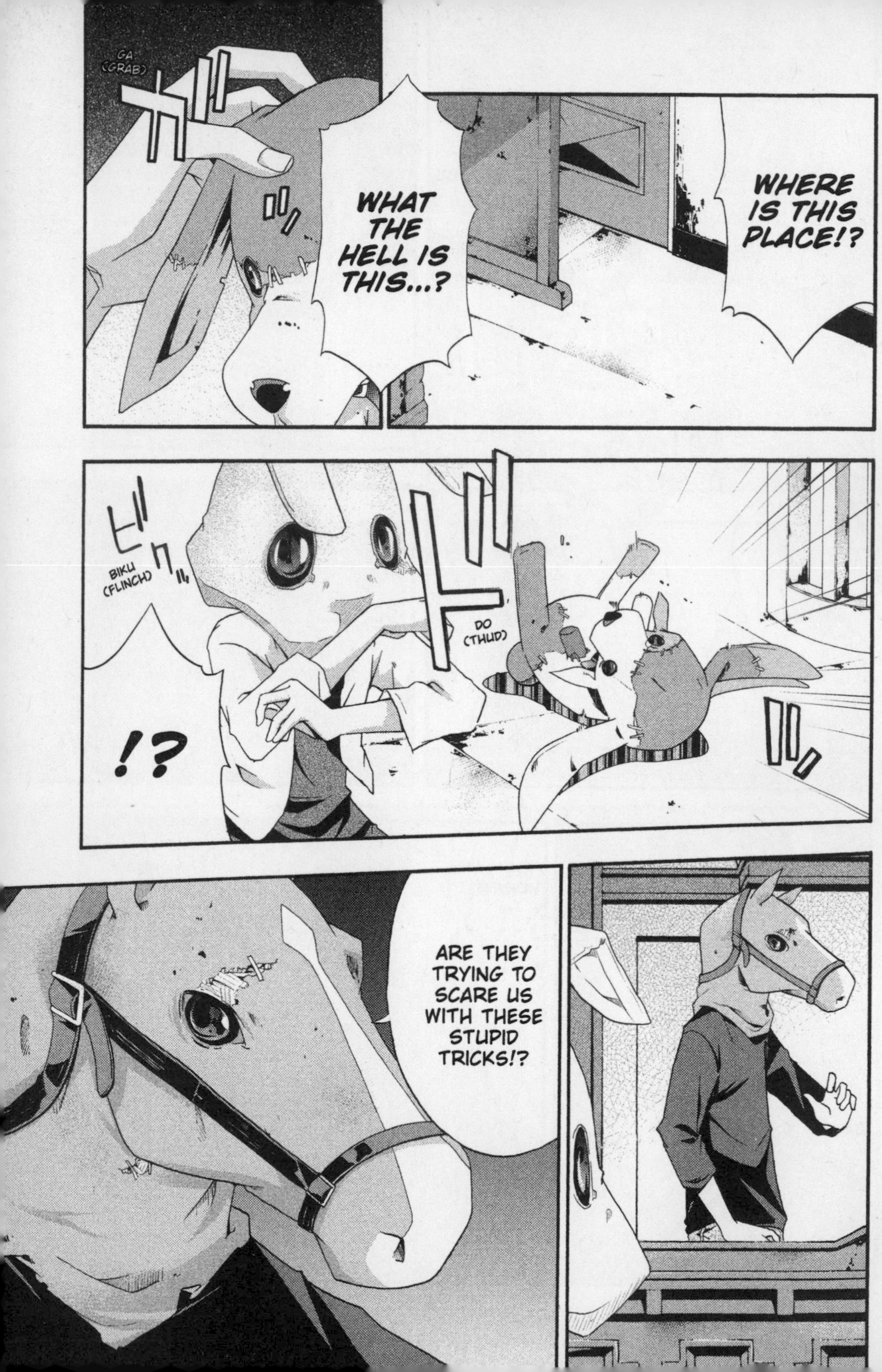
GA (GRAB)
WHERE IS THIS PLACE!?
WHAT THE HELL IS THIS...?
DO (THUD)
BIKU (FLINCH)
!?
ARE THEY TRYING TO SCARE US WITH THESE STUPID TRICKS!?

IF THEY AREN'T THE ONES...

...WHO BROUGHT ME HERE, THEN WHO ...?

THIS FREAKY THING...

SHIT!

HUFF ...

HUFF ...

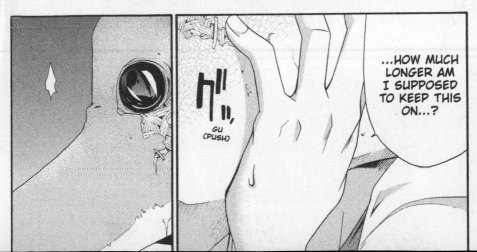

グ
GU
(PUSH)

...HOW MUCH LONGER AM I SUPPOSED TO KEEP THIS ON...?

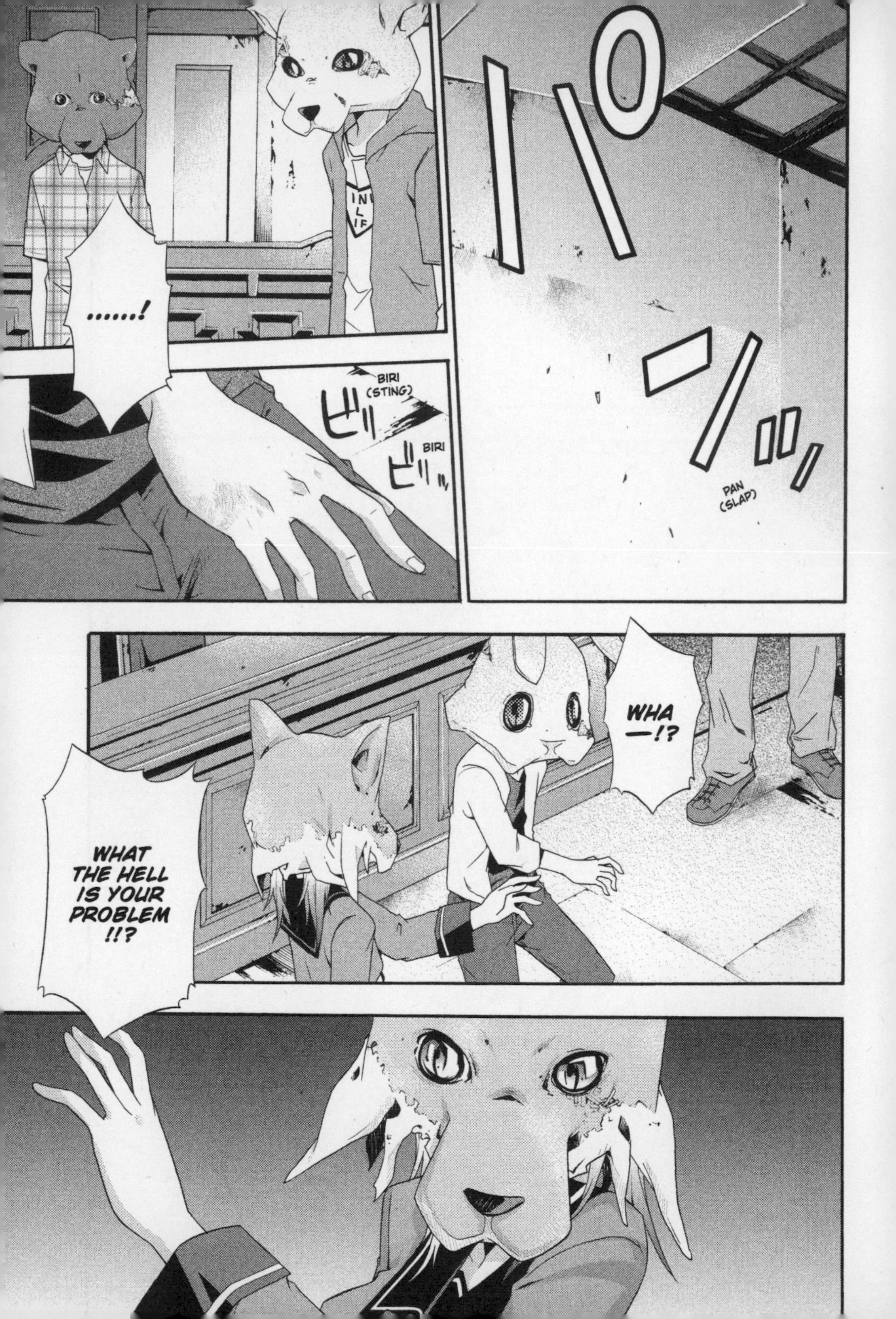
PAN
(SLAP)
......!
BIRI
(STING)
BIRI
WHA—!?
WHAT THE HELL IS YOUR PROBLEM!!?

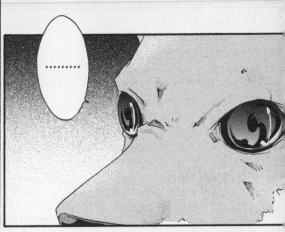

DON'T JUST STAND THERE, SAY SOMETHING!

....

UNLESS YOU WANNA DIE, YOU PROBABLY SHOULDN'T TAKE THAT OFF.

DON'T YOUR LIFE

OTHERWISE YOU COULD END UP LIKE THAT GUY.

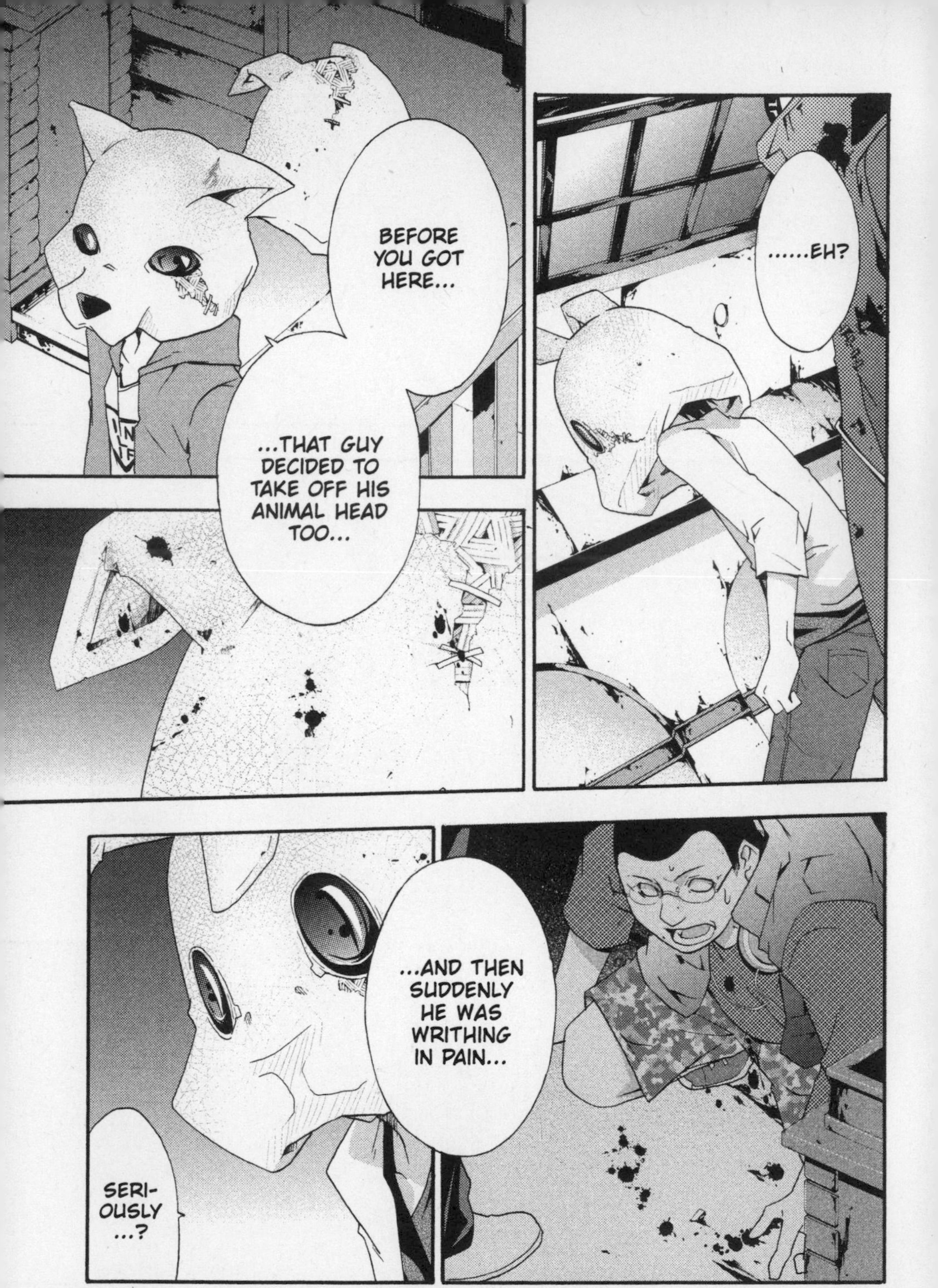
......EH?
BEFORE YOU GOT HERE...
...THAT GUY DECIDED TO TAKE OFF HIS ANIMAL HEAD TOO...
...AND THEN SUDDENLY HE WAS WRITHING IN PAIN...
SERI-OUSLY ...?

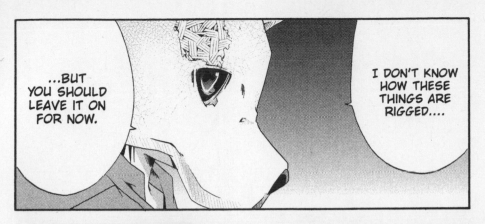

I DON'T KNOW HOW THESE THINGS ARE RIGGED....
...BUT YOU SHOULD LEAVE IT ON FOR NOW.
WHO......
WHO ARE YOU PEOPLE ...?
DON'T YOU GET IT?
EH......?

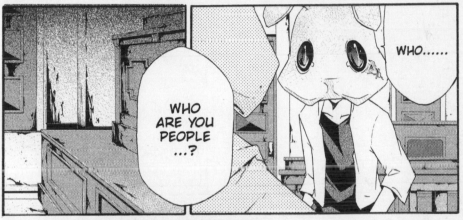

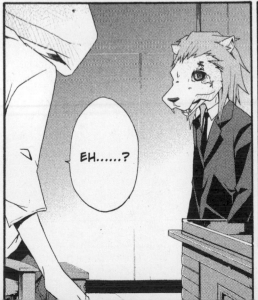

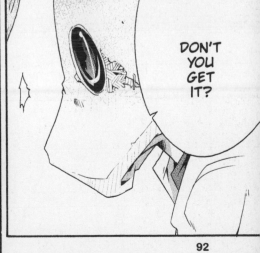

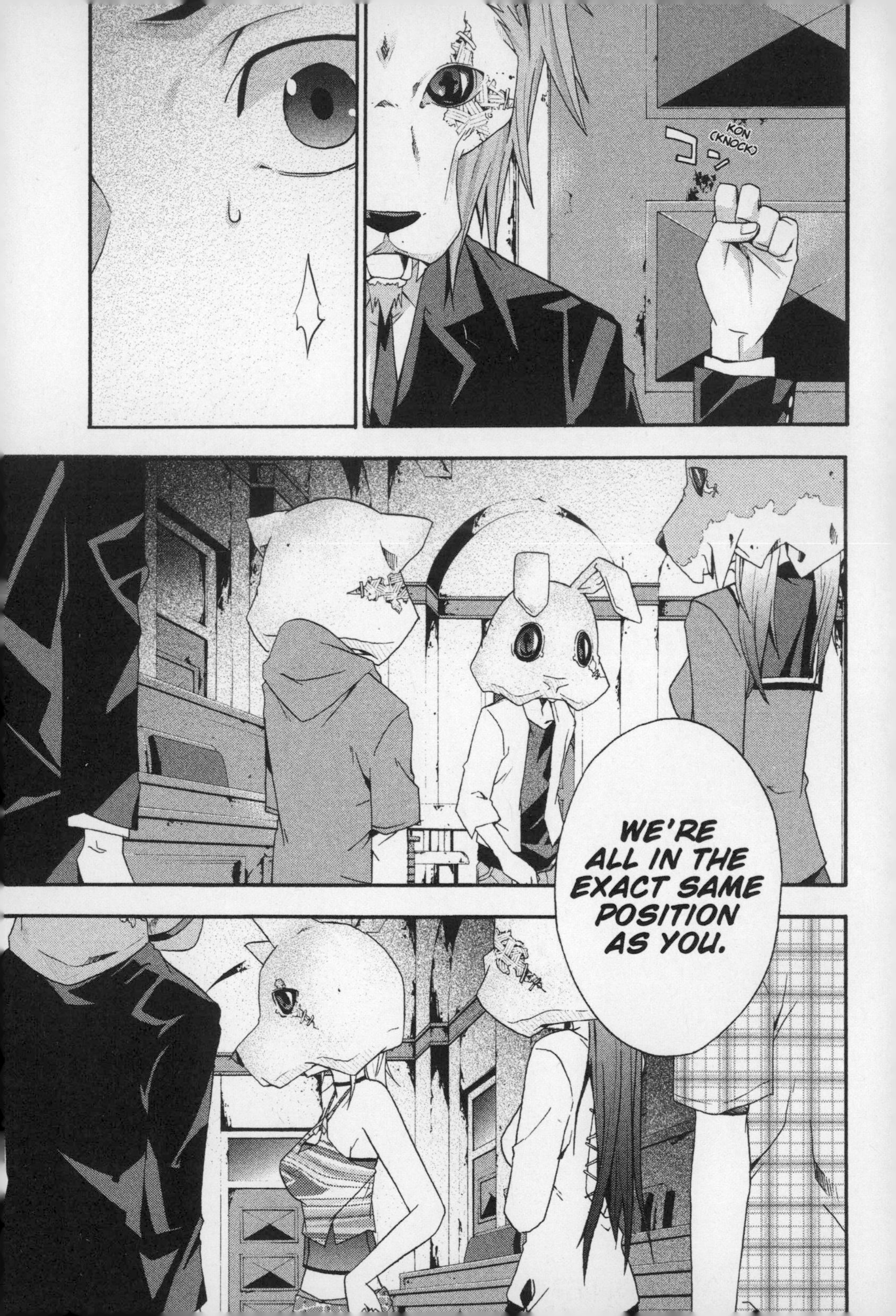
KON (KNOCK)
WE'RE ALL IN THE EXACT SAME POSITION AS YOU.

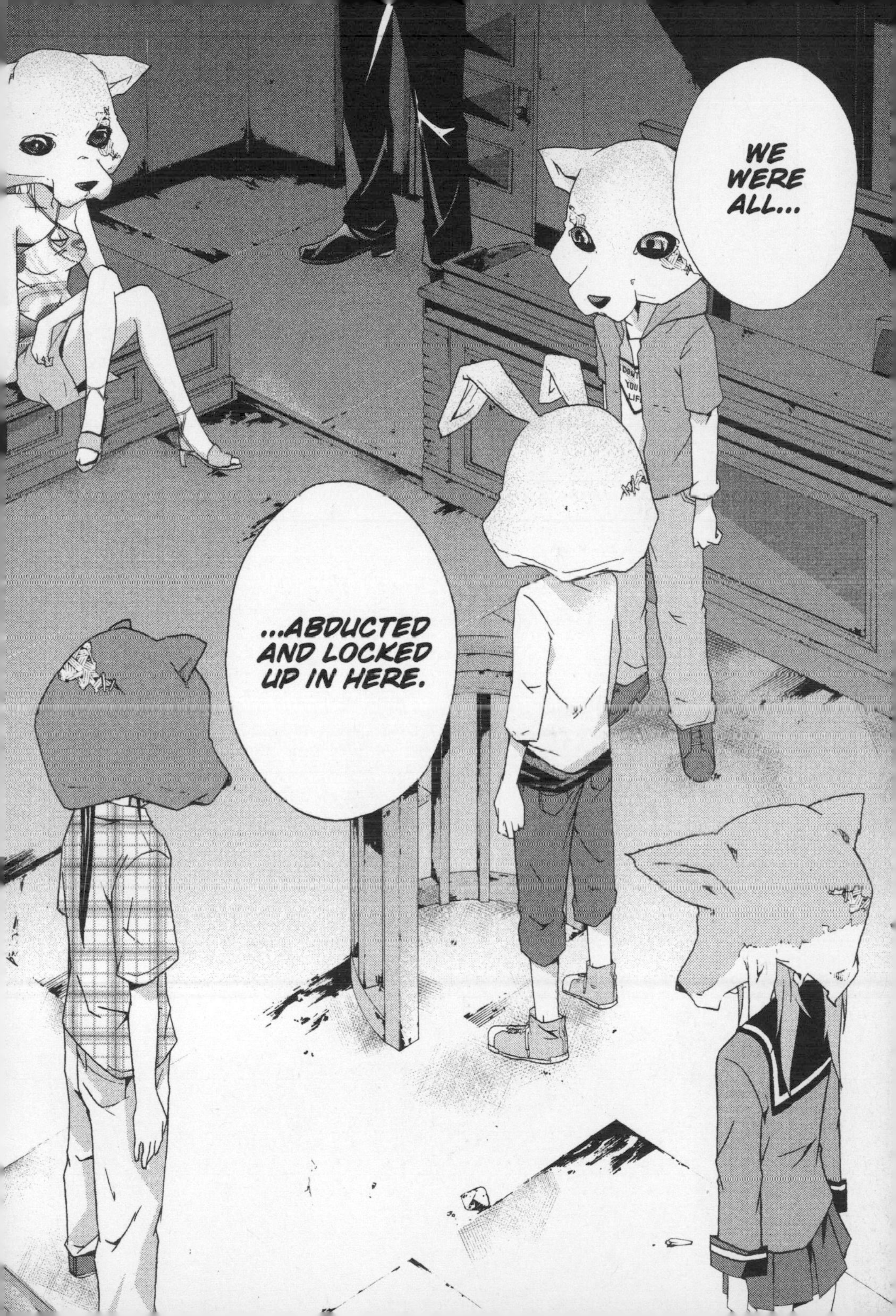
WE WERE ALL...
...ABDUCTED AND LOCKED UP IN HERE.

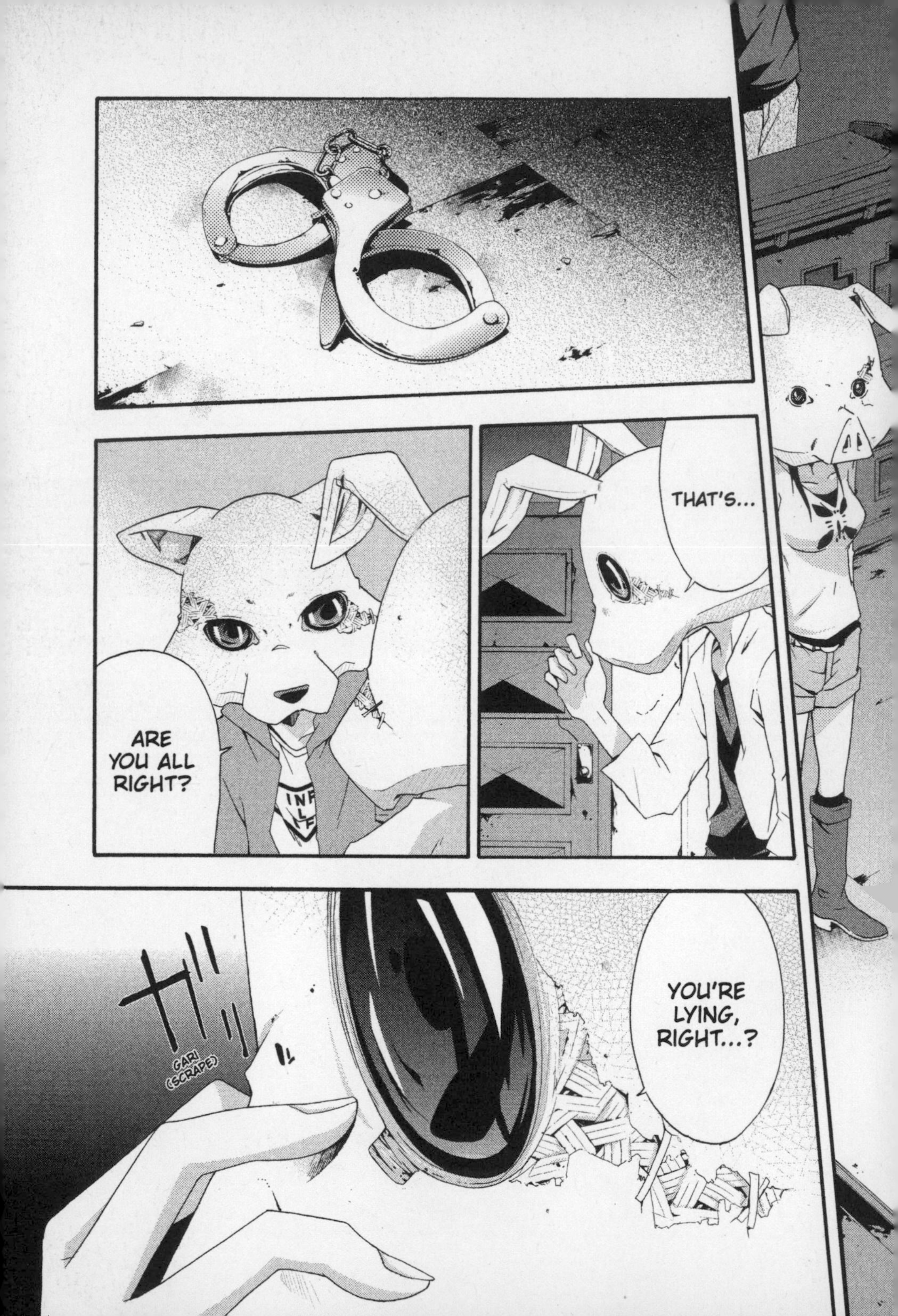
THAT'S...
ARE YOU ALL RIGHT?
YOU'RE LYING, RIGHT...?
GARI (SCRAPE)

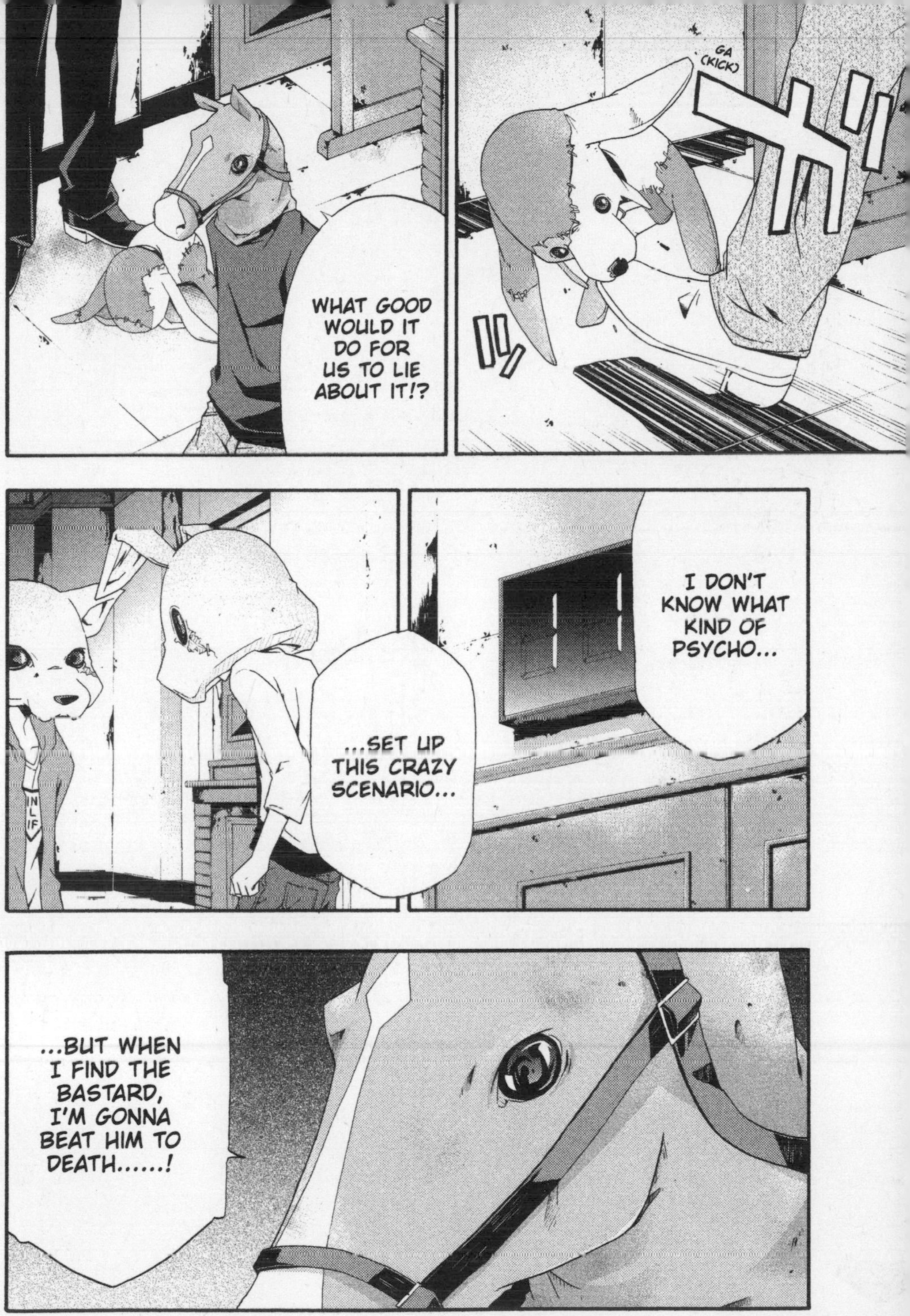
GA (KICK)
WHAT GOOD WOULD IT DO FOR US TO LIE ABOUT IT!?
I DON'T KNOW WHAT KIND OF PSYCHO...
...SET UP THIS CRAZY SCENARIO...
...BUT WHEN I FIND THE BASTARD, I'M GONNA BEAT HIM TO DEATH......!

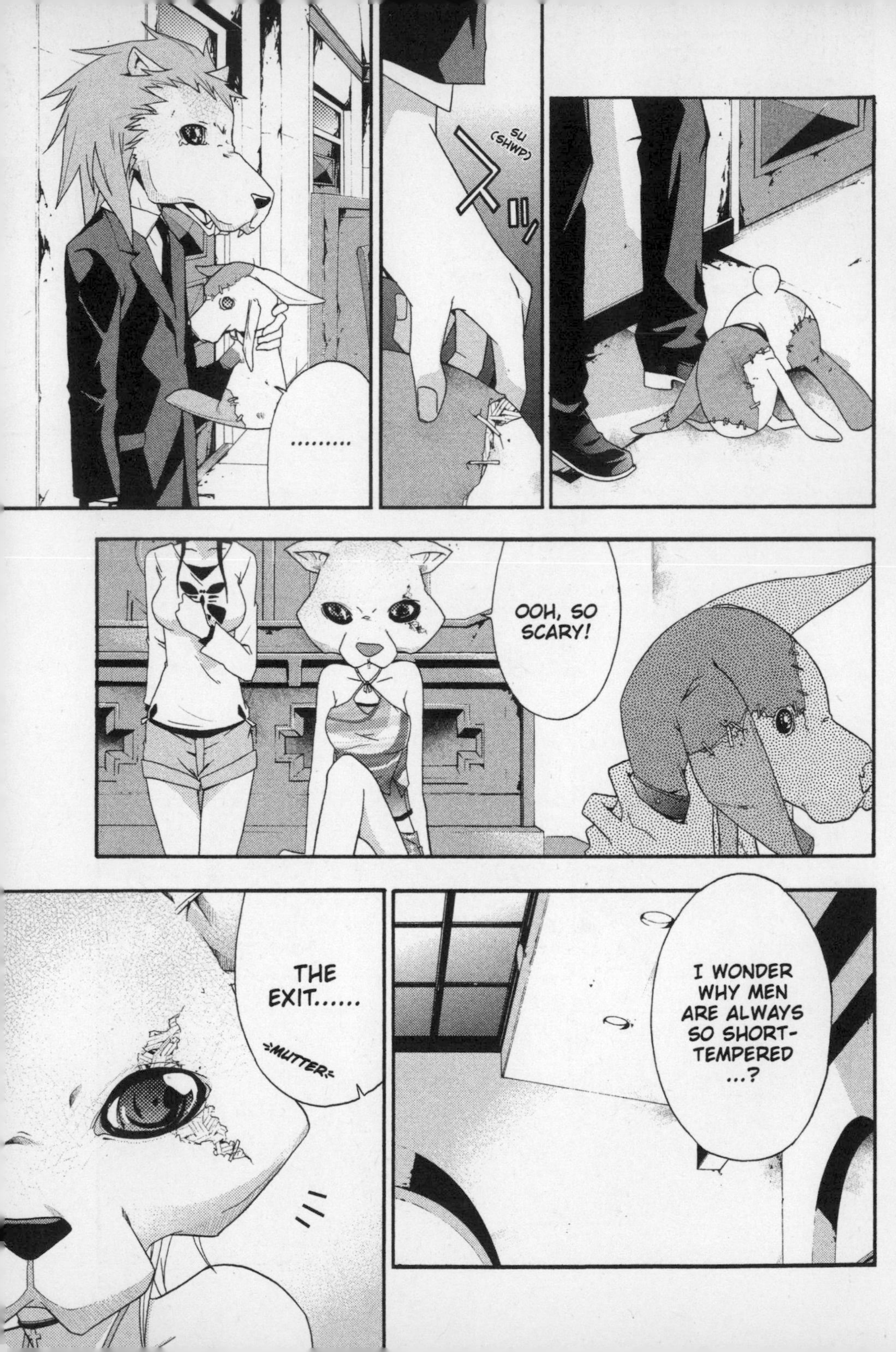
SU (SHWP)
....
OOH, SO SCARY!
I WONDER WHY MEN ARE ALWAYS SO SHORT-TEMPERED ...?
THE EXIT......
MUTTER

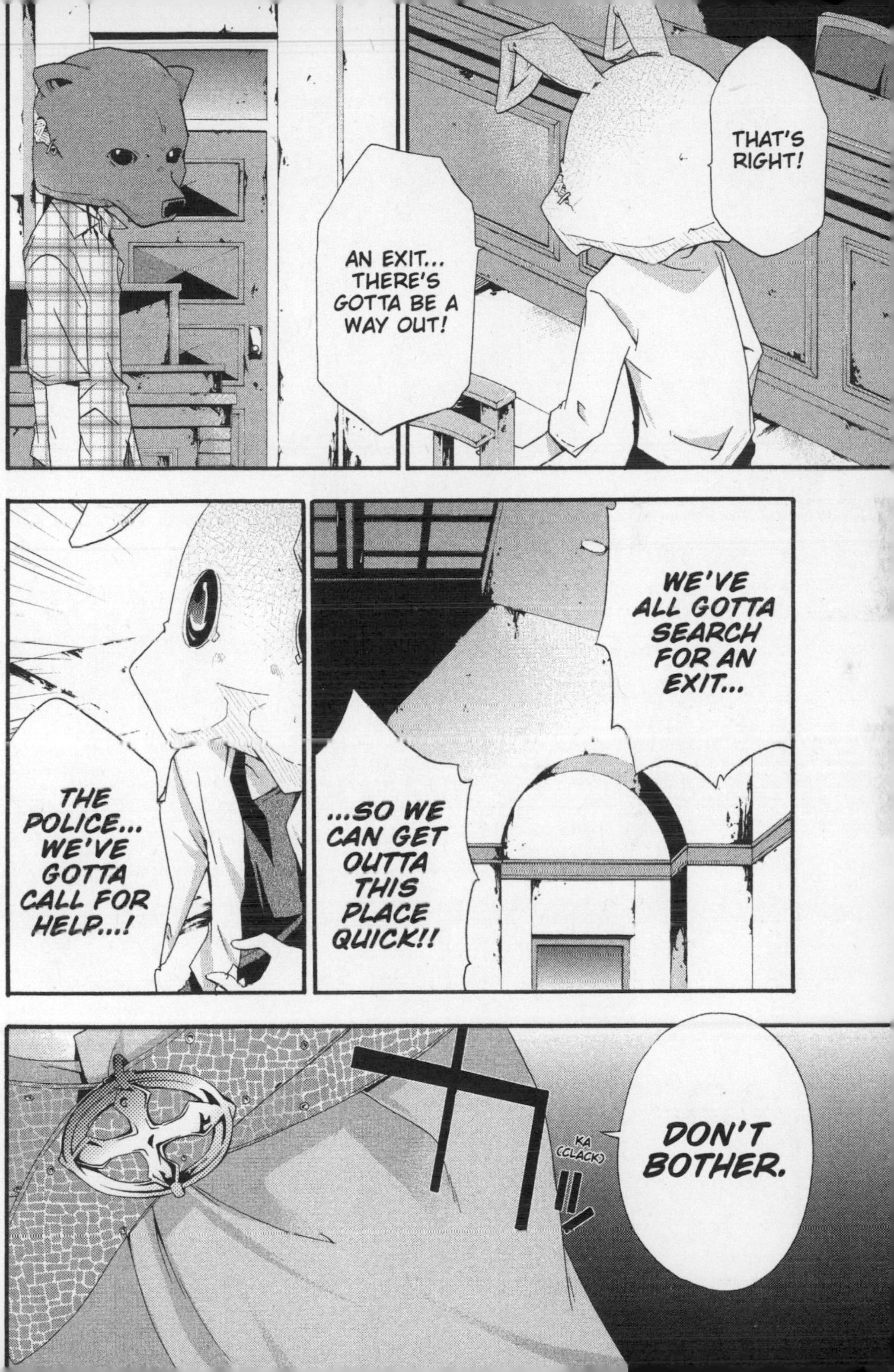
THAT'S RIGHT!
AN EXIT... THERE'S GOTTA BE A WAY OUT!
WE'VE ALL GOTTA SEARCH FOR AN EXIT...
...SO WE CAN GET OUTTA THIS PLACE QUICK!!
THE POLICE... WE'VE GOTTA CALL FOR HELP...!
DON'T BOTHER.
KA (CLACK)

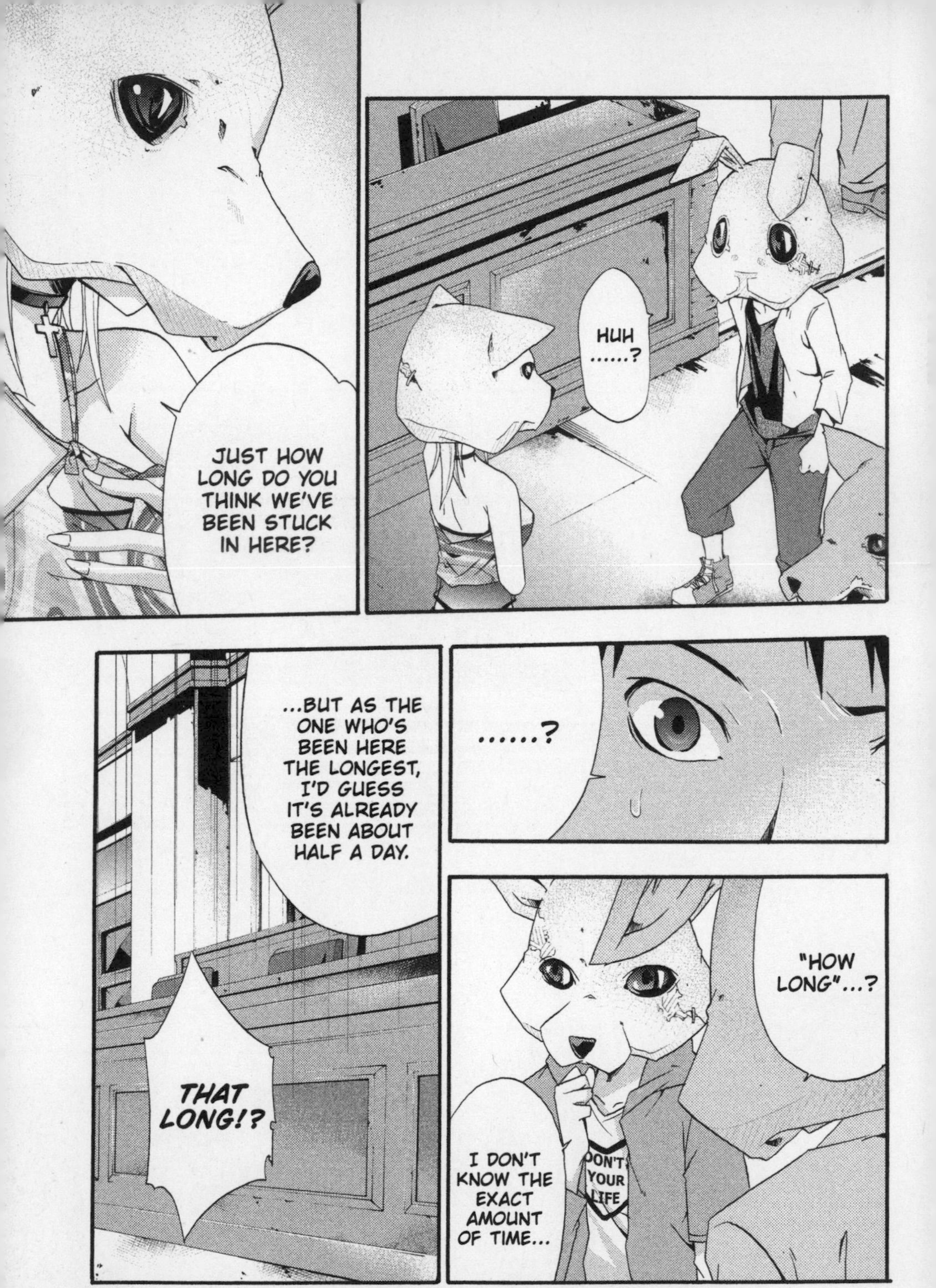
HUH ......?
JUST HOW LONG DO YOU THINK WE'VE BEEN STUCK IN HERE?
......?
"HOW LONG"...?
I DON'T KNOW THE EXACT AMOUNT OF TIME...
...BUT AS THE ONE WHO'S BEEN HERE THE LONGEST, I'D GUESS IT'S ALREADY BEEN ABOUT HALF A DAY.
THAT LONG!?

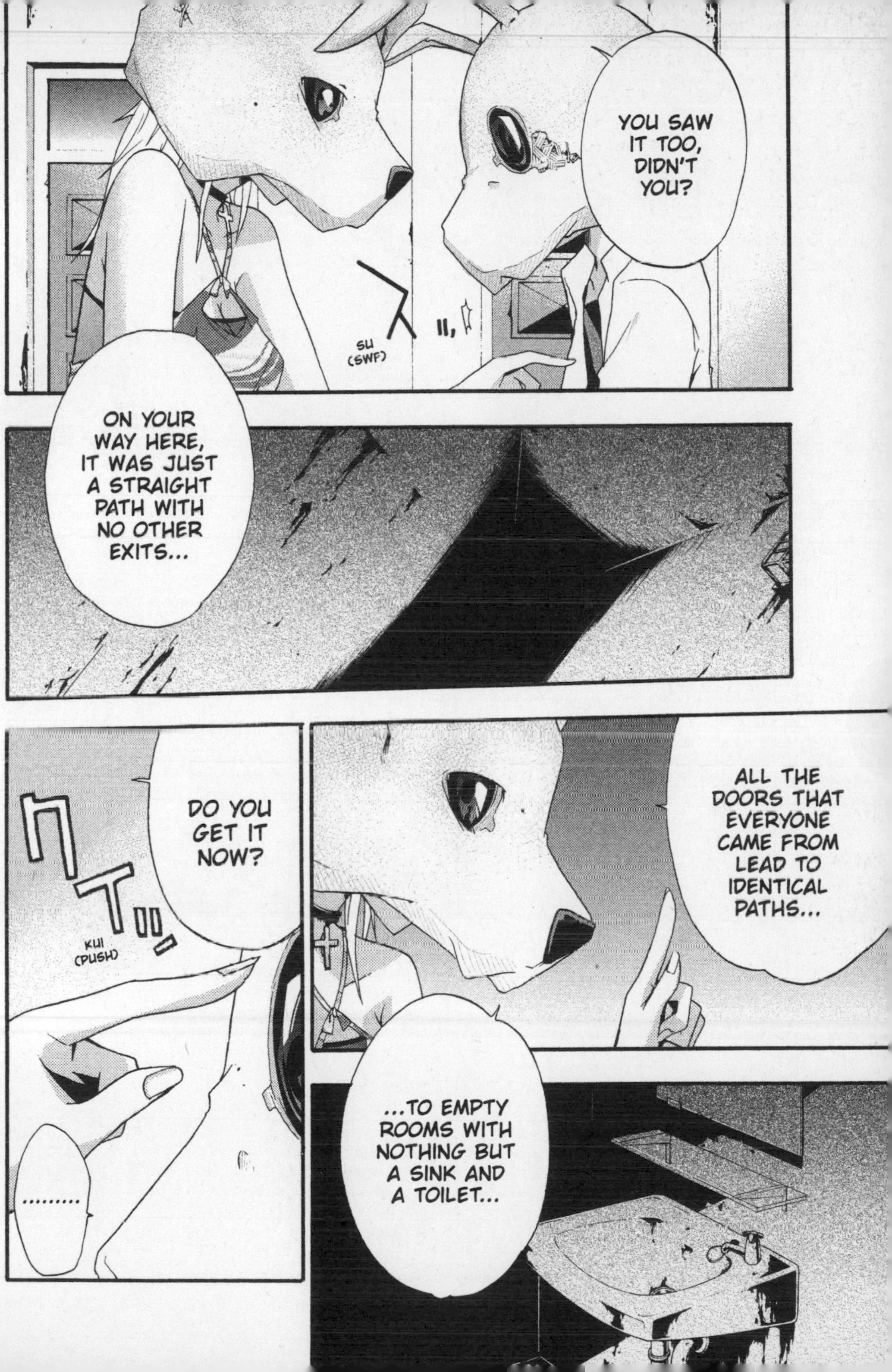
YOU SAW IT TOO, DIDN'T YOU?
SU (SWF)
ON YOUR WAY HERE, IT WAS JUST A STRAIGHT PATH WITH NO OTHER EXITS...
ALL THE DOORS THAT EVERYONE CAME FROM LEAD TO IDENTICAL PATHS...
...TO EMPTY ROOMS WITH NOTHING BUT A SINK AND A TOILET...
DO YOU GET IT NOW?
KUI (PUSH)
....

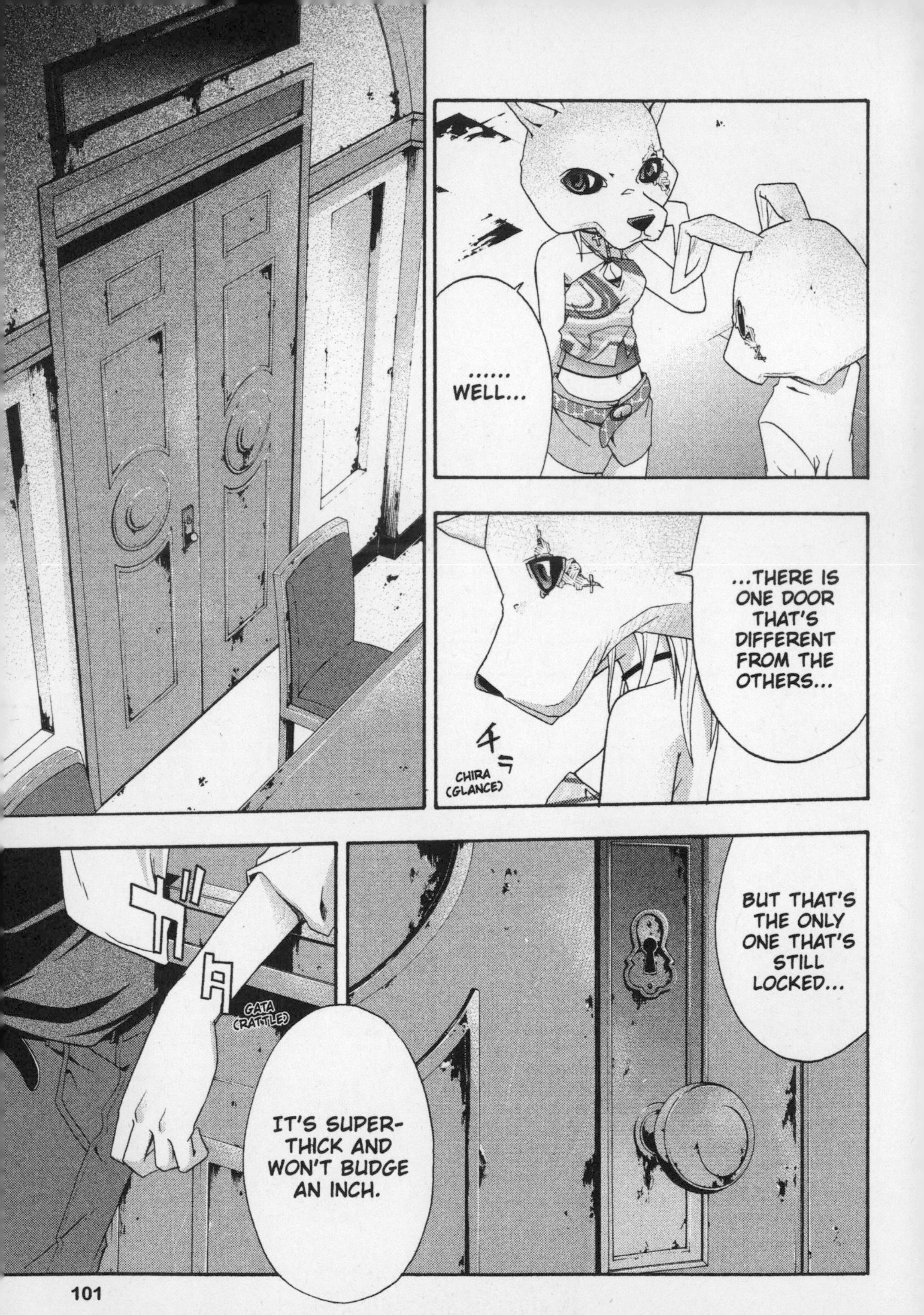
......
WELL...
...THERE IS ONE DOOR THAT'S DIFFERENT FROM THE OTHERS...
CHIRA (GLANCE)
BUT THAT'S THE ONLY ONE THAT'S STILL LOCKED...
GATA (RATTLE)
IT'S SUPER-THICK AND WON'T BUDGE AN INCH.

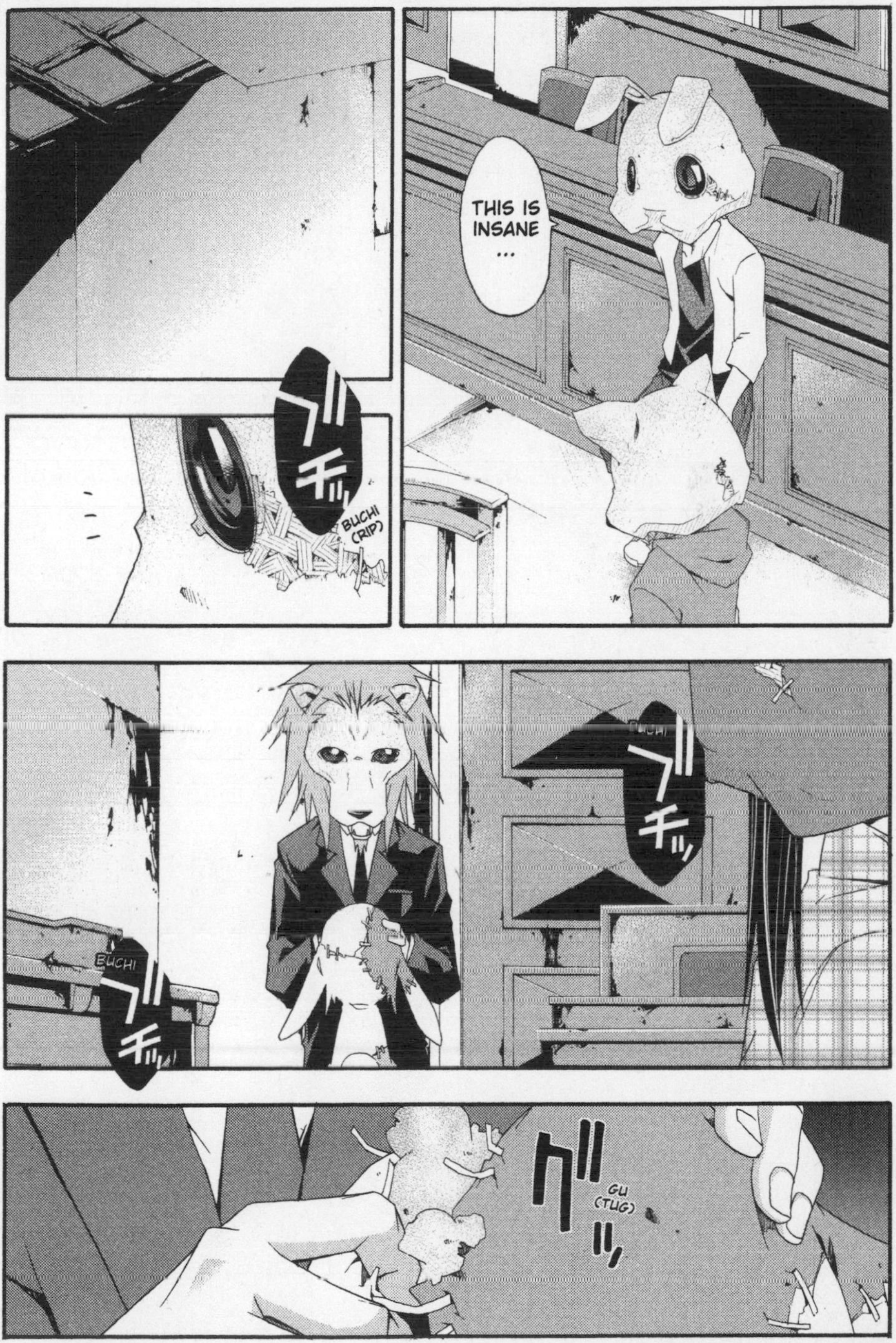
THIS IS INSANE ...
ブチッ
BUCHI (RIP)
ブチッ
BUCHI
ブチッ
BUCHI
グッ
GU (TUG)

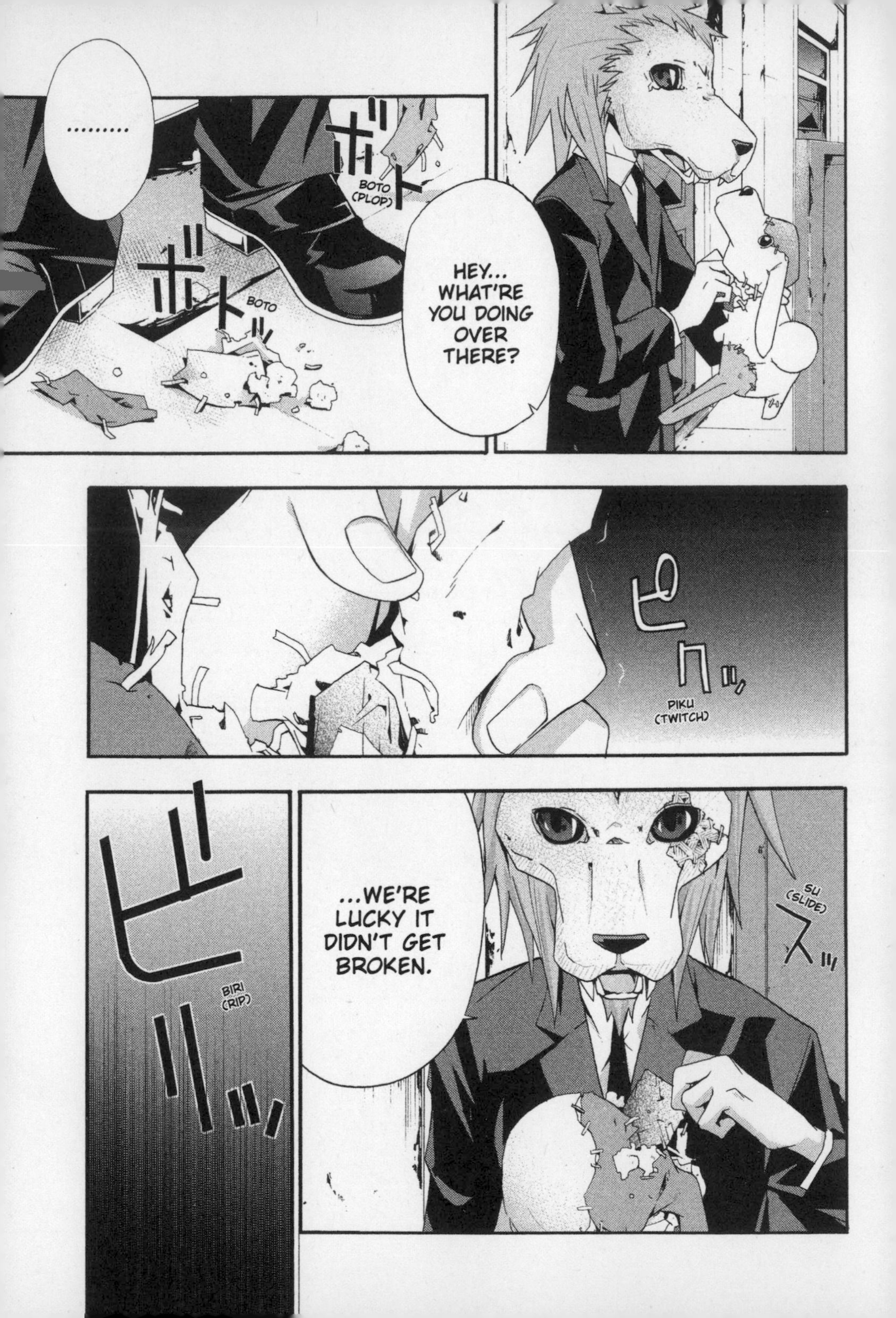
HEY... WHAT'RE YOU DOING OVER THERE?
BOTO (PLOP)
....
BOTO
PIKU (TWITCH)
SU (SLIDE)
...WE'RE LUCKY IT DIDN'T GET BROKEN.
BIRI (RIP)

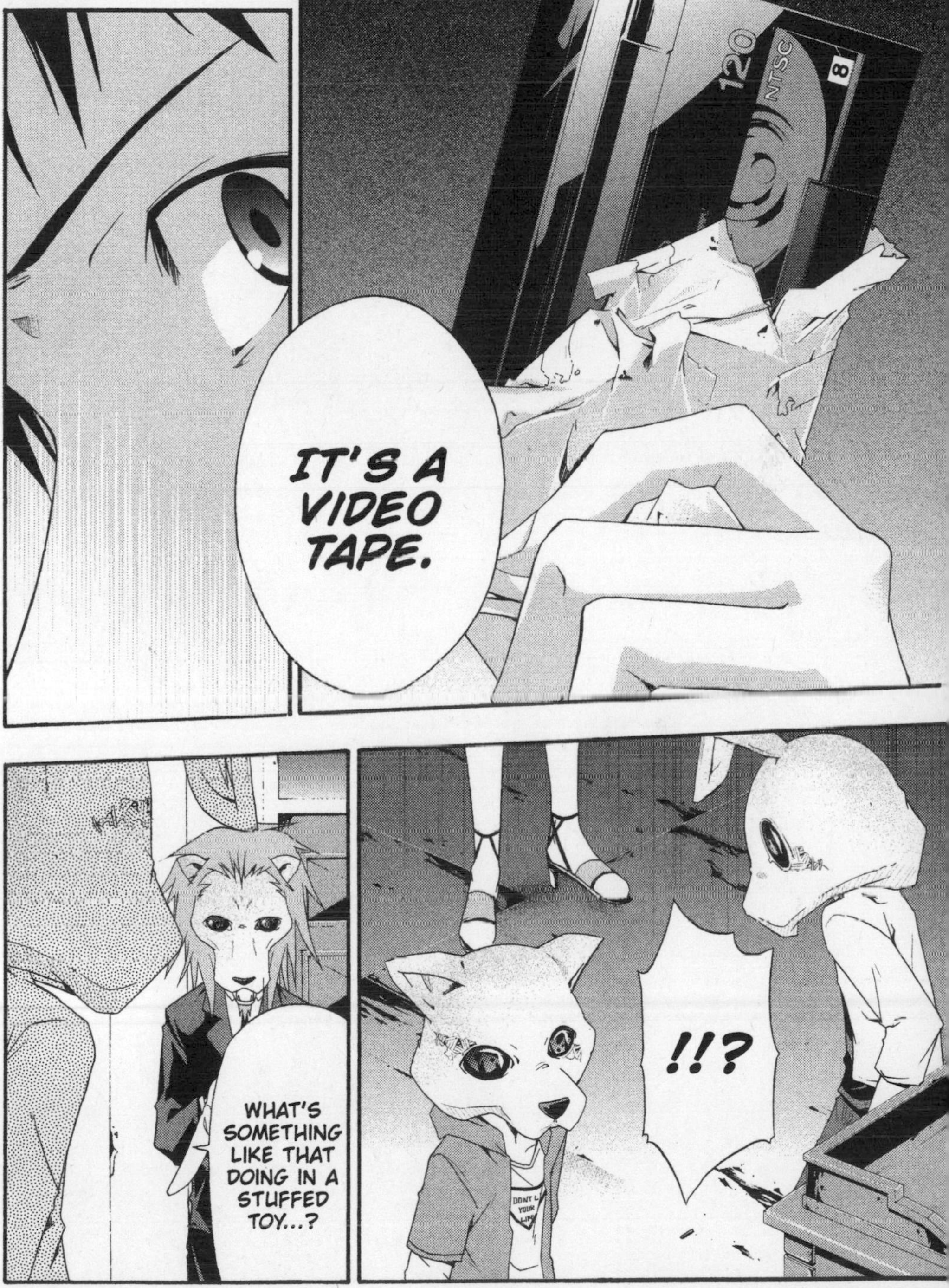
120
NTSC
8
IT'S A VIDEO TAPE.
!!?
WHAT'S SOMETHING LIKE THAT DOING IN A STUFFED TOY...?

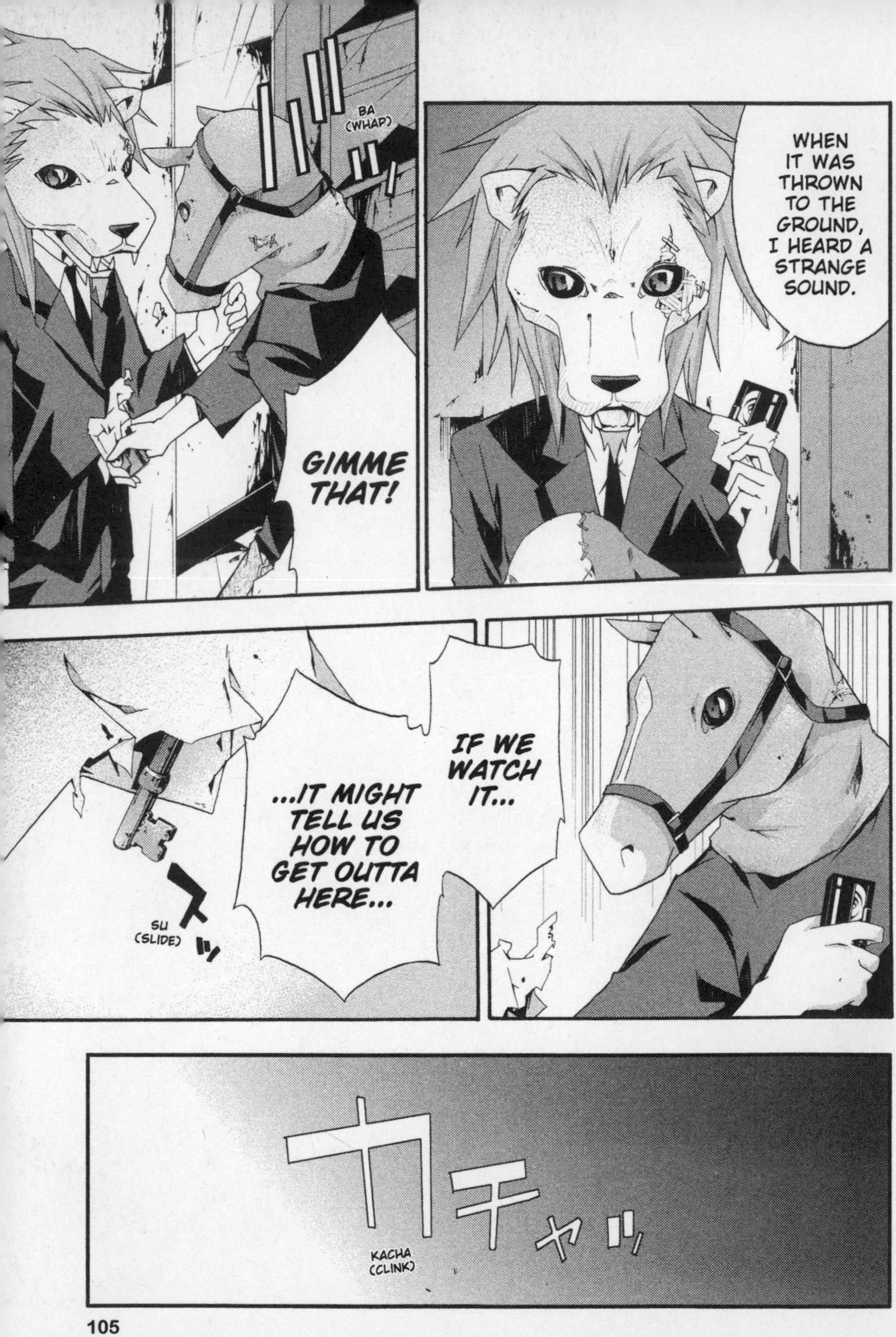
WHEN IT WAS THROWN TO THE GROUND, I HEARD A STRANGE SOUND.
BA (WHAP)
GIMME THAT!
IF WE WATCH IT...
...IT MIGHT TELL US HOW TO GET OUTTA HERE...
SU (SLIDE)
KACHA (CLINK)

HNN?
SU
(SWF)
ズッ
....
A KEY......

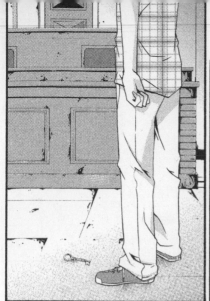

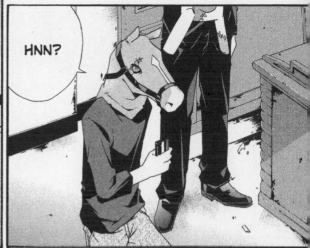

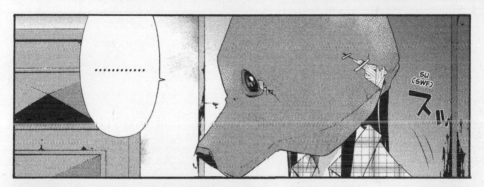

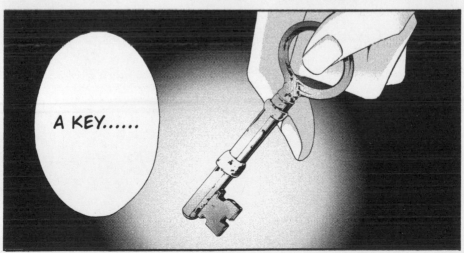

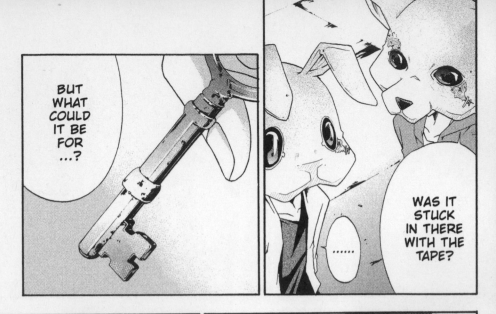

WAS IT STUCK IN THERE WITH THE TAPE?
......
BUT WHAT COULD IT BE FOR ...?
MAYBE ...!

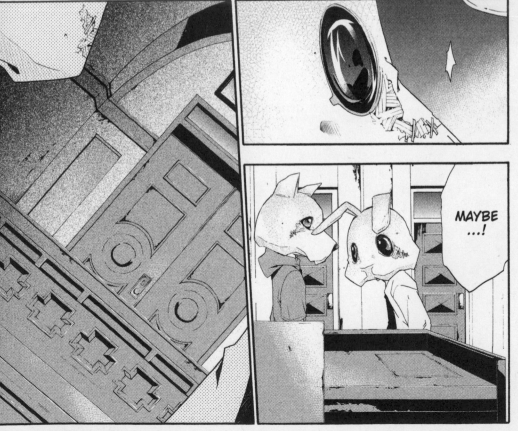

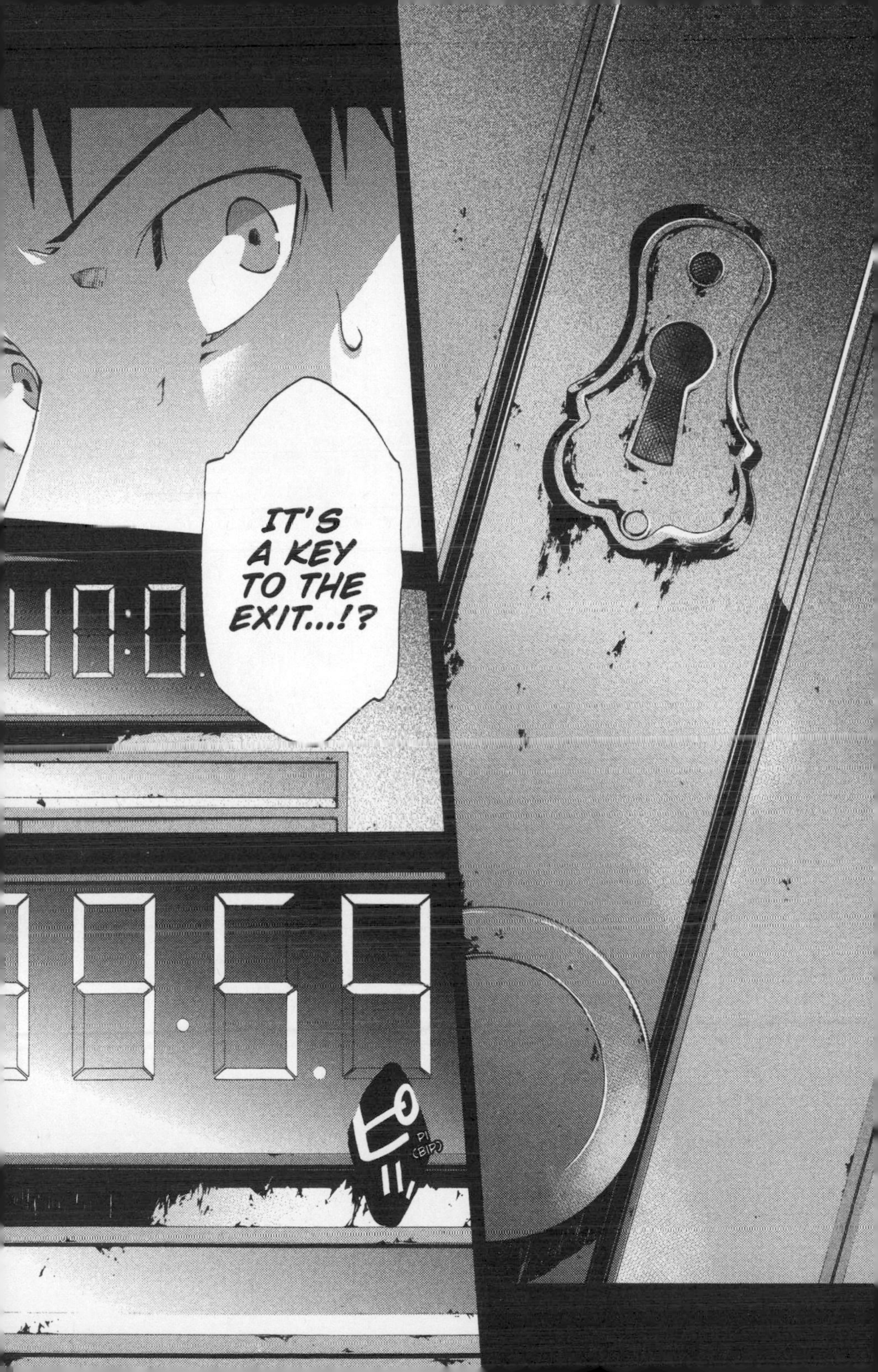
IT'S A KEY TO THE EXIT...!?
PI (BIP)

Sloth

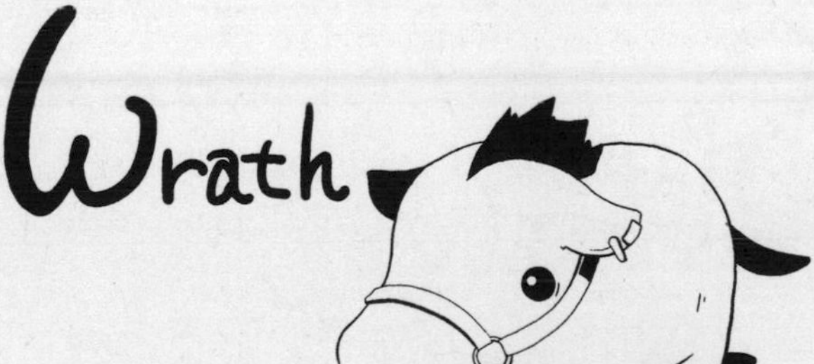
Wrath

CHAPTER 3 SINNERS

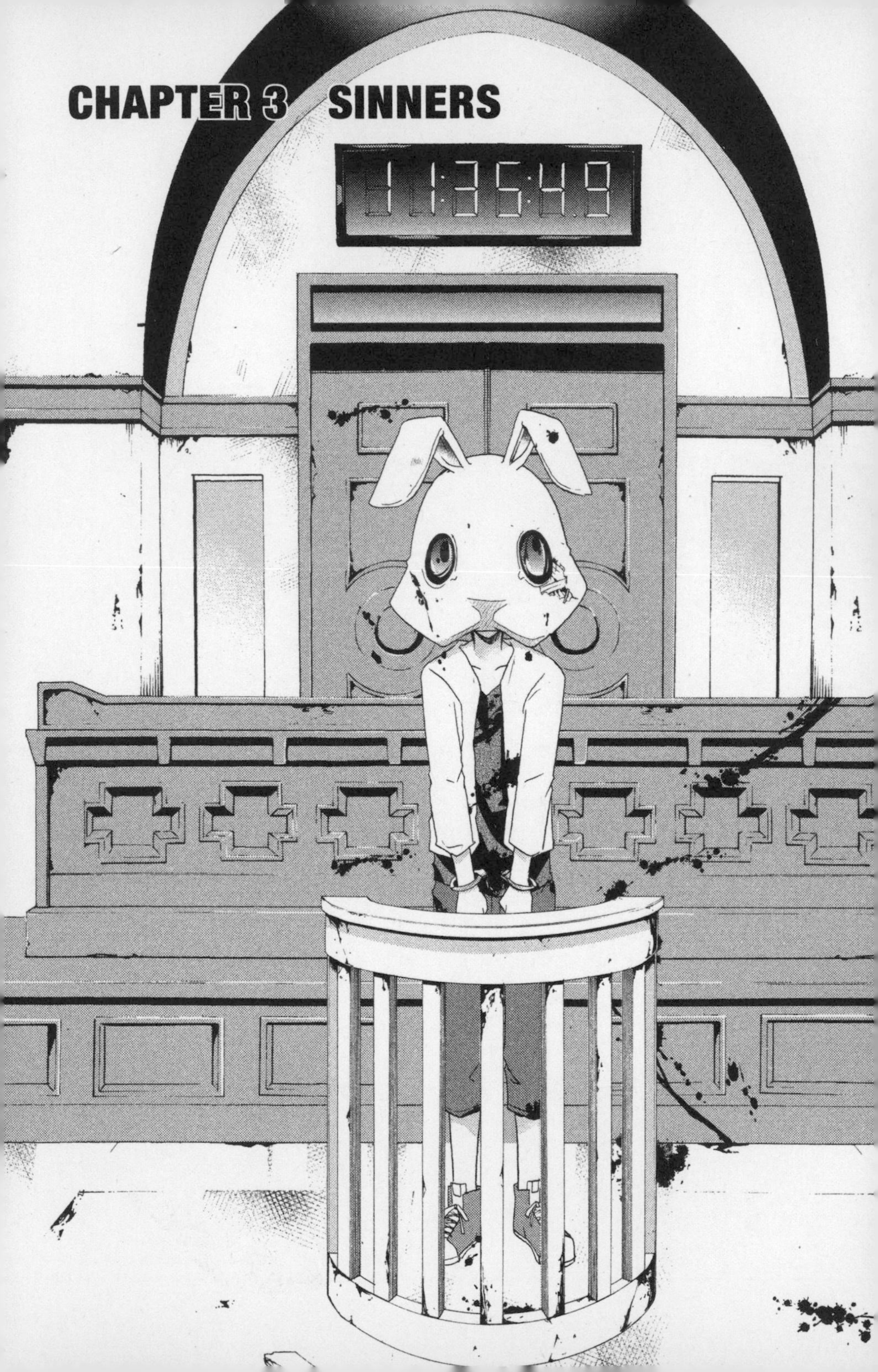
11:35:49

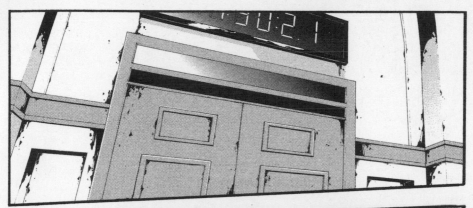

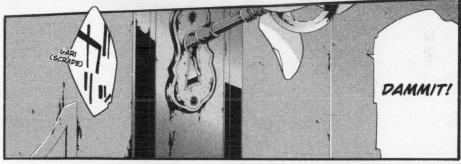

DAMMIT!
GARI (SCRAPE)
GA (WHACK)
WHY WON'T IT OPEN !!?
SO THIS ISN'T THE RIGHT KEY...?

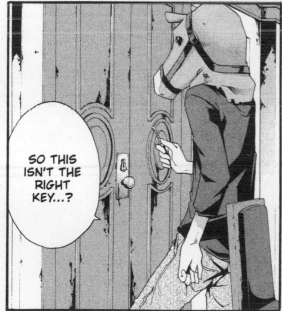

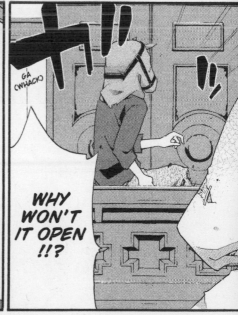

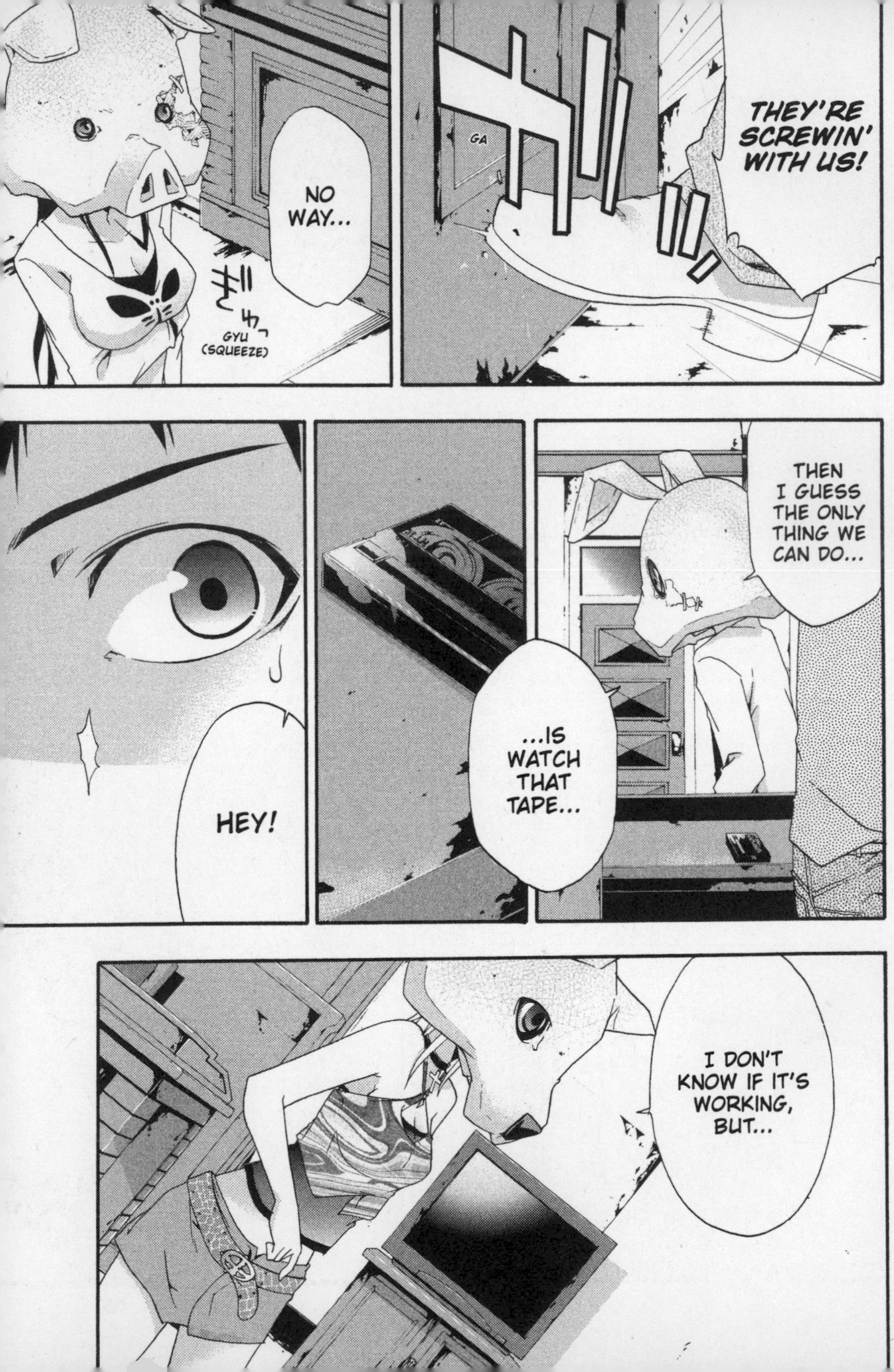
THEY'RE SCREWIN' WITH US!
GA
NO WAY...
ぎゅっ
GYU (SQUEEZE)
THEN I GUESS THE ONLY THING WE CAN DO...
...IS WATCH THAT TAPE...
HEY!
I DON'T KNOW IF IT'S WORKING, BUT...

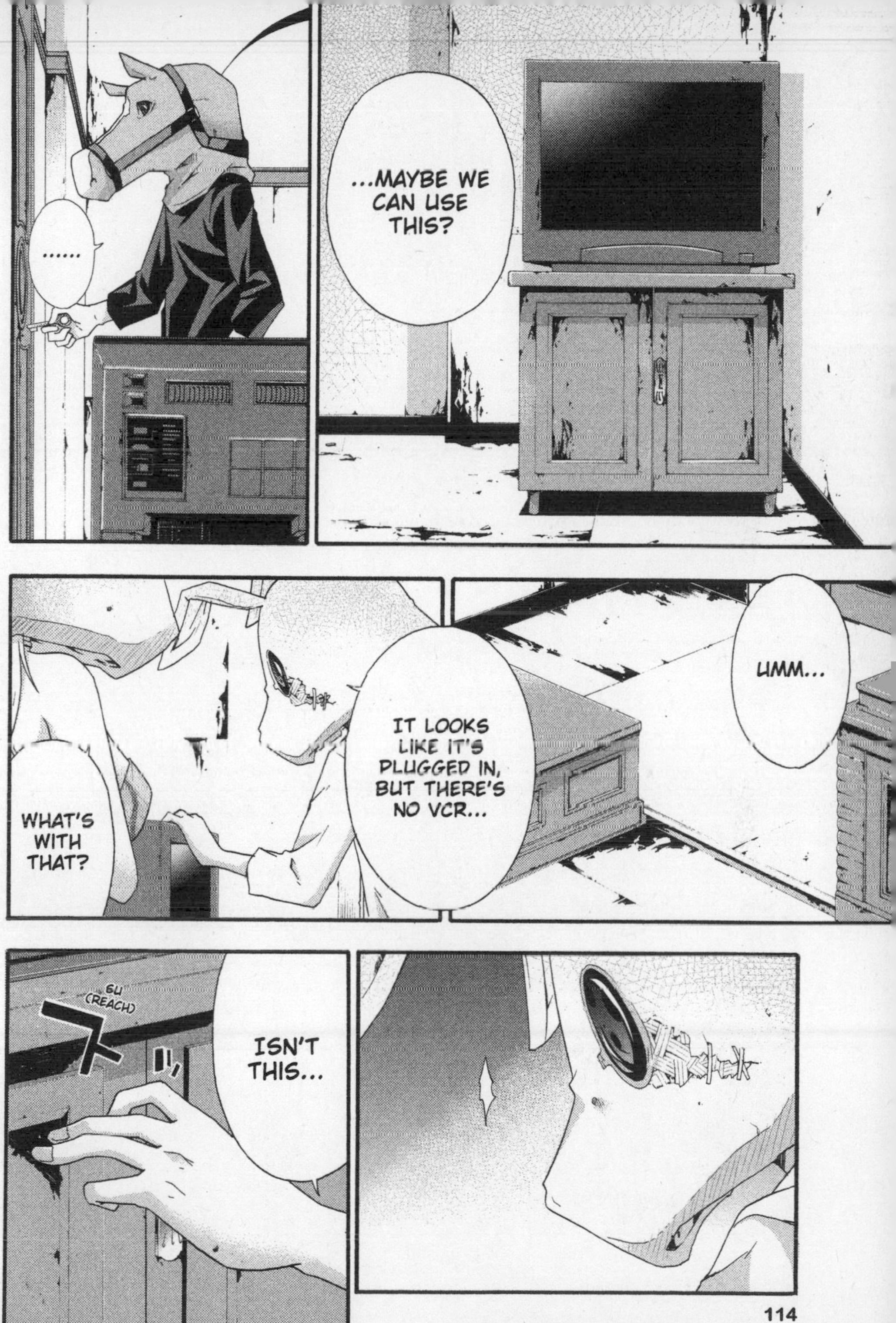
...MAYBE WE CAN USE THIS?
......
UMM...
IT LOOKS LIKE IT'S PLUGGED IN, BUT THERE'S NO VCR...
WHAT'S WITH THAT?
ISN'T THIS...
GU (REACH)

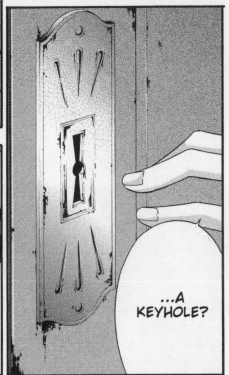

...A KEYHOLE?

MOVE IT!

GA
(GRAB)

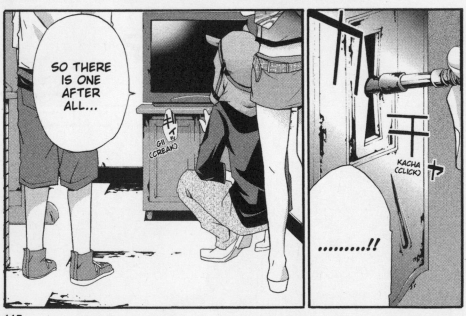

SO THERE IS ONE AFTER ALL...

GII
(CREAK)

KACHA
(CLICK)

..........!!

115

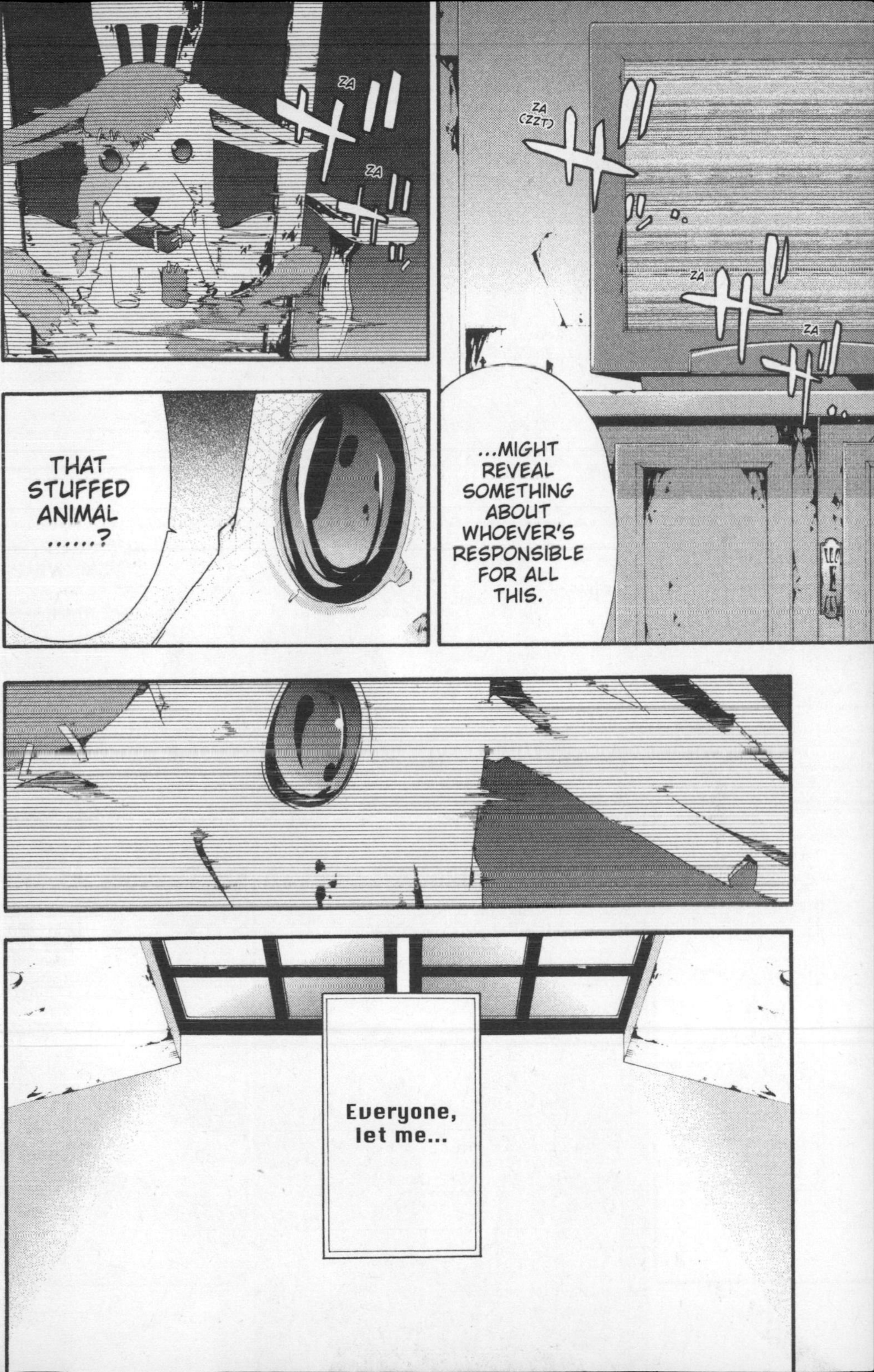
ZA (ZZT)
ZA
ZA
...MIGHT REVEAL SOMETHING ABOUT WHOEVER'S RESPONSIBLE FOR ALL THIS.
ZA
ZA
THAT STUFFED ANIMAL ......?
Everyone, let me...

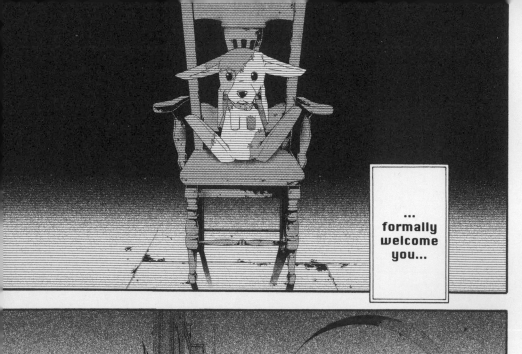

... **formally welcome you...**

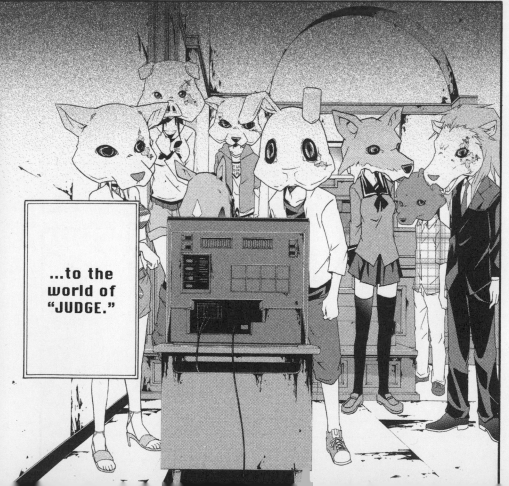

...to the world of "JUDGE."

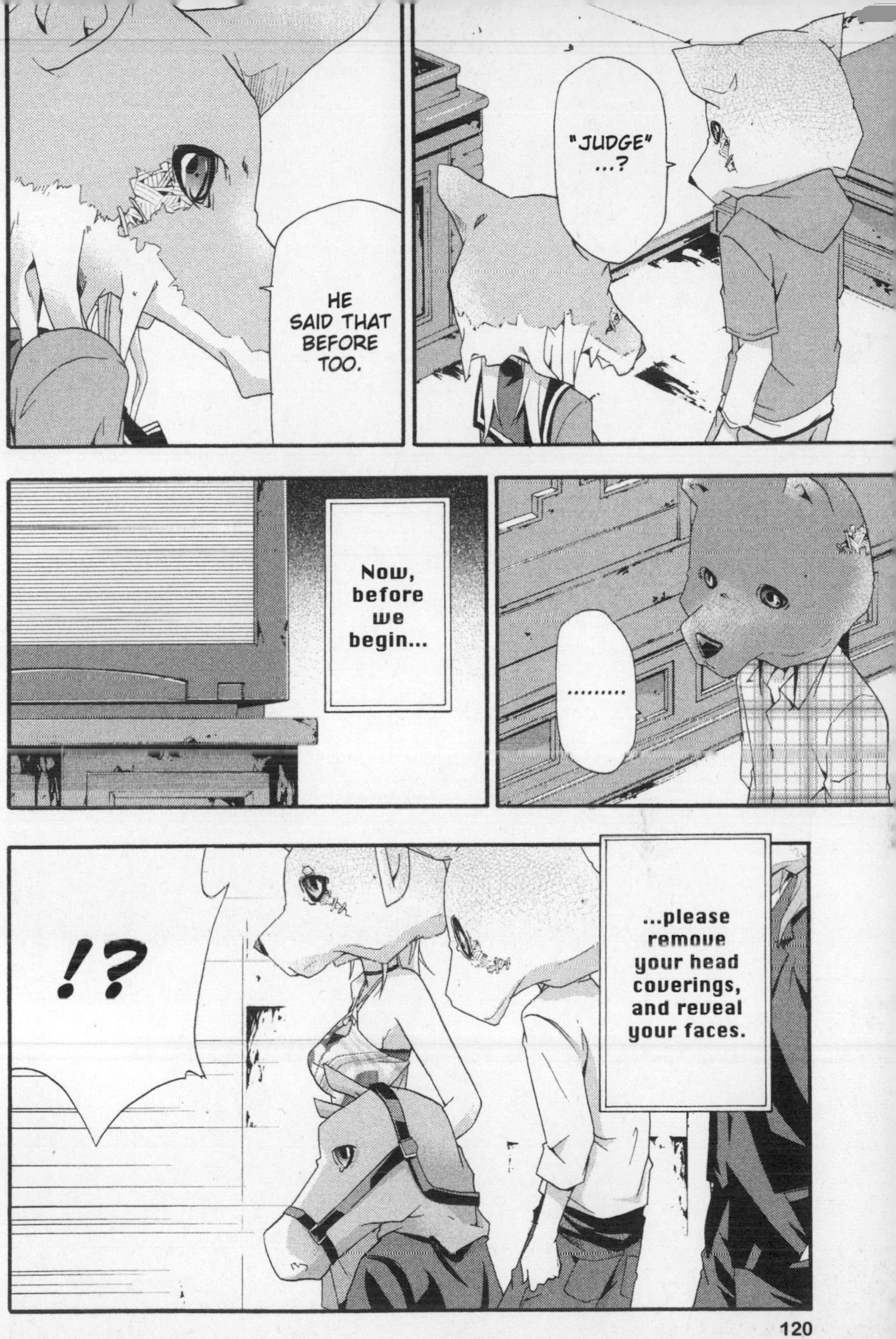
"JUDGE" ...?
HE SAID THAT BEFORE TOO.
....
Now, before we begin...
...please remove your head coverings, and reveal your faces.
!?

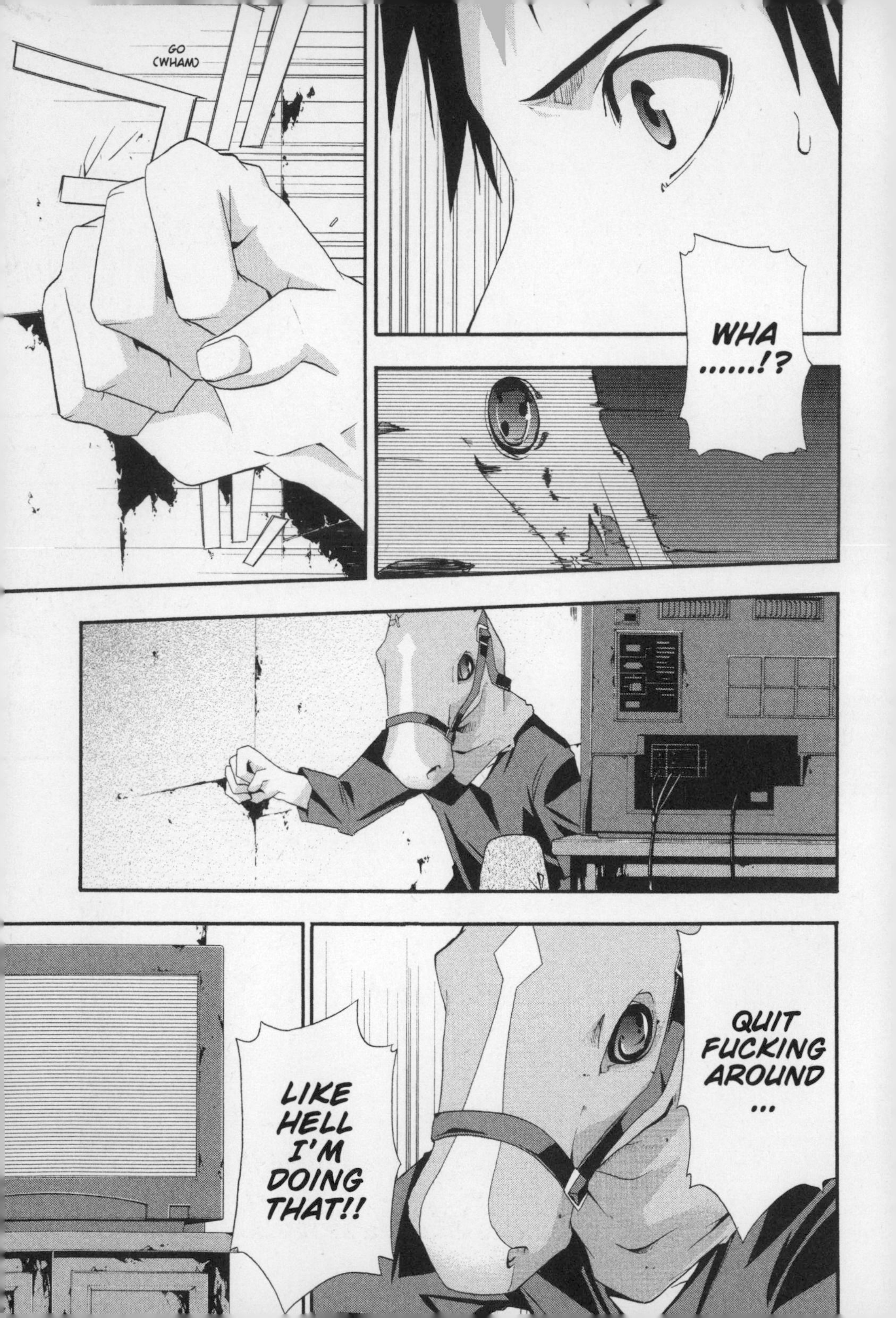

WHA ......!?
GO (WHAM)
QUIT FUCKING AROUND ...
LIKE HELL I'M DOING THAT!!

YOU'RE JUST TRYIN' TO TRICK US...

...INTO KILLIN' OURSELVES, LIKE THAT GUY DID!

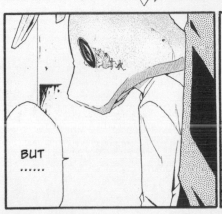

BUT
......

Y-YEAH!

GYU
(SQUEEZE)

HEY!

GASA
(RUSTLE)

WHAT...

...DO YOU THINK YOU'RE DOING!?

SU
(SLIDE)

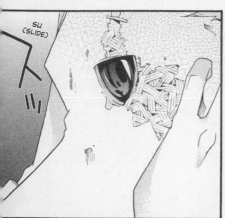

......

D—! DON'T DO IT...

BA
(LUNGE)

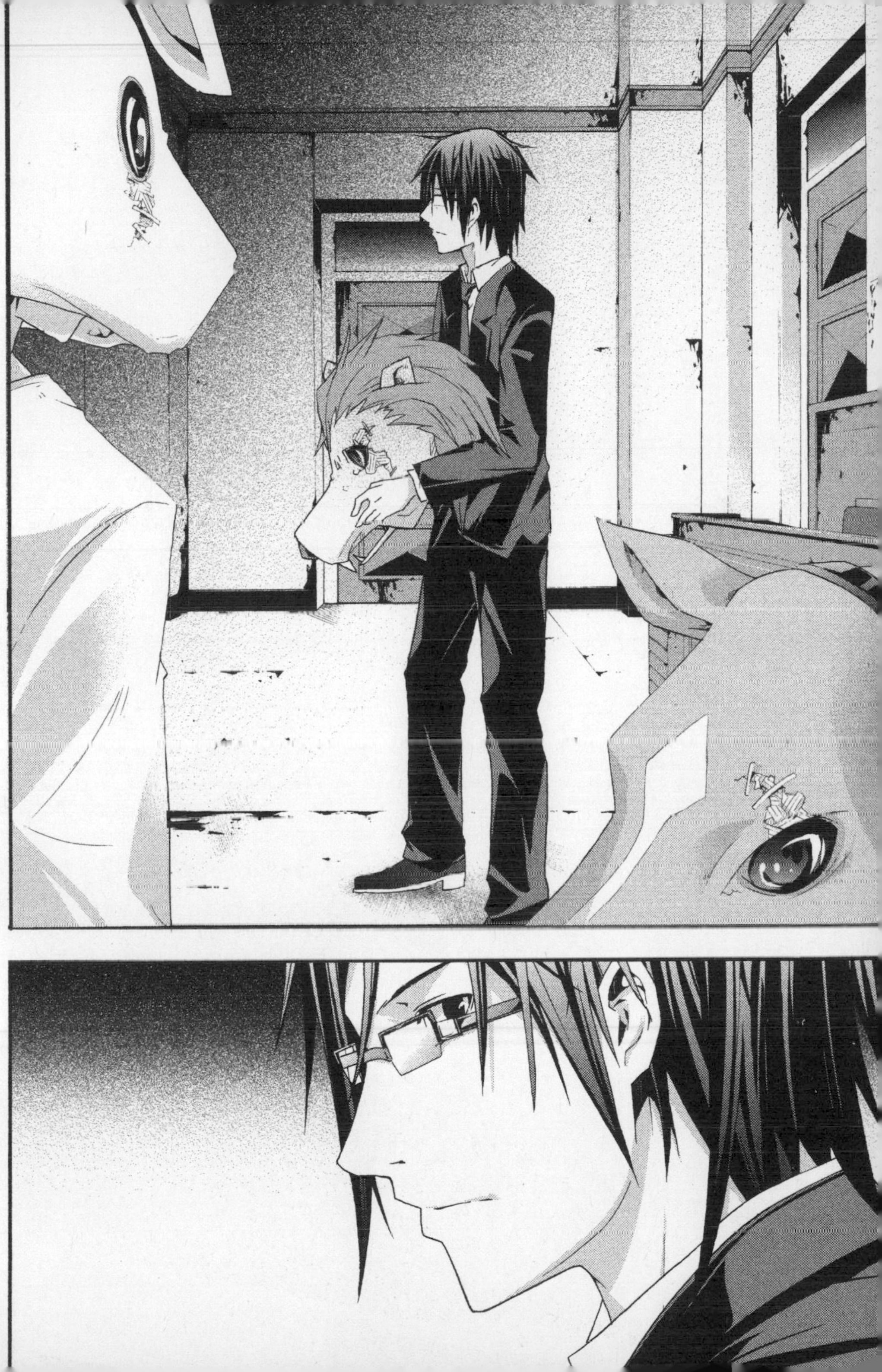

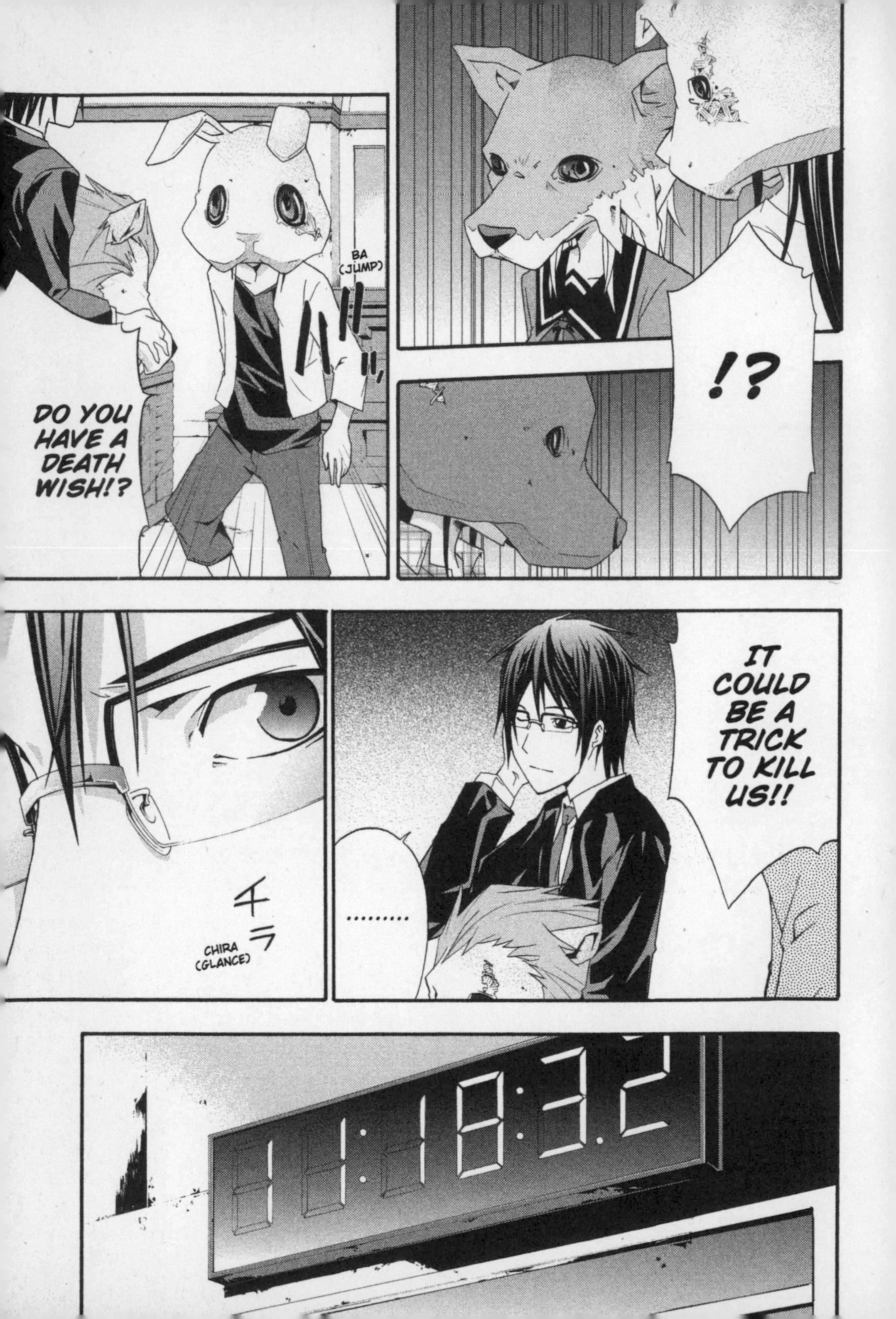
!?
BA (JUMP)
DO YOU HAVE A DEATH WISH!?
IT COULD BE A TRICK TO KILL US!!
....
チラ
CHIRA (GLANCE)

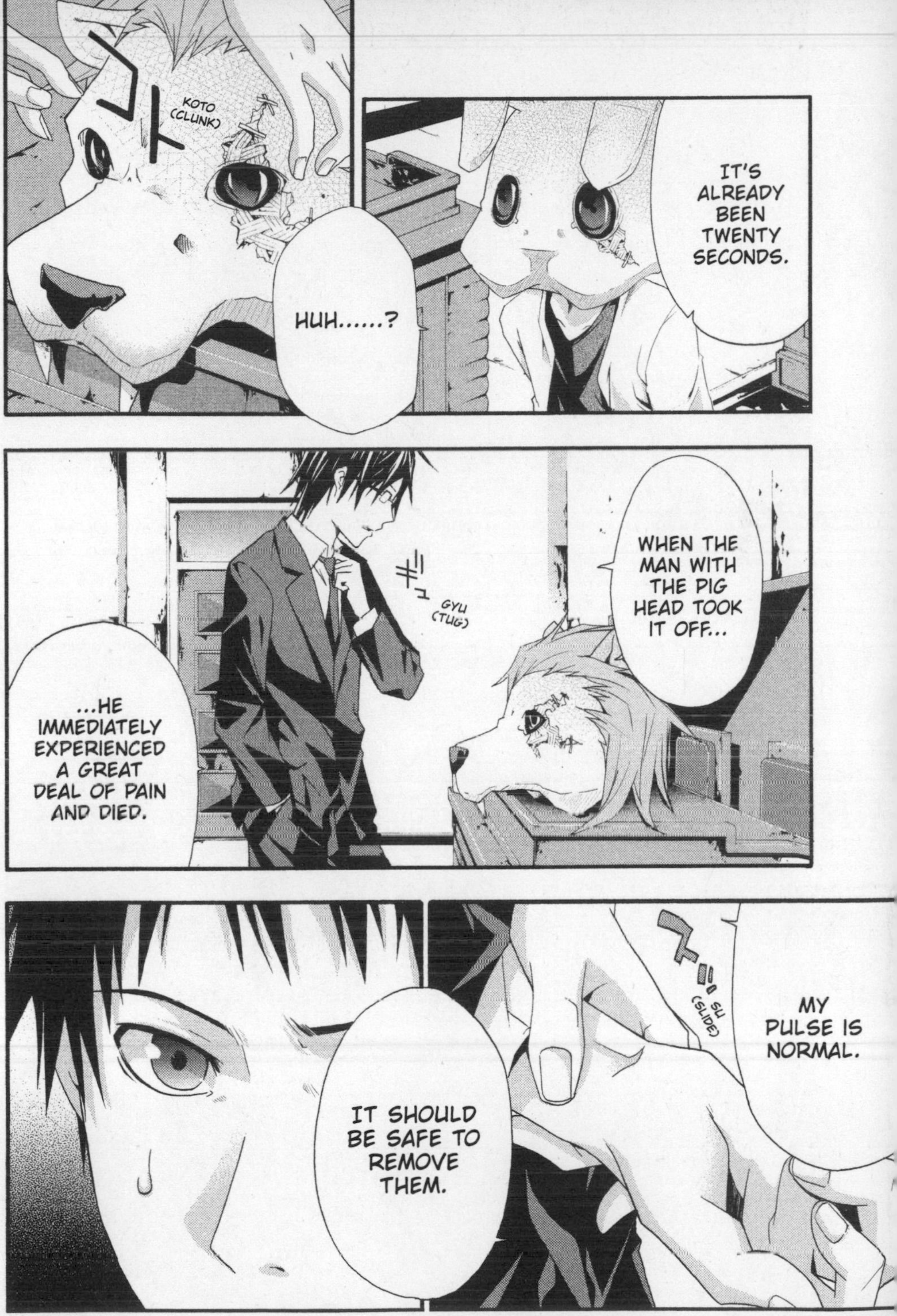
IT'S ALREADY BEEN TWENTY SECONDS.
KOTO (CLUNK)
HUH......?
WHEN THE MAN WITH THE PIG HEAD TOOK IT OFF...
GYU (TUG)
...HE IMMEDIATELY EXPERIENCED A GREAT DEAL OF PAIN AND DIED.
SU (SLIDE)
MY PULSE IS NORMAL.
IT SHOULD BE SAFE TO REMOVE THEM.

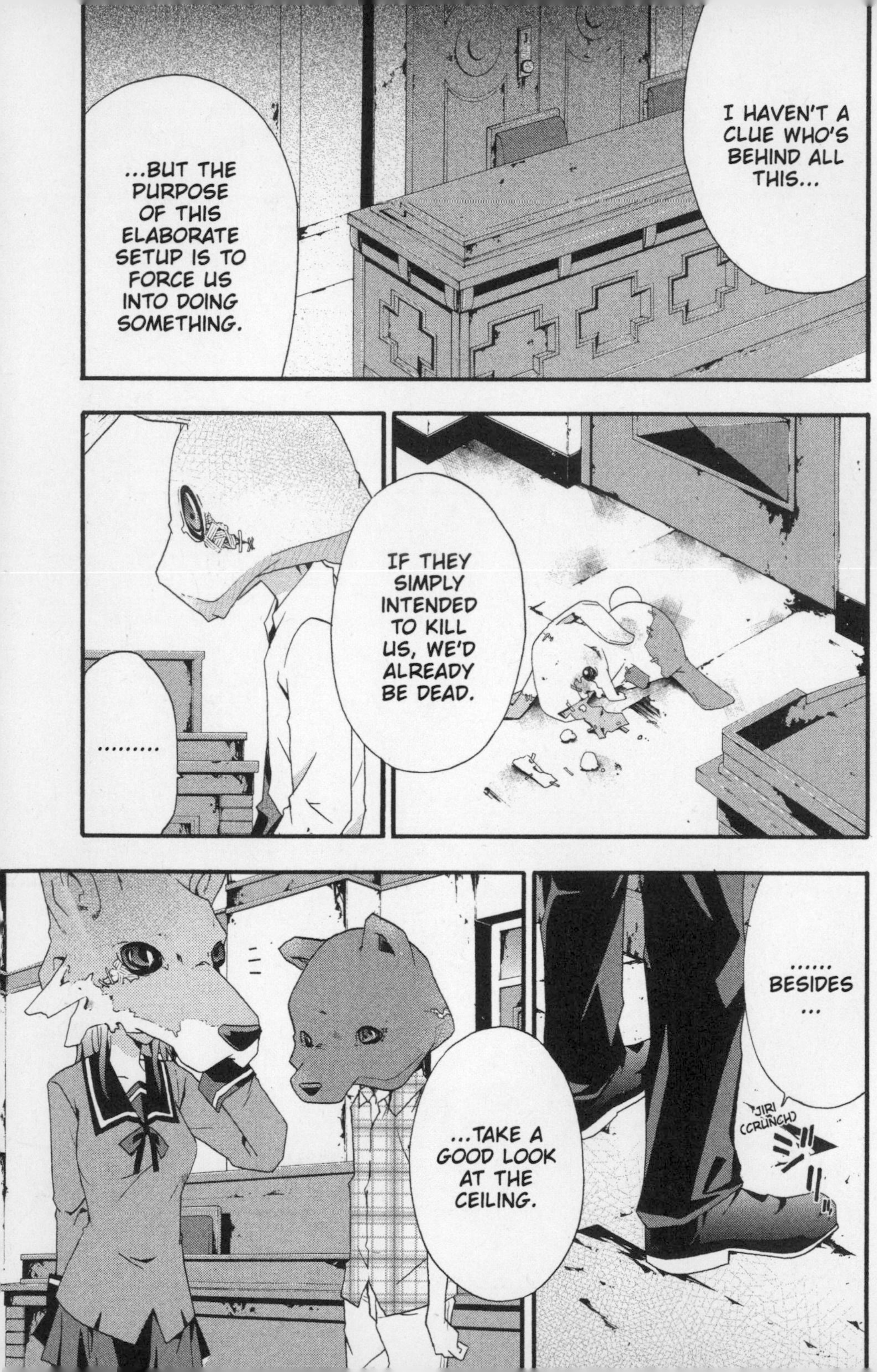
I HAVEN'T A CLUE WHO'S BEHIND ALL THIS...
...BUT THE PURPOSE OF THIS ELABORATE SETUP IS TO FORCE US INTO DOING SOMETHING.
IF THEY SIMPLY INTENDED TO KILL US, WE'D ALREADY BE DEAD.
....
......BESIDES...
JIRI (CRUNCH)
...TAKE A GOOD LOOK AT THE CEILING.

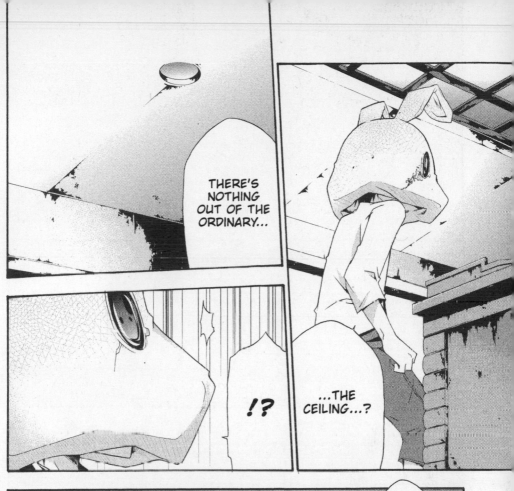

THERE'S NOTHING OUT OF THE ORDINARY...

!?

...THE CEILING...?

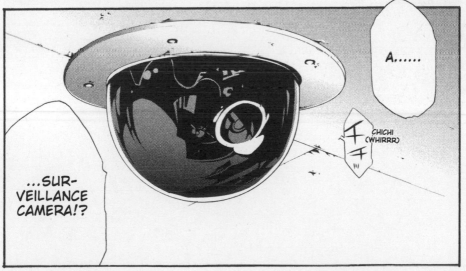

A......

CHICHI
(WHIRRR)

...SUR-VEILLANCE CAMERA!?

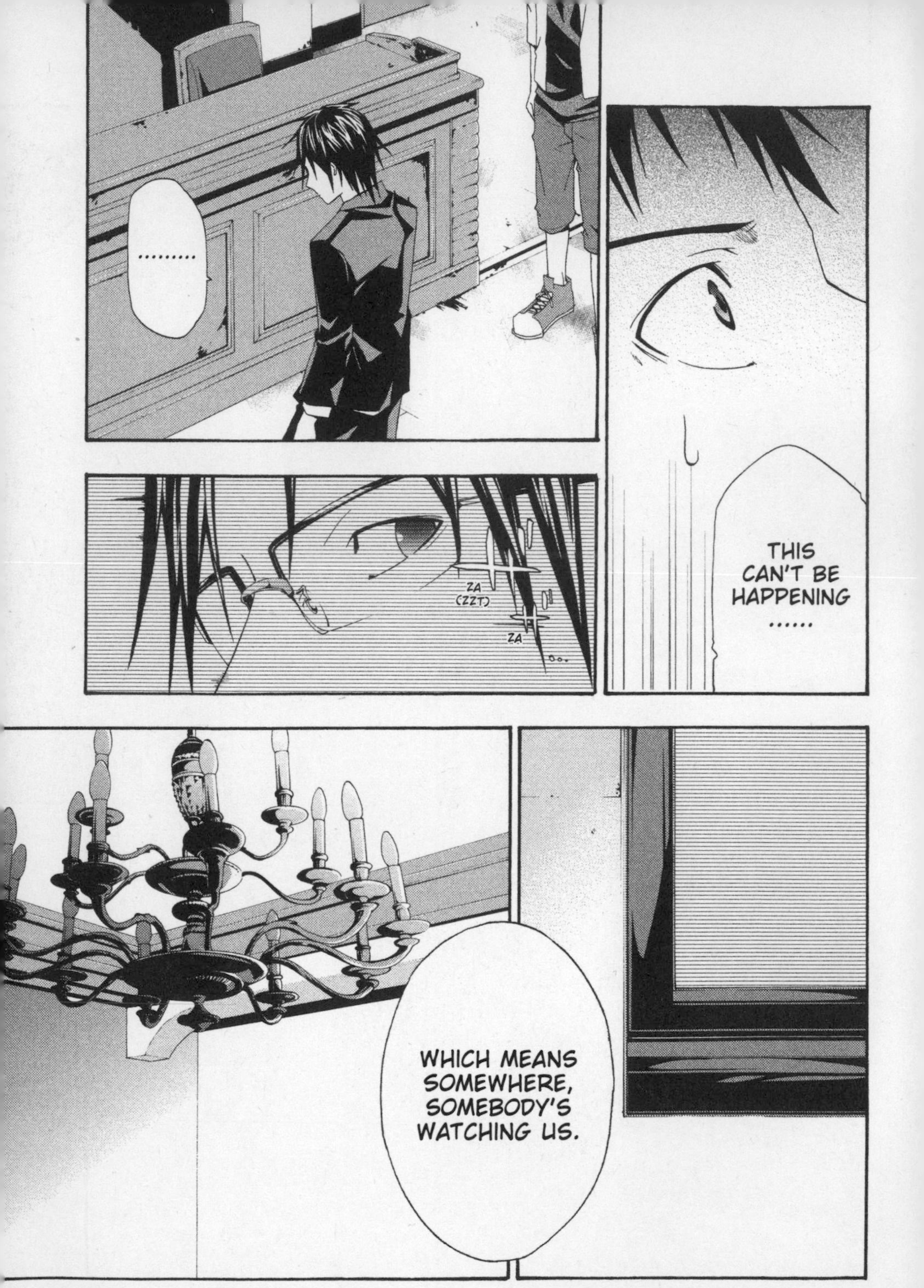
THIS CAN'T BE HAPPENING......
....
ZA (ZZT)
ZA
WHICH MEANS SOMEWHERE, SOMEBODY'S WATCHING US.

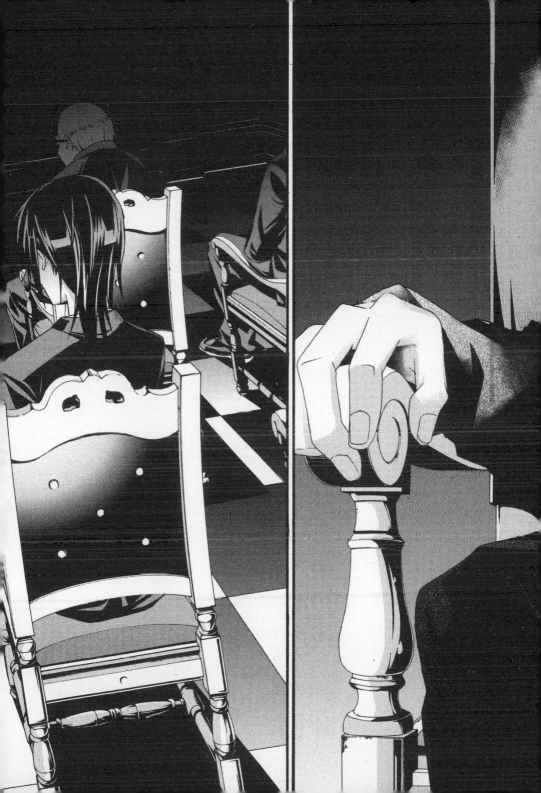

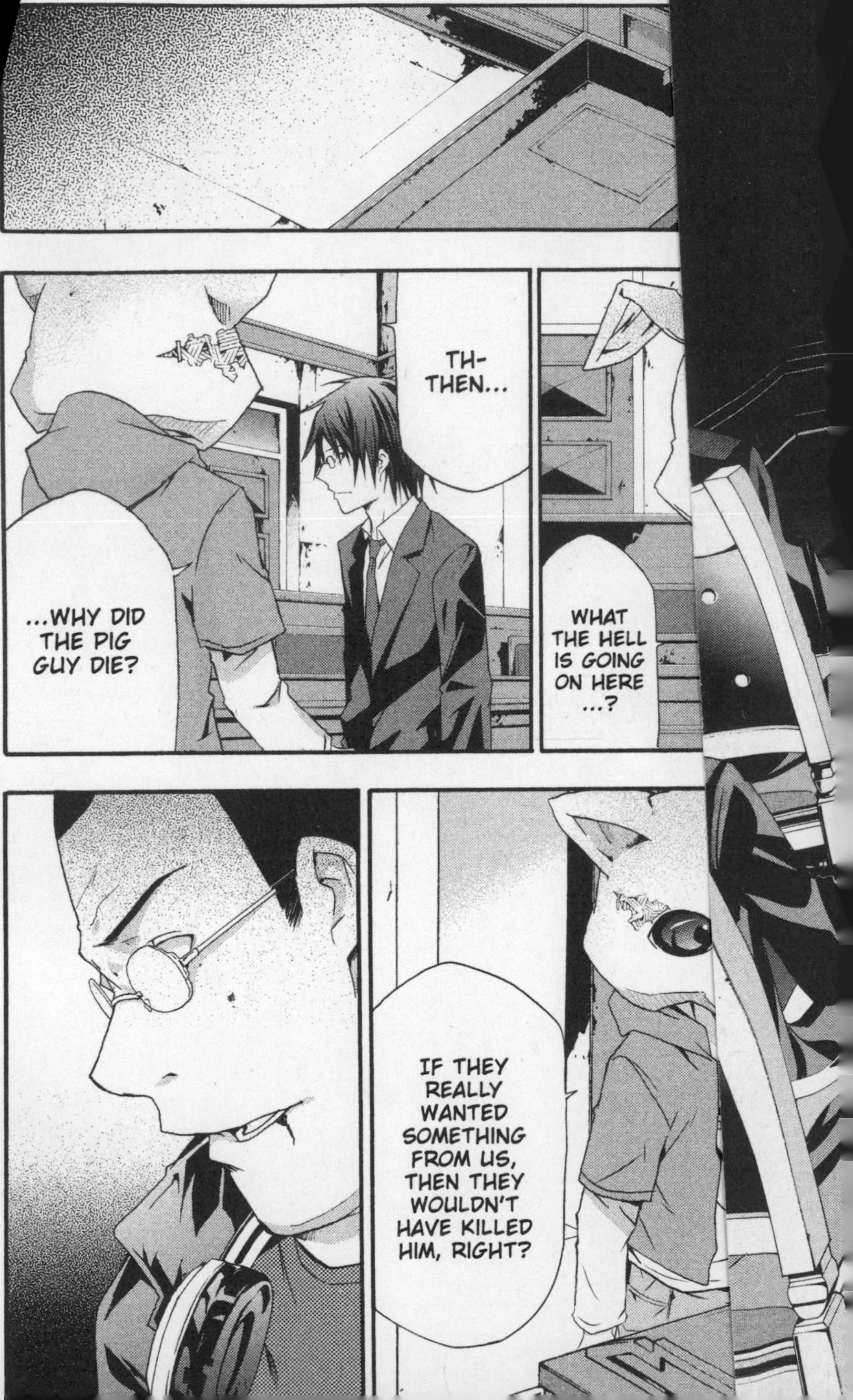
WHAT THE HELL IS GOING ON HERE ...?
TH- THEN...
...WHY DID THE PIG GUY DIE?
IF THEY REALLY WANTED SOMETHING FROM US, THEN THEY WOULDN'T HAVE KILLED HIM, RIGHT?

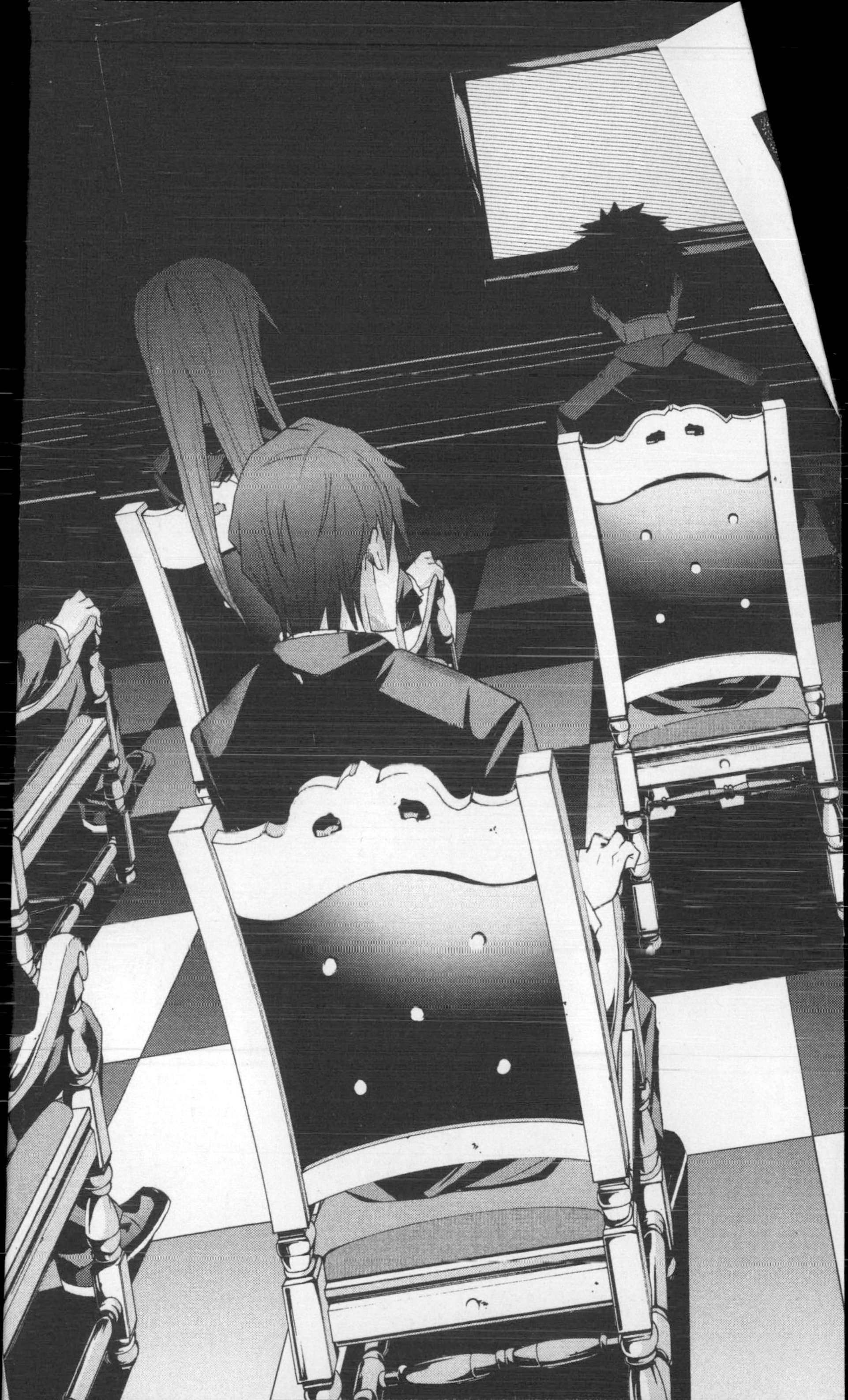

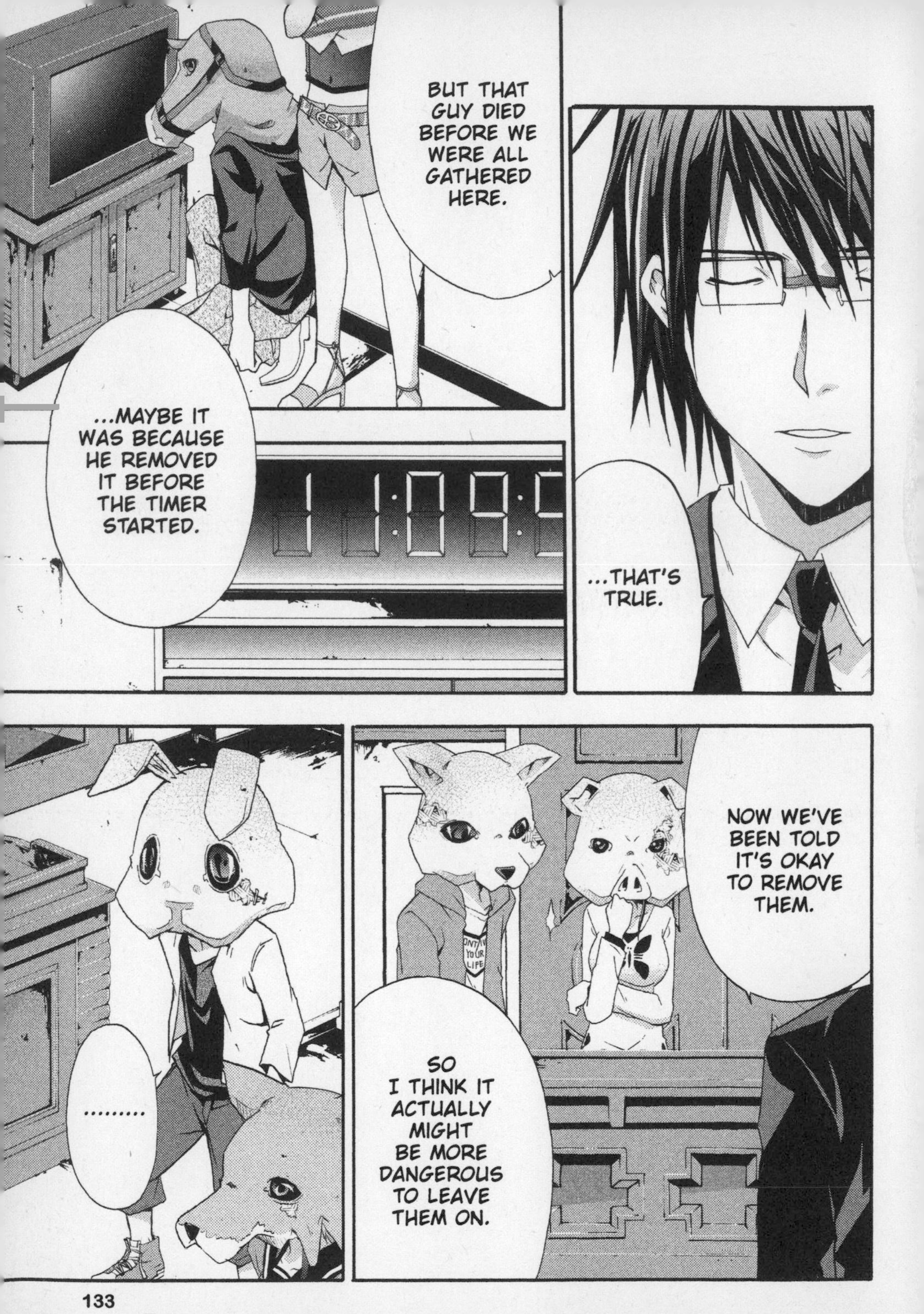
...THAT'S TRUE.
BUT THAT GUY DIED BEFORE WE WERE ALL GATHERED HERE.
...MAYBE IT WAS BECAUSE HE REMOVED IT BEFORE THE TIMER STARTED.
NOW WE'VE BEEN TOLD IT'S OKAY TO REMOVE THEM.
SO I THINK IT ACTUALLY MIGHT BE MORE DANGEROUS TO LEAVE THEM ON.
....

HOLD ON...

I'M TAKING MINE OFF.

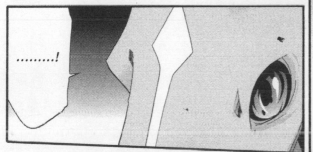

.........!

I-I'M TAKING MINE OFF TOO!

GU (TUG)

LIKE I'M GONNA BE SCARED OF SOMETHIN' LIKE THIS!

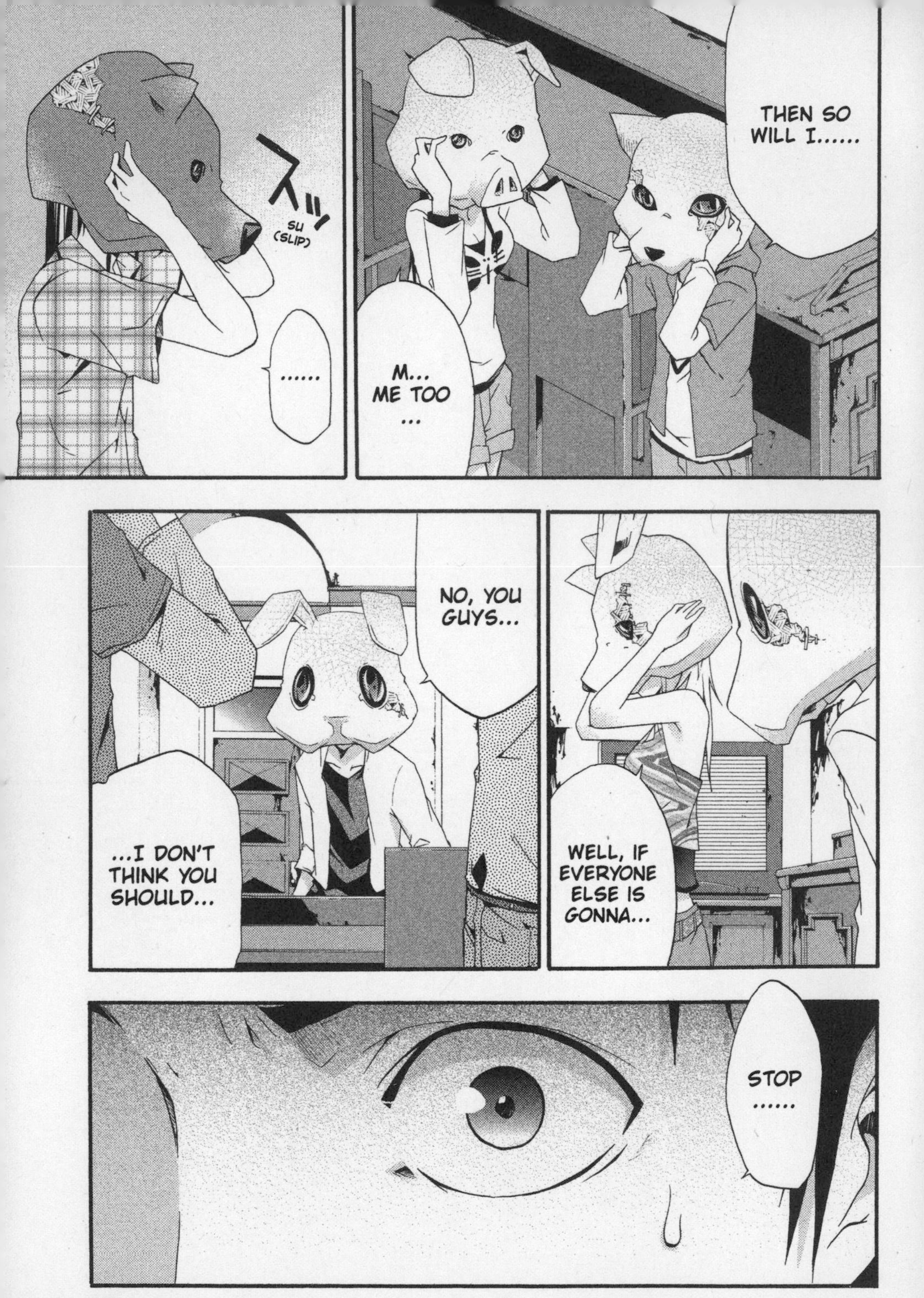
THEN SO WILL I......
M... ME TOO ...
スッ
SU (SLIP)
......
WELL, IF EVERYONE ELSE IS GONNA...
NO, YOU GUYS...
...I DON'T THINK YOU SHOULD...
STOP ......

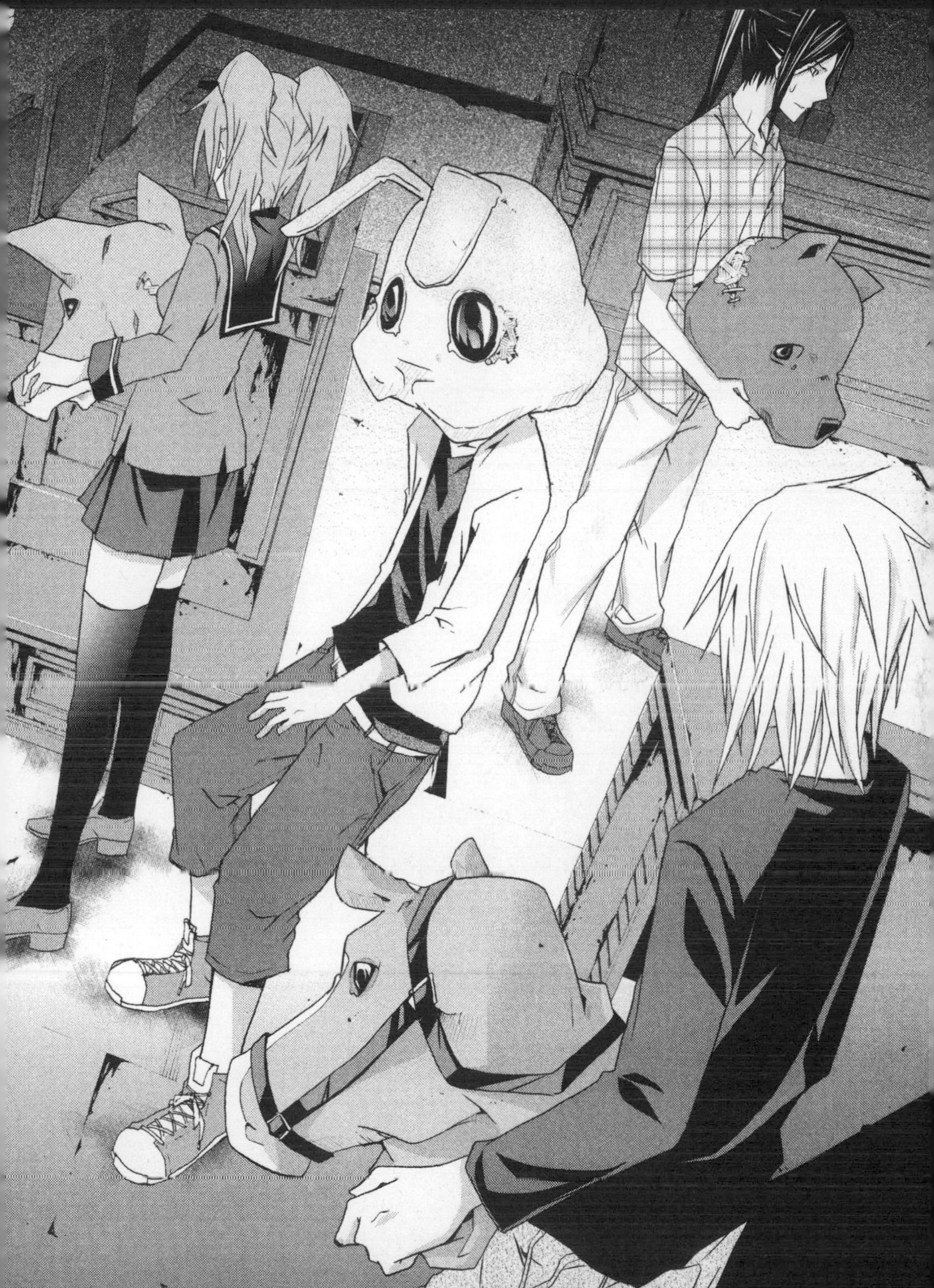

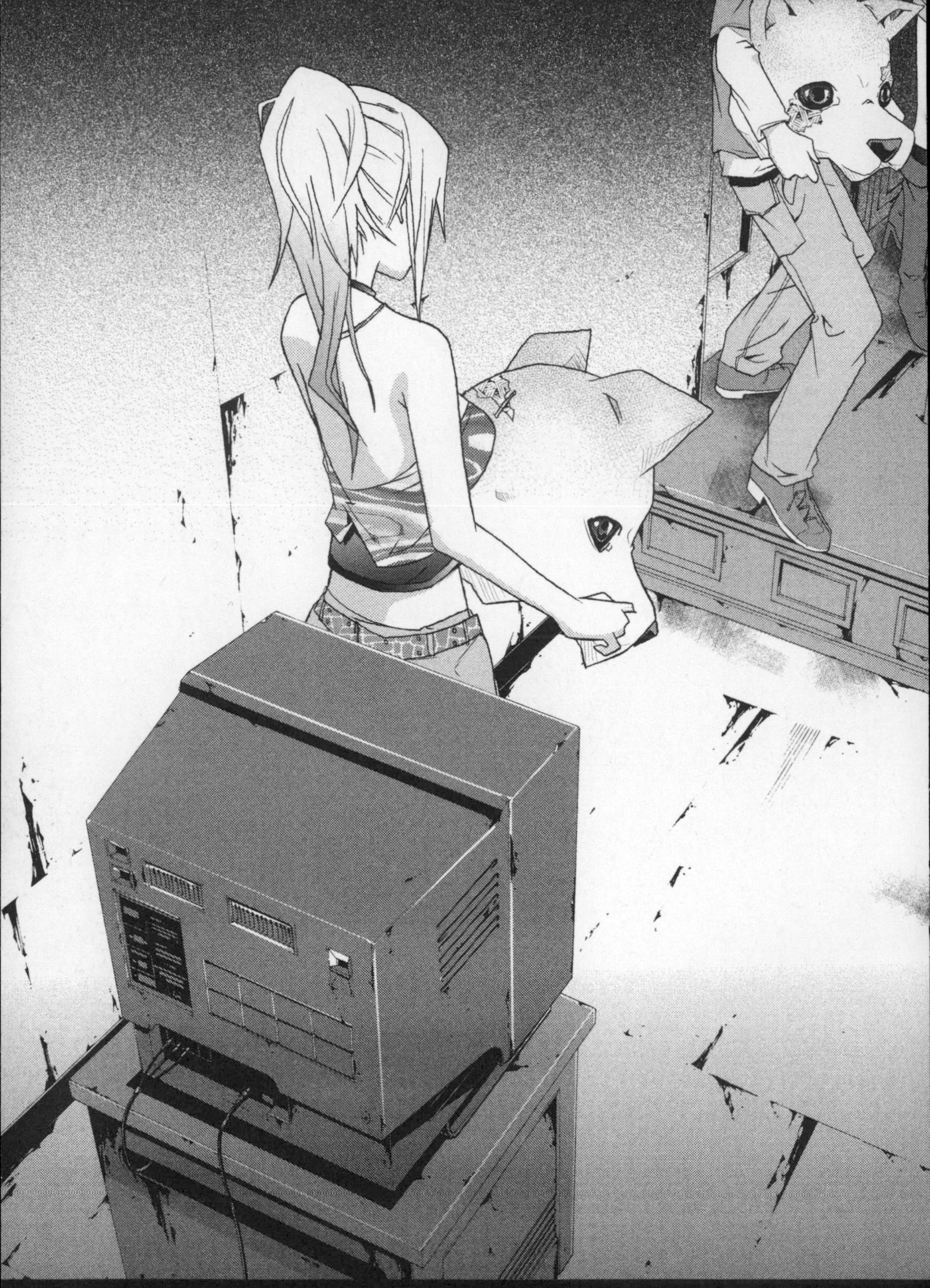

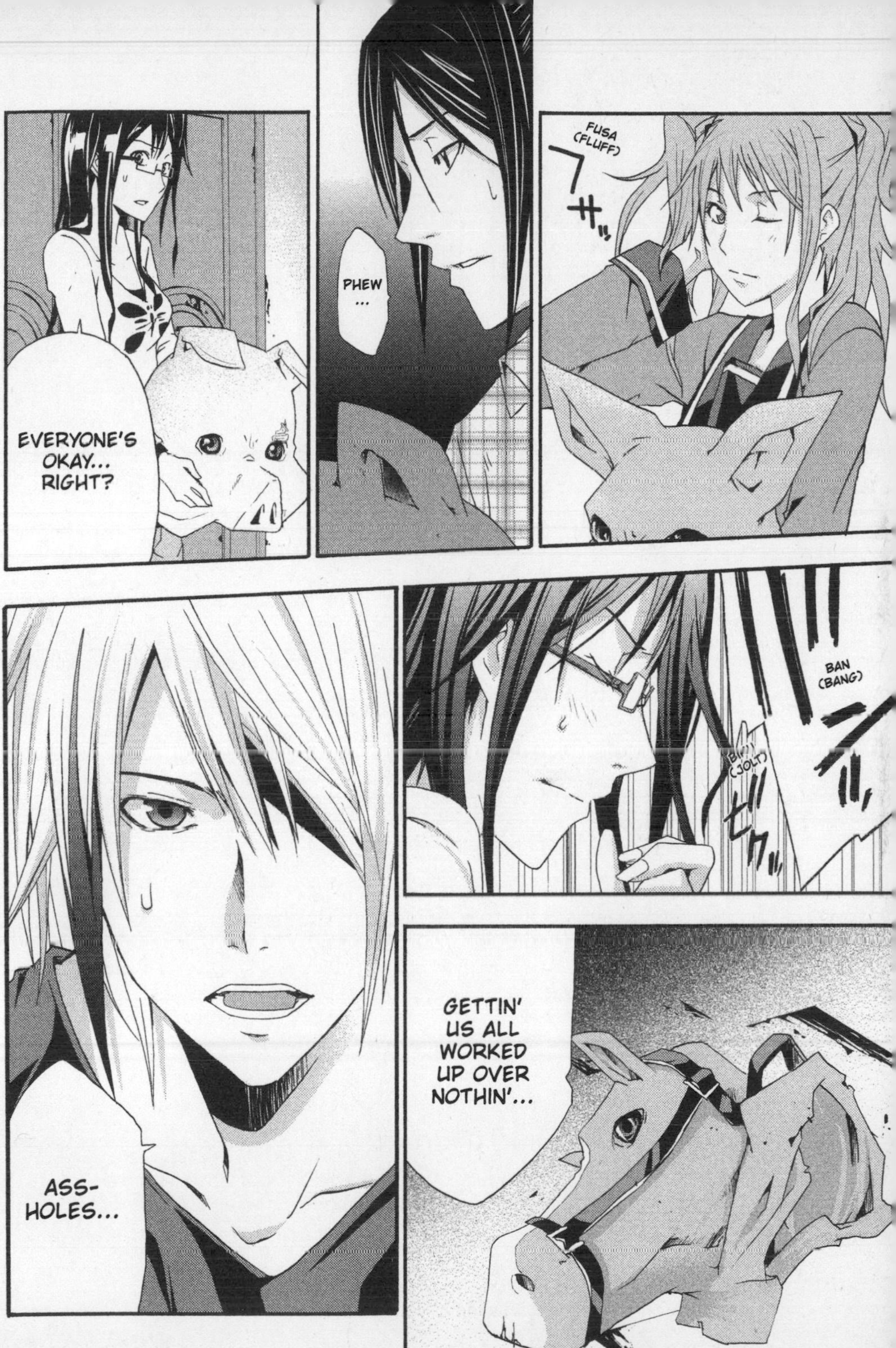
FUSA
(FLUFF)
PHEW...
EVERYONE'S OKAY... RIGHT?
BAN
(BANG)
(JOLT)
GETTIN' US ALL WORKED UP OVER NOTHIN'...
ASS-HOLES...

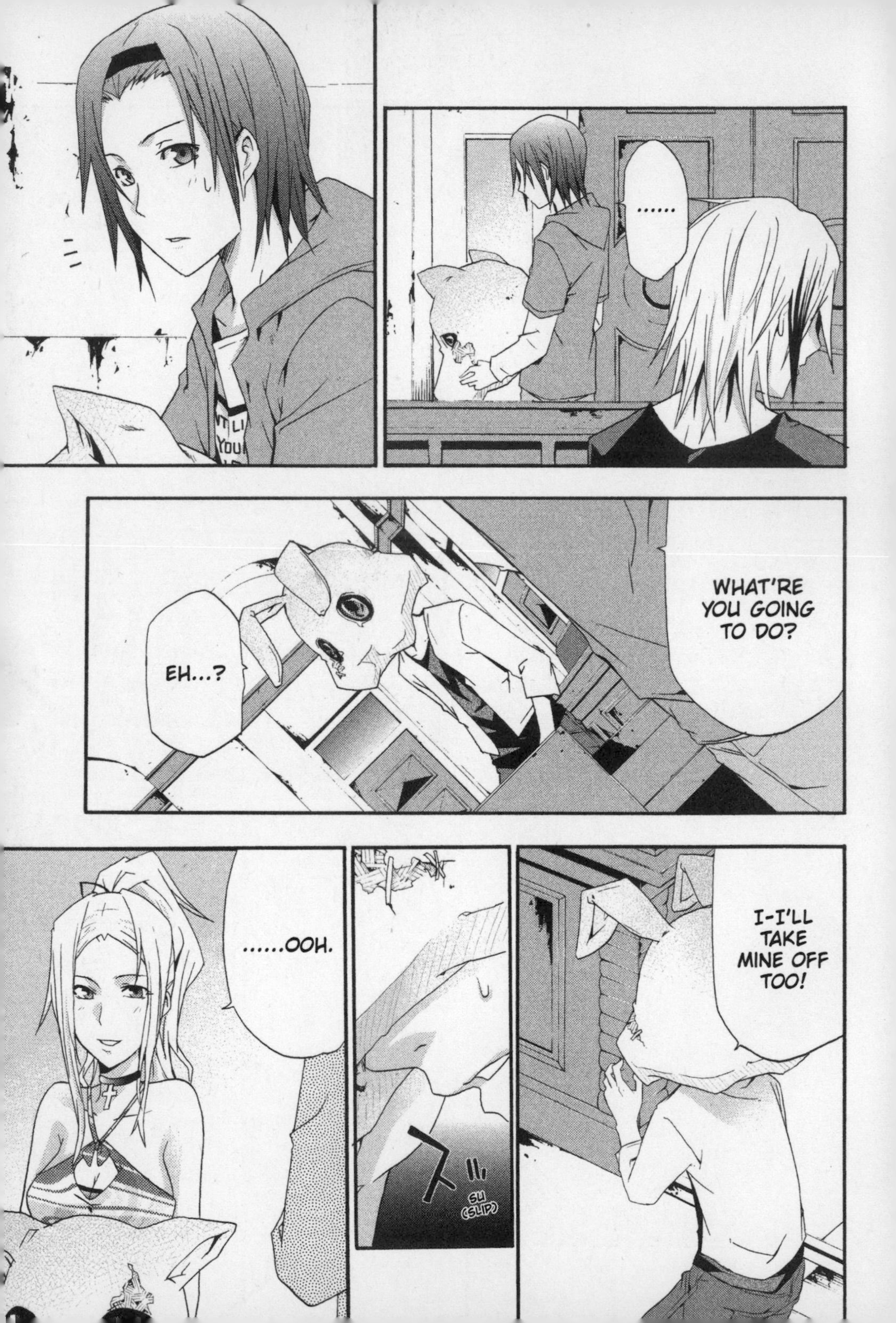
......
WHAT'RE YOU GOING TO DO?
EH...?
I-I'LL TAKE MINE OFF TOO!
SU (SLIP)
......OOH.

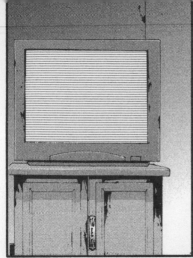

YOU'RE NOT
TOO BAD
LOOKING!

....

Envy.

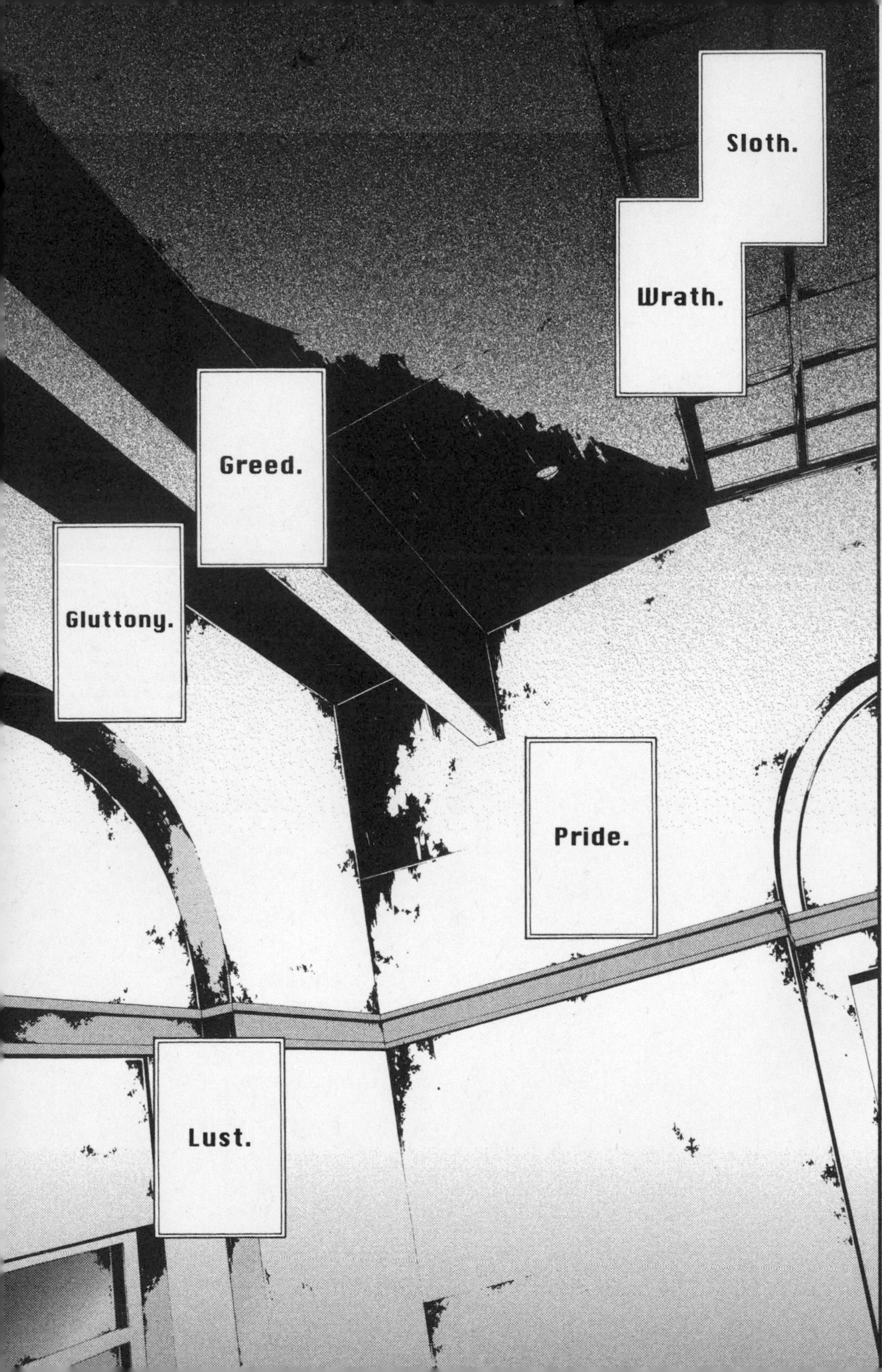
Sloth.
Wrath.
Greed.
Gluttony.
Pride.
Lust.

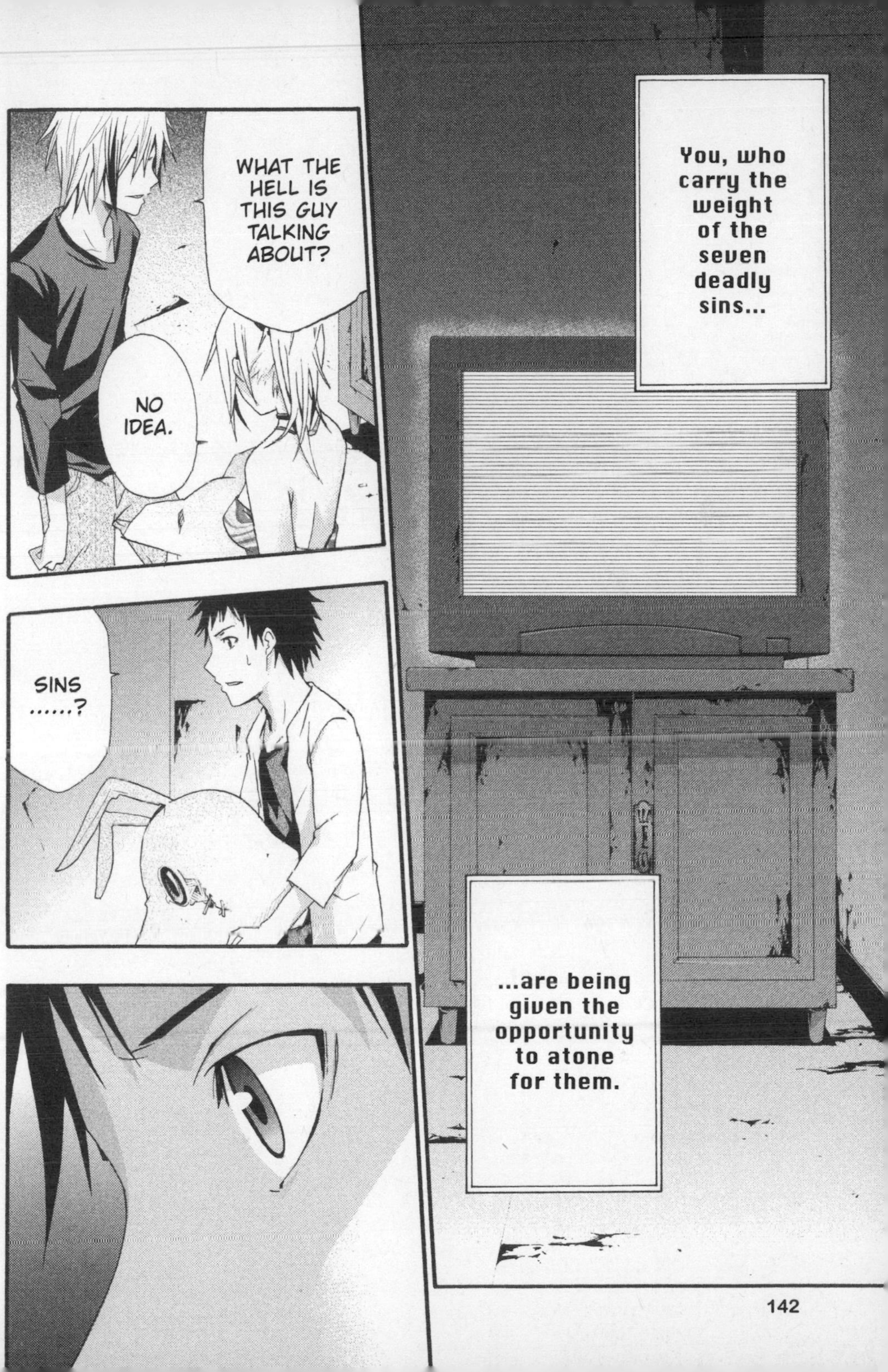
You, who carry the weight of the seven deadly sins...
...are being given the opportunity to atone for them.
WHAT THE HELL IS THIS GUY TALKING ABOUT?
NO IDEA.
SINS ......?

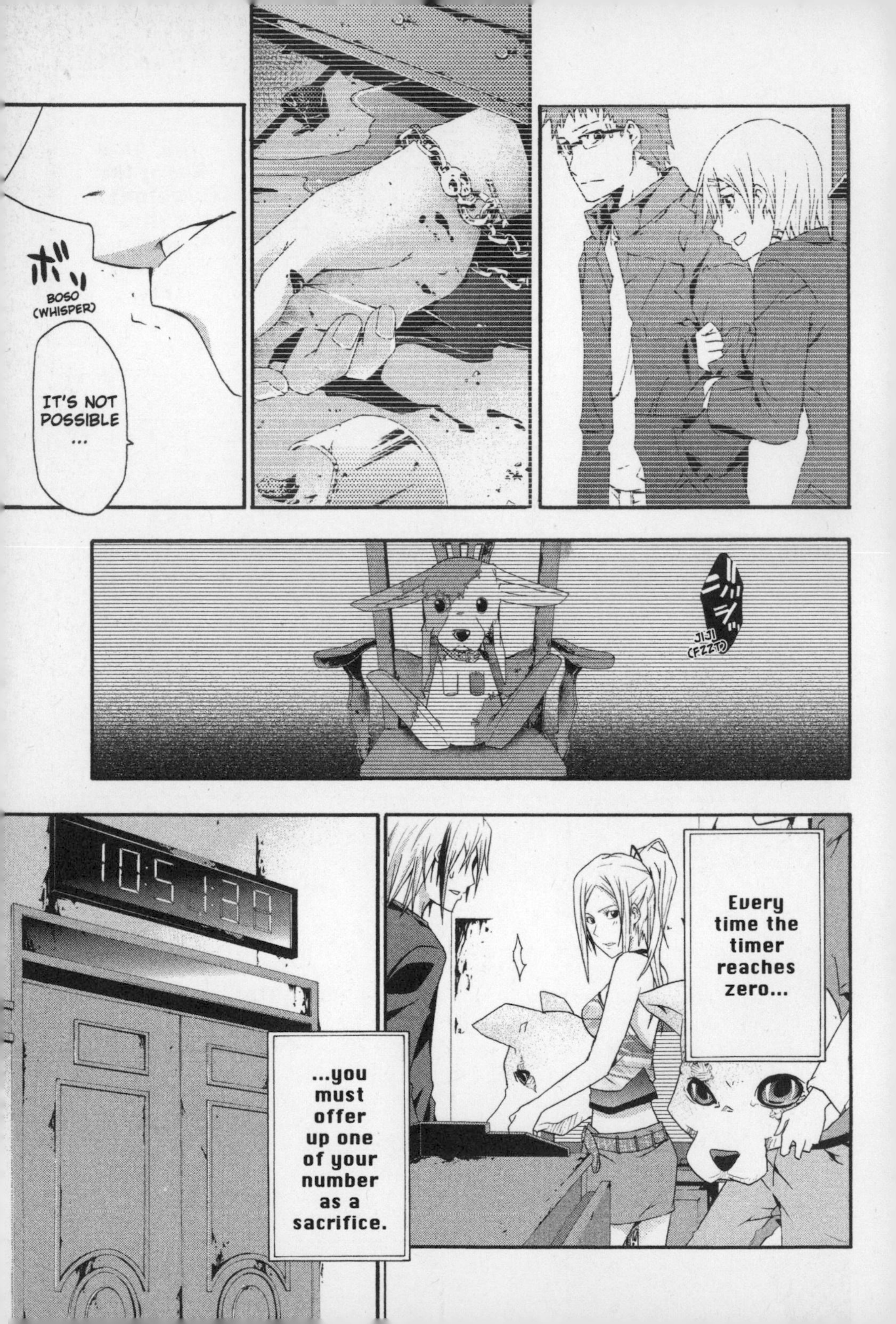

ボソッ
BOSO
(WHISPER)
IT'S NOT POSSIBLE ...
ジジ
JIJI
(FZZT)
Every time the timer reaches zero...
...you must offer up one of your number as a sacrifice.

Only four people will survive in the end.

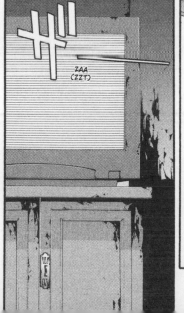

ZAA
(ZZT)

WHAT
......!?

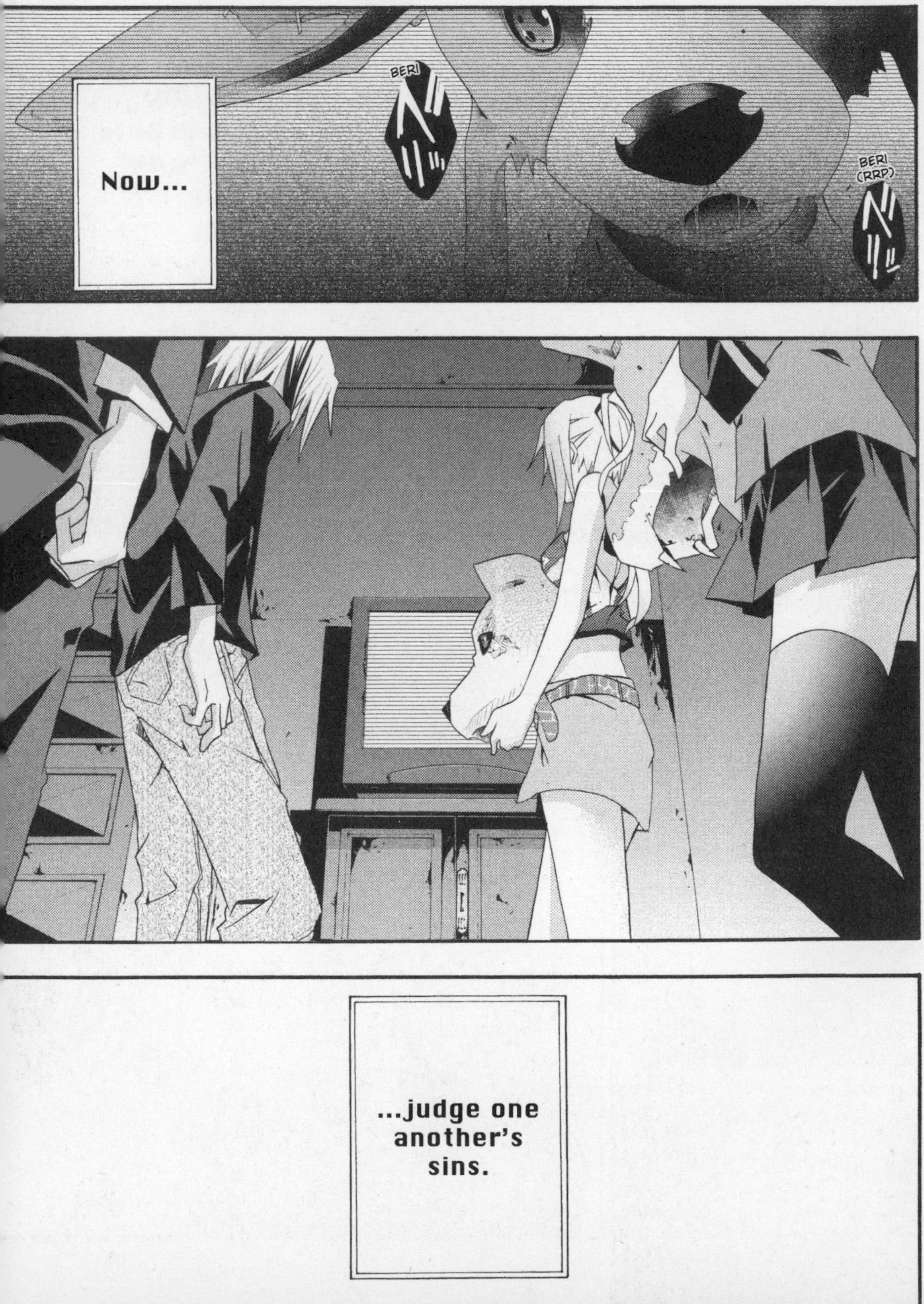
BERI (RRP)
BERI
Now...
...judge one another's sins.

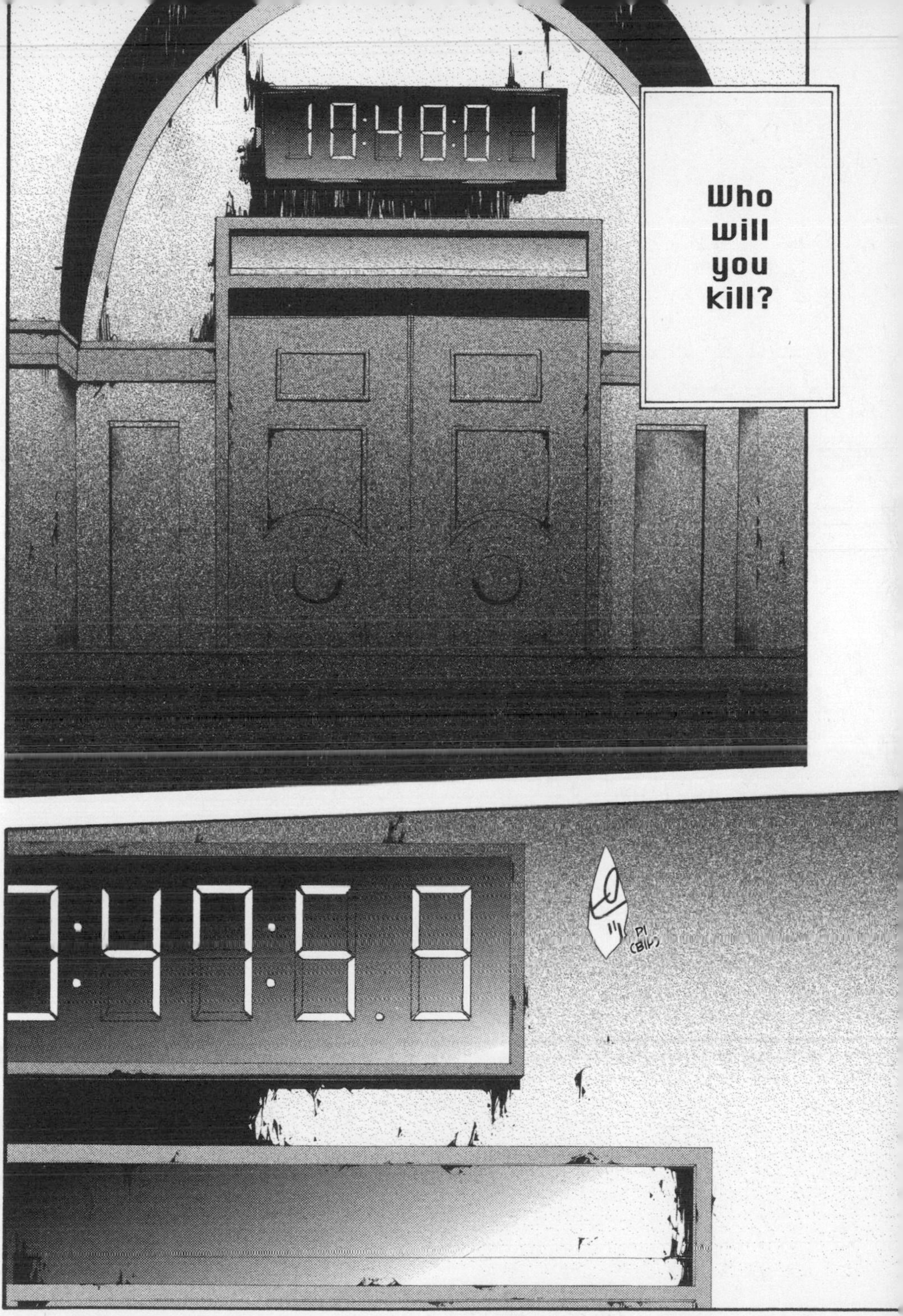
Who will you kill?
PI (BIP)

Greed

Gluttony

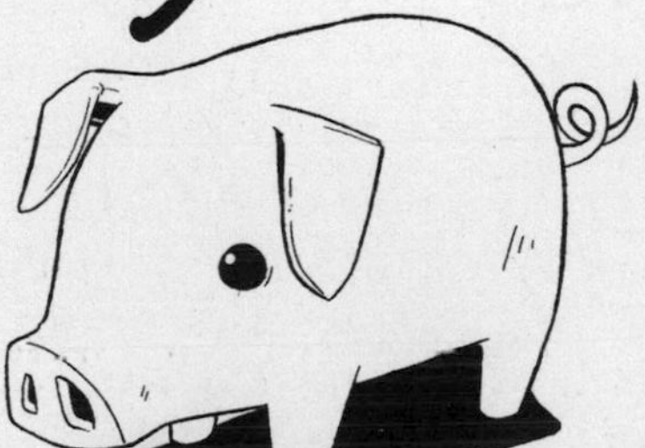

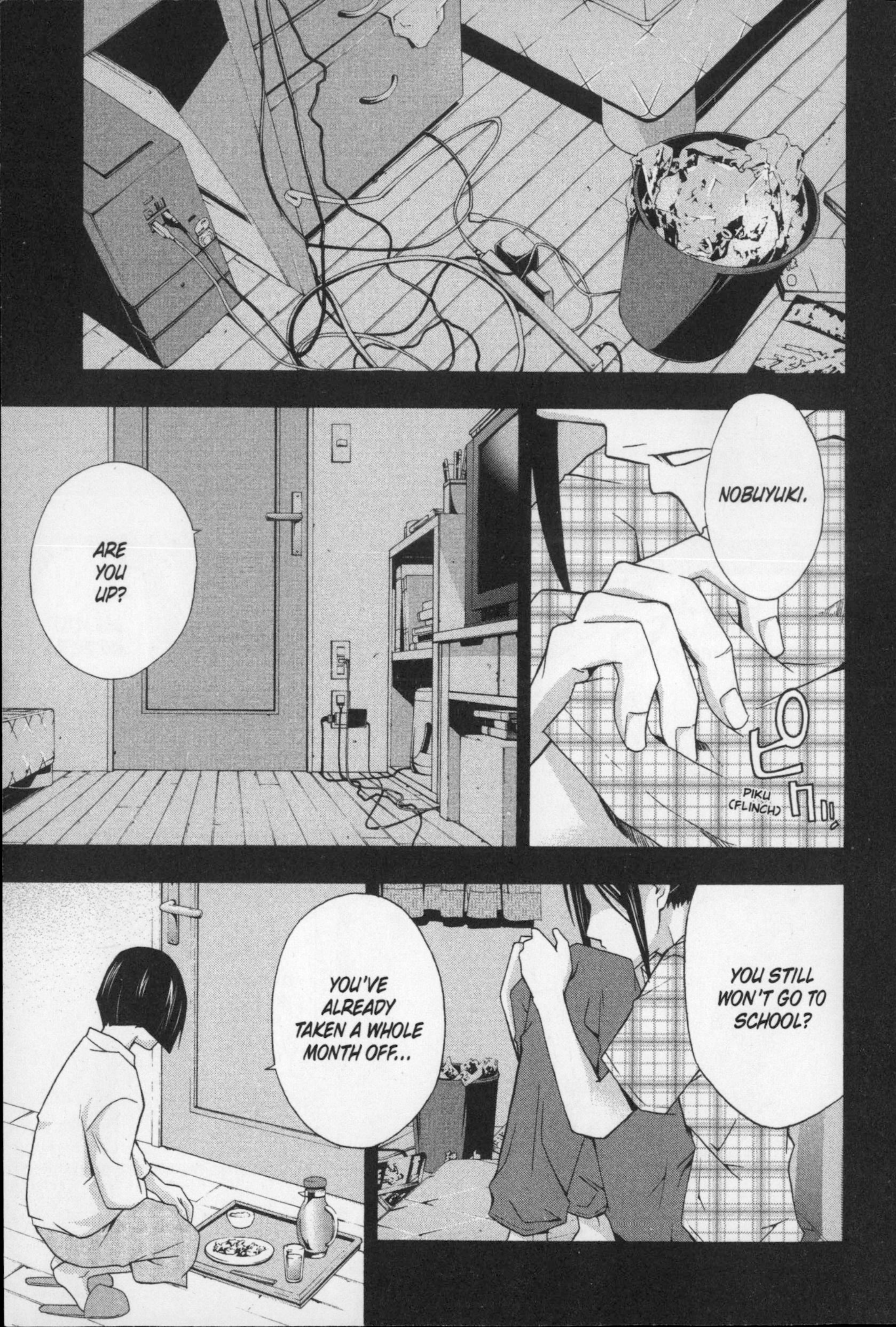
NOBUYUKI.
PIKU (FLINCH)
ARE YOU UP?
YOU STILL WON'T GO TO SCHOOL?
YOU'VE ALREADY TAKEN A WHOLE MONTH OFF...

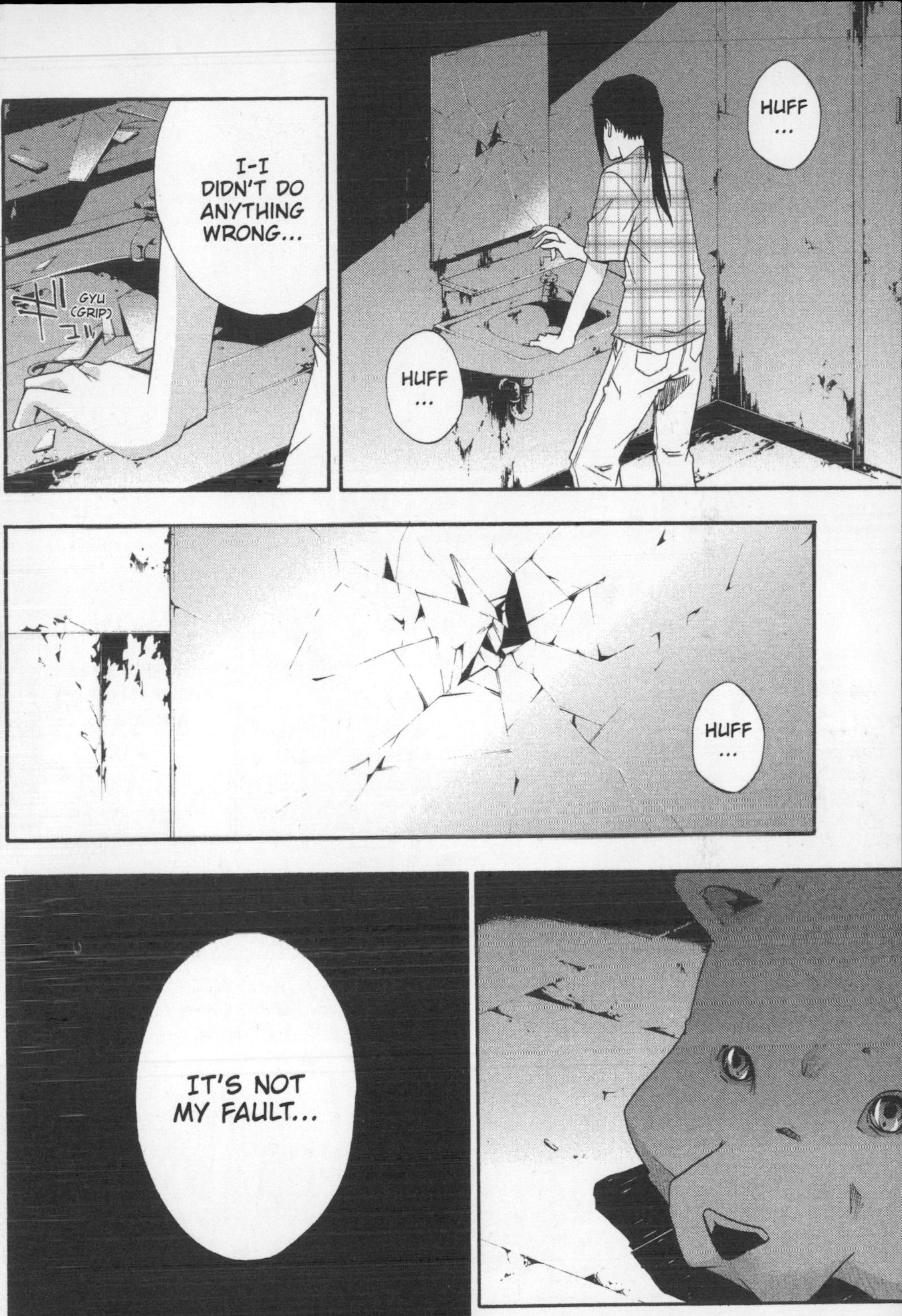
HUFF ...
HUFF ...
I-I DIDN'T DO ANYTHING WRONG...
GYU (GRIP)
HUFF ...
IT'S NOT MY FAULT...

CHAPTER 4 RECLUSE

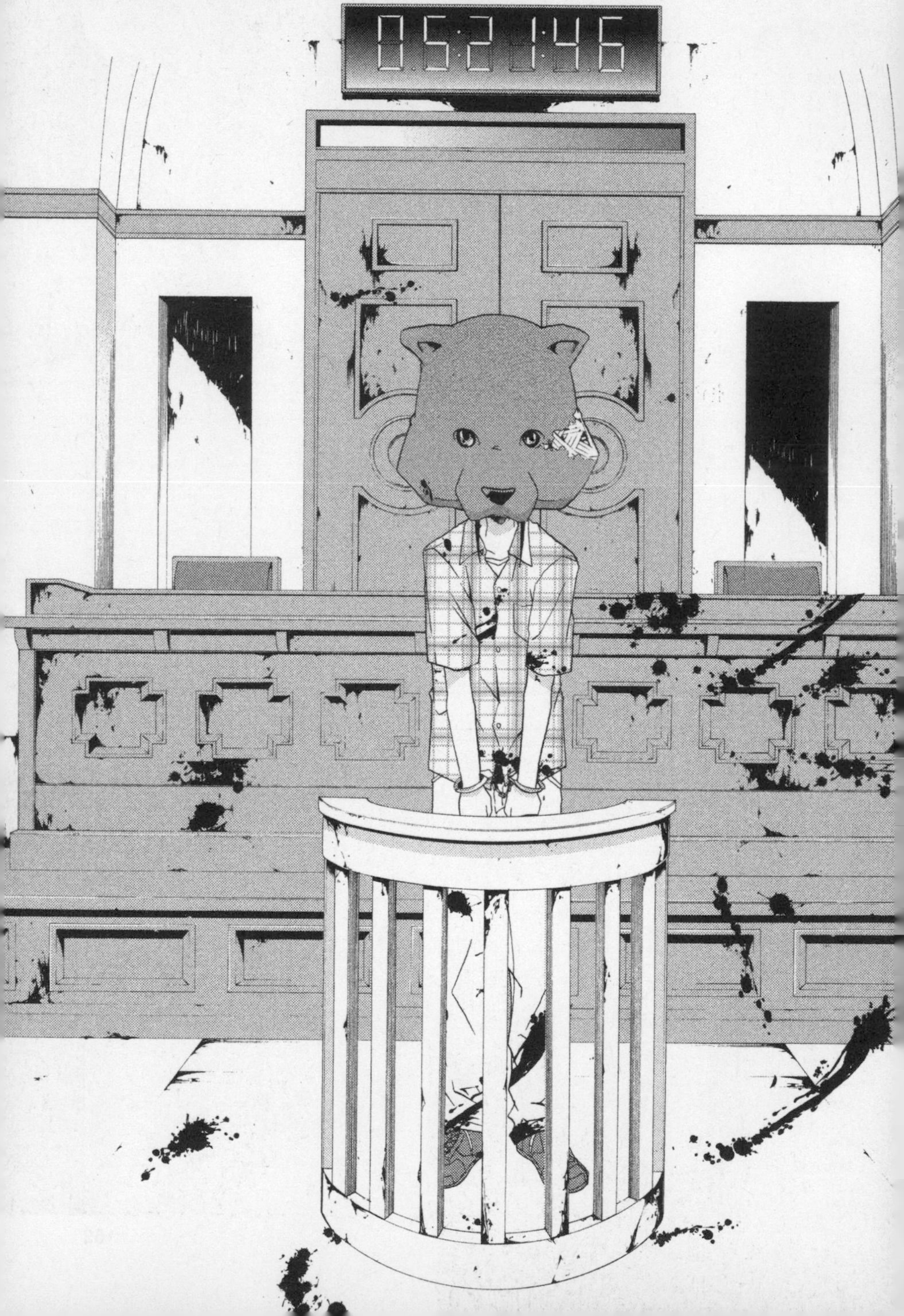

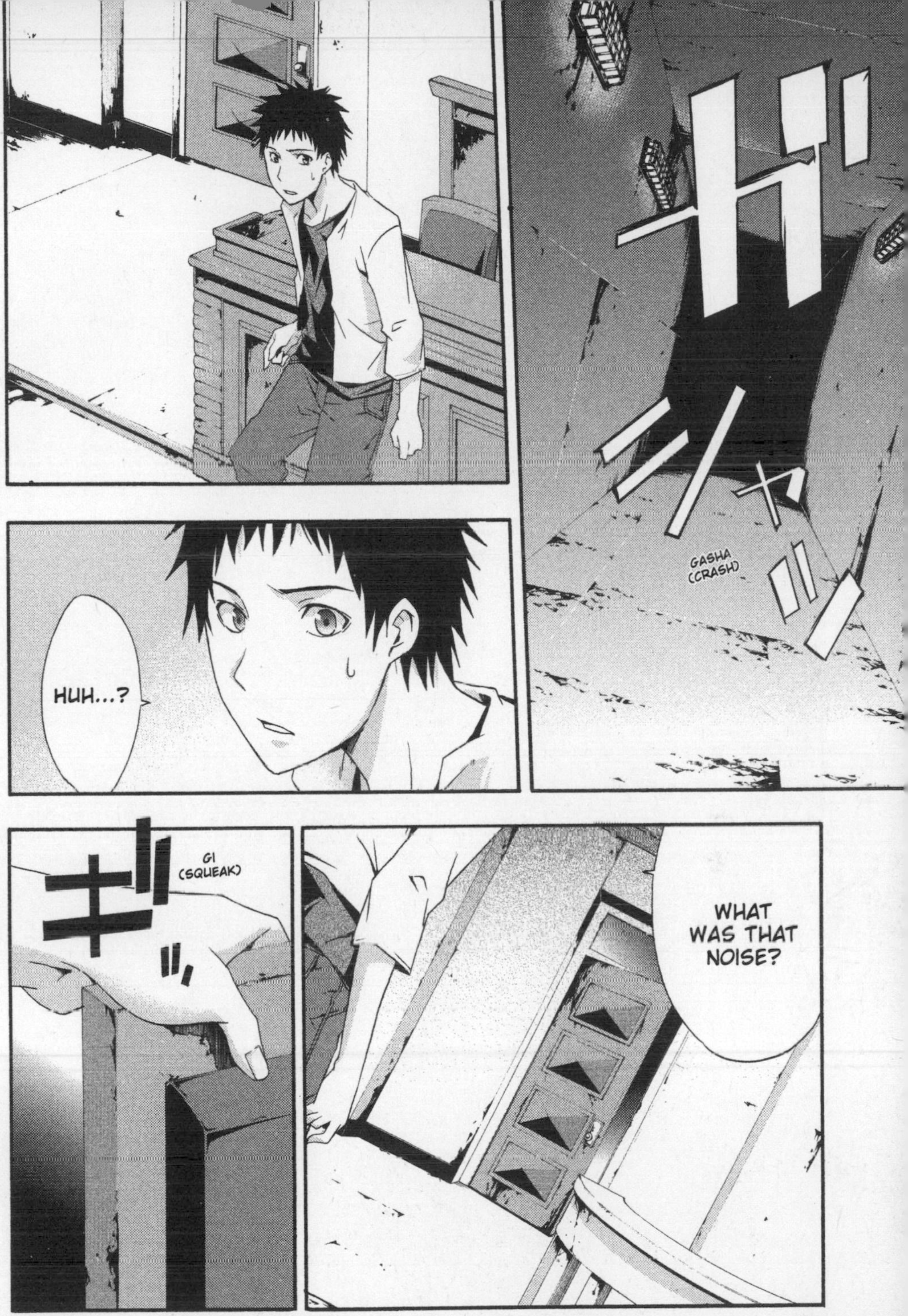
GASHA
(CRASH)
HUH...?
WHAT WAS THAT NOISE?
GI
(SQUEAK)

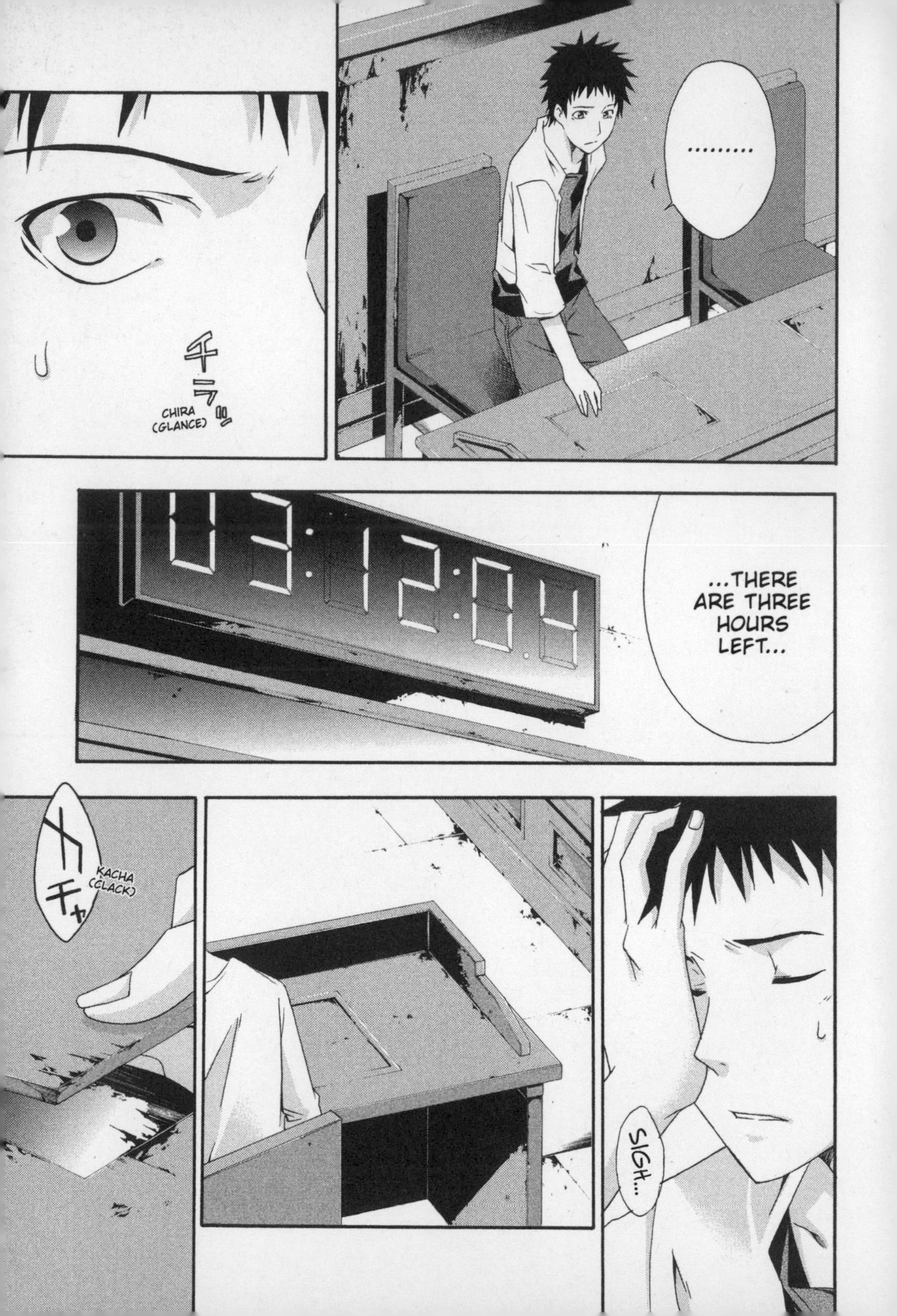
....
チラッ
CHIRA (GLANCE)
03:12:04
...THERE ARE THREE HOURS LEFT...
SIGH...
カチャ
KACHA (CLACK)

JUDGE......

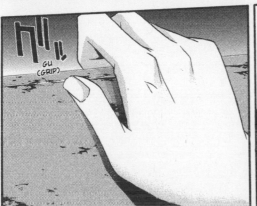

GU
(GRIP)

....

Please
choose a
person to
kill every
twelve
hours.

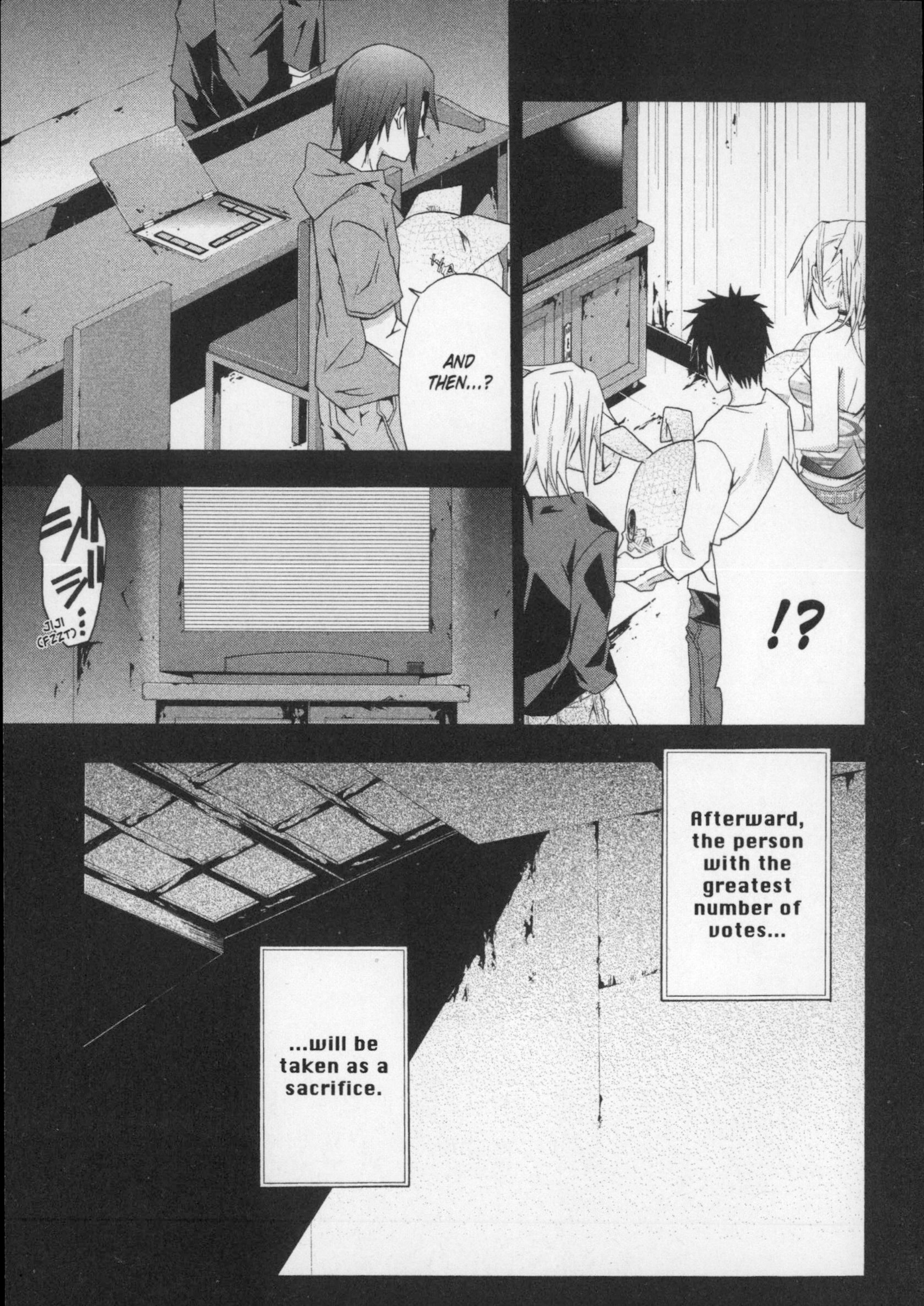
!?
AND THEN...?
ジジ...
JIJI (FZZT)
Afterward, the person with the greatest number of votes...
...will be taken as a sacrifice.

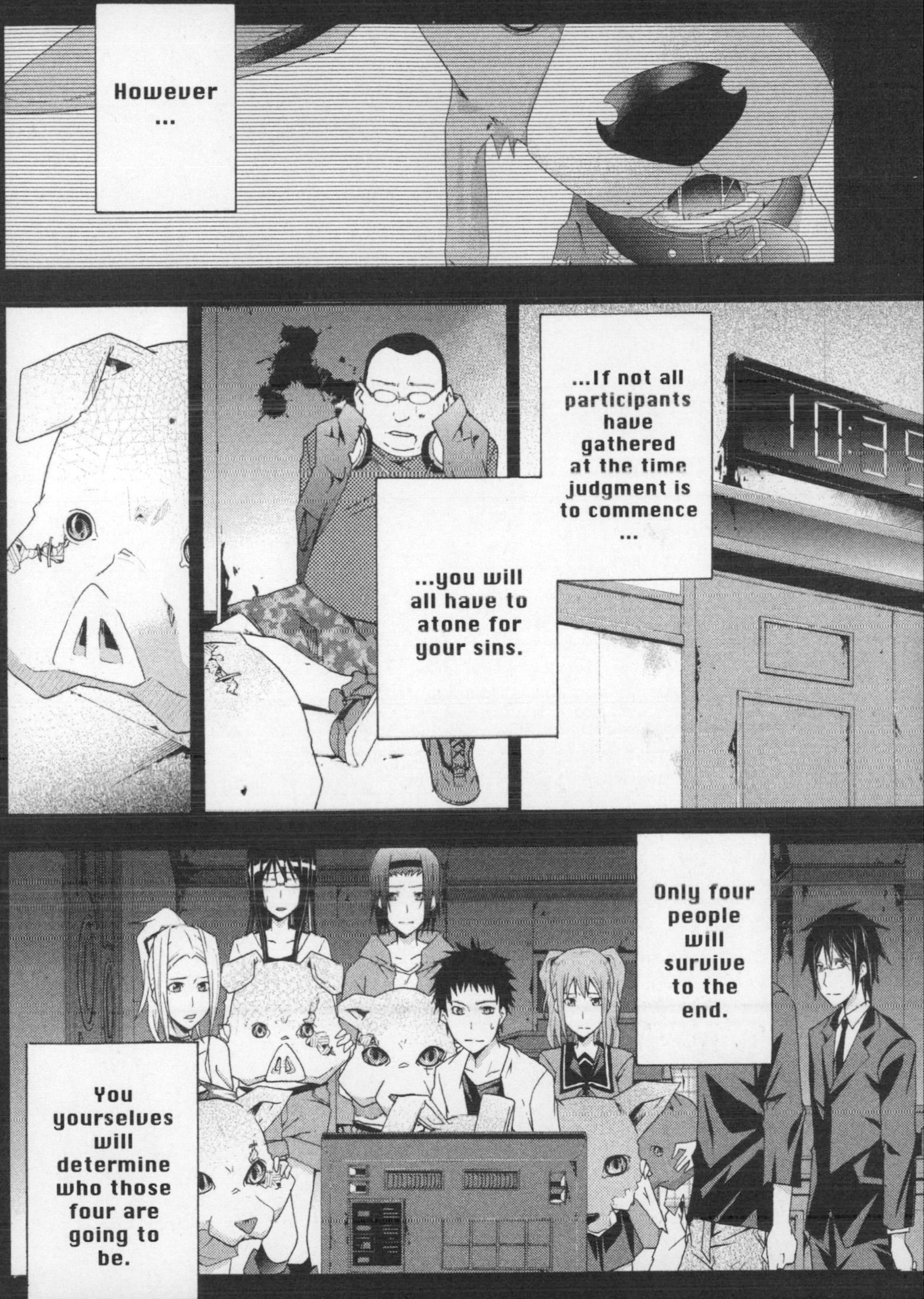
However ...
...If not all participants have gathered at the time judgment is to commence ...
...you will all have to atone for your sins.
Only four people will survive to the end.
You yourselves will determine who those four are going to be.

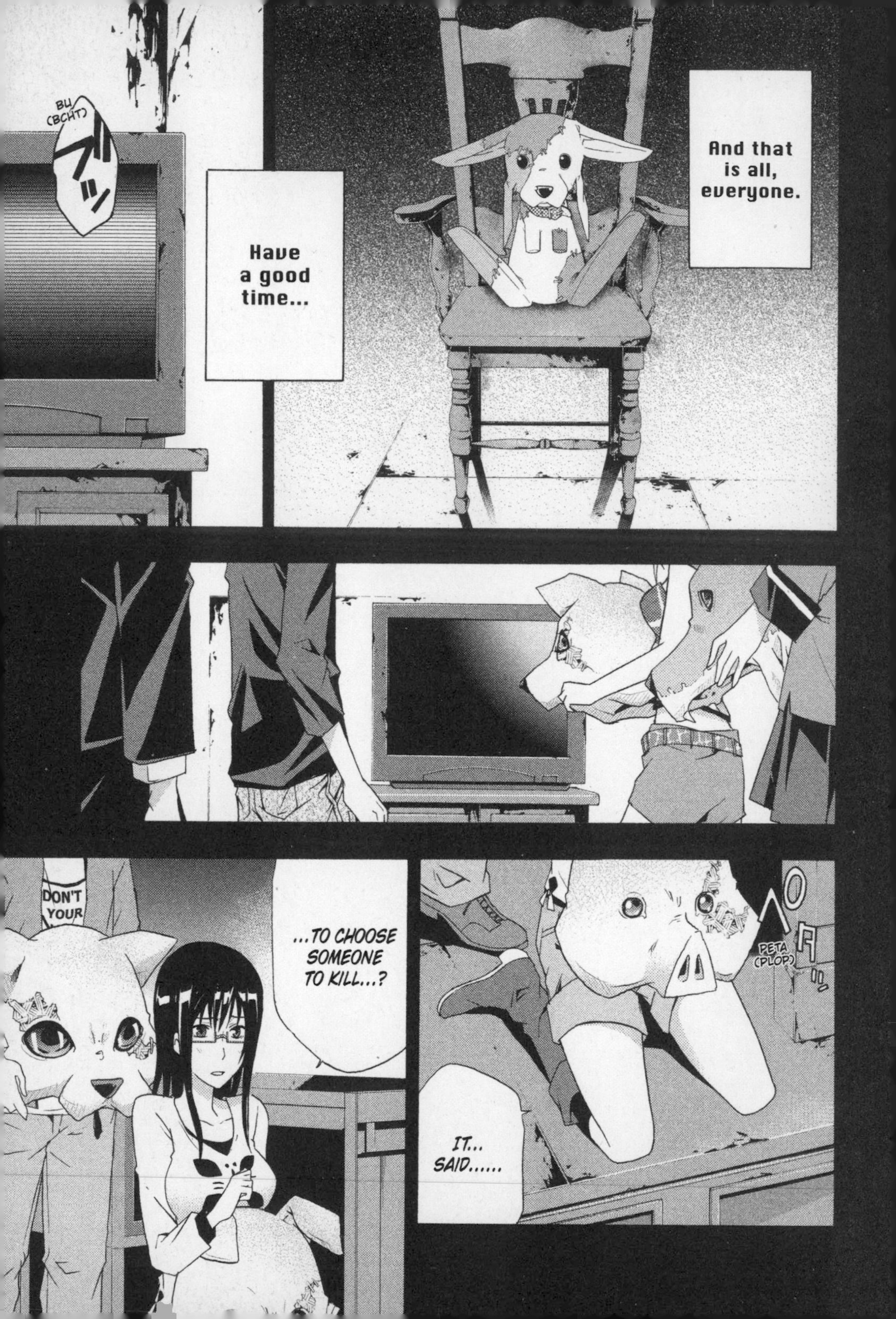
And that is all, everyone.
Have a good time...
BU (BCHT)
PETA (PLOP)
IT... SAID......
...TO CHOOSE SOMEONE TO KILL...?
DON'T YOUR

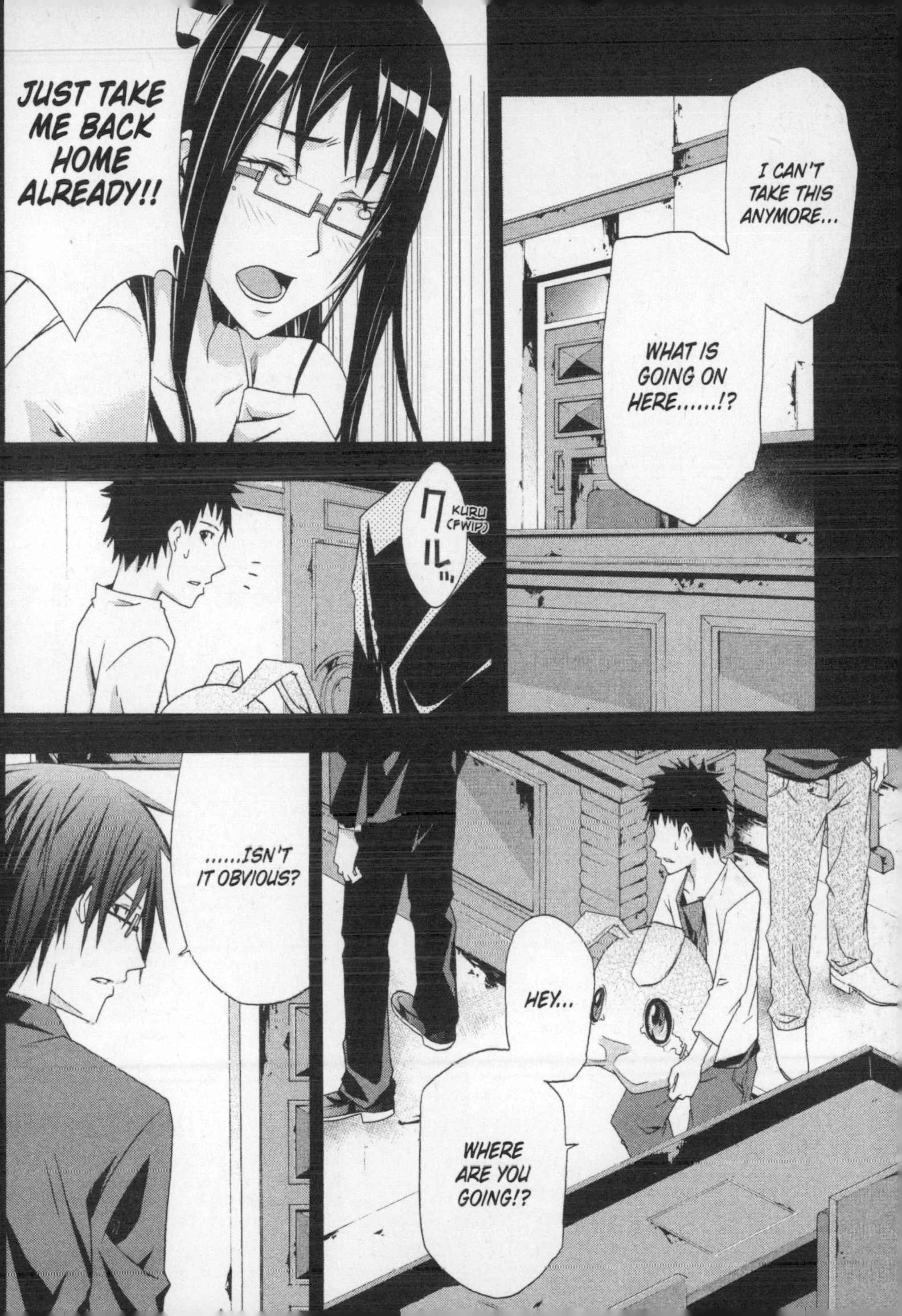
I CAN'T TAKE THIS ANYMORE...
WHAT IS GOING ON HERE......!?
JUST TAKE ME BACK HOME ALREADY!!
クル
KURU (FWIP)
HEY...
WHERE ARE YOU GOING!?
......ISN'T IT OBVIOUS?

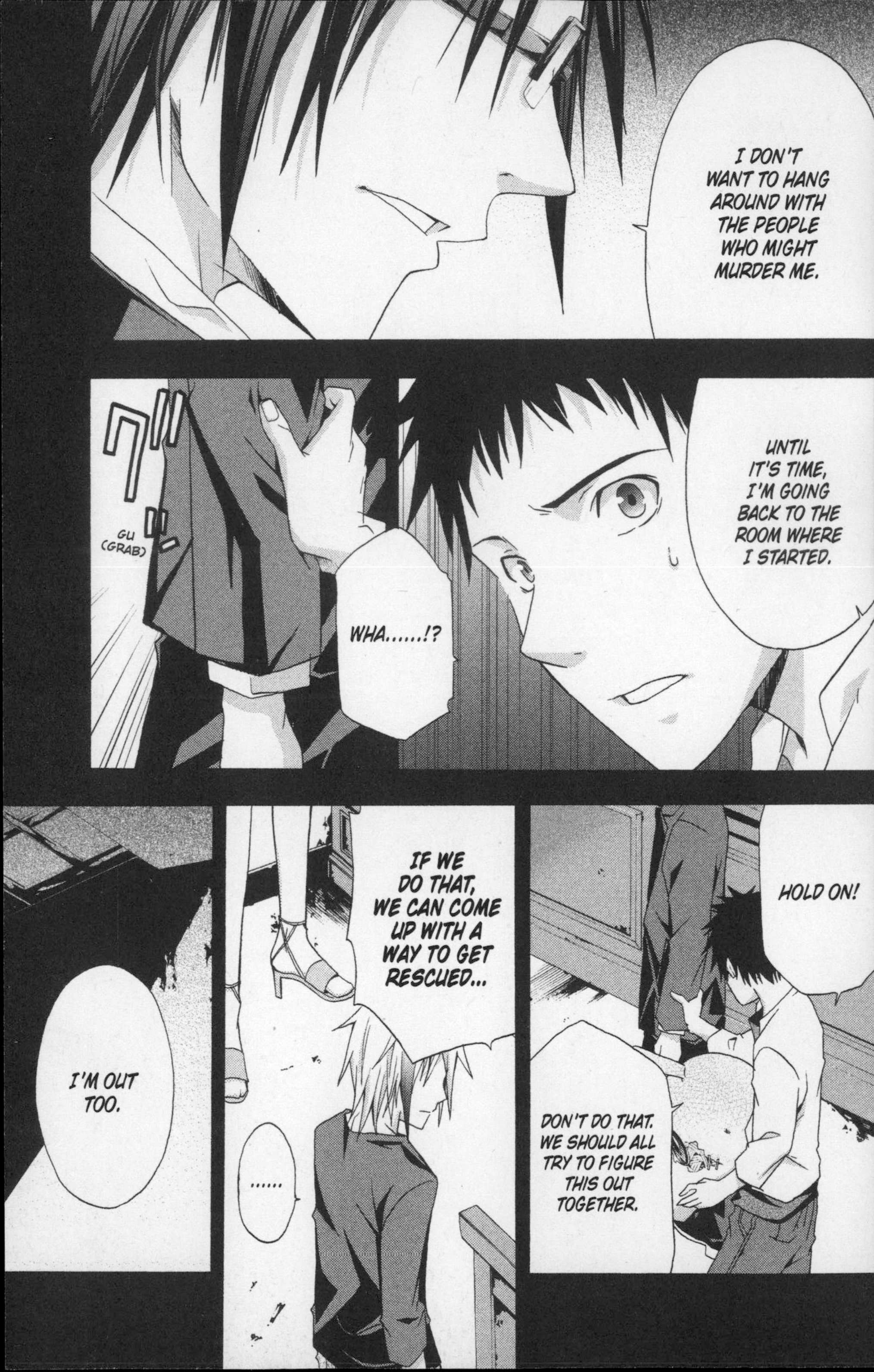
I DON'T WANT TO HANG AROUND WITH THE PEOPLE WHO MIGHT MURDER ME.
UNTIL IT'S TIME, I'M GOING BACK TO THE ROOM WHERE I STARTED.
GU (GRAB)
WHA......!?
HOLD ON!
DON'T DO THAT. WE SHOULD ALL TRY TO FIGURE THIS OUT TOGETHER.
IF WE DO THAT, WE CAN COME UP WITH A WAY TO GET RESCUED...
......
I'M OUT TOO.

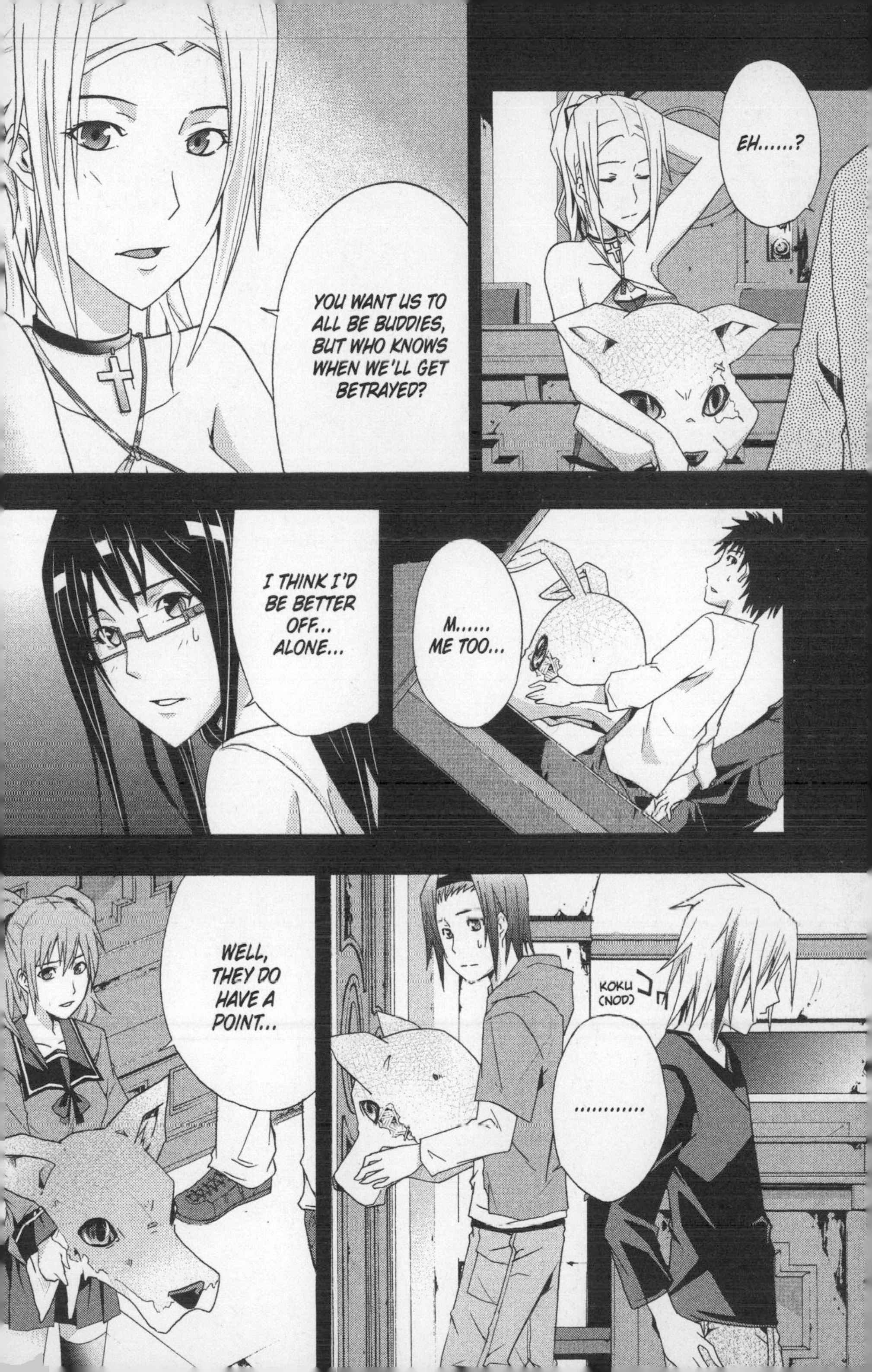
EH......?
YOU WANT US TO ALL BE BUDDIES, BUT WHO KNOWS WHEN WE'LL GET BETRAYED?
M...... ME TOO...
I THINK I'D BE BETTER OFF... ALONE...
KOKU (NOD)
....
WELL, THEY DO HAVE A POINT...

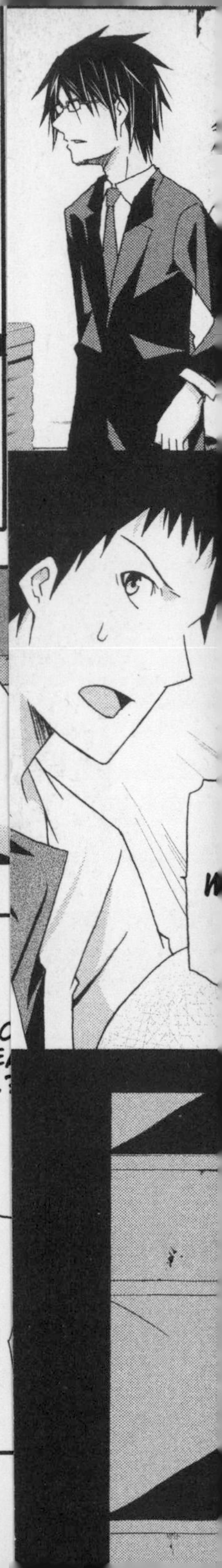

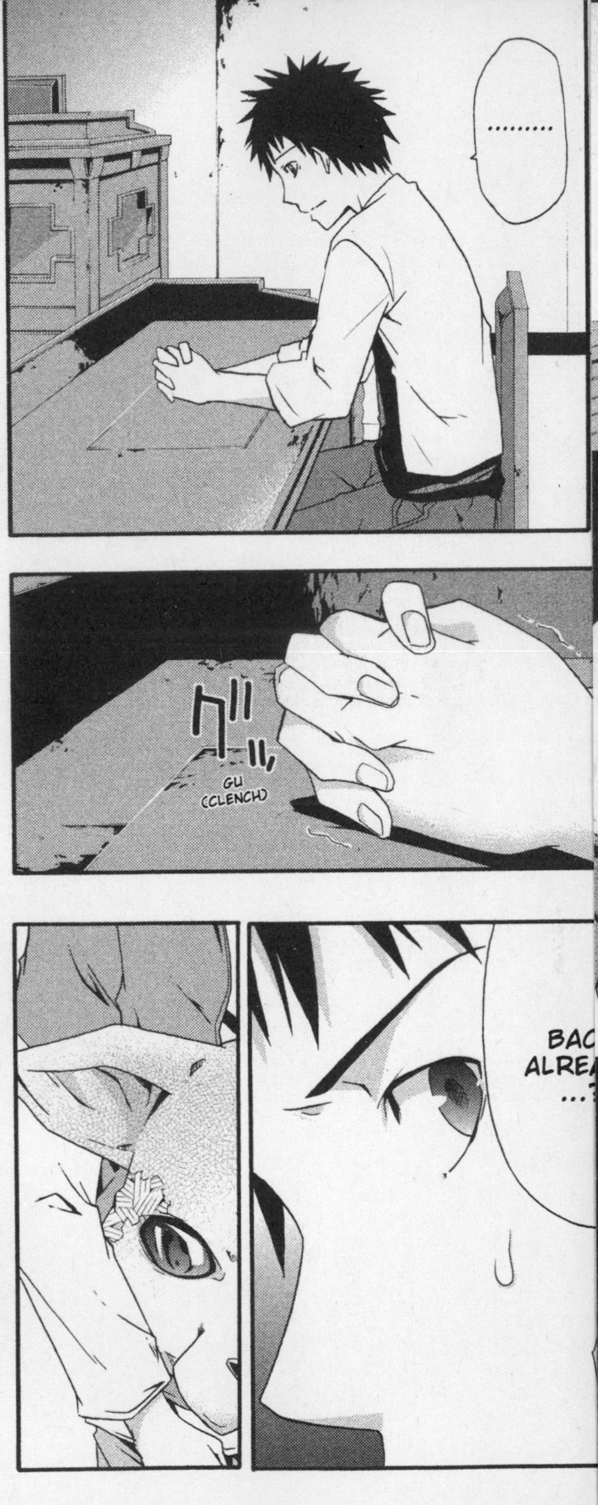
....
グッ
GU (CLENCH)

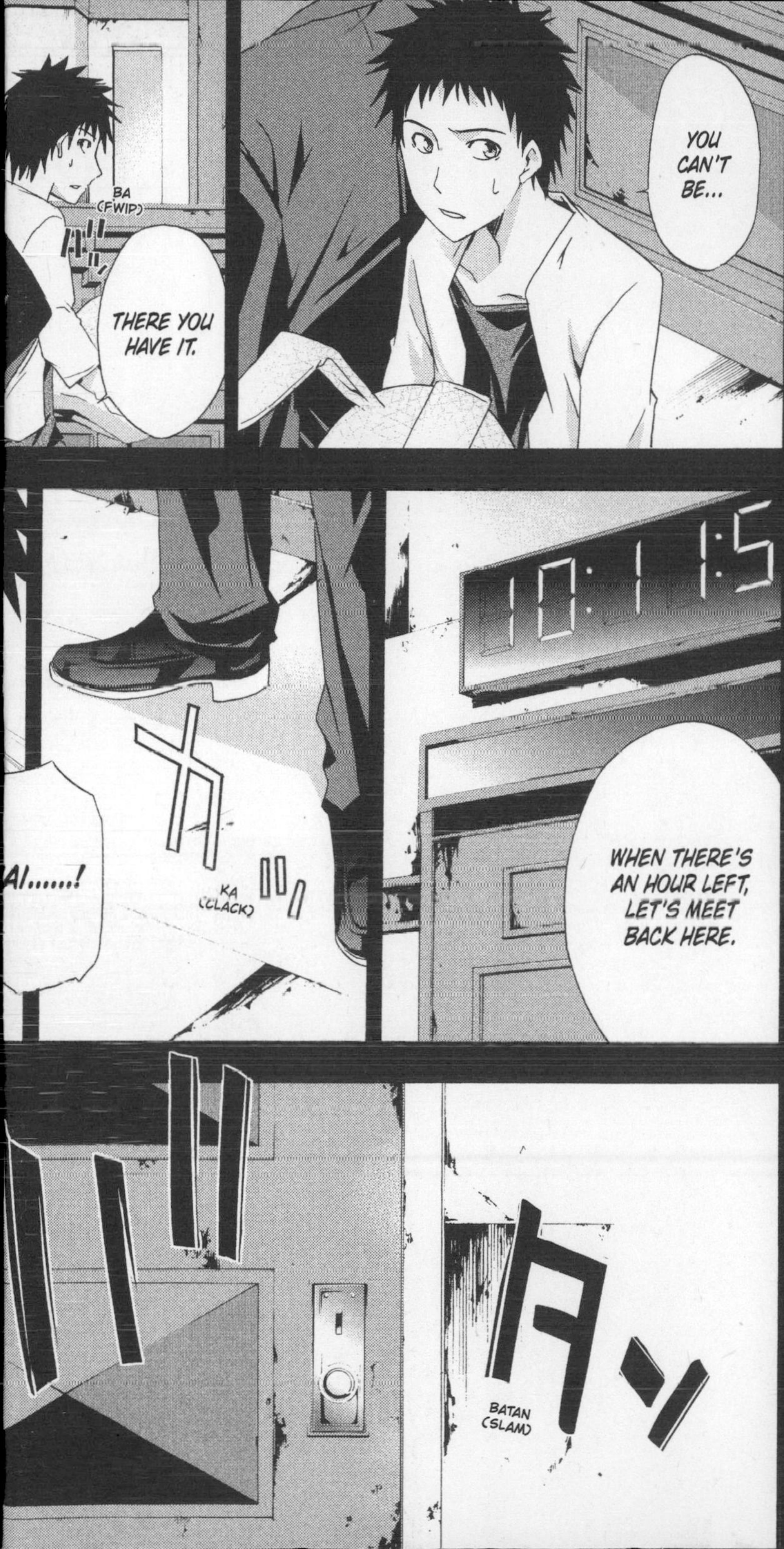
YOU CAN'T BE...
BA (FWIP)
THERE YOU HAVE IT.
10:11:5
WHEN THERE'S AN HOUR LEFT, LET'S MEET BACK HERE.
KA (CLACK)
AI......!
BATAN (SLAM)

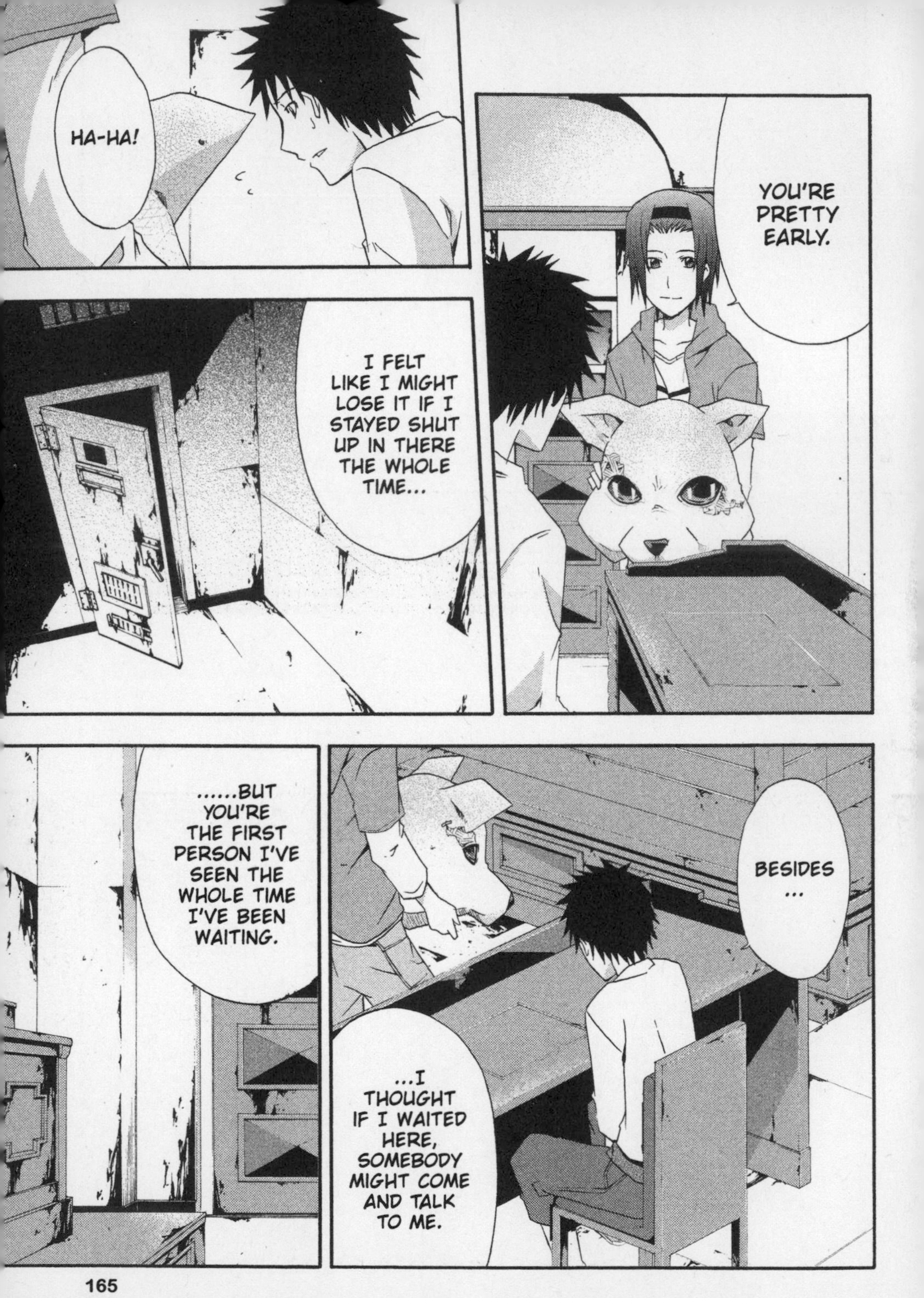
YOU'RE PRETTY EARLY.
HA-HA!
I FELT LIKE I MIGHT LOSE IT IF I STAYED SHUT UP IN THERE THE WHOLE TIME...
BESIDES...
...I THOUGHT IF I WAITED HERE, SOMEBODY MIGHT COME AND TALK TO ME.
......BUT YOU'RE THE FIRST PERSON I'VE SEEN THE WHOLE TIME I'VE BEEN WAITING.

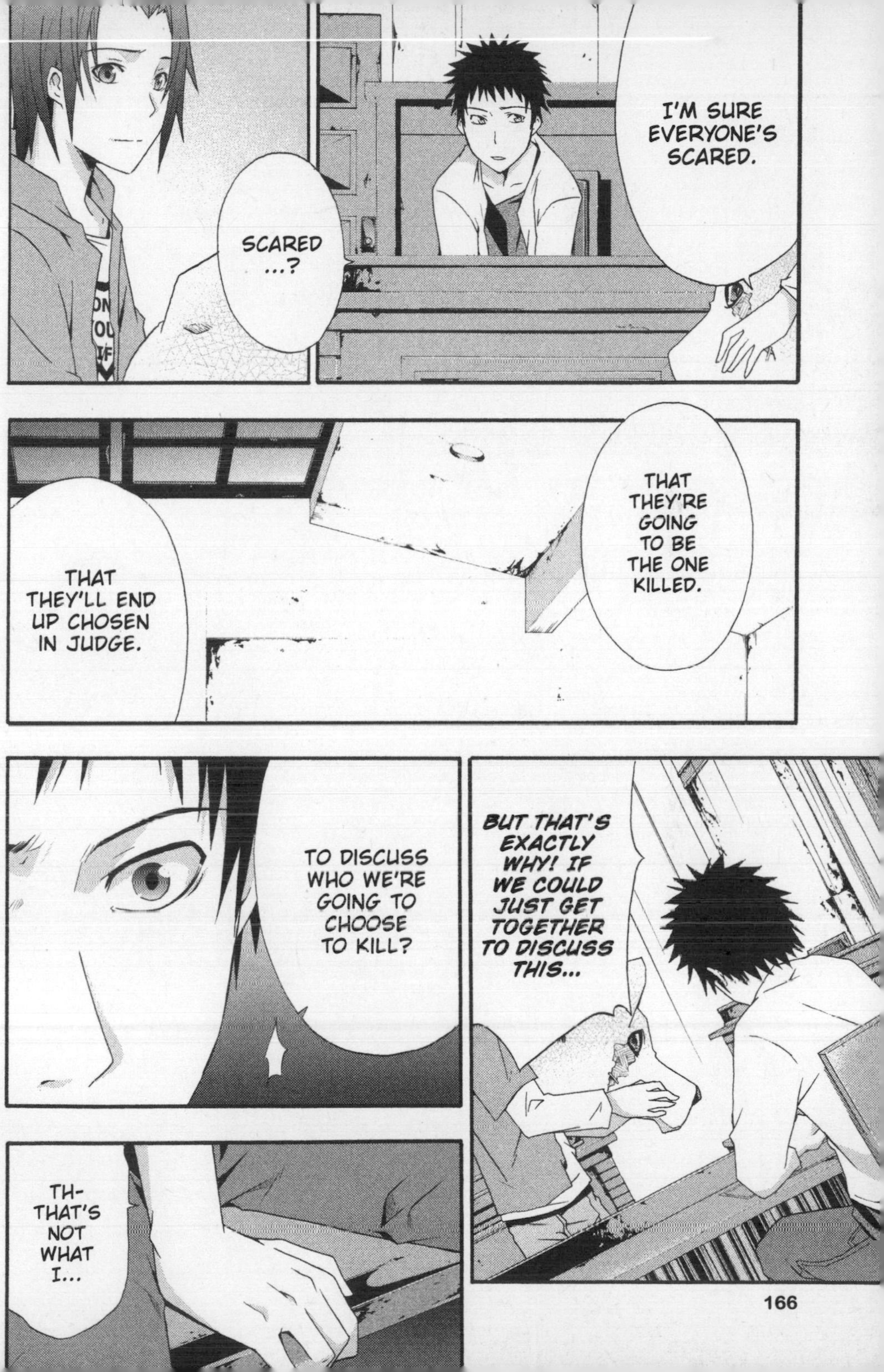
I'M SURE EVERYONE'S SCARED.
SCARED ...?
THAT THEY'RE GOING TO BE THE ONE KILLED.
THAT THEY'LL END UP CHOSEN IN JUDGE.
BUT THAT'S EXACTLY WHY! IF WE COULD JUST GET TOGETHER TO DISCUSS THIS...
TO DISCUSS WHO WE'RE GOING TO CHOOSE TO KILL?
TH- THAT'S NOT WHAT I...

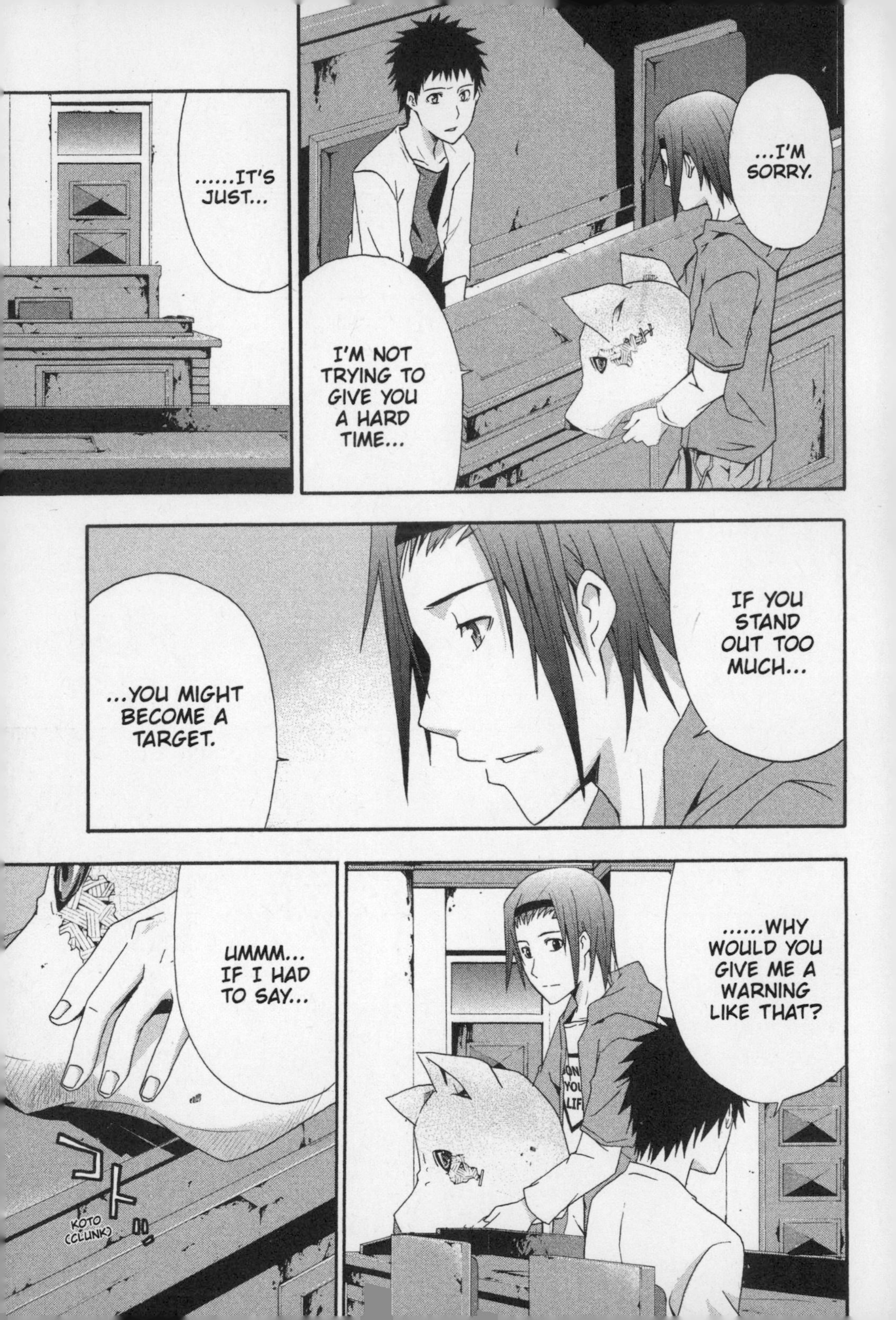
...I'M SORRY.
I'M NOT TRYING TO GIVE YOU A HARD TIME...
......IT'S JUST...
IF YOU STAND OUT TOO MUCH...
...YOU MIGHT BECOME A TARGET.
......WHY WOULD YOU GIVE ME A WARNING LIKE THAT?
UMMM... IF I HAD TO SAY...
KOTO (CLUNK)

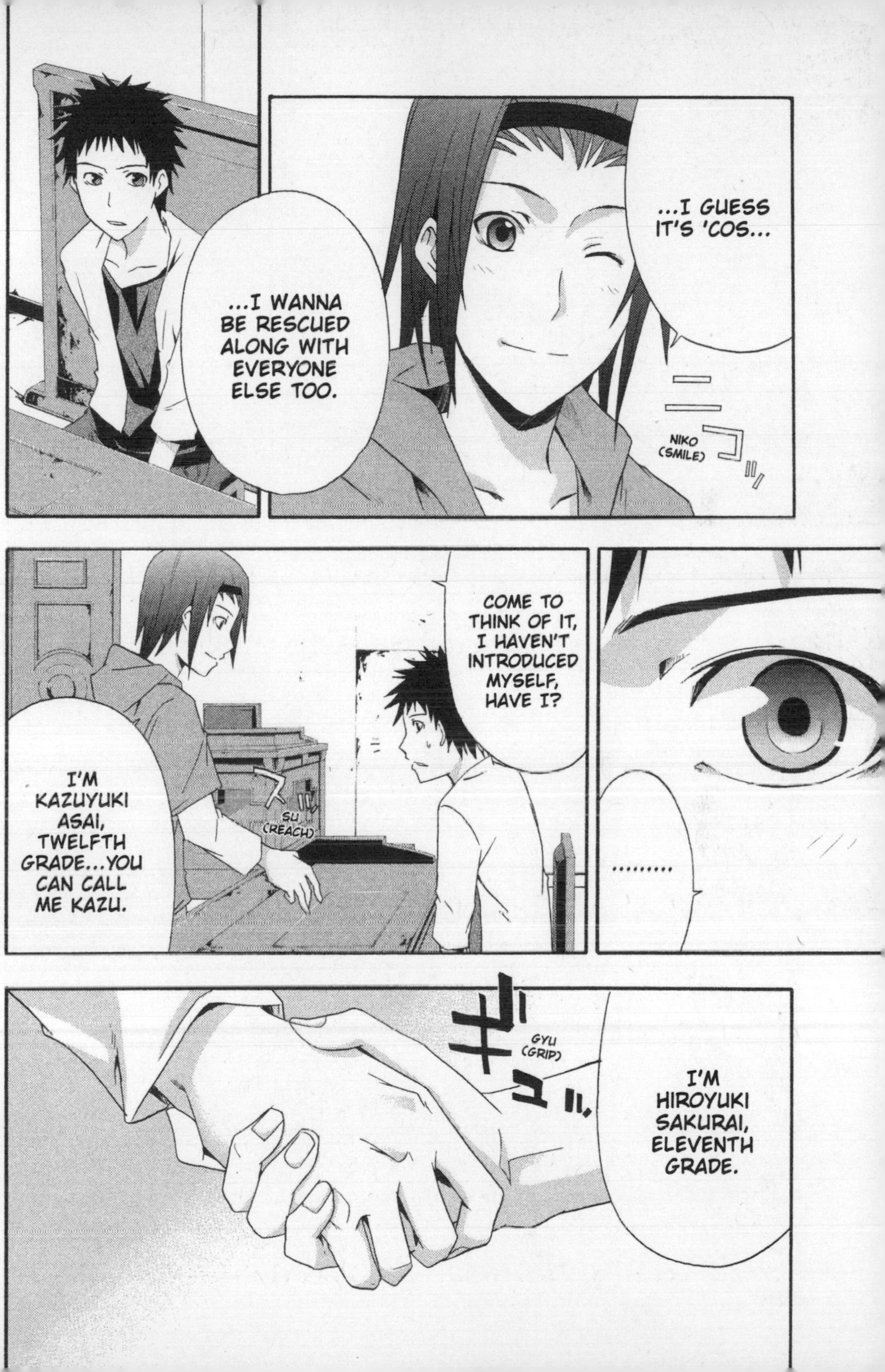
...I GUESS IT'S 'COS...
NIKO (SMILE)
...I WANNA BE RESCUED ALONG WITH EVERYONE ELSE TOO.
....
COME TO THINK OF IT, I HAVEN'T INTRODUCED MYSELF, HAVE I?
SU (REACH)
I'M KAZUYUKI ASAI, TWELFTH GRADE...YOU CAN CALL ME KAZU.
GYU (GRIP)
I'M HIROYUKI SAKURAI, ELEVENTH GRADE.

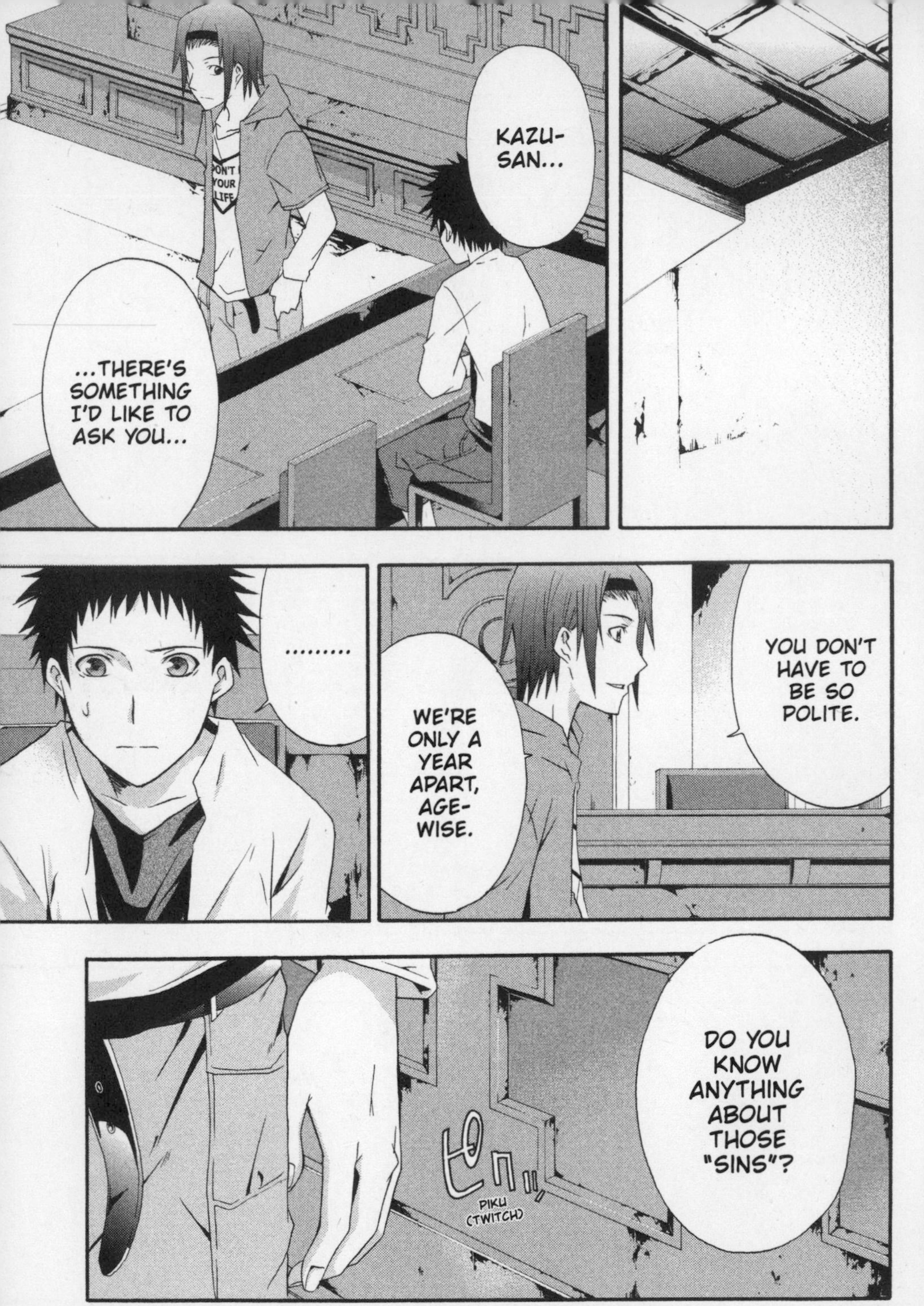
KAZU-SAN...
...THERE'S SOMETHING I'D LIKE TO ASK YOU...
YOU DON'T HAVE TO BE SO POLITE.
WE'RE ONLY A YEAR APART, AGE-WISE.
....
DO YOU KNOW ANYTHING ABOUT THOSE "SINS"?
PIKU (TWITCH)

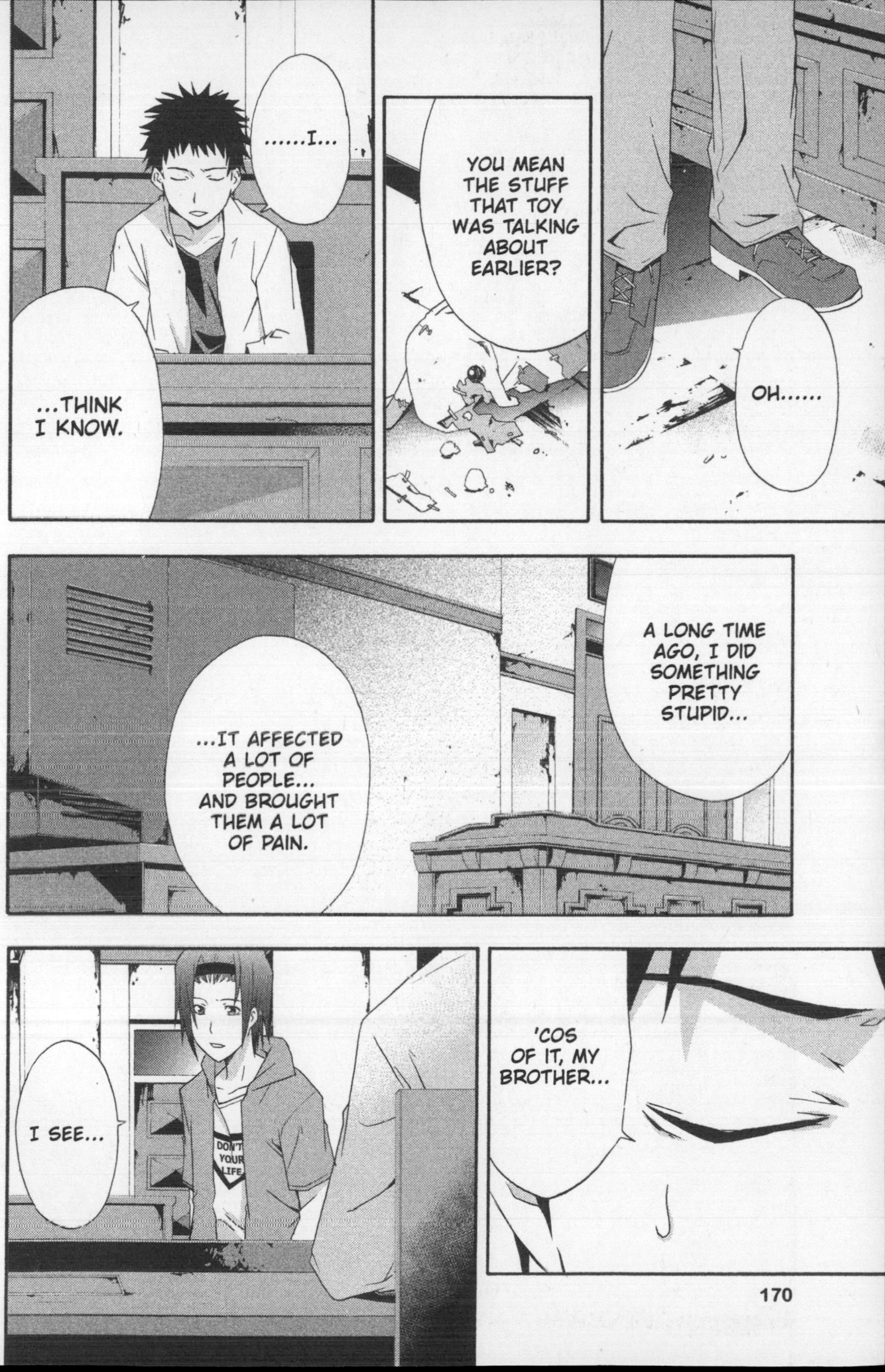
OH......
YOU MEAN THE STUFF THAT TOY WAS TALKING ABOUT EARLIER?
......I...
...THINK I KNOW.
A LONG TIME AGO, I DID SOMETHING PRETTY STUPID...
...IT AFFECTED A LOT OF PEOPLE... AND BROUGHT THEM A LOT OF PAIN.
'COS OF IT, MY BROTHER...
I SEE...

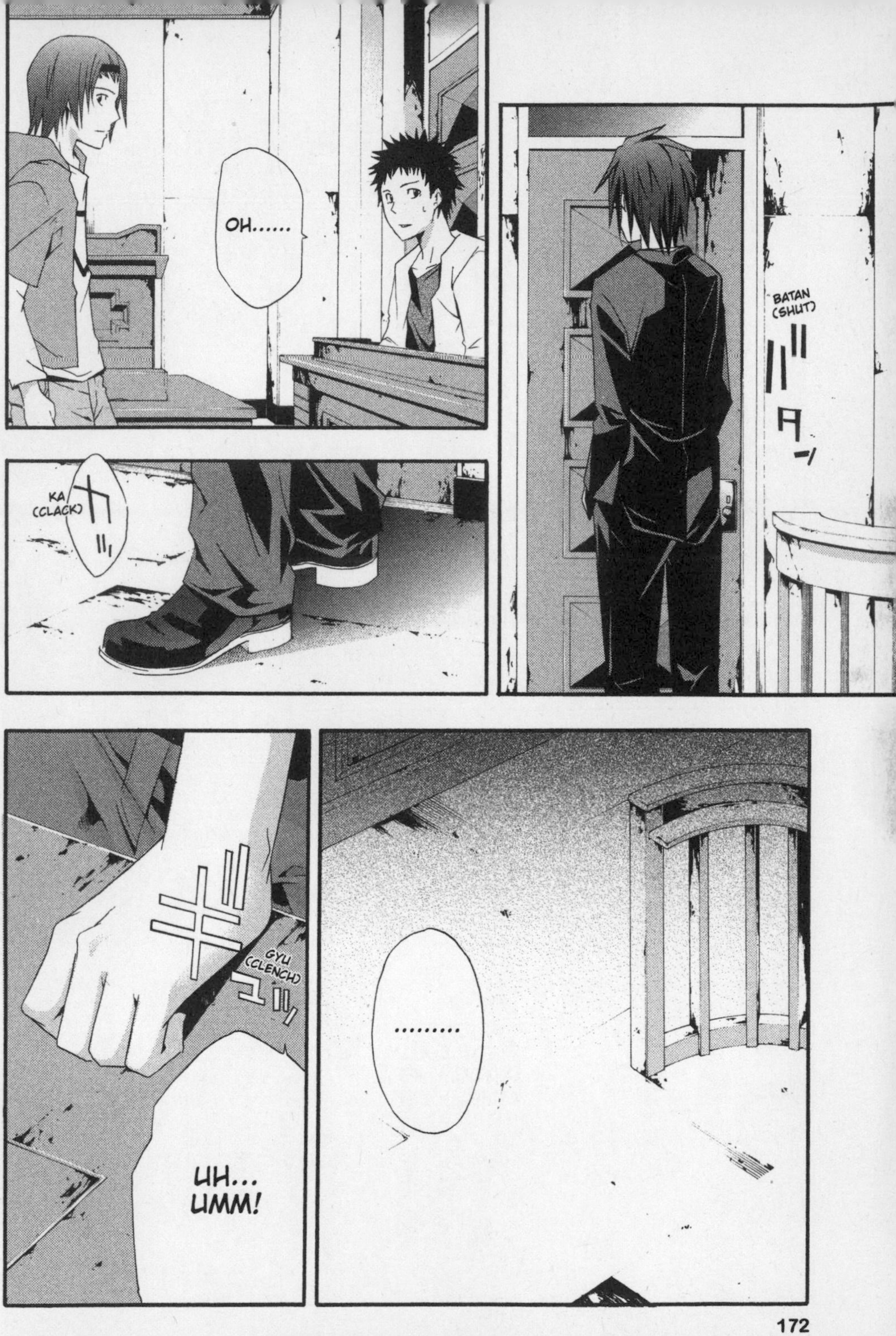
BATAN (SHUT)
バタン
OH......
KA (CLACK)
カッ
....
GYU (CLENCH)
ギュッ
UH... UMM!

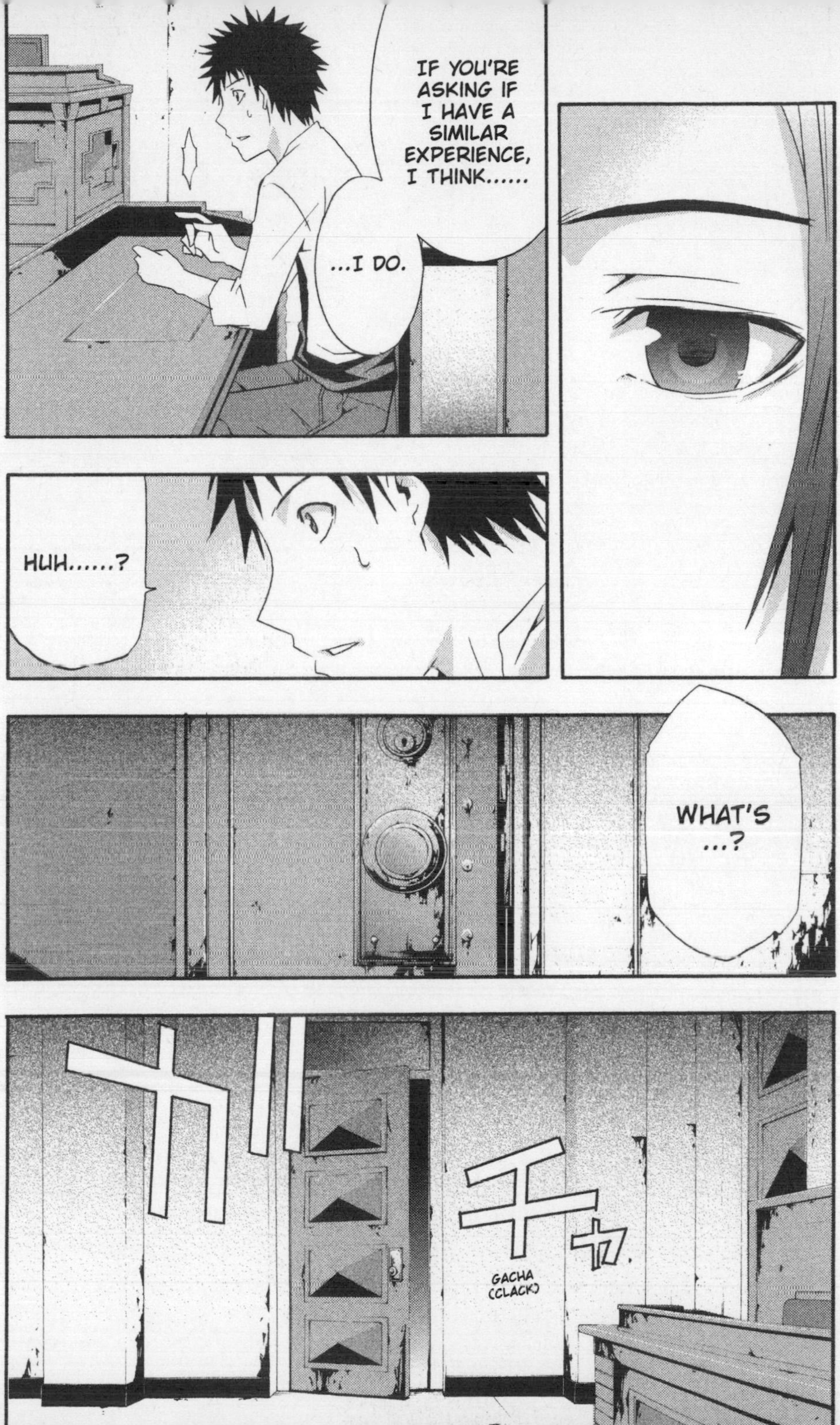
IF YOU'RE ASKING IF I HAVE A SIMILAR EXPERIENCE, I THINK......
...I DO.
HUH......?
WHAT'S ...?
カチャ
GACHA (CLACK)

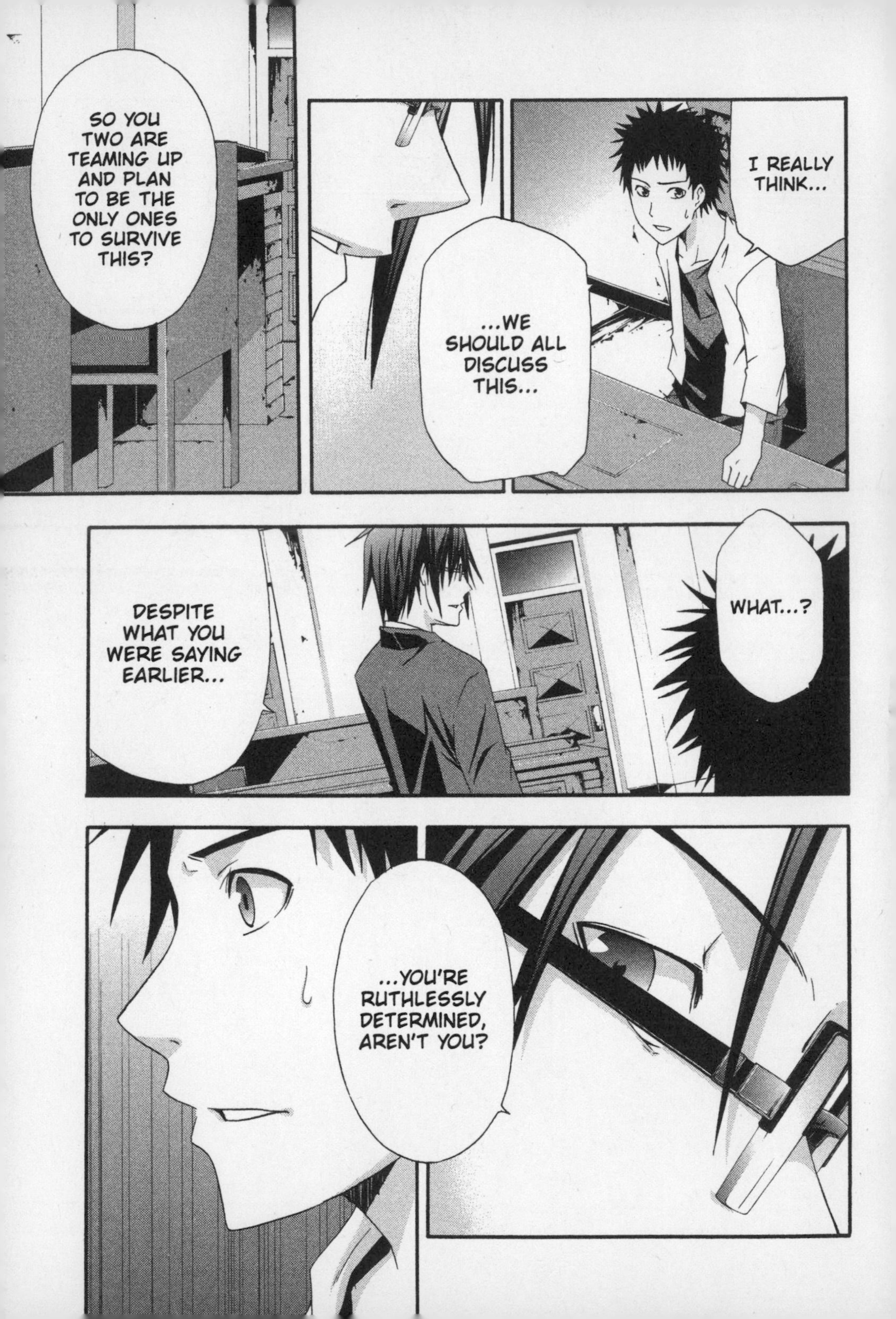
I REALLY THINK...
...WE SHOULD ALL DISCUSS THIS...
SO YOU TWO ARE TEAMING UP AND PLAN TO BE THE ONLY ONES TO SURVIVE THIS?
WHAT...?
DESPITE WHAT YOU WERE SAYING EARLIER...
...YOU'RE RUTHLESSLY DETERMINED, AREN'T YOU?

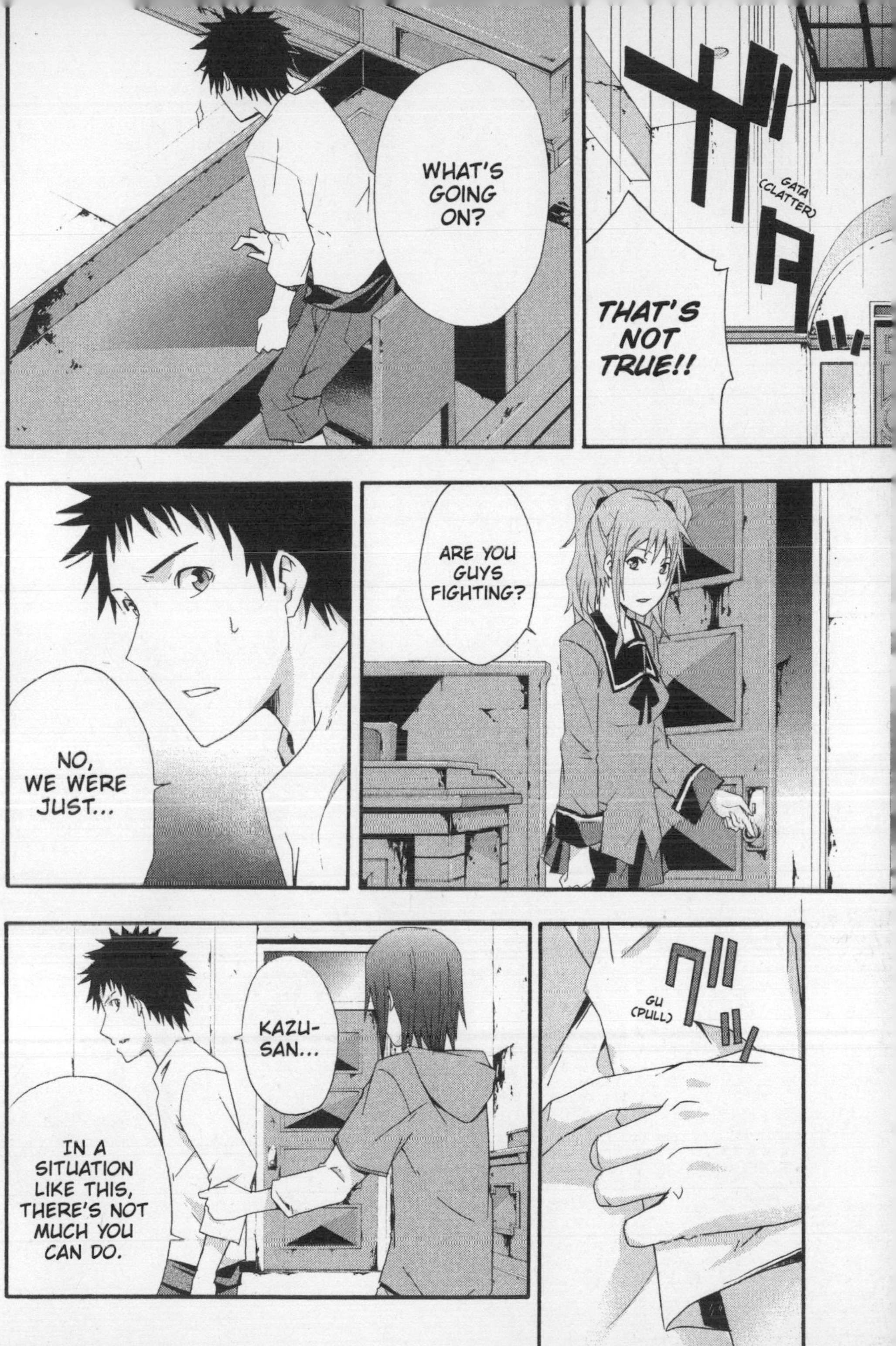
GATA (CLATTER)
THAT'S NOT TRUE!!
WHAT'S GOING ON?
ARE YOU GUYS FIGHTING?
NO, WE WERE JUST...
GU (PULL)
KAZU-SAN...
IN A SITUATION LIKE THIS, THERE'S NOT MUCH YOU CAN DO.

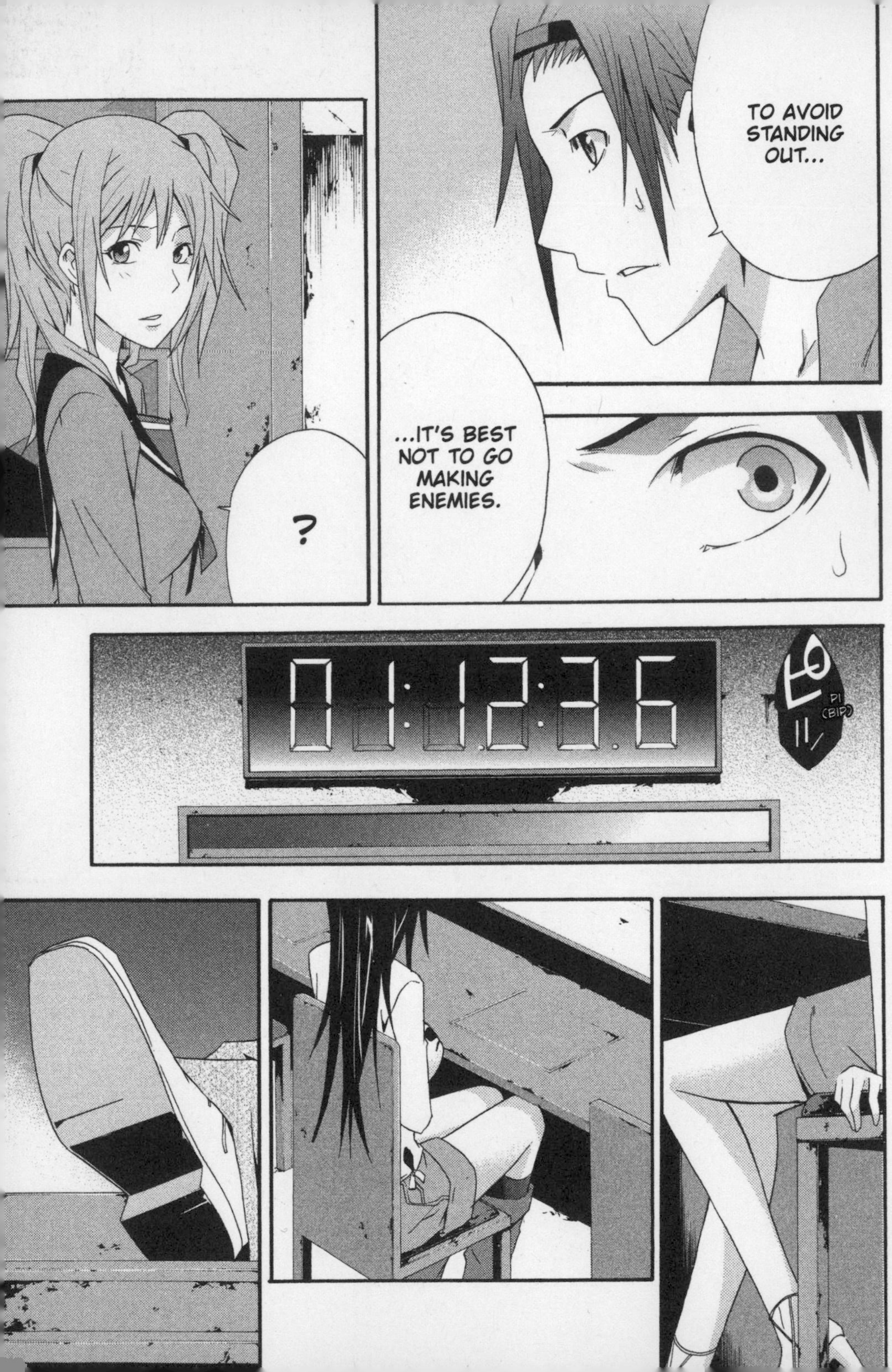
TO AVOID STANDING OUT...
...IT'S BEST NOT TO GO MAKING ENEMIES.
?
01:12:23.6
PI (BIP)

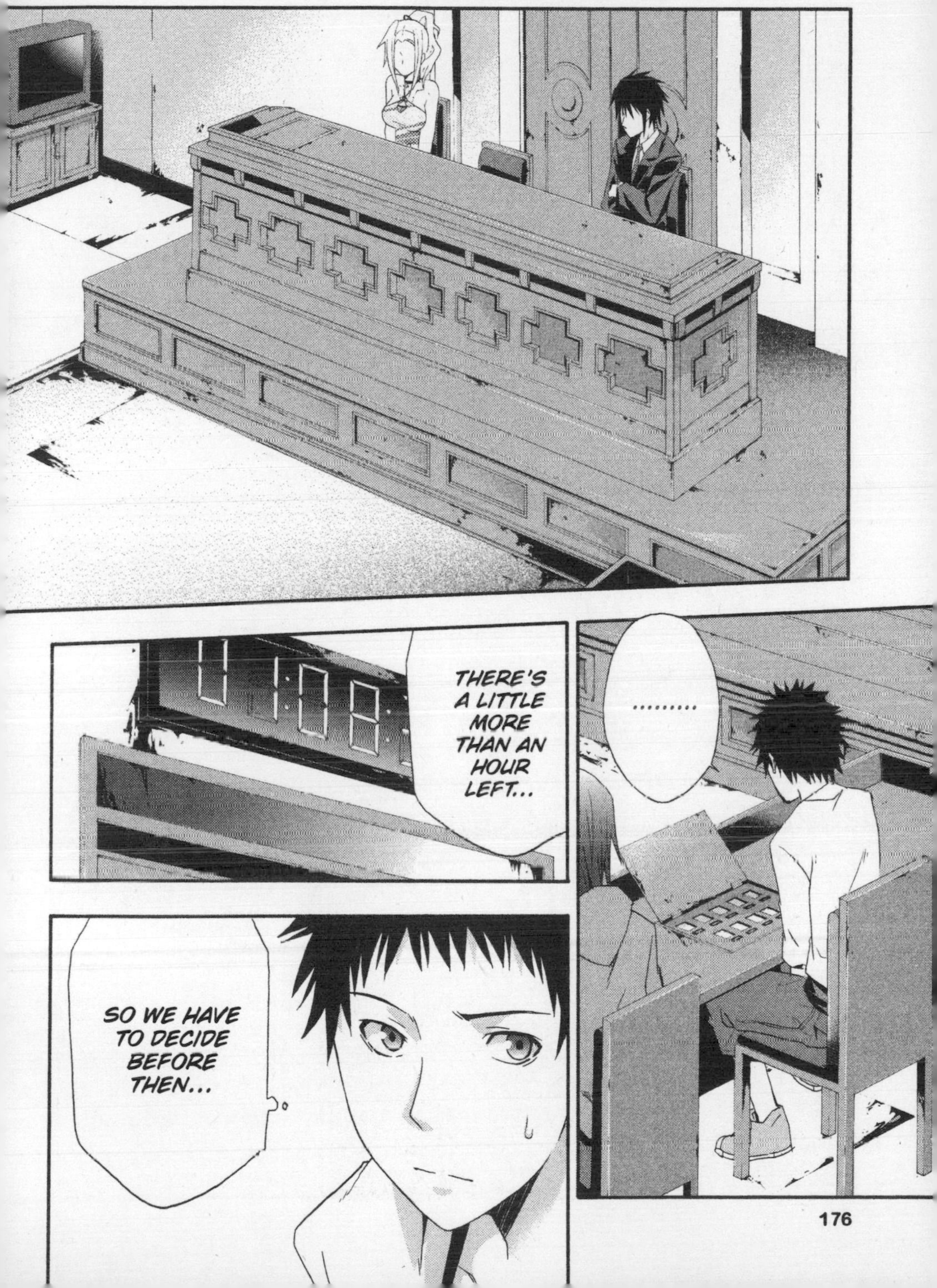
....
THERE'S A LITTLE MORE THAN AN HOUR LEFT...
SO WE HAVE TO DECIDE BEFORE THEN...

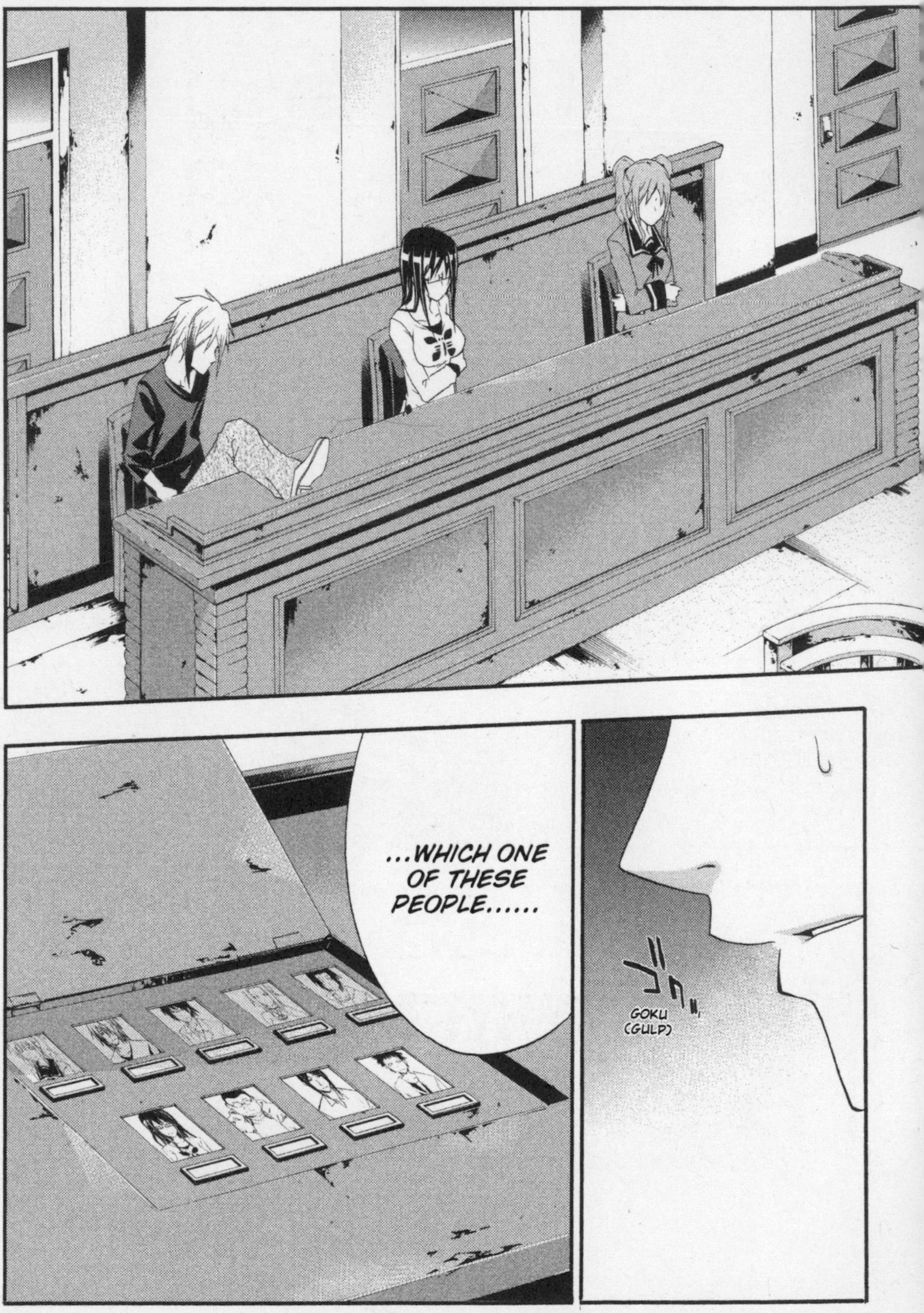
...WHICH ONE OF THESE PEOPLE......
GOKU (GULP)

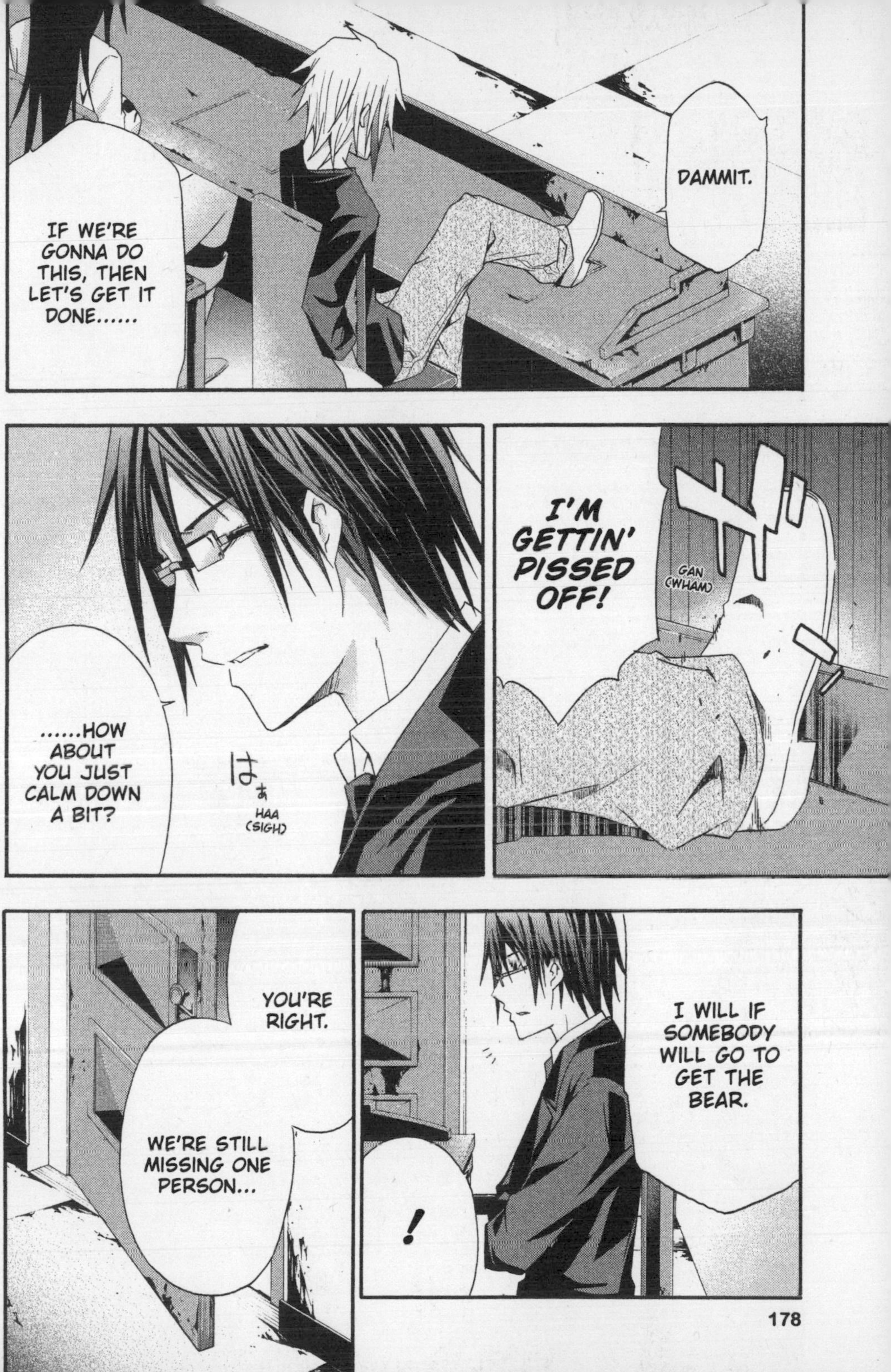

DAMMIT.
IF WE'RE GONNA DO THIS, THEN LET'S GET IT DONE......
I'M GETTIN' PISSED OFF!
GAN (WHAM)
......HOW ABOUT YOU JUST CALM DOWN A BIT?
はぁ
HAA (SIGH)
I WILL IF SOMEBODY WILL GO TO GET THE BEAR.
!
YOU'RE RIGHT.
WE'RE STILL MISSING ONE PERSON...

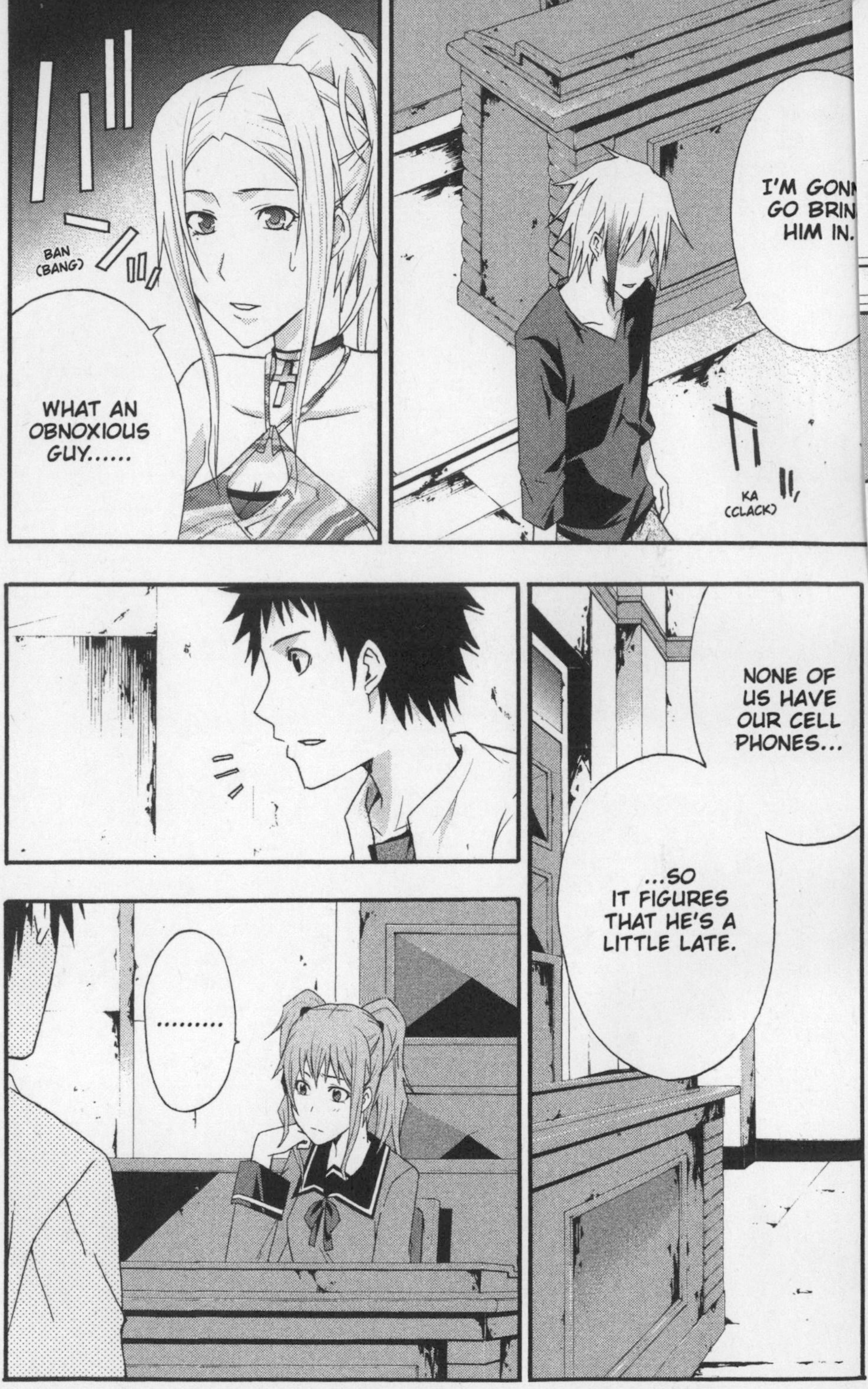
I'M GONN GO BRIN HIM IN.
KA (CLACK)
BAN (BANG)
WHAT AN OBNOXIOUS GUY......
NONE OF US HAVE OUR CELL PHONES...
...SO IT FIGURES THAT HE'S A LITTLE LATE.
....

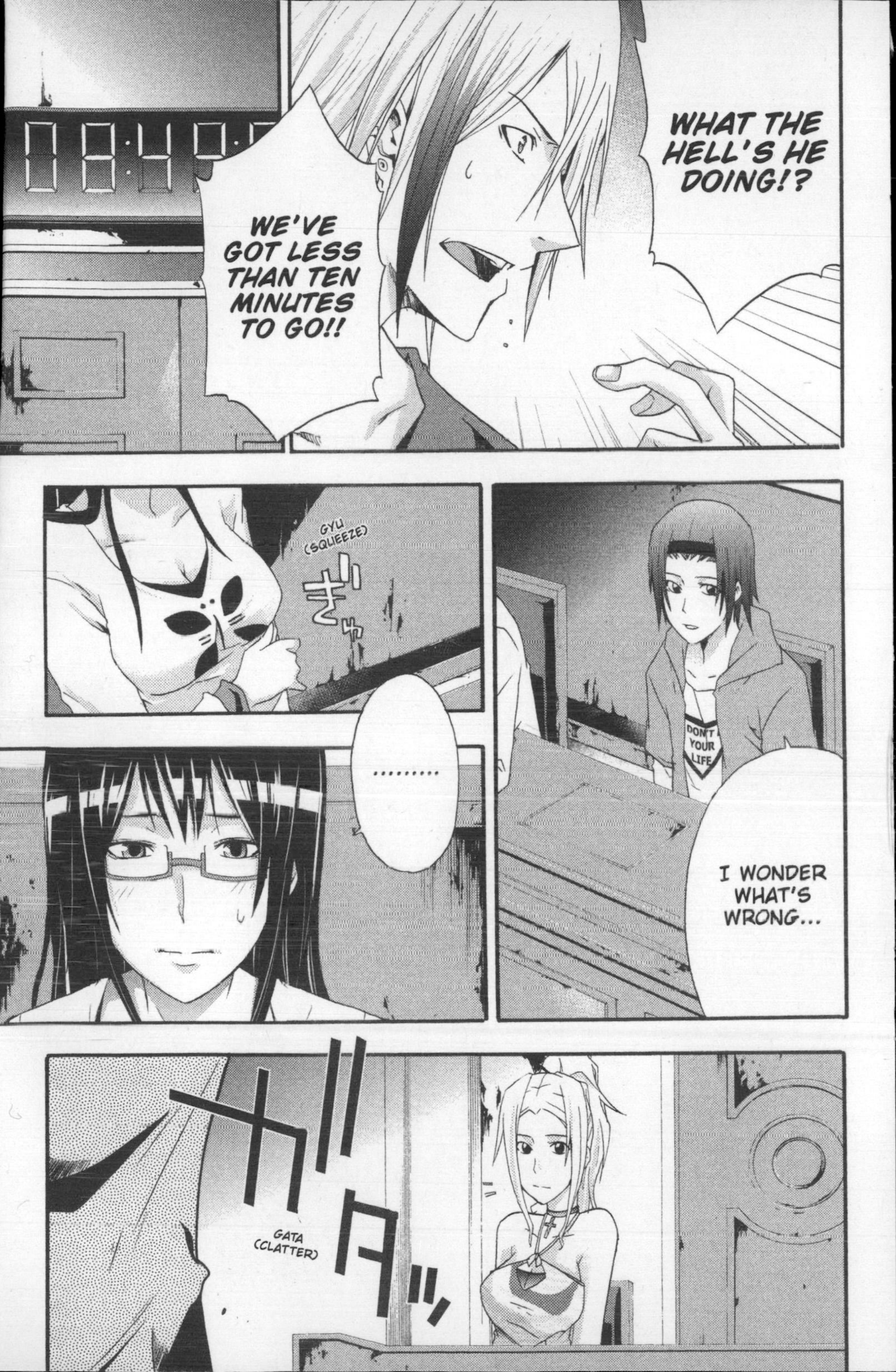
WHAT THE HELL'S HE DOING!?
WE'VE GOT LESS THAN TEN MINUTES TO GO!!
I WONDER WHAT'S WRONG...
GYU (SQUEEZE)
....
GATA (CLATTER)

JUST A LITTLE SOMETHING...

WHAT IS IT?

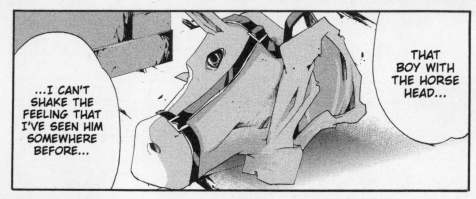

THAT BOY WITH THE HORSE HEAD...

...I CAN'T SHAKE THE FEELING THAT I'VE SEEN HIM SOMEWHERE BEFORE...

ARGH... NEVER MIND!

I CAN'T SEEM TO PUT MY FINGER ON IT.

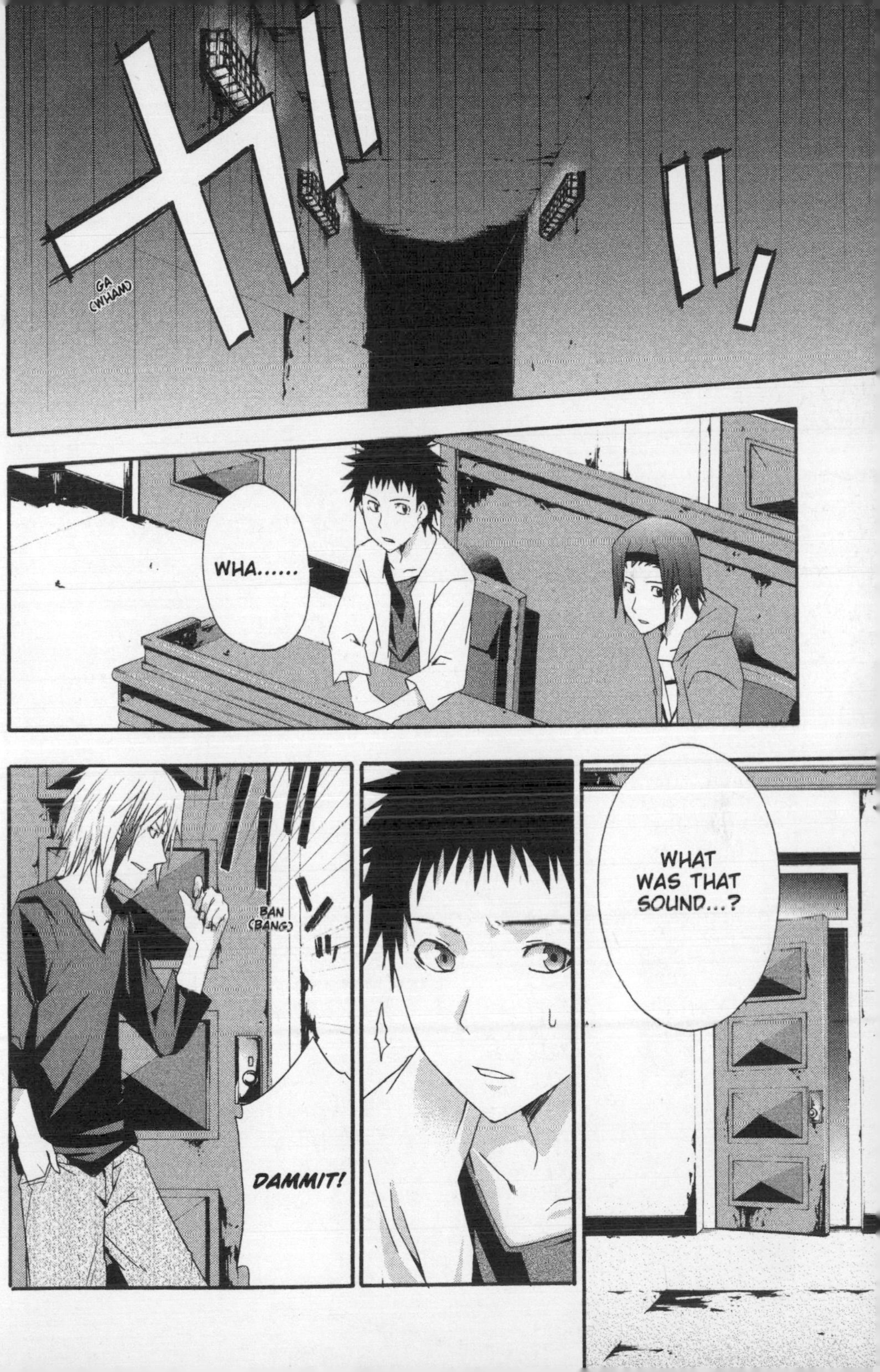
GA (WHAM)
WHA......
WHAT WAS THAT SOUND...?
BAN (BANG)
DAMMIT!

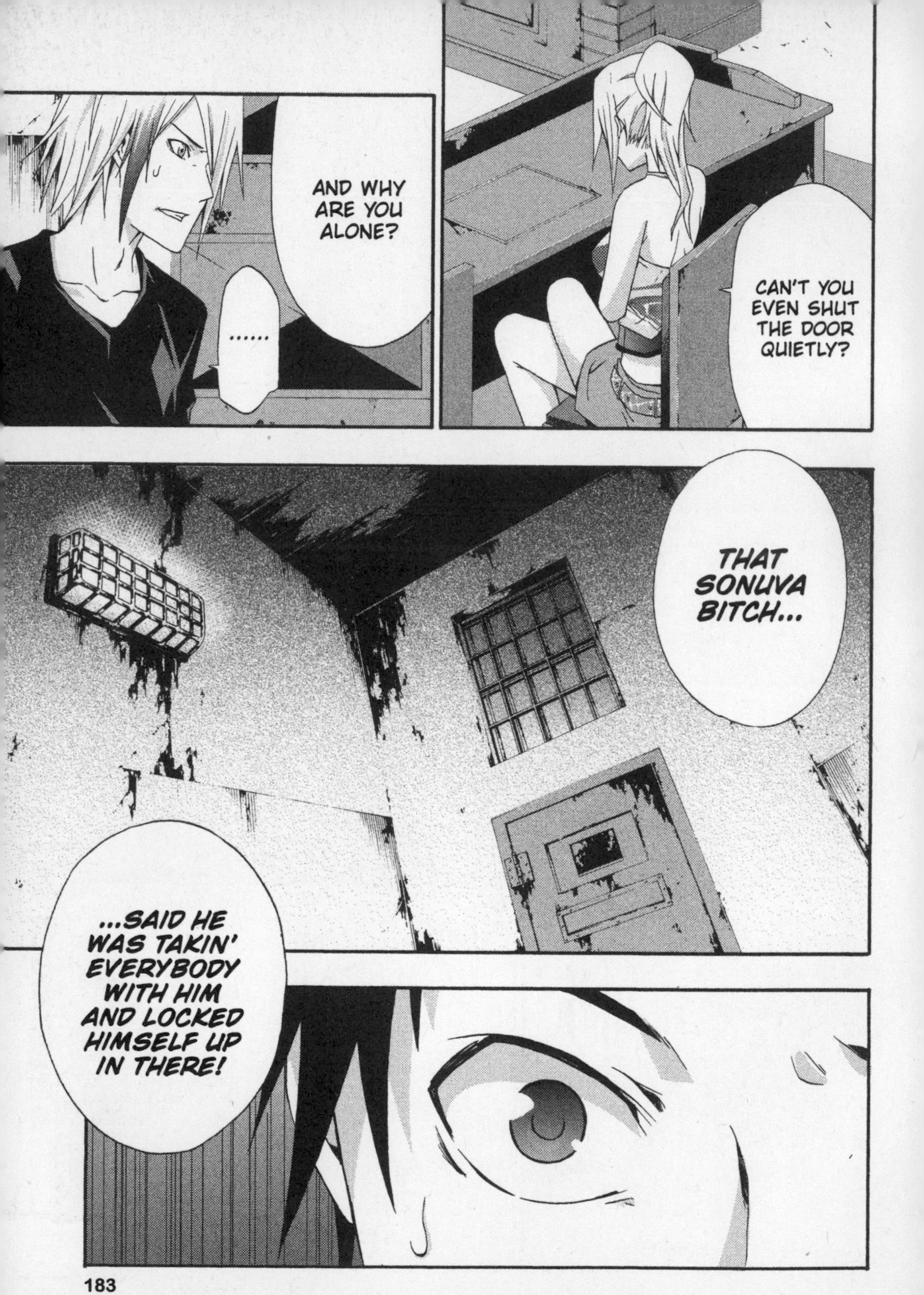
CAN'T YOU EVEN SHUT THE DOOR QUIETLY?
AND WHY ARE YOU ALONE?
......
THAT SONUVA BITCH...
...SAID HE WAS TAKIN' EVERYBODY WITH HIM AND LOCKED HIMSELF UP IN THERE!

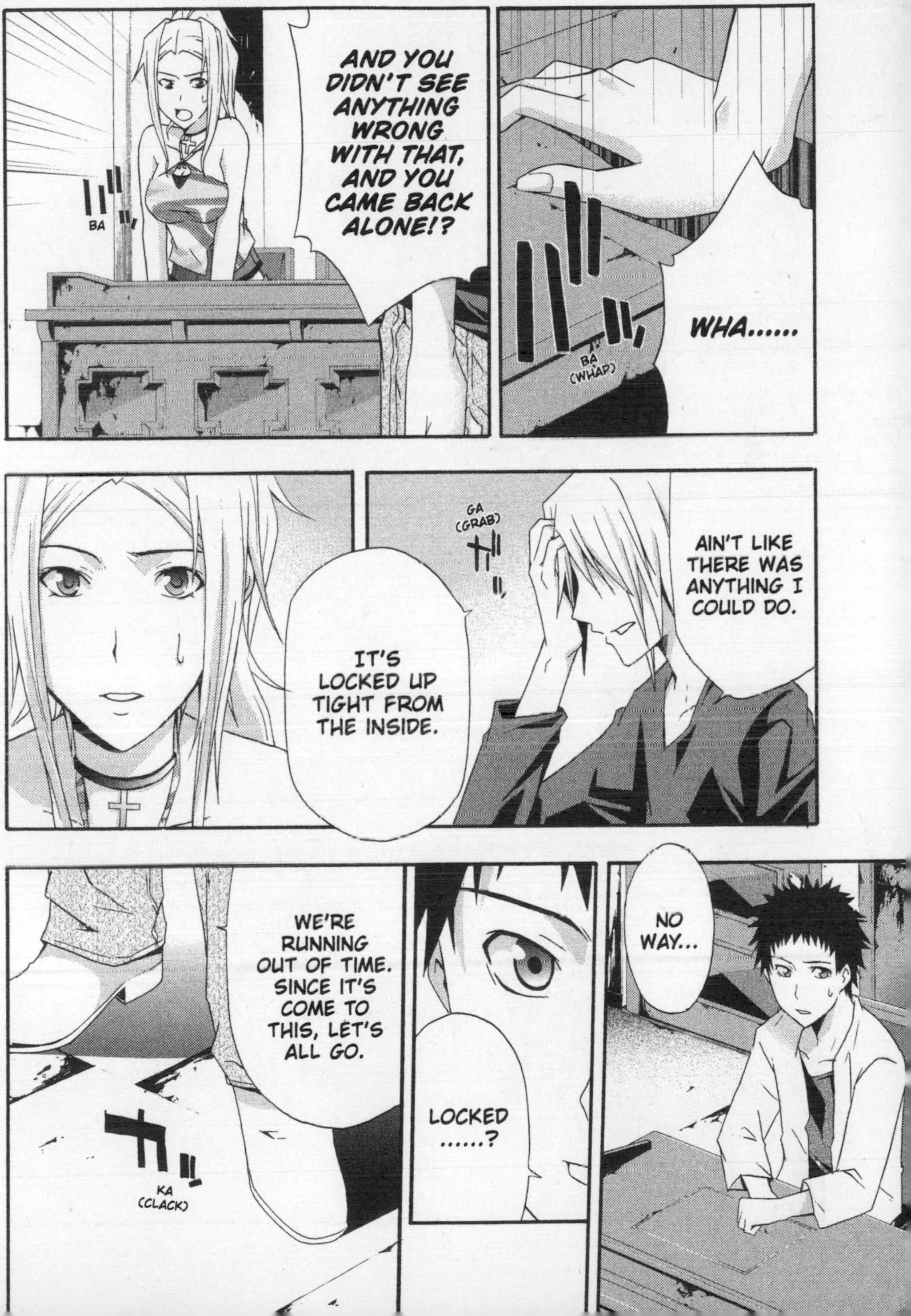
WHA......
BA (WHAP)
BA
AND YOU DIDN'T SEE ANYTHING WRONG WITH THAT, AND YOU CAME BACK ALONE!?
AIN'T LIKE THERE WAS ANYTHING I COULD DO.
GA (GRAB)
IT'S LOCKED UP TIGHT FROM THE INSIDE.
NO WAY...
LOCKED ......?
WE'RE RUNNING OUT OF TIME. SINCE IT'S COME TO THIS, LET'S ALL GO.
KA (CLACK)

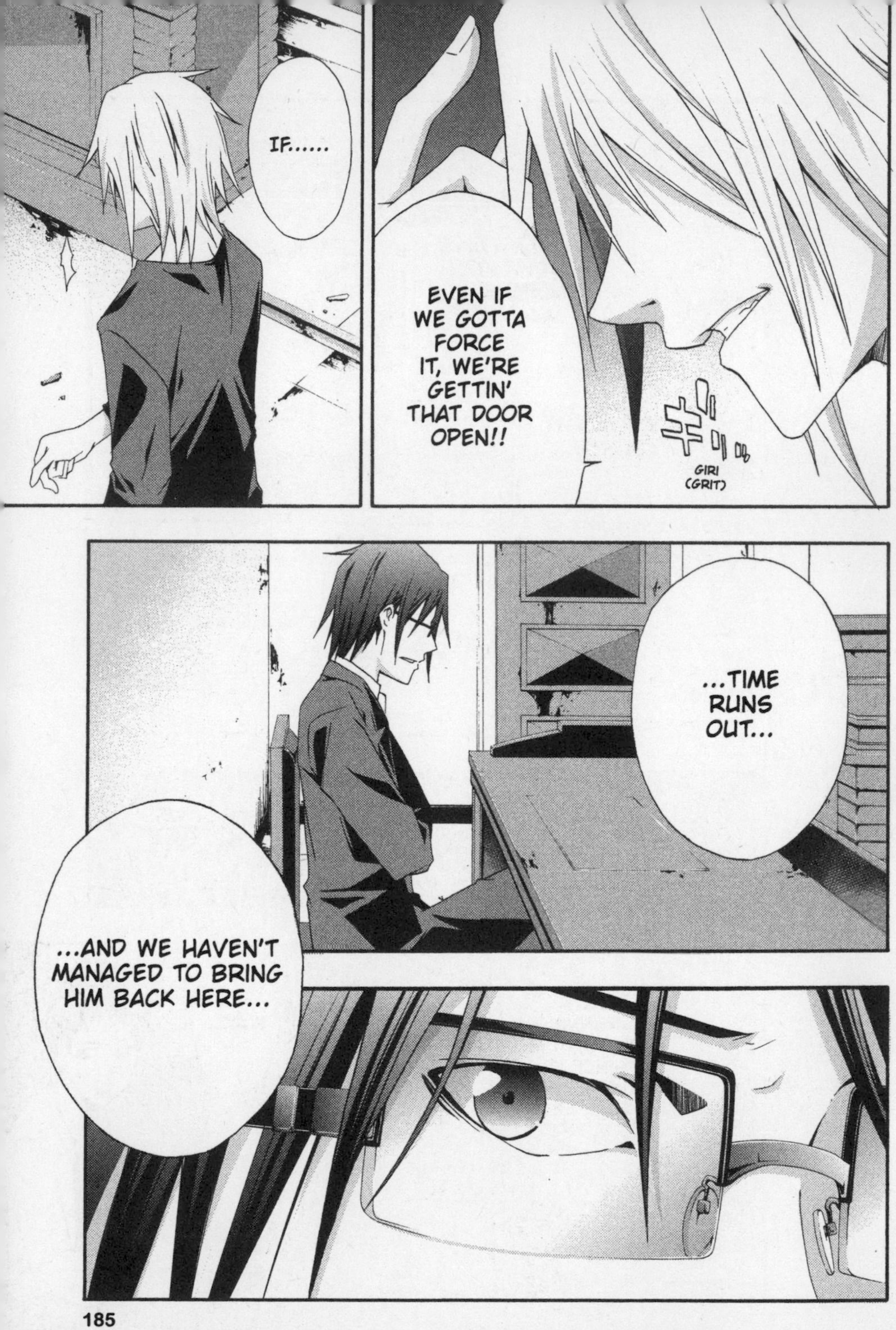
EVEN IF WE GOTTA FORCE IT, WE'RE GETTIN' THAT DOOR OPEN!!
ギリッ
GIRI (GRIT)
IF......
...TIME RUNS OUT...
...AND WE HAVEN'T MANAGED TO BRING HIM BACK HERE...

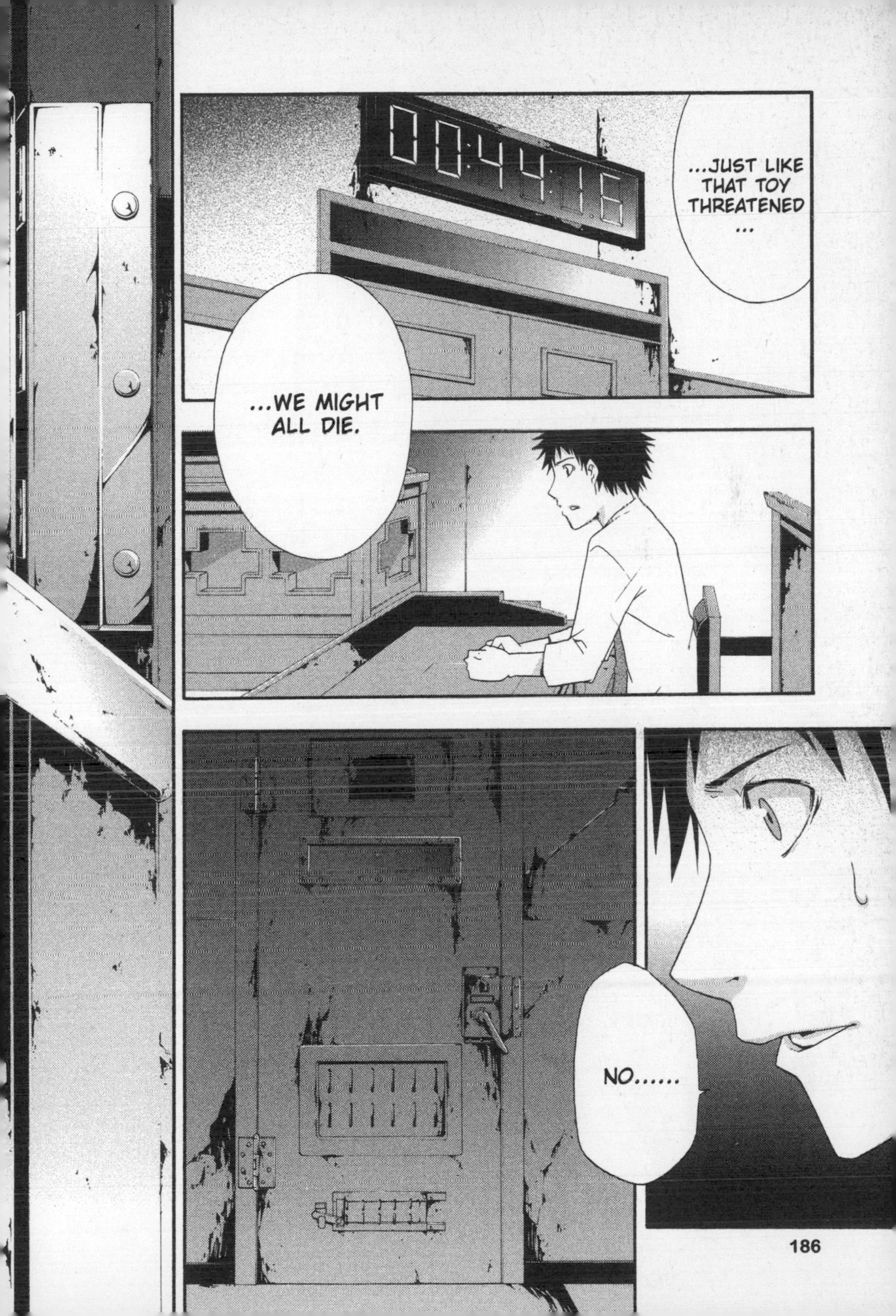
...JUST LIKE THAT TOY THREATENED ...
...WE MIGHT ALL DIE.
NO......

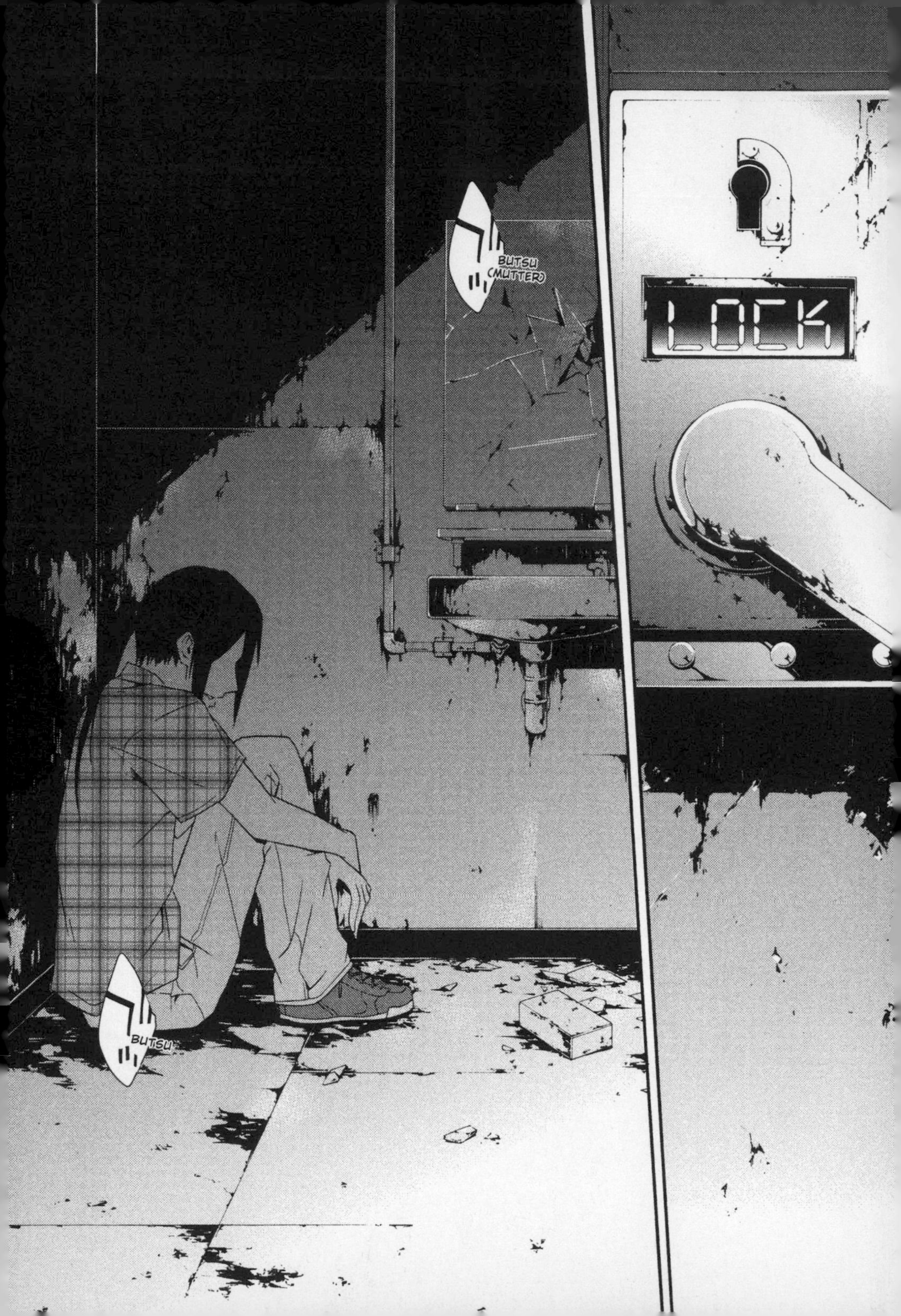
LOCK
BUTSU (MUTTER)
BUTSU

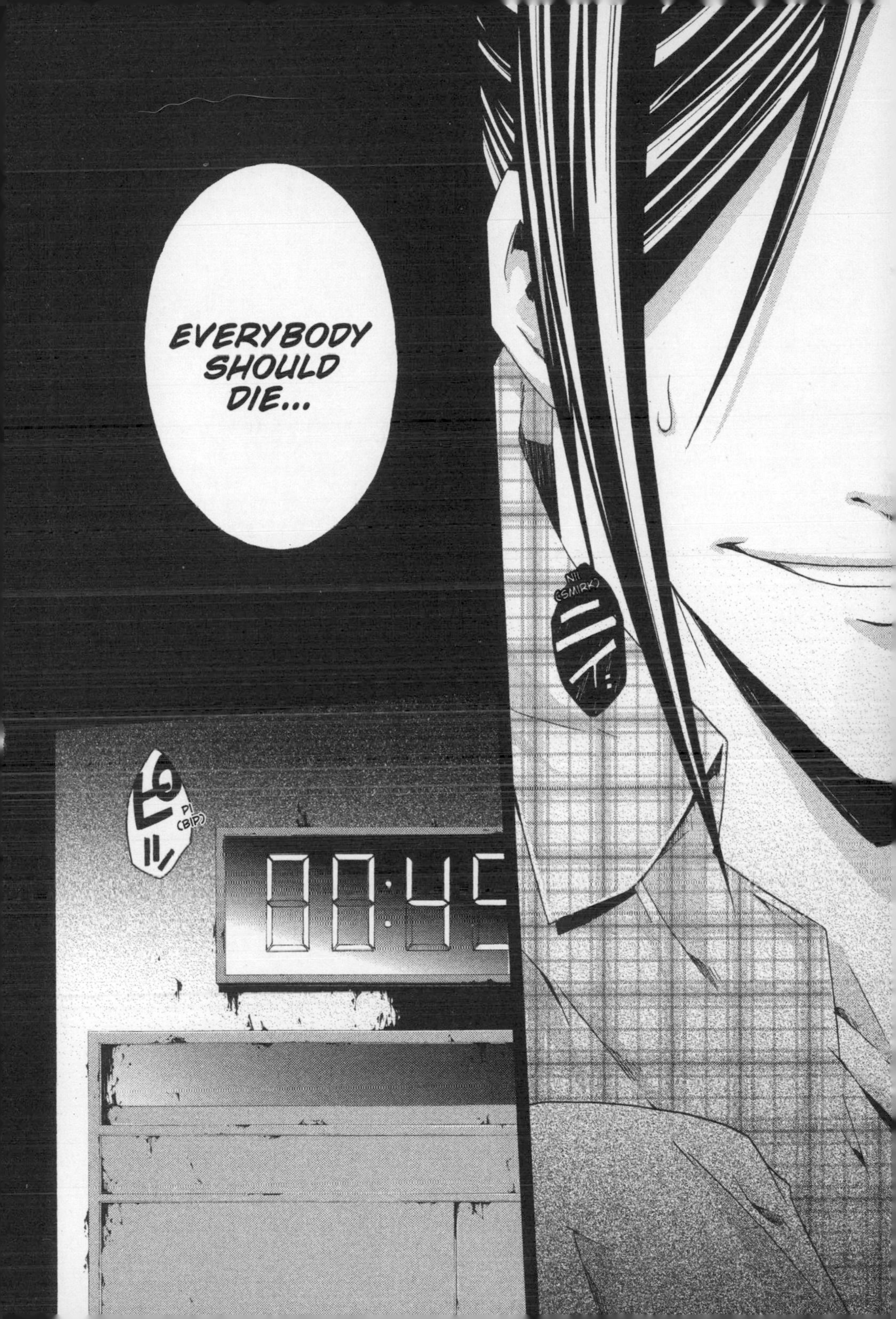
NII (SMIRK)
EVERYBODY SHOULD DIE...
PI (BIP)

Pride

Lust

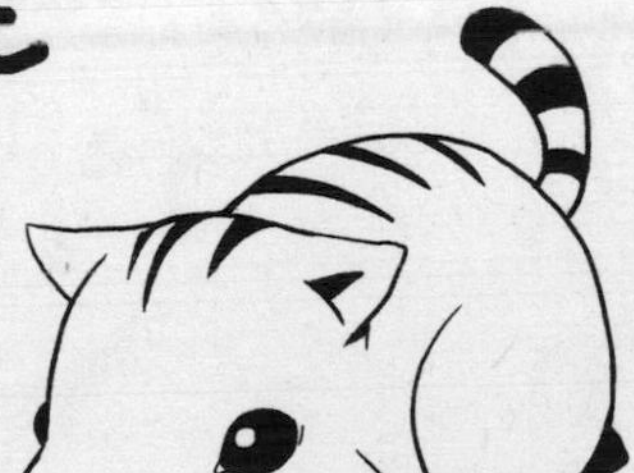

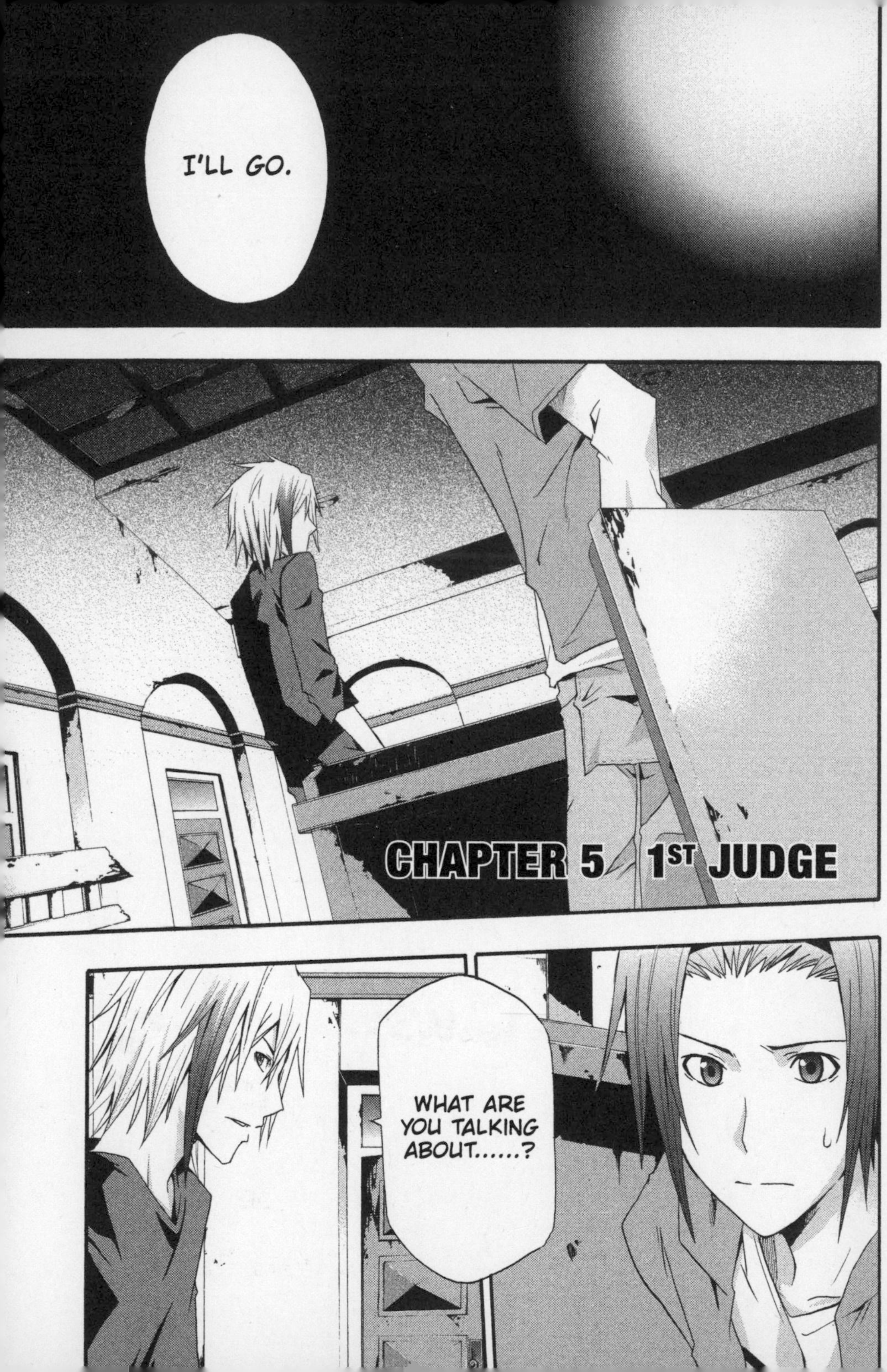
I'LL GO.
CHAPTER 5 1ST JUDGE
WHAT ARE YOU TALKING ABOUT......?

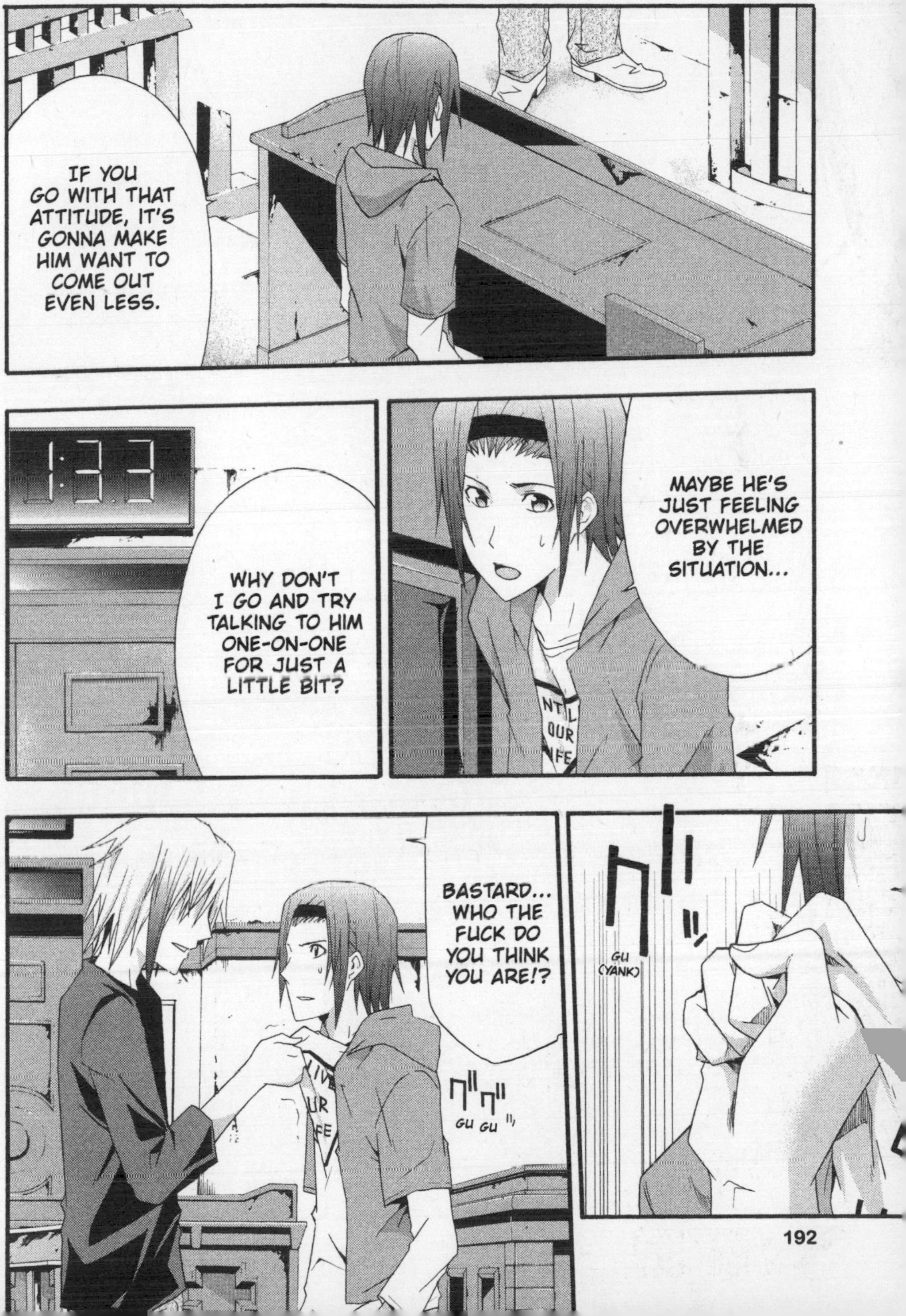
IF YOU GO WITH THAT ATTITUDE, IT'S GONNA MAKE HIM WANT TO COME OUT EVEN LESS.
MAYBE HE'S JUST FEELING OVERWHELMED BY THE SITUATION...
WHY DON'T I GO AND TRY TALKING TO HIM ONE-ON-ONE FOR JUST A LITTLE BIT?
GU (YANK)
BASTARD... WHO THE FUCK DO YOU THINK YOU ARE!?
GU GU

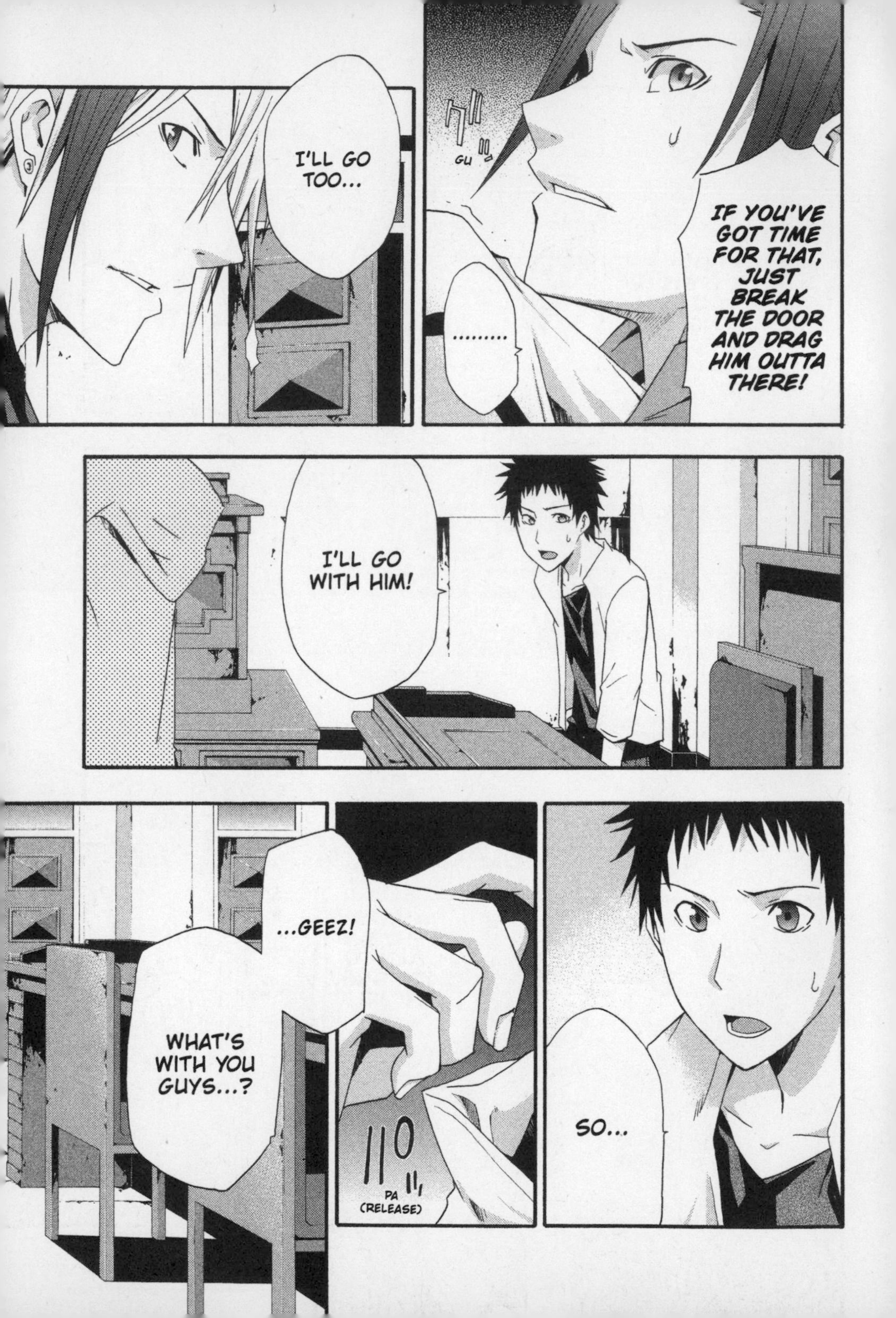
IF YOU'VE GOT TIME FOR THAT, JUST BREAK THE DOOR AND DRAG HIM OUTTA THERE!
GU
....
I'LL GO TOO...
I'LL GO WITH HIM!
SO...
PA (RELEASE)
...GEEZ!
WHAT'S WITH YOU GUYS...?

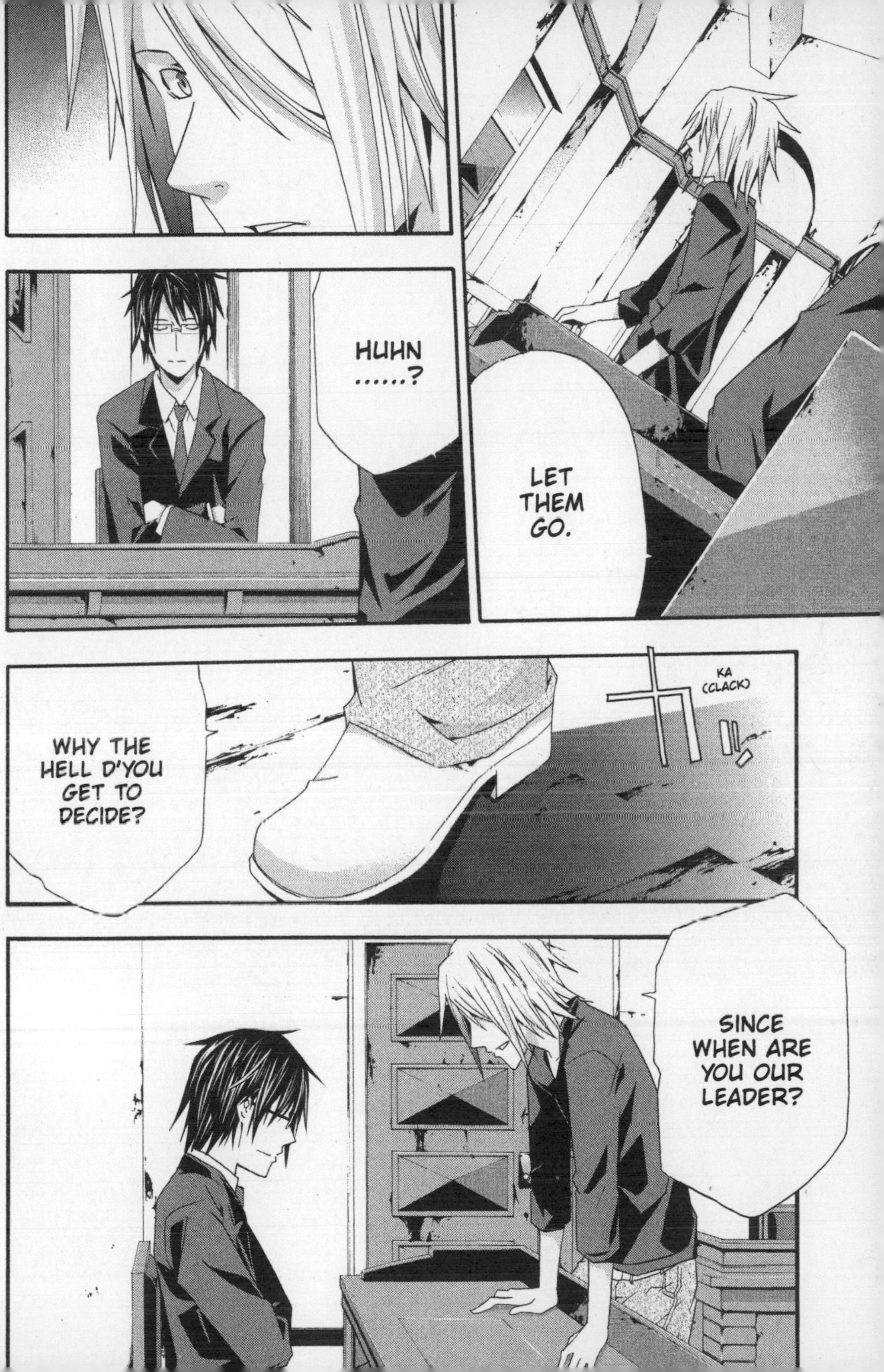
LET THEM GO.
HUHN ......?
KA (CLACK)
WHY THE HELL D'YOU GET TO DECIDE?
SINCE WHEN ARE YOU OUR LEADER?

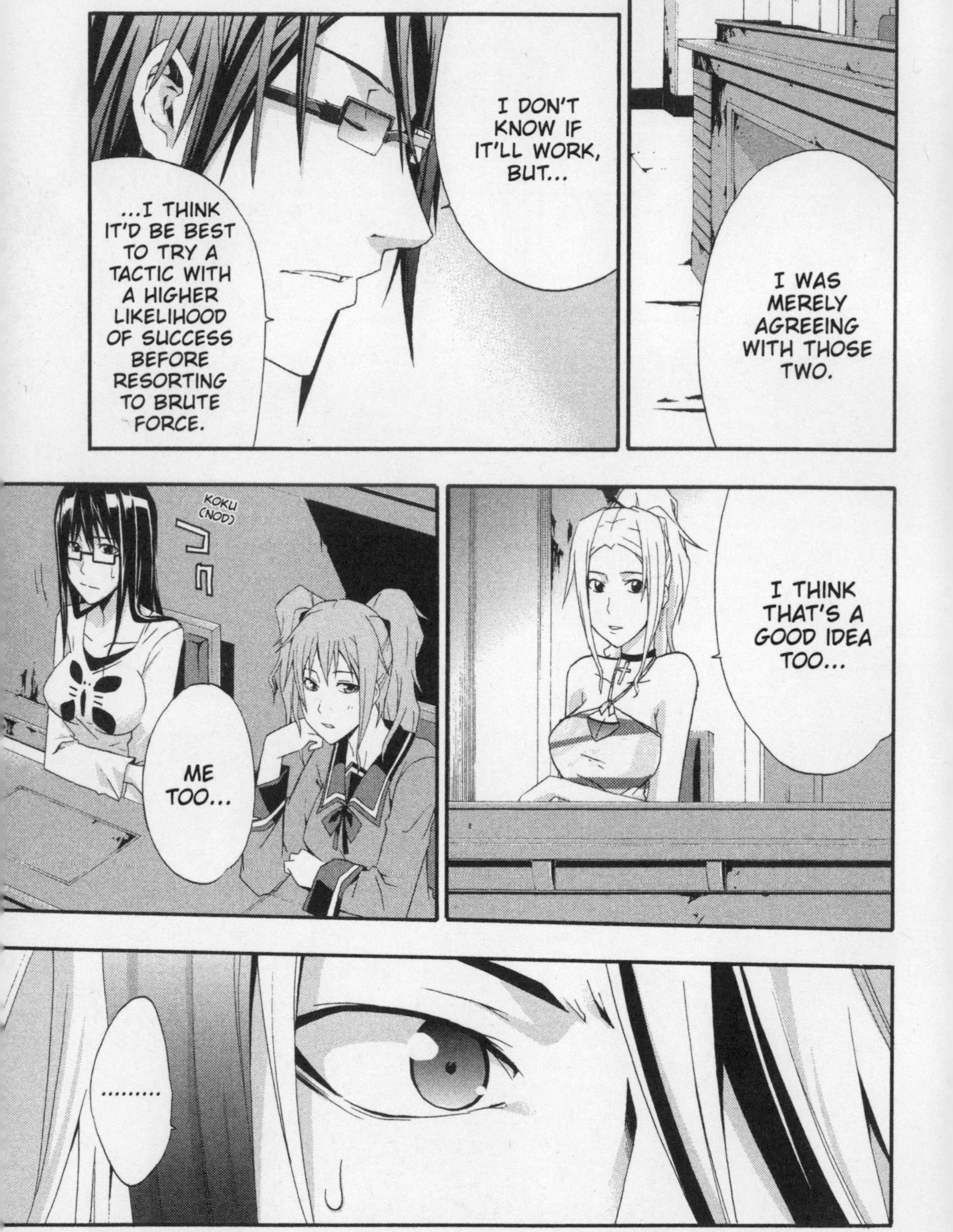
I WAS MERELY AGREEING WITH THOSE TWO.
I DON'T KNOW IF IT'LL WORK, BUT...
...I THINK IT'D BE BEST TO TRY A TACTIC WITH A HIGHER LIKELIHOOD OF SUCCESS BEFORE RESORTING TO BRUTE FORCE.
I THINK THAT'S A GOOD IDEA TOO...
KOKU (NOD)
ME TOO...
....

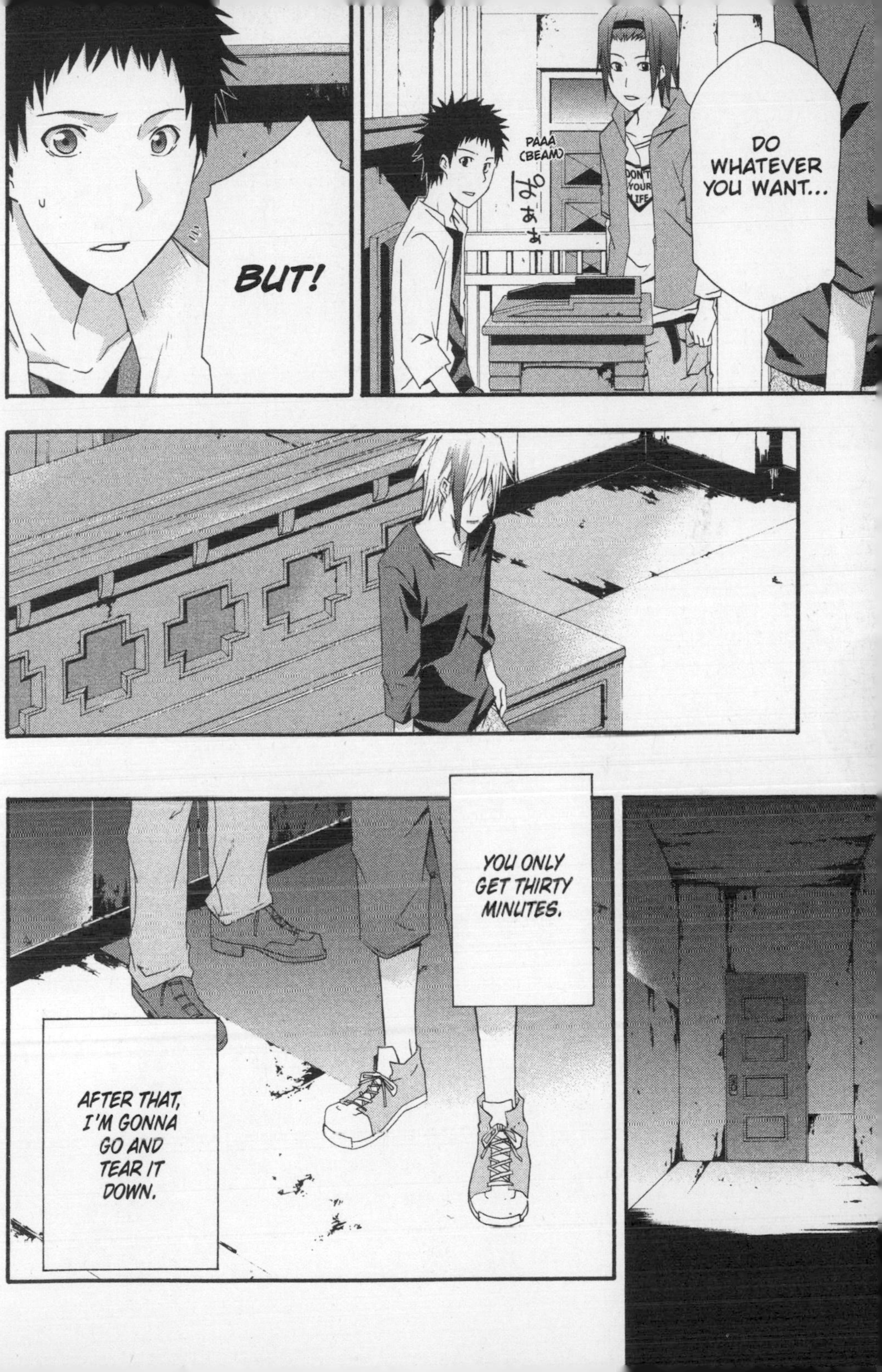
DO WHATEVER YOU WANT...
PAAA (BEAM)
BUT!
YOU ONLY GET THIRTY MINUTES.
AFTER THAT, I'M GONNA GO AND TEAR IT DOWN.

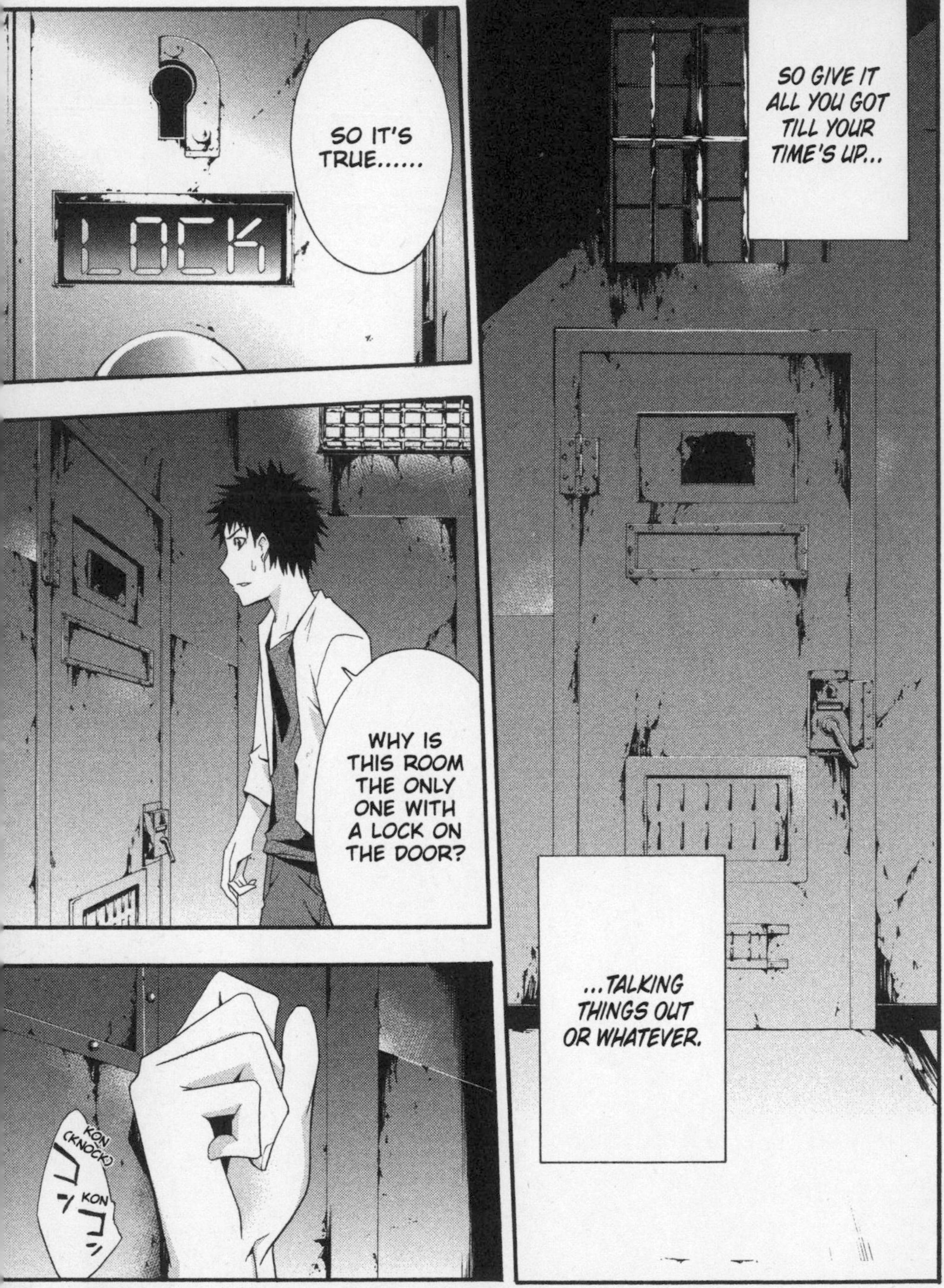
SO GIVE IT ALL YOU GOT TILL YOUR TIME'S UP...
...TALKING THINGS OUT OR WHATEVER.
LOCK
SO IT'S TRUE......
WHY IS THIS ROOM THE ONLY ONE WITH A LOCK ON THE DOOR?
KON (KNOCK)
KON

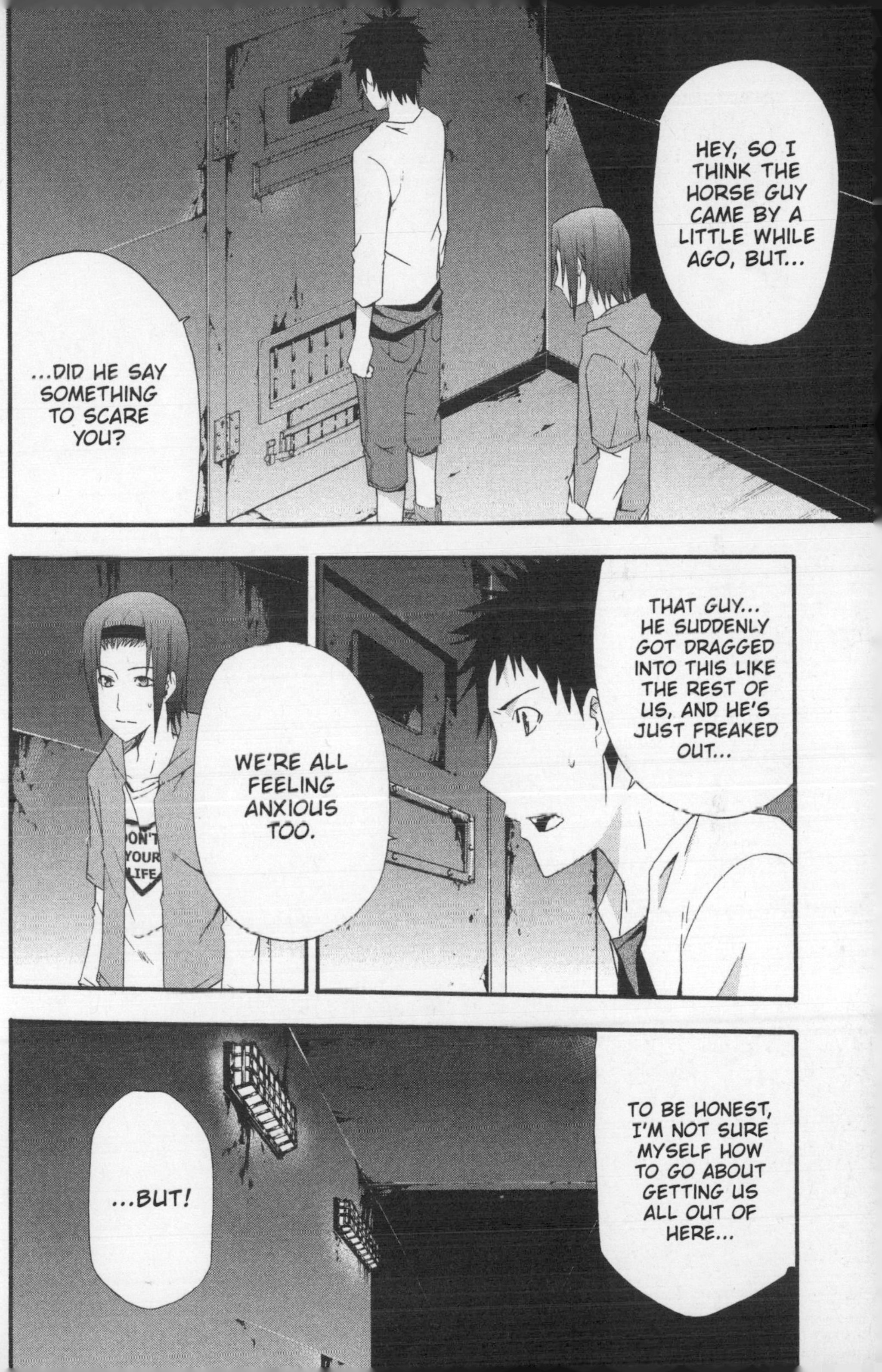
HEY, SO I THINK THE HORSE GUY CAME BY A LITTLE WHILE AGO, BUT...
...DID HE SAY SOMETHING TO SCARE YOU?
THAT GUY... HE SUDDENLY GOT DRAGGED INTO THIS LIKE THE REST OF US, AND HE'S JUST FREAKED OUT...
WE'RE ALL FEELING ANXIOUS TOO.
TO BE HONEST, I'M NOT SURE MYSELF HOW TO GO ABOUT GETTING US ALL OUT OF HERE...
...BUT!

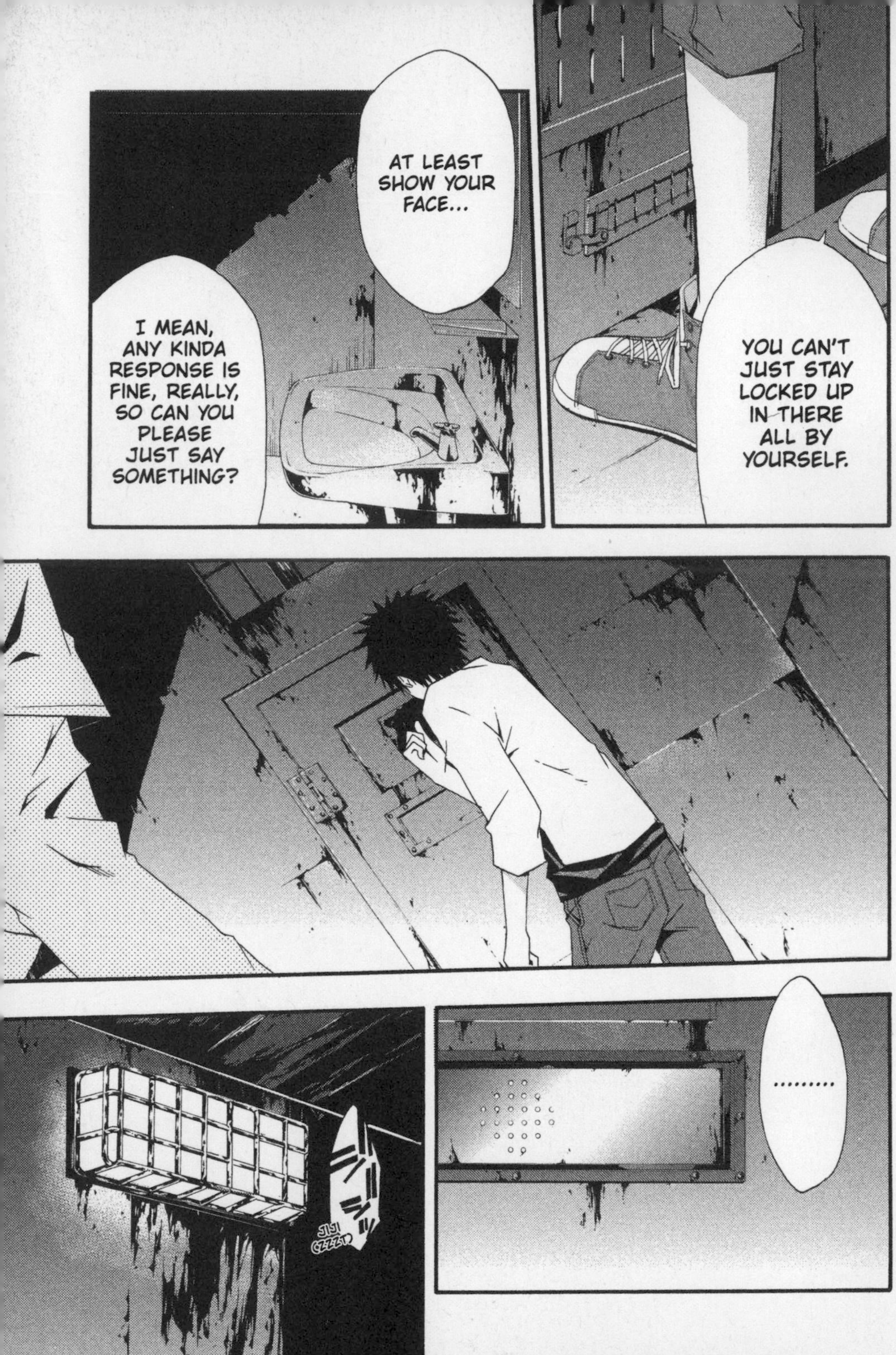
YOU CAN'T JUST STAY LOCKED UP IN THERE ALL BY YOURSELF.
AT LEAST SHOW YOUR FACE...
I MEAN, ANY KINDA RESPONSE IS FINE, REALLY, SO CAN YOU PLEASE JUST SAY SOMETHING?
....
JIJI (ZZZT)

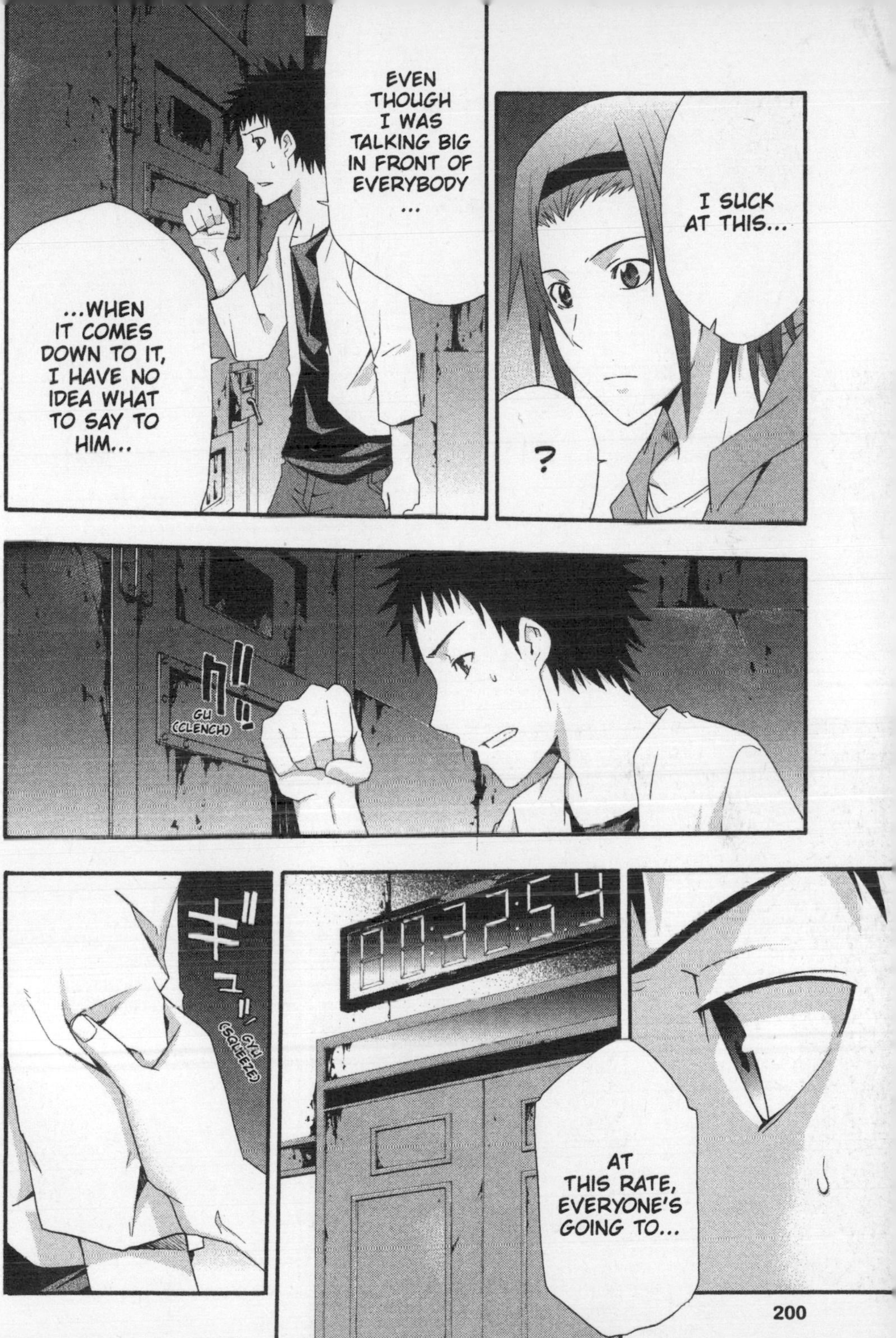
I SUCK AT THIS...
?
EVEN THOUGH I WAS TALKING BIG IN FRONT OF EVERYBODY ...
...WHEN IT COMES DOWN TO IT, I HAVE NO IDEA WHAT TO SAY TO HIM...
GU (CLENCH)
AT THIS RATE, EVERYONE'S GOING TO...
GYU (SQUEEZE)

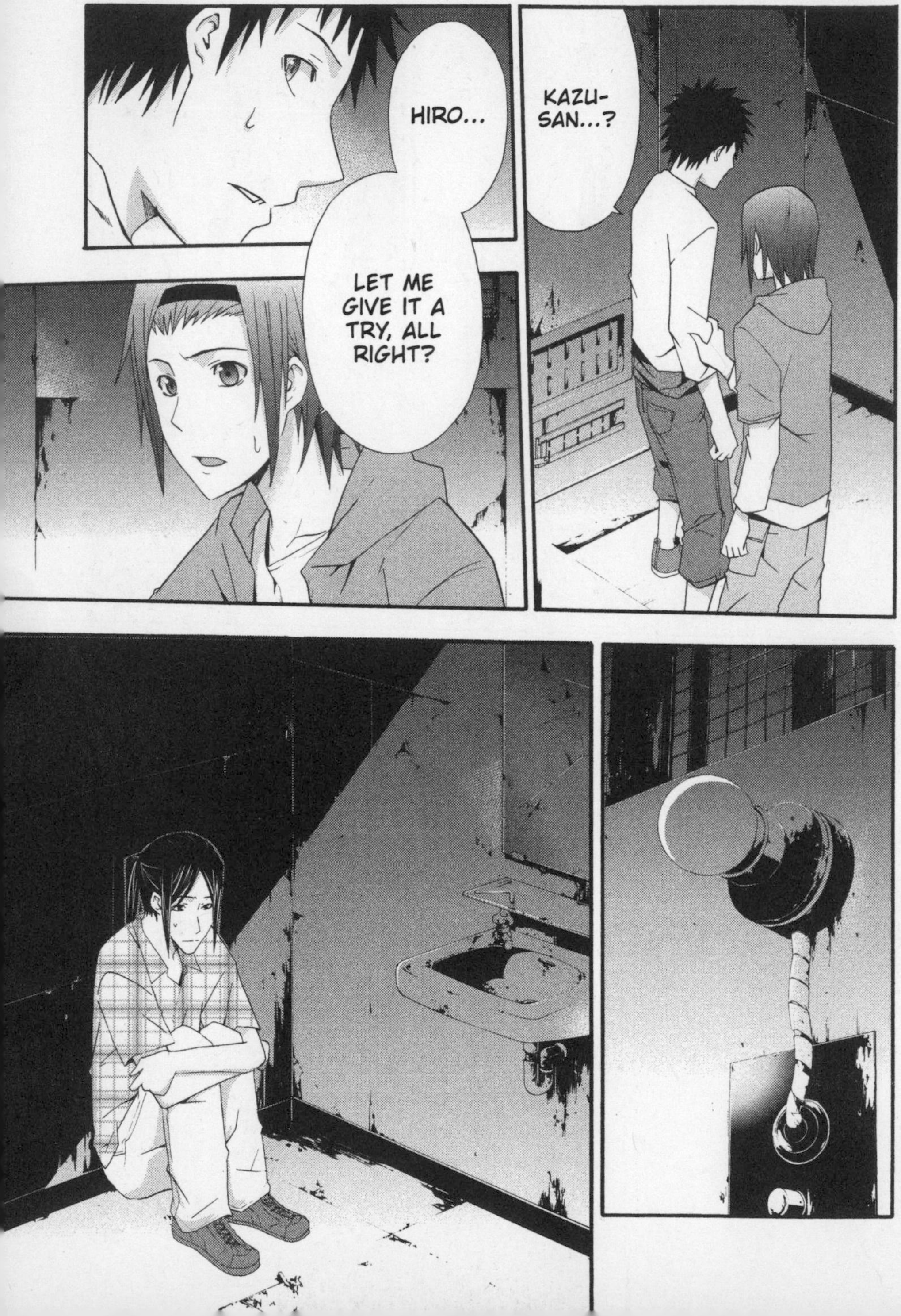
KAZU-SAN...?
HIRO...
LET ME GIVE IT A TRY, ALL RIGHT?

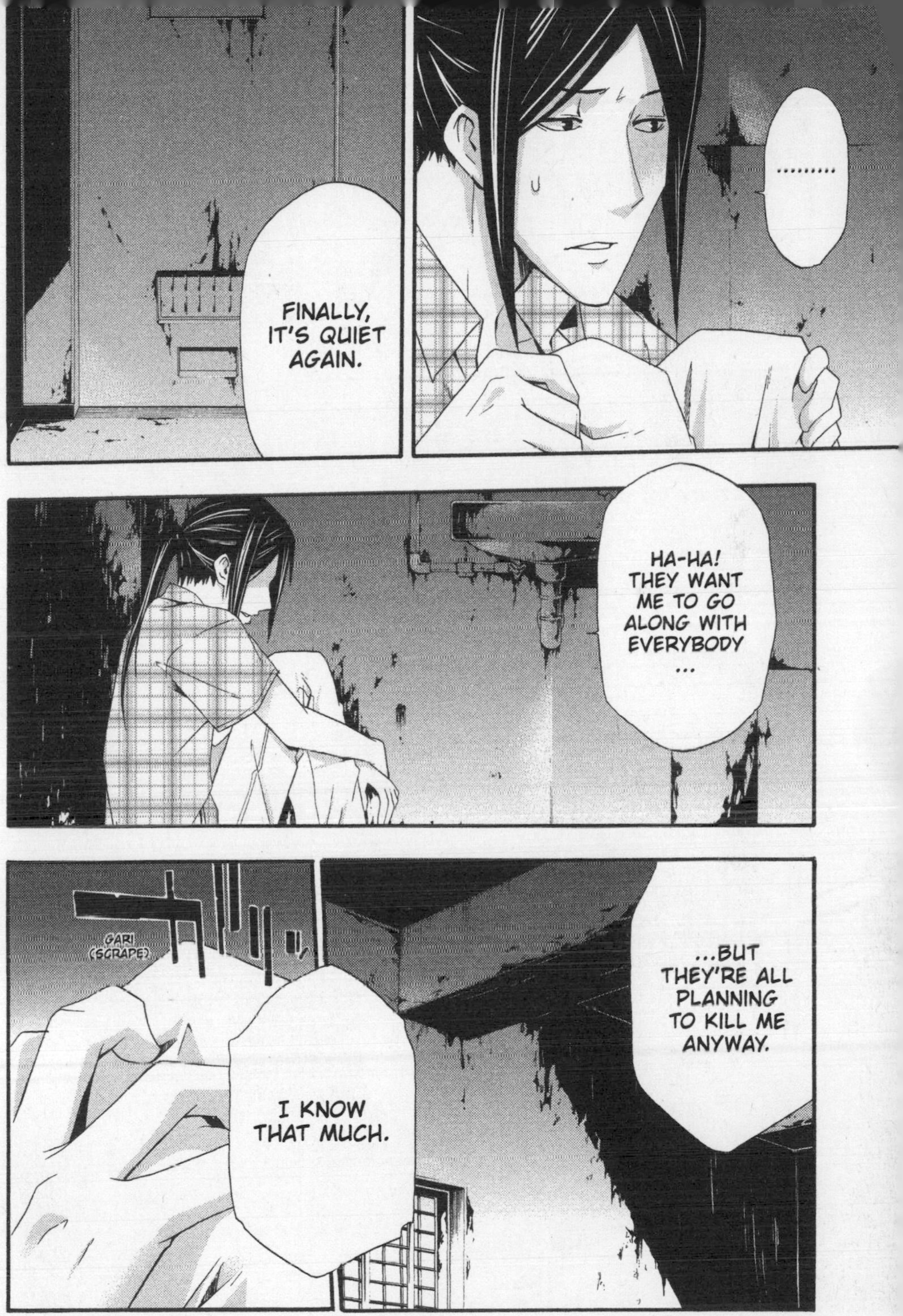

....
FINALLY, IT'S QUIET AGAIN.
HA-HA! THEY WANT ME TO GO ALONG WITH EVERYBODY ...
...BUT THEY'RE ALL PLANNING TO KILL ME ANYWAY.
GARI (SCRAPE)
I KNOW THAT MUCH.

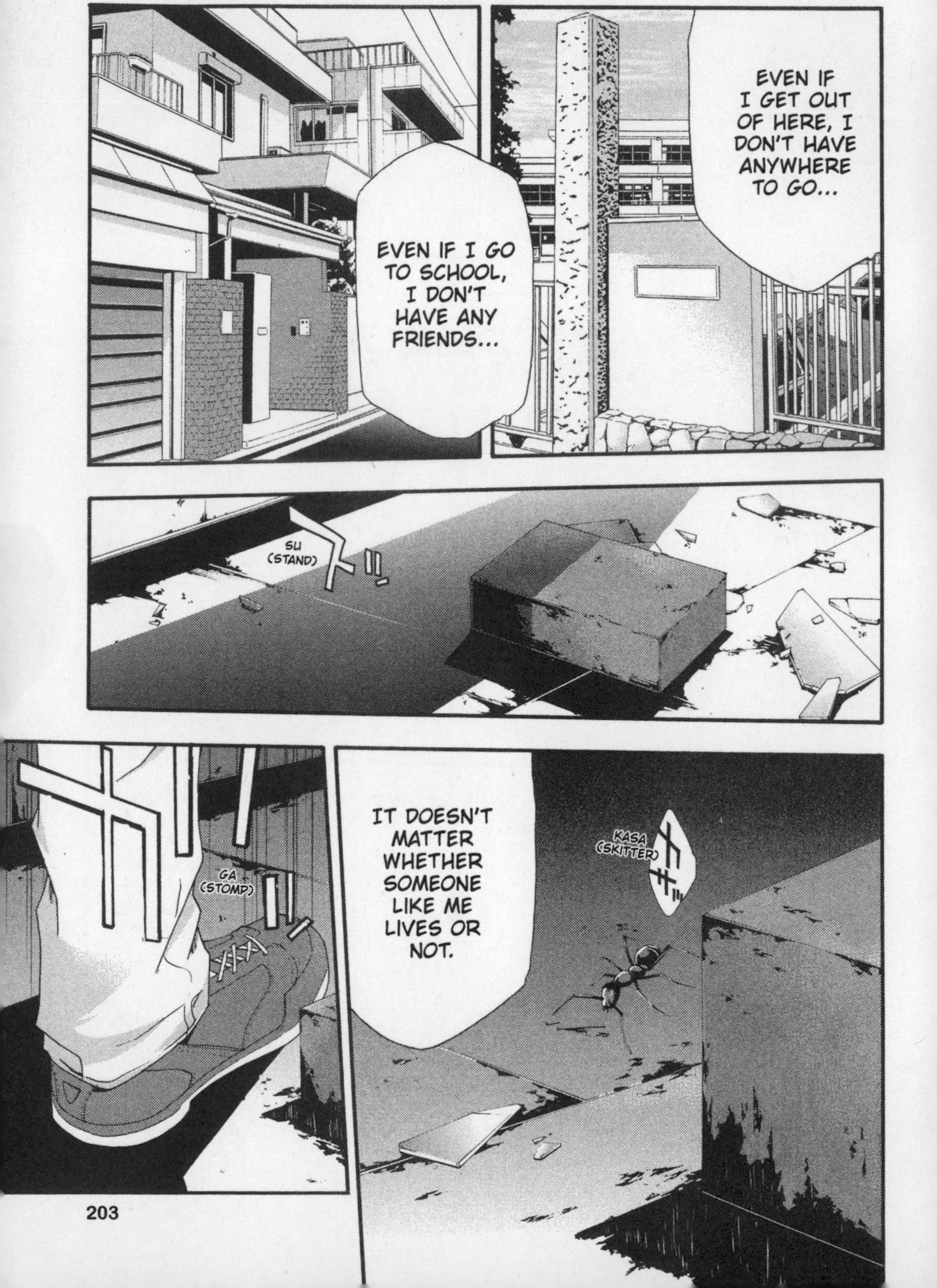
EVEN IF I GET OUT OF HERE, I DON'T HAVE ANYWHERE TO GO...
EVEN IF I GO TO SCHOOL, I DON'T HAVE ANY FRIENDS...
SU (STAND)
IT DOESN'T MATTER WHETHER SOMEONE LIKE ME LIVES OR NOT.
KASA (SKITTER)
GA (STOMP)

...SO I MIGHT AS WELL GET IT OVER WITH...

JUST LIKE THIS, WITH EVERYBODY ELSE...

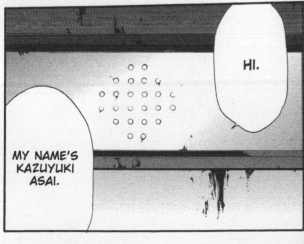

HI.

MY NAME'S KAZUYUKI ASAI.

コン (KON) (KNOCK)

コン KON

ビク, (BIKU) (FLINCH)

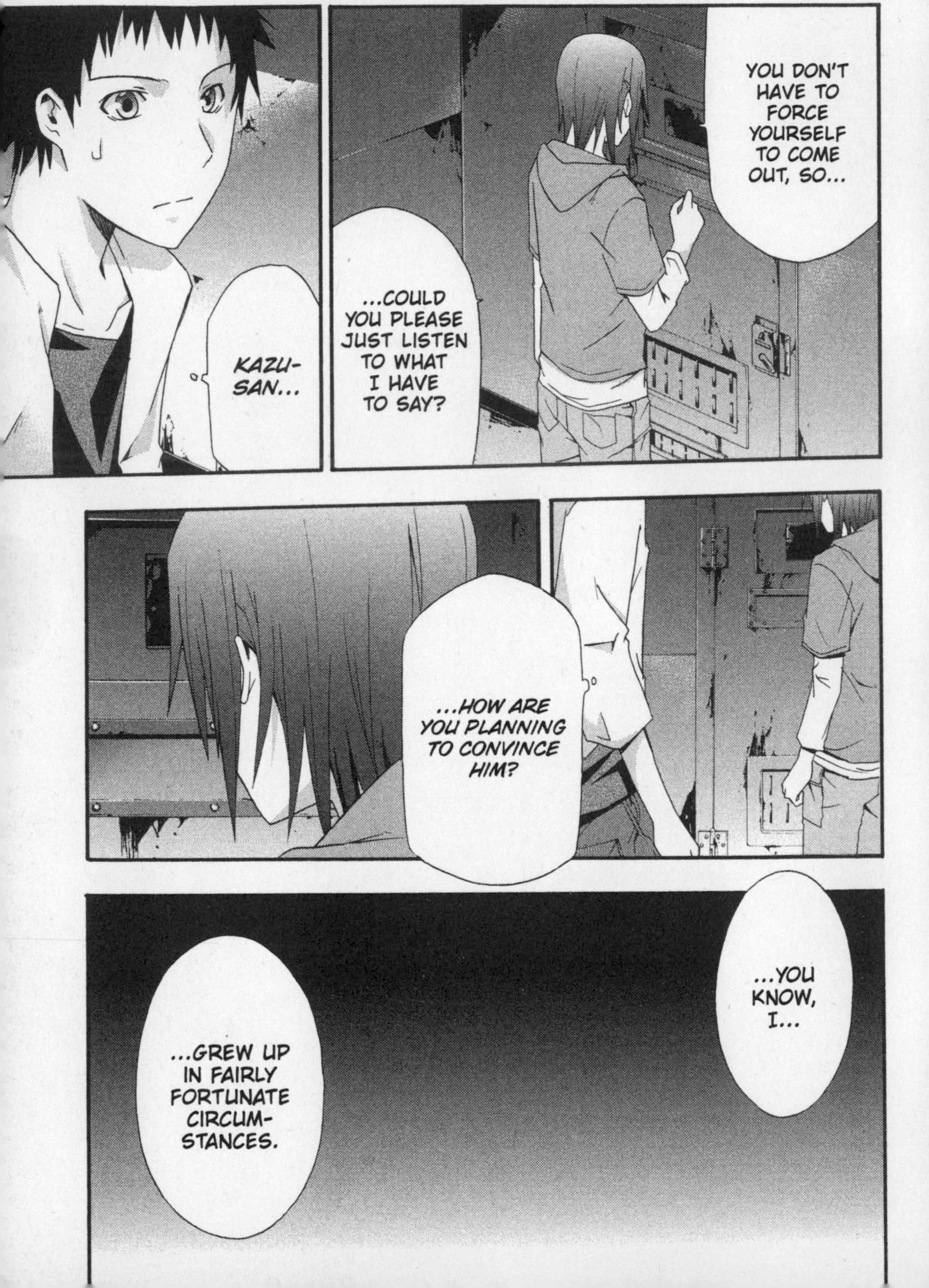
YOU DON'T HAVE TO FORCE YOURSELF TO COME OUT, SO...
...COULD YOU PLEASE JUST LISTEN TO WHAT I HAVE TO SAY?
KAZU-SAN...
...HOW ARE YOU PLANNING TO CONVINCE HIM?
...YOU KNOW, I...
...GREW UP IN FAIRLY FORTUNATE CIRCUM-STANCES.

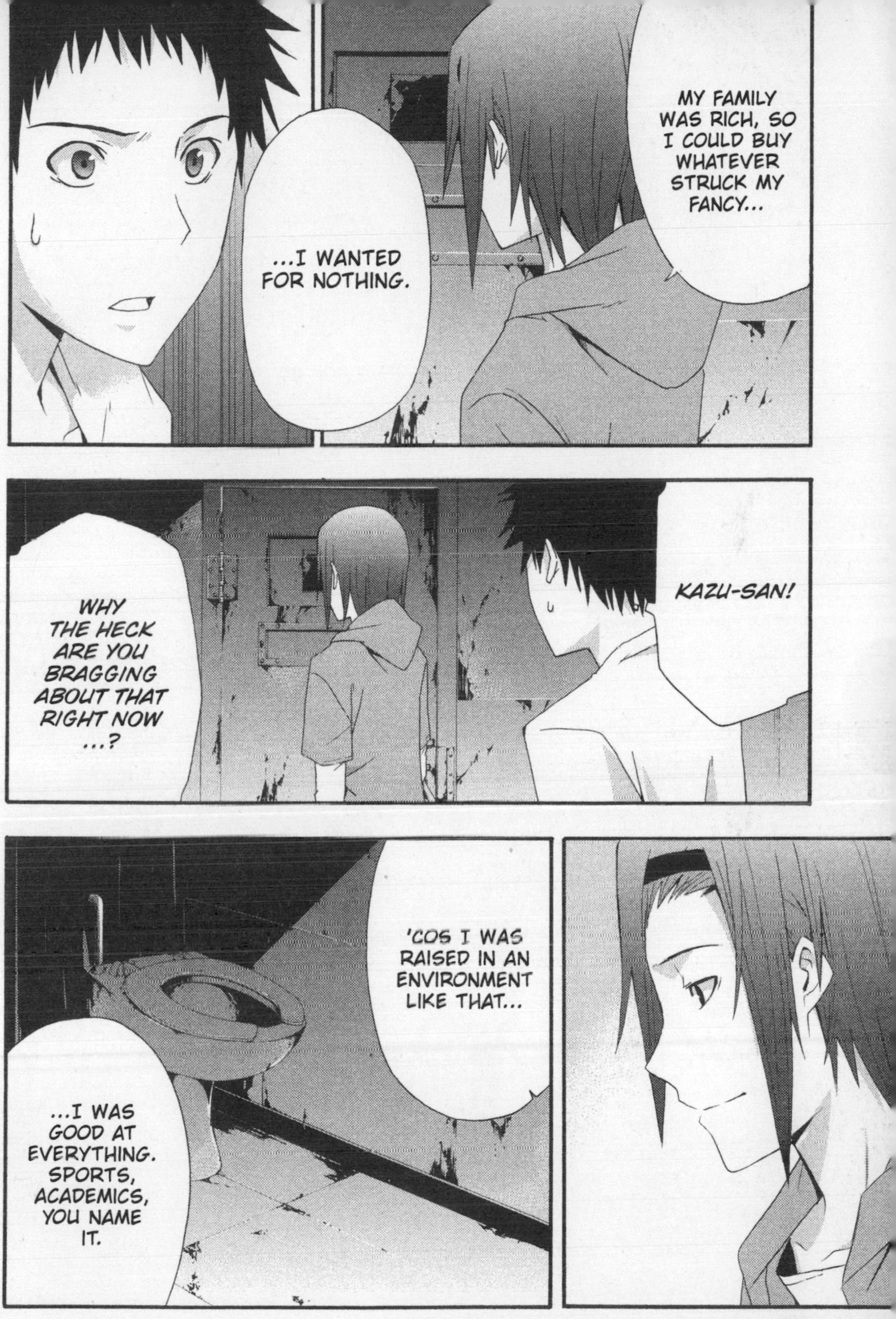
MY FAMILY WAS RICH, SO I COULD BUY WHATEVER STRUCK MY FANCY...
...I WANTED FOR NOTHING.
KAZU-SAN!
WHY THE HECK ARE YOU BRAGGING ABOUT THAT RIGHT NOW ...?
'COS I WAS RAISED IN AN ENVIRONMENT LIKE THAT...
...I WAS GOOD AT EVERYTHING. SPORTS, ACADEMICS, YOU NAME IT.

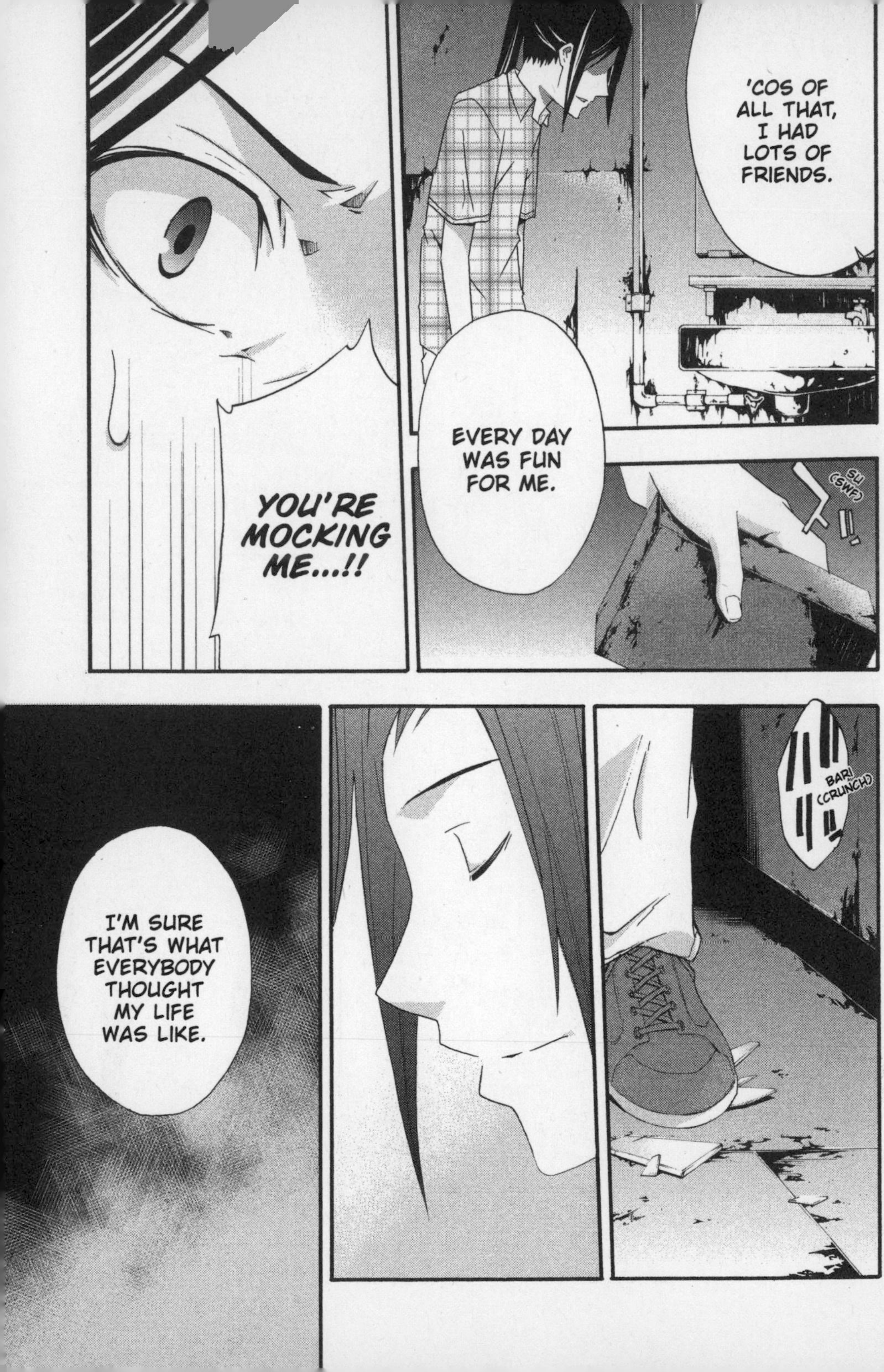
'COS OF ALL THAT, I HAD LOTS OF FRIENDS.
EVERY DAY WAS FUN FOR ME.
SU (SWF)
YOU'RE MOCKING ME...!!
BARI (CRUNCH)
I'M SURE THAT'S WHAT EVERYBODY THOUGHT MY LIFE WAS LIKE.

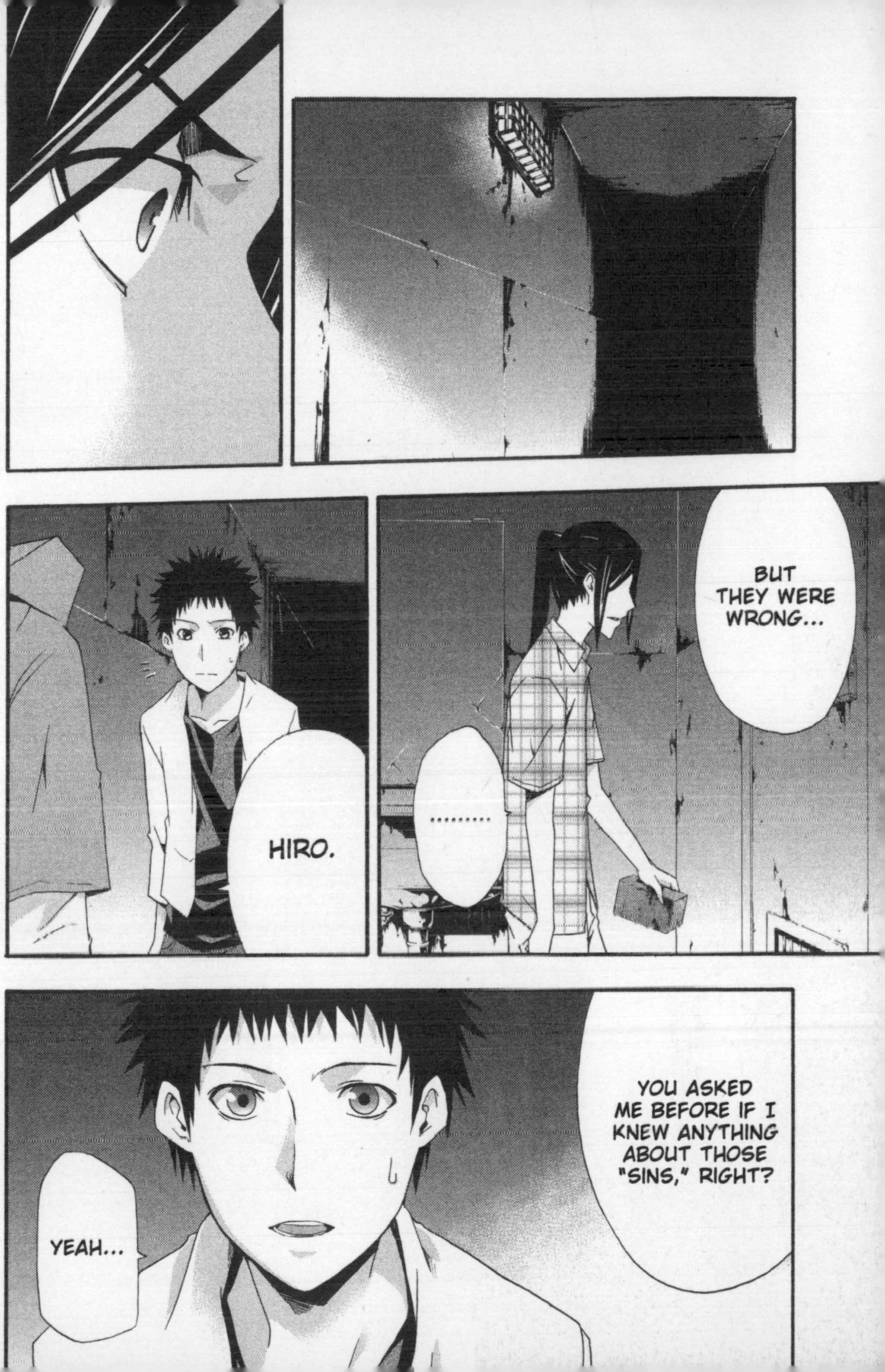
BUT THEY WERE WRONG...
....
HIRO.
YOU ASKED ME BEFORE IF I KNEW ANYTHING ABOUT THOSE "SINS," RIGHT?
YEAH...

TO BE TOLD IT'S A SIN IS HURTFUL, BUT...
...I THINK I KNOW WHAT IT MEANS.
I...
WHAT IS IT!?

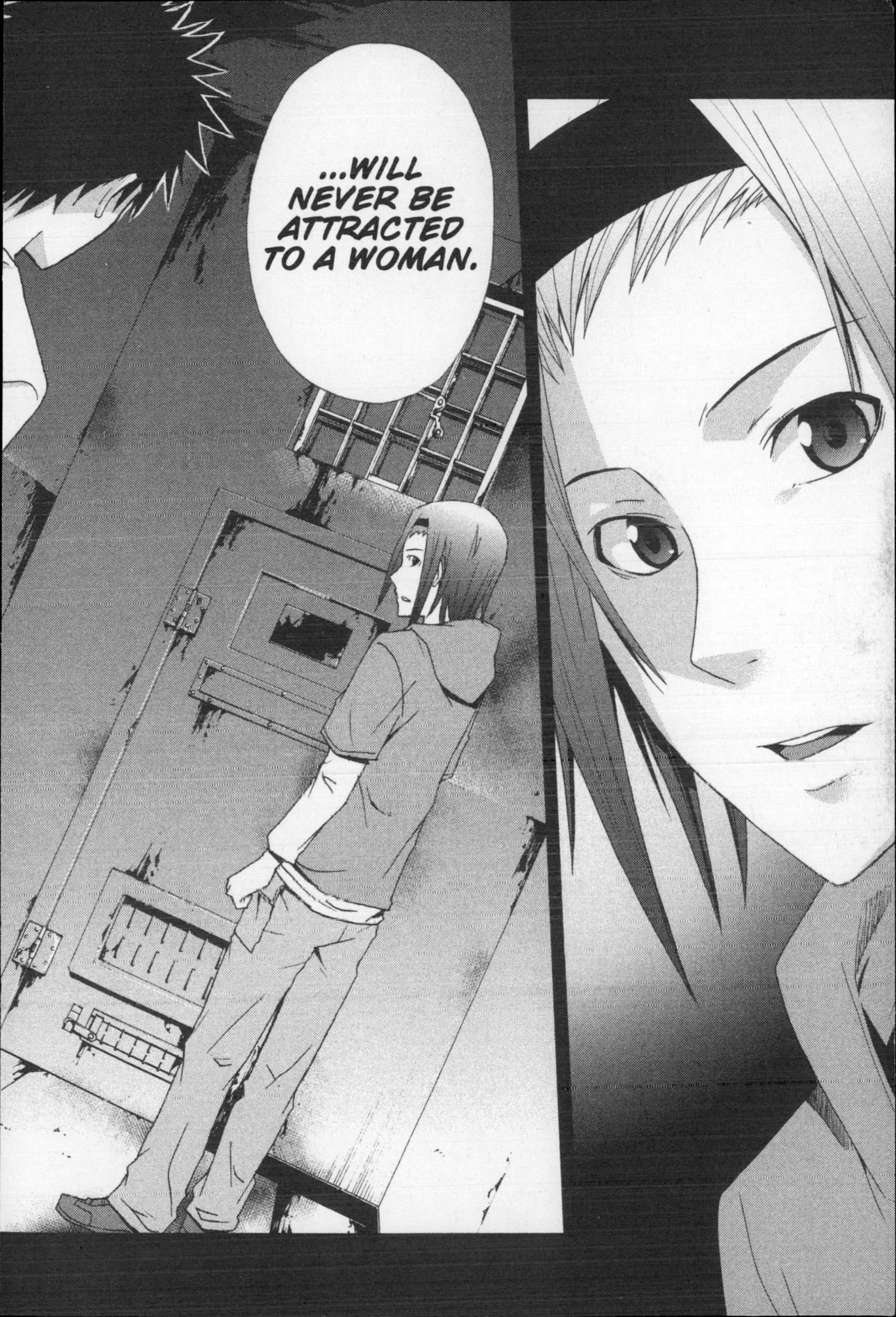
...WILL NEVER BE ATTRACTED TO A WOMAN.

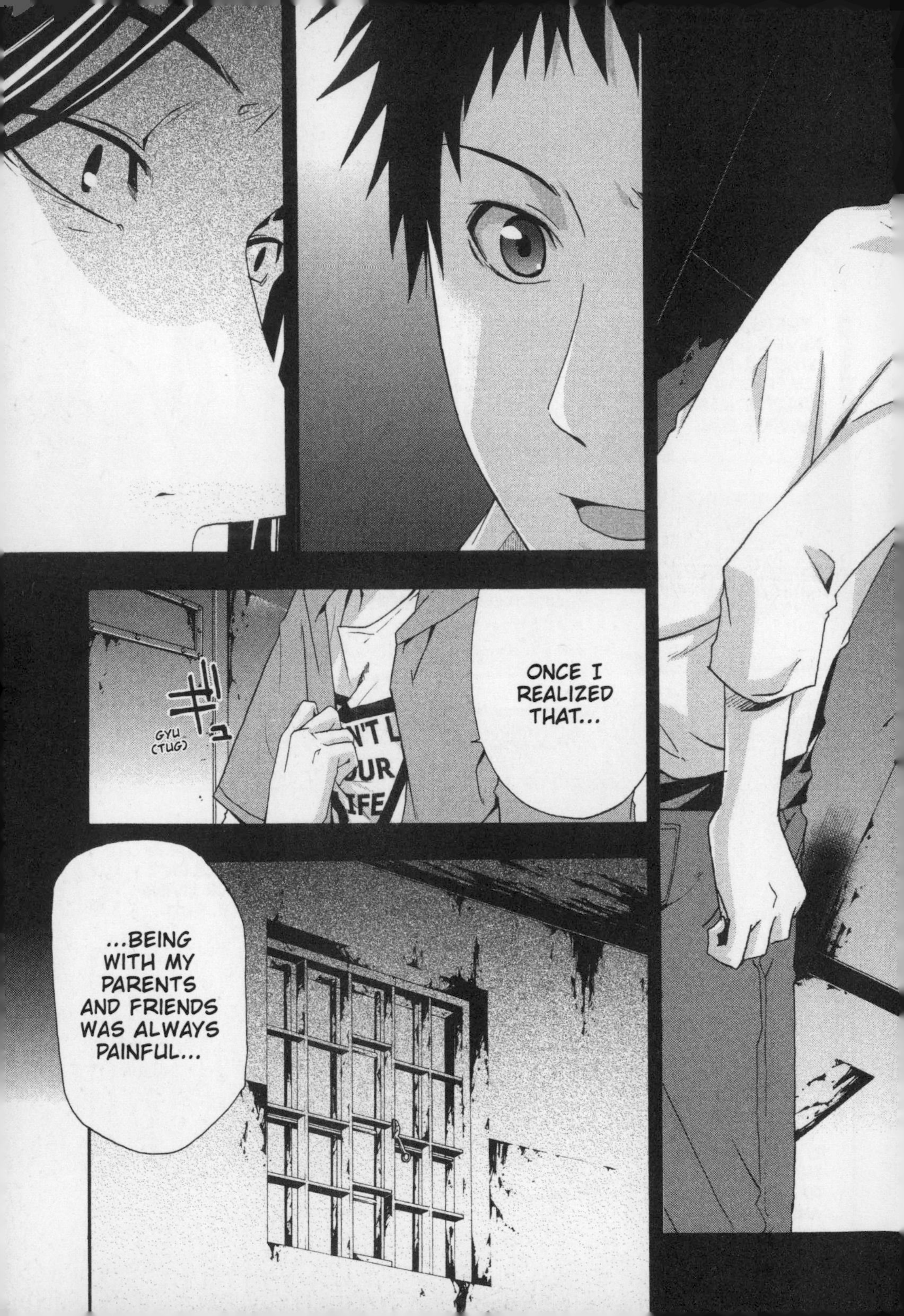
ONCE I REALIZED THAT...
ギュ
GYU (TUG)
...BEING WITH MY PARENTS AND FRIENDS WAS ALWAYS PAINFUL...

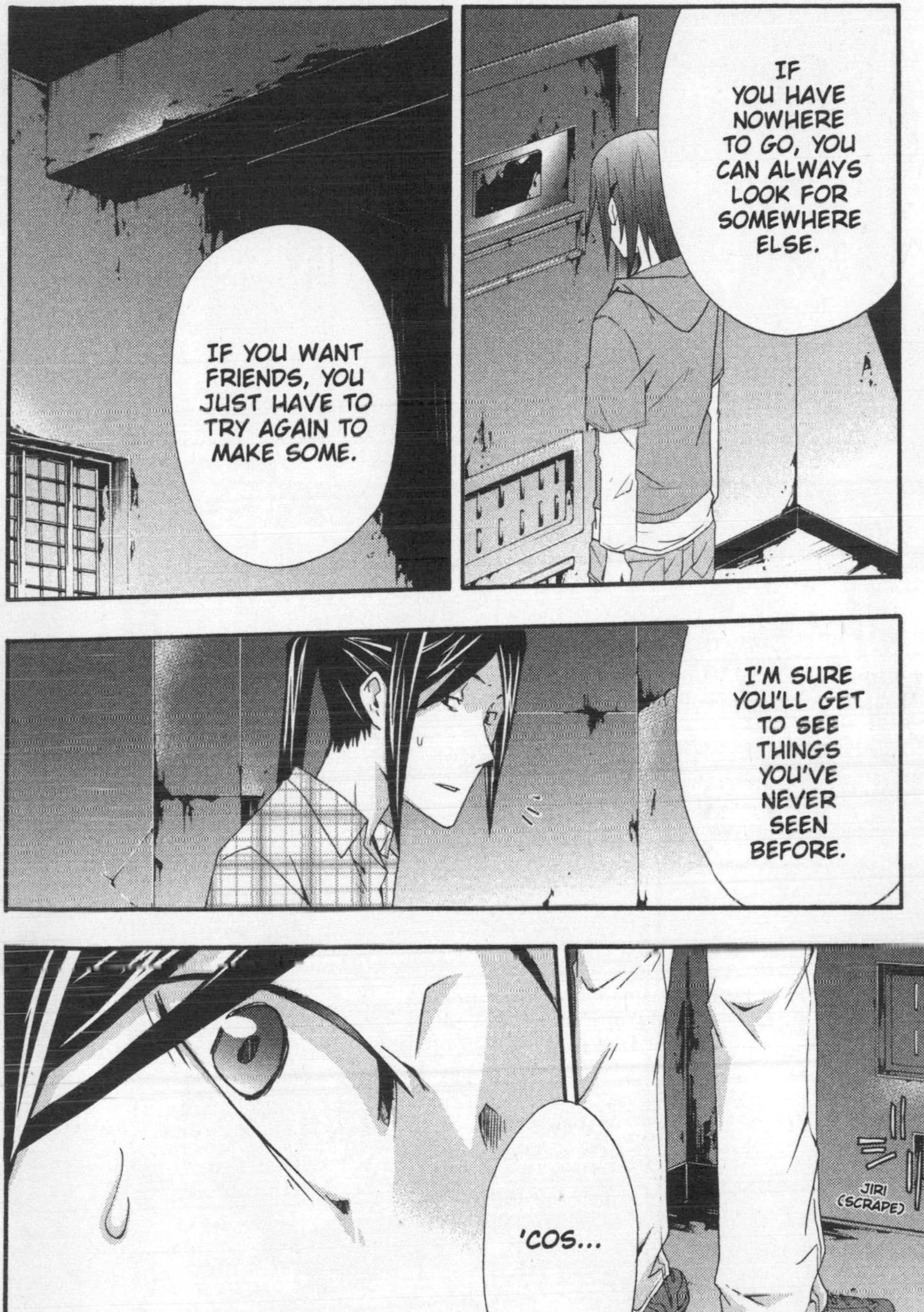
IF YOU HAVE NOWHERE TO GO, YOU CAN ALWAYS LOOK FOR SOMEWHERE ELSE.
IF YOU WANT FRIENDS, YOU JUST HAVE TO TRY AGAIN TO MAKE SOME.
I'M SURE YOU'LL GET TO SEE THINGS YOU'VE NEVER SEEN BEFORE.
JIRI (SCRAPE)
'COS...

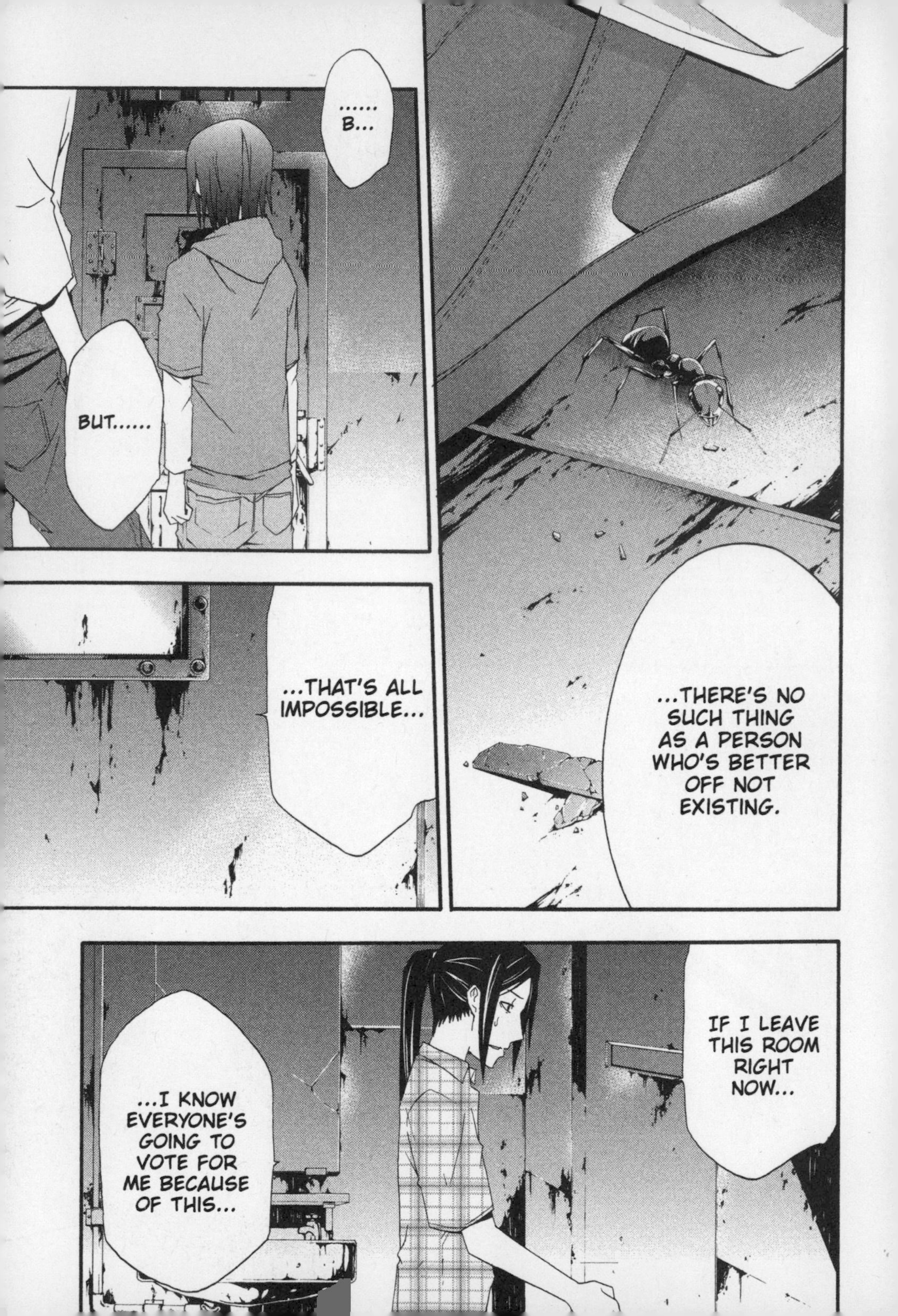
...THERE'S NO SUCH THING AS A PERSON WHO'S BETTER OFF NOT EXISTING.
......B...
BUT......
...THAT'S ALL IMPOSSIBLE...
IF I LEAVE THIS ROOM RIGHT NOW...
...I KNOW EVERYONE'S GOING TO VOTE FOR ME BECAUSE OF THIS...

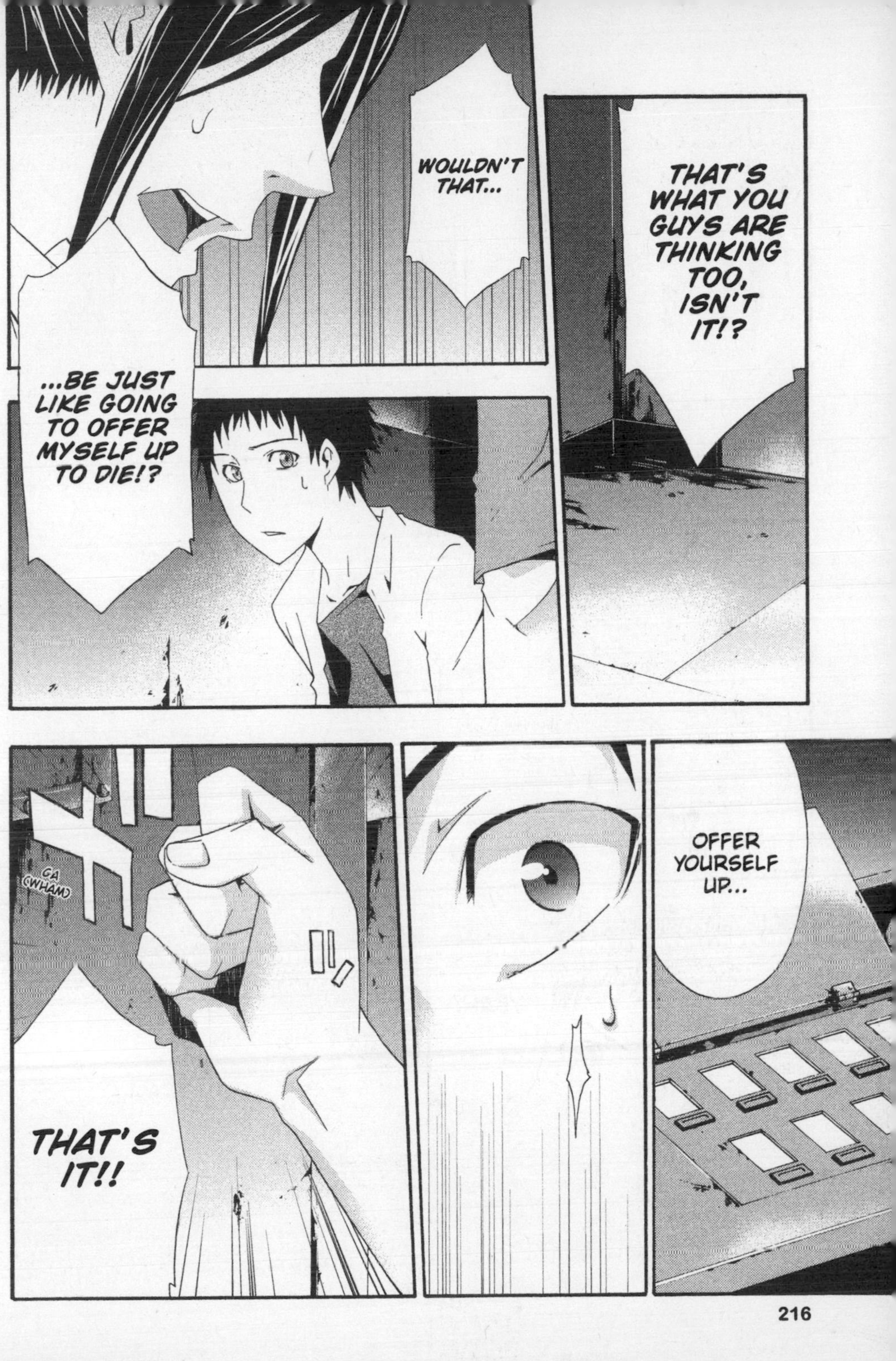
THAT'S WHAT YOU GUYS ARE THINKING TOO, ISN'T IT!?
WOULDN'T THAT...
...BE JUST LIKE GOING TO OFFER MYSELF UP TO DIE!?
OFFER YOURSELF UP...
GA (WHAM)
THAT'S IT!!

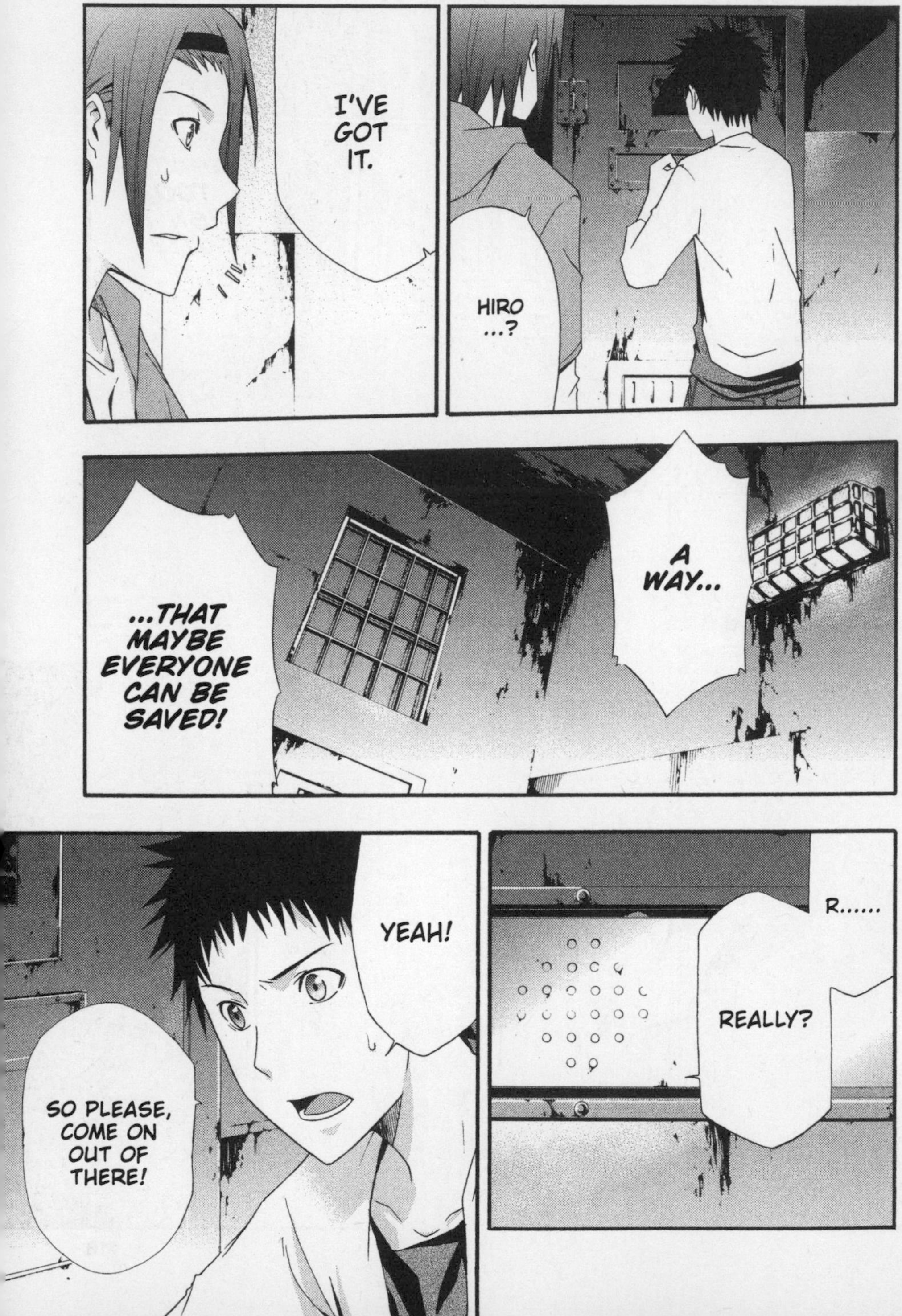
HIRO ...?
I'VE GOT IT.
A WAY...
...THAT MAYBE EVERYONE CAN BE SAVED!
R......
REALLY?
YEAH!
SO PLEASE, COME ON OUT OF THERE!

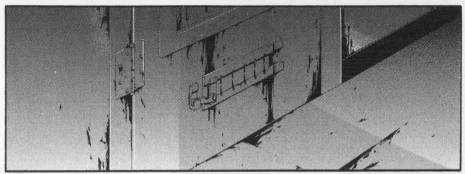

IF
YOU'RE
LYING...

GII
(CREAK)

OPEN

......!

BI
(BEEP)

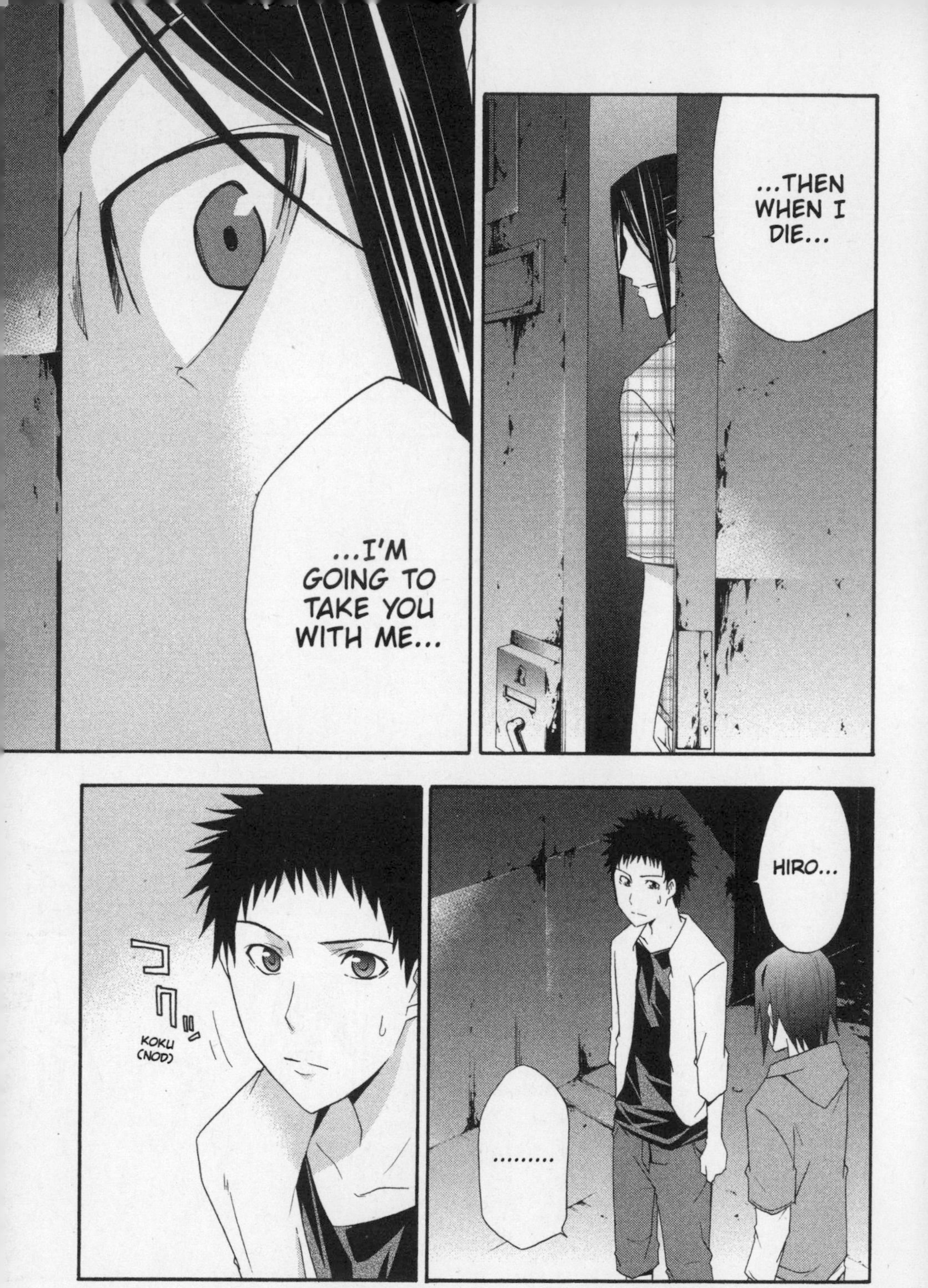
...THEN WHEN I DIE...
...I'M GOING TO TAKE YOU WITH ME...
HIRO...
....
KOKU (NOD)

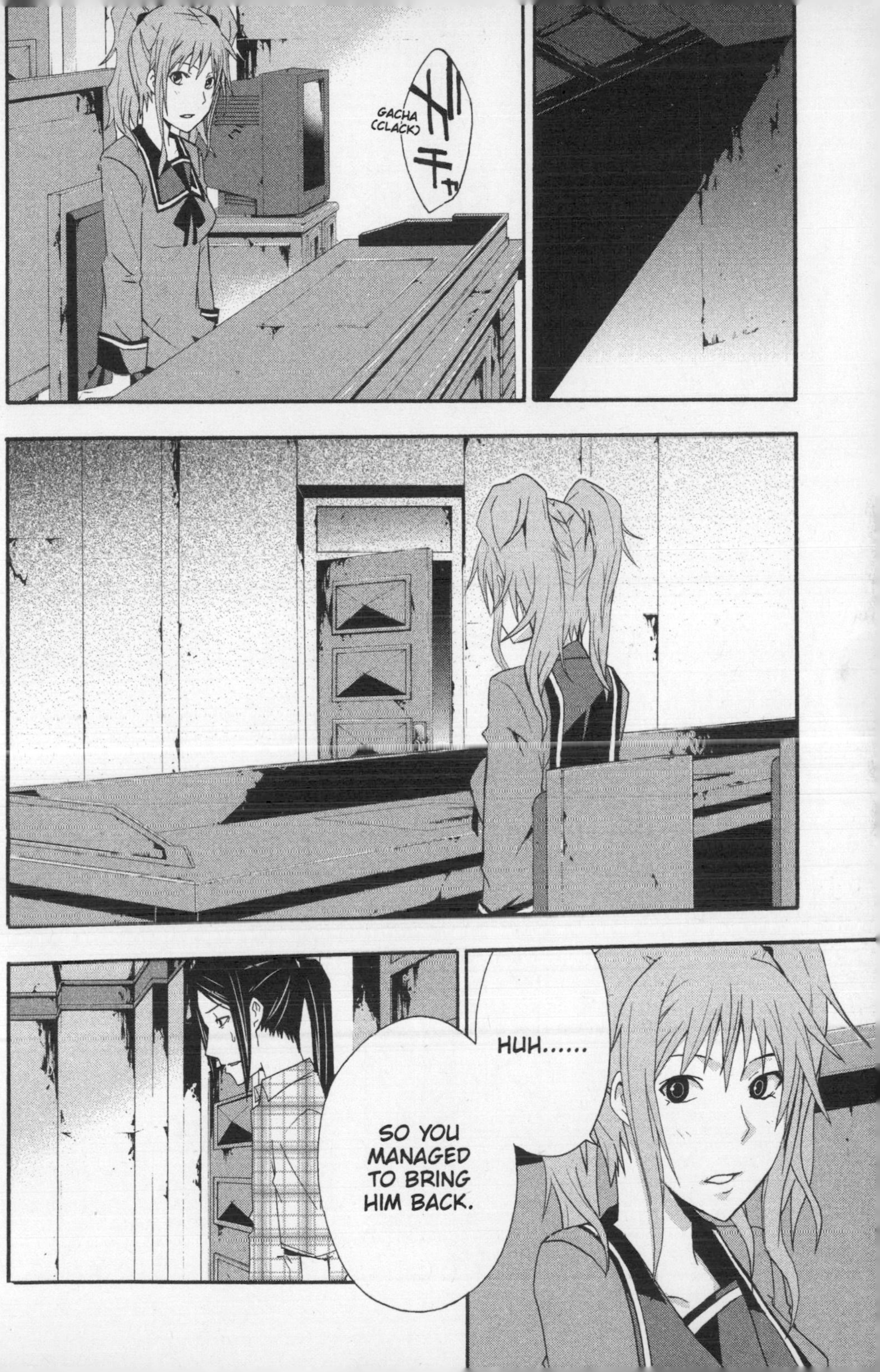
ガチャ
GACHA (CLACK)
HUH......
SO YOU MANAGED TO BRING HIM BACK.

YOU DUMB SHIT...

UGH......

...SO YOU FINALLY DECIDED TO SHOW YOUR MUG IN HERE...

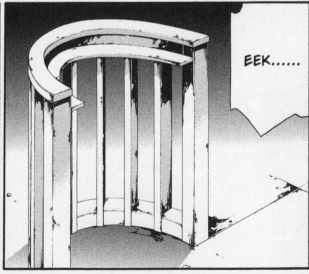

EEK......

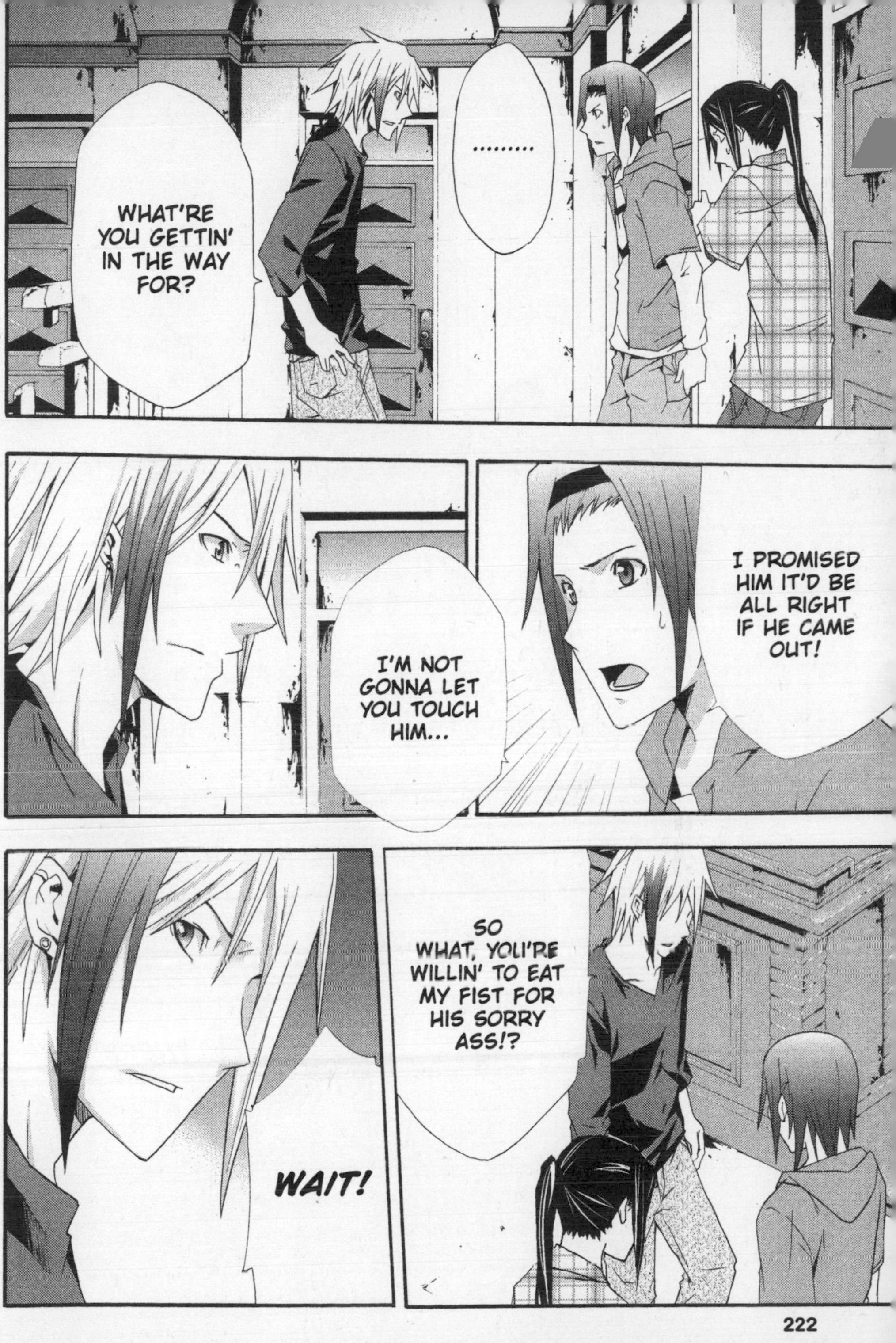
....
WHAT'RE YOU GETTIN' IN THE WAY FOR?
I PROMISED HIM IT'D BE ALL RIGHT IF HE CAME OUT!
I'M NOT GONNA LET YOU TOUCH HIM...
SO WHAT, YOU'RE WILLIN' TO EAT MY FIST FOR HIS SORRY ASS!?
WAIT!

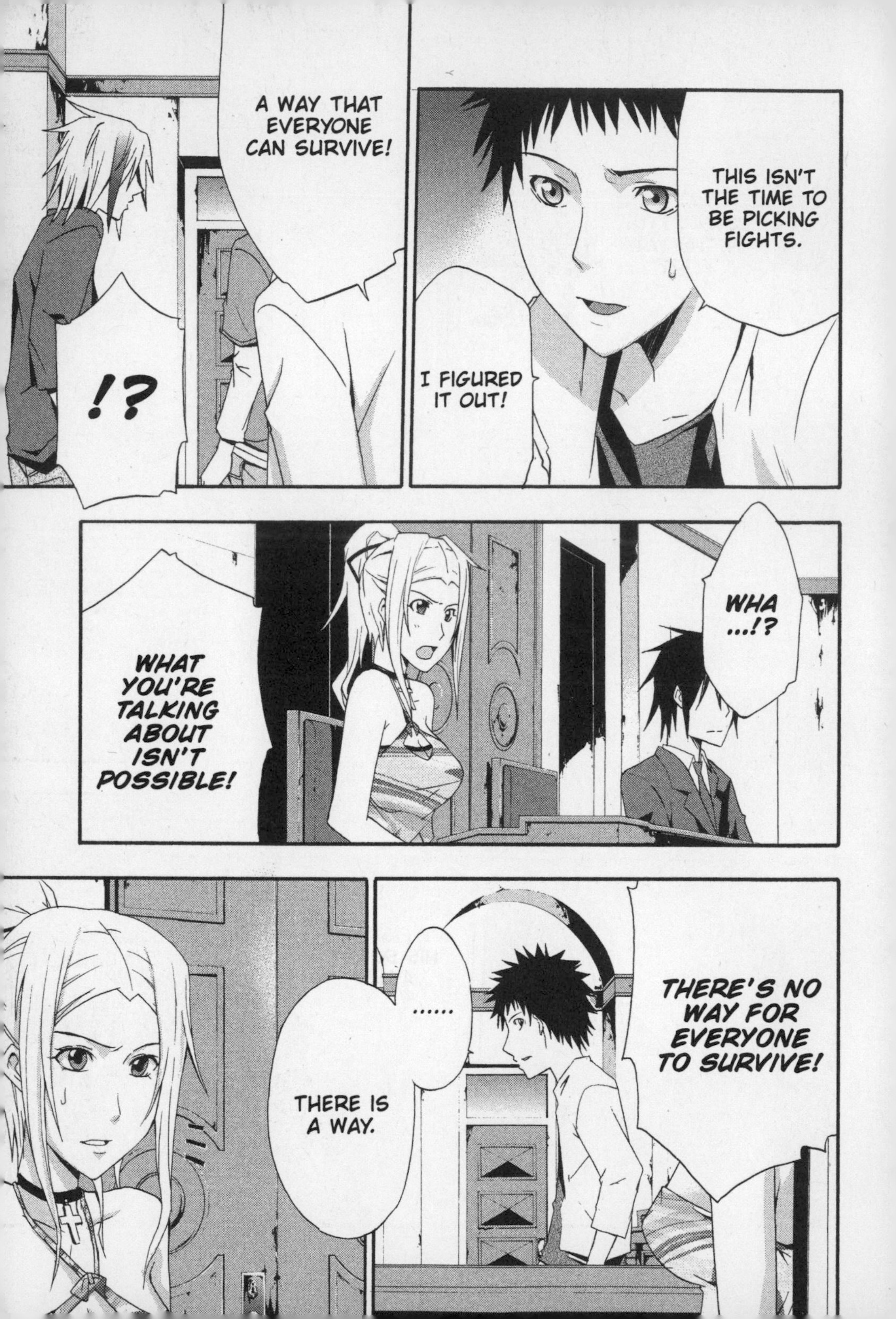
THIS ISN'T THE TIME TO BE PICKING FIGHTS.
I FIGURED IT OUT!
A WAY THAT EVERYONE CAN SURVIVE!
!?
WHA ...!?
WHAT YOU'RE TALKING ABOUT ISN'T POSSIBLE!
THERE'S NO WAY FOR EVERYONE TO SURVIVE!
......
THERE IS A WAY.

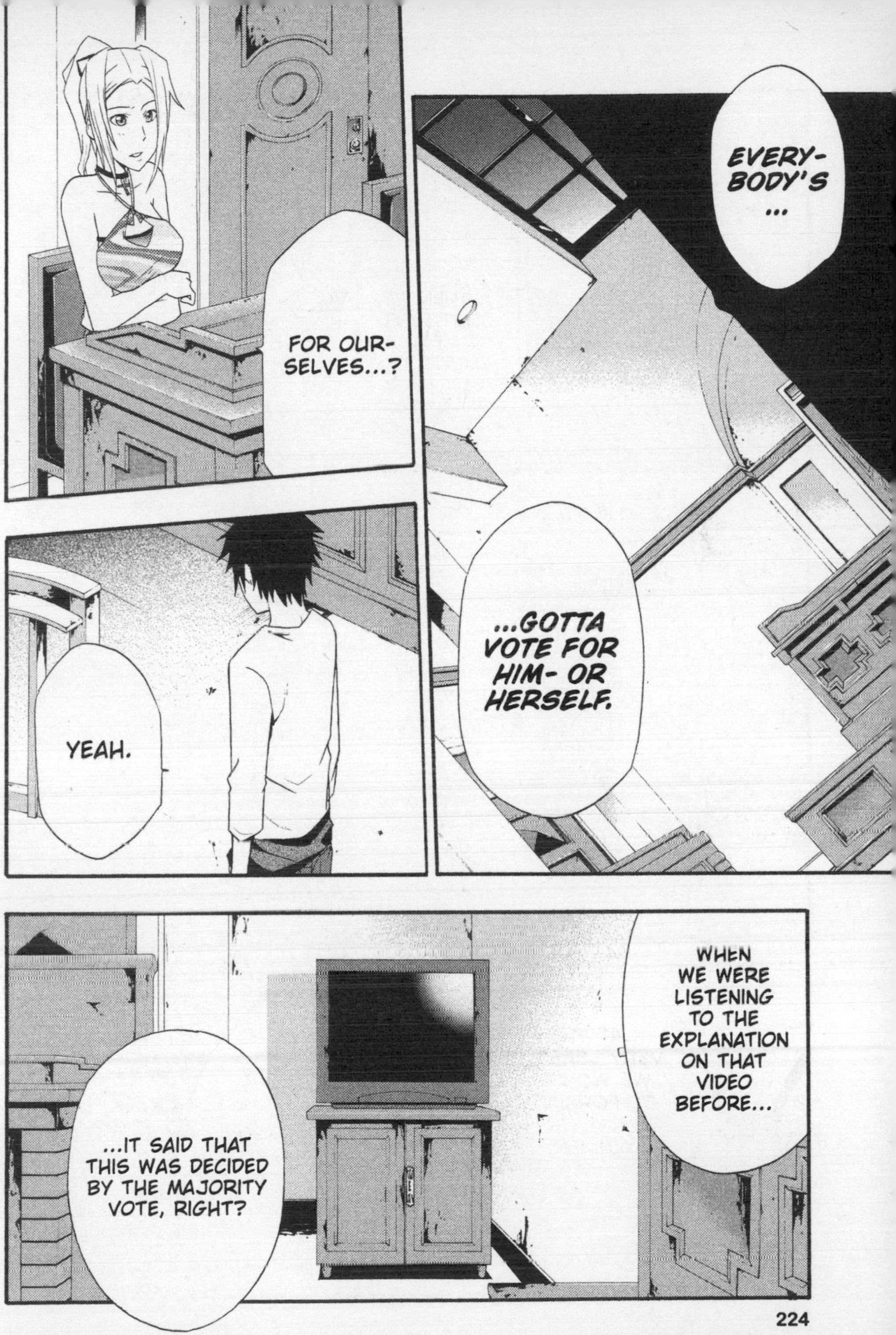
EVERY-BODY'S ...
...GOTTA VOTE FOR HIM- OR HERSELF.
FOR OUR-SELVES...?
YEAH.
WHEN WE WERE LISTENING TO THE EXPLANATION ON THAT VIDEO BEFORE...
...IT SAID THAT THIS WAS DECIDED BY THE MAJORITY VOTE, RIGHT?

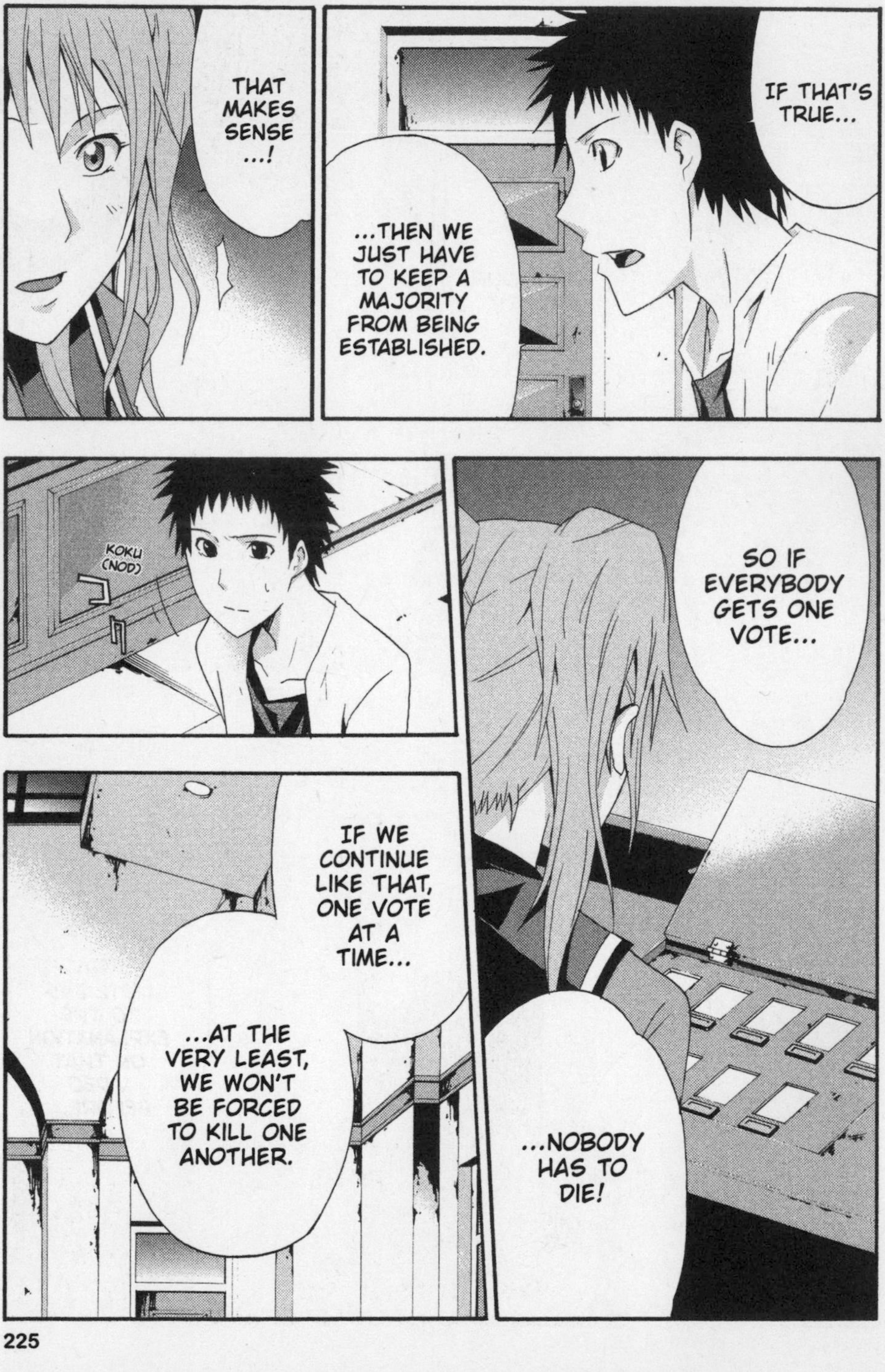
IF THAT'S TRUE...
...THEN WE JUST HAVE TO KEEP A MAJORITY FROM BEING ESTABLISHED.
THAT MAKES SENSE ...!
SO IF EVERYBODY GETS ONE VOTE...
...NOBODY HAS TO DIE!
KOKU (NOD)
IF WE CONTINUE LIKE THAT, ONE VOTE AT A TIME...
...AT THE VERY LEAST, WE WON'T BE FORCED TO KILL ONE ANOTHER.

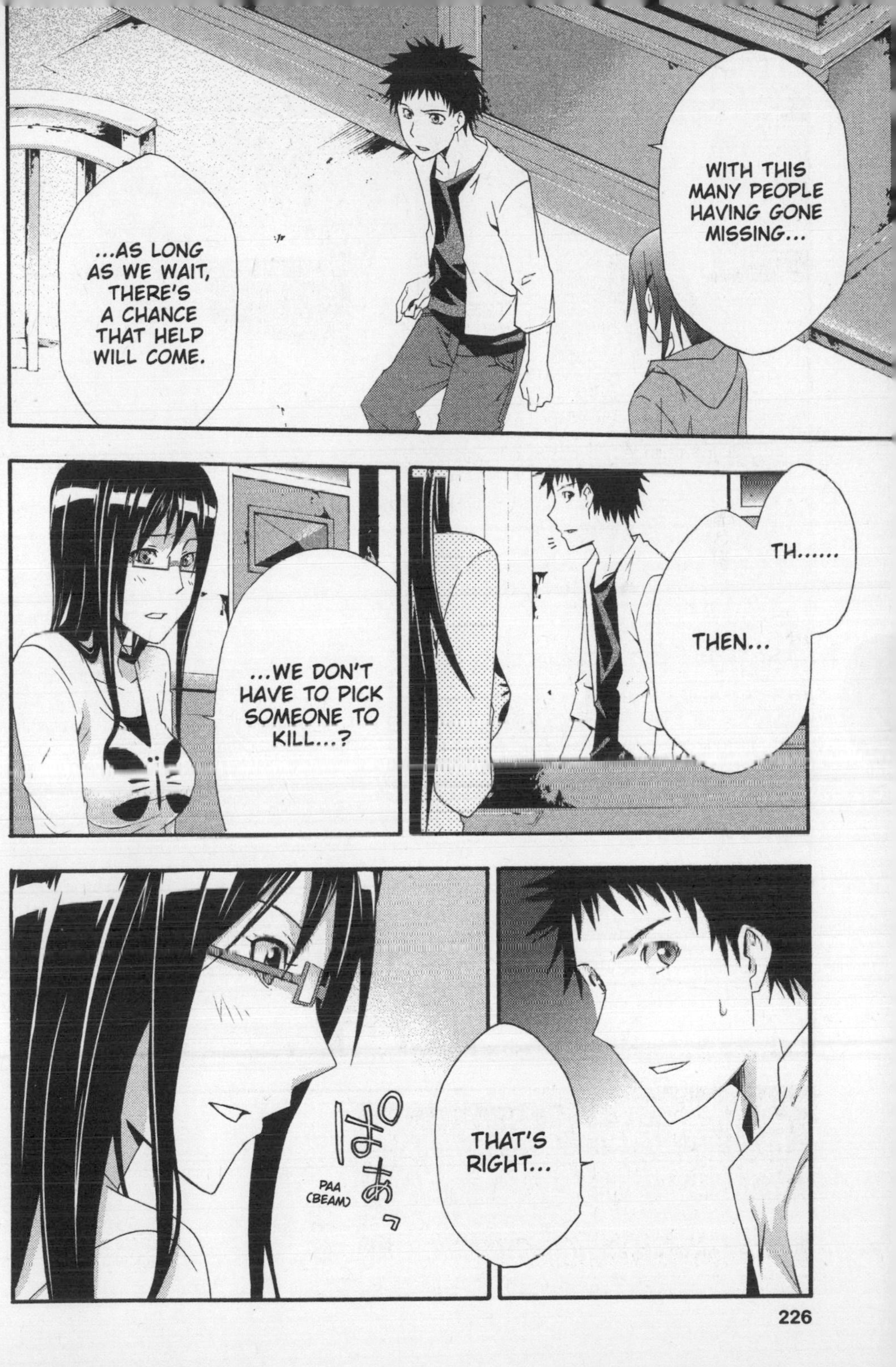
WITH THIS MANY PEOPLE HAVING GONE MISSING...
...AS LONG AS WE WAIT, THERE'S A CHANCE THAT HELP WILL COME.
TH......
THEN...
...WE DON'T HAVE TO PICK SOMEONE TO KILL...?
THAT'S RIGHT...
ぱあっ
PAA (BEAM)

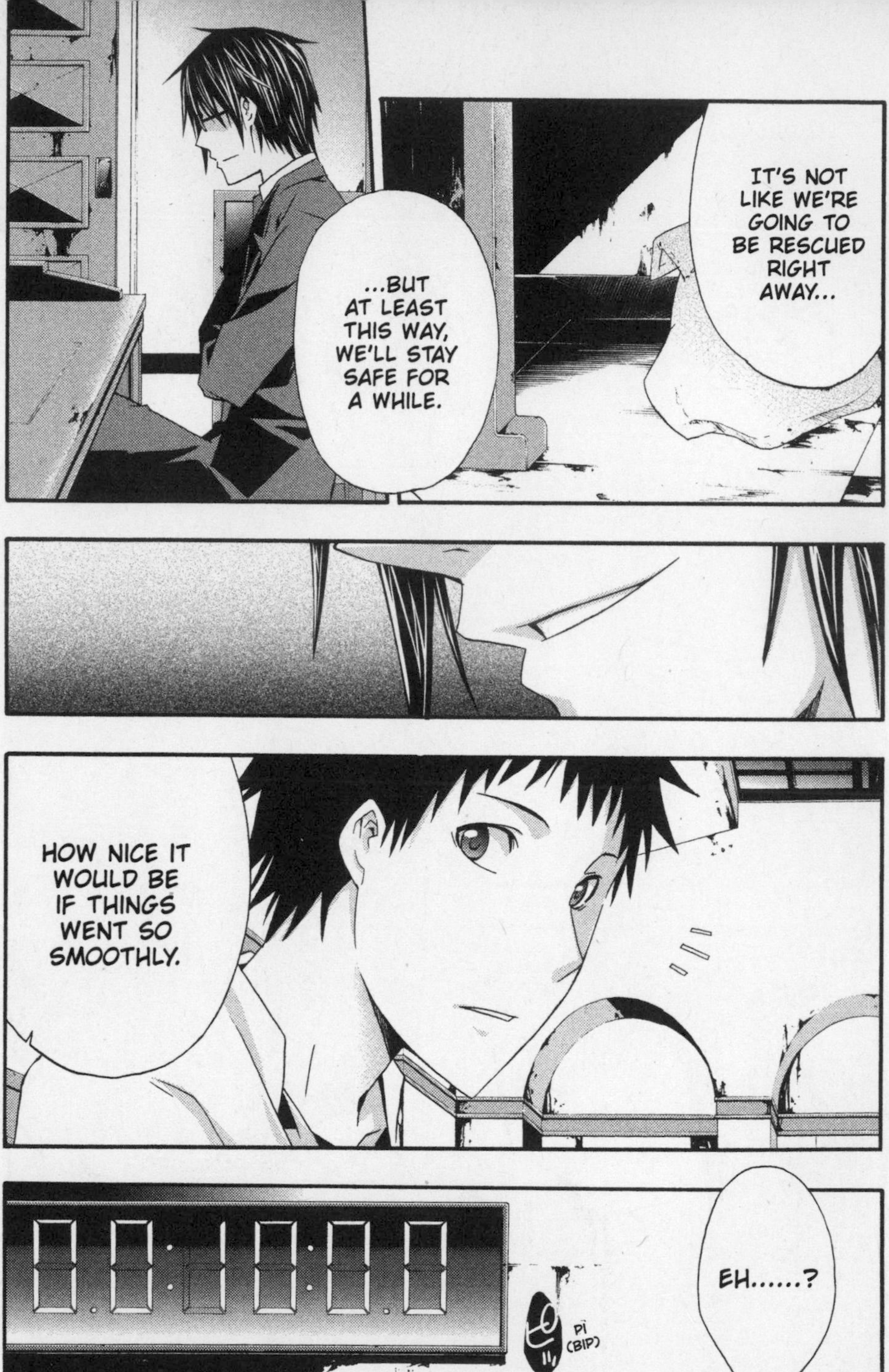
IT'S NOT LIKE WE'RE GOING TO BE RESCUED RIGHT AWAY...
...BUT AT LEAST THIS WAY, WE'LL STAY SAFE FOR A WHILE.
HOW NICE IT WOULD BE IF THINGS WENT SO SMOOTHLY.
EH......?
PI (BIP)

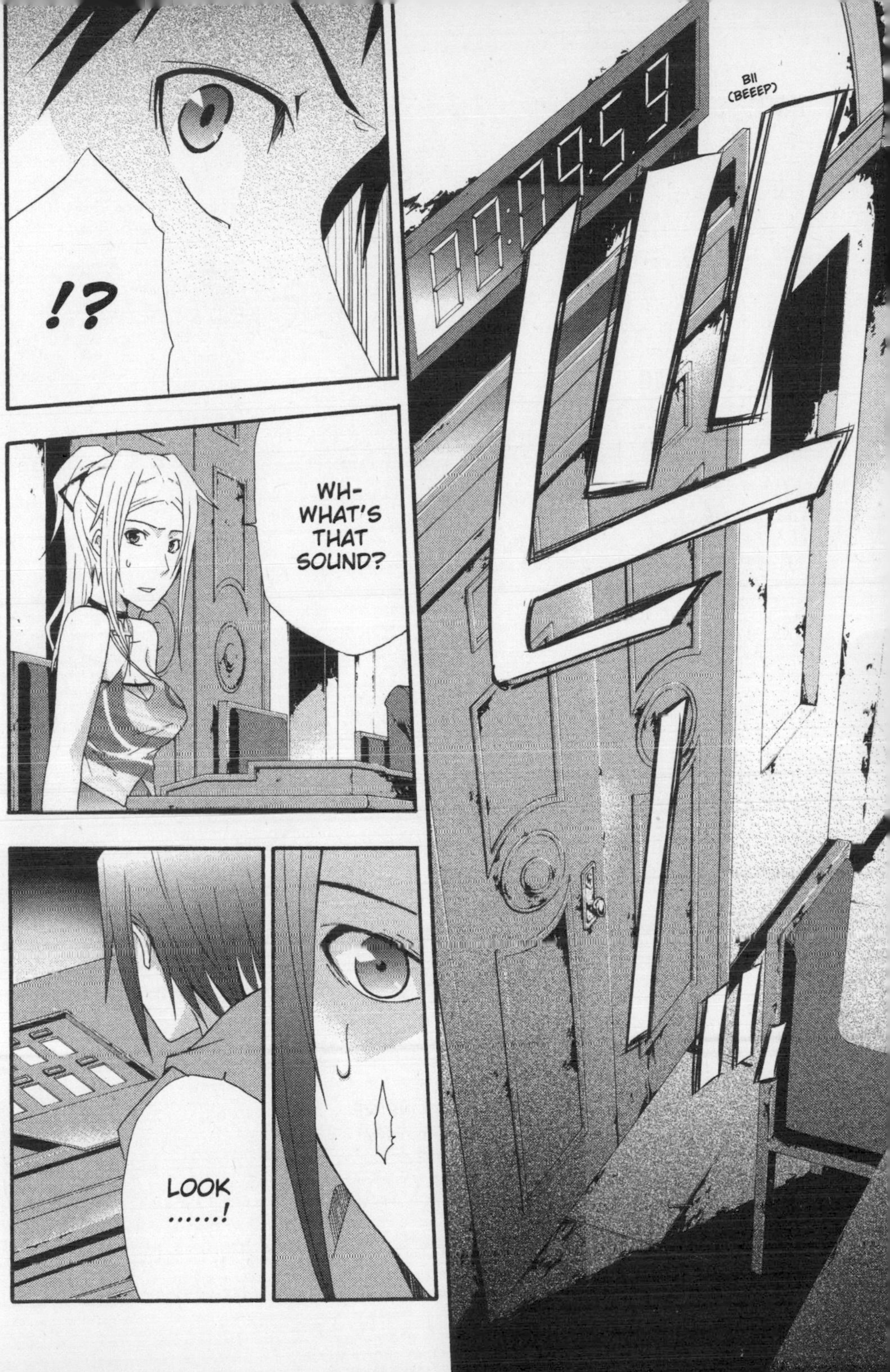
BII
(BEEEP)
!?
WH-
WHAT'S
THAT
SOUND?
LOOK
......!

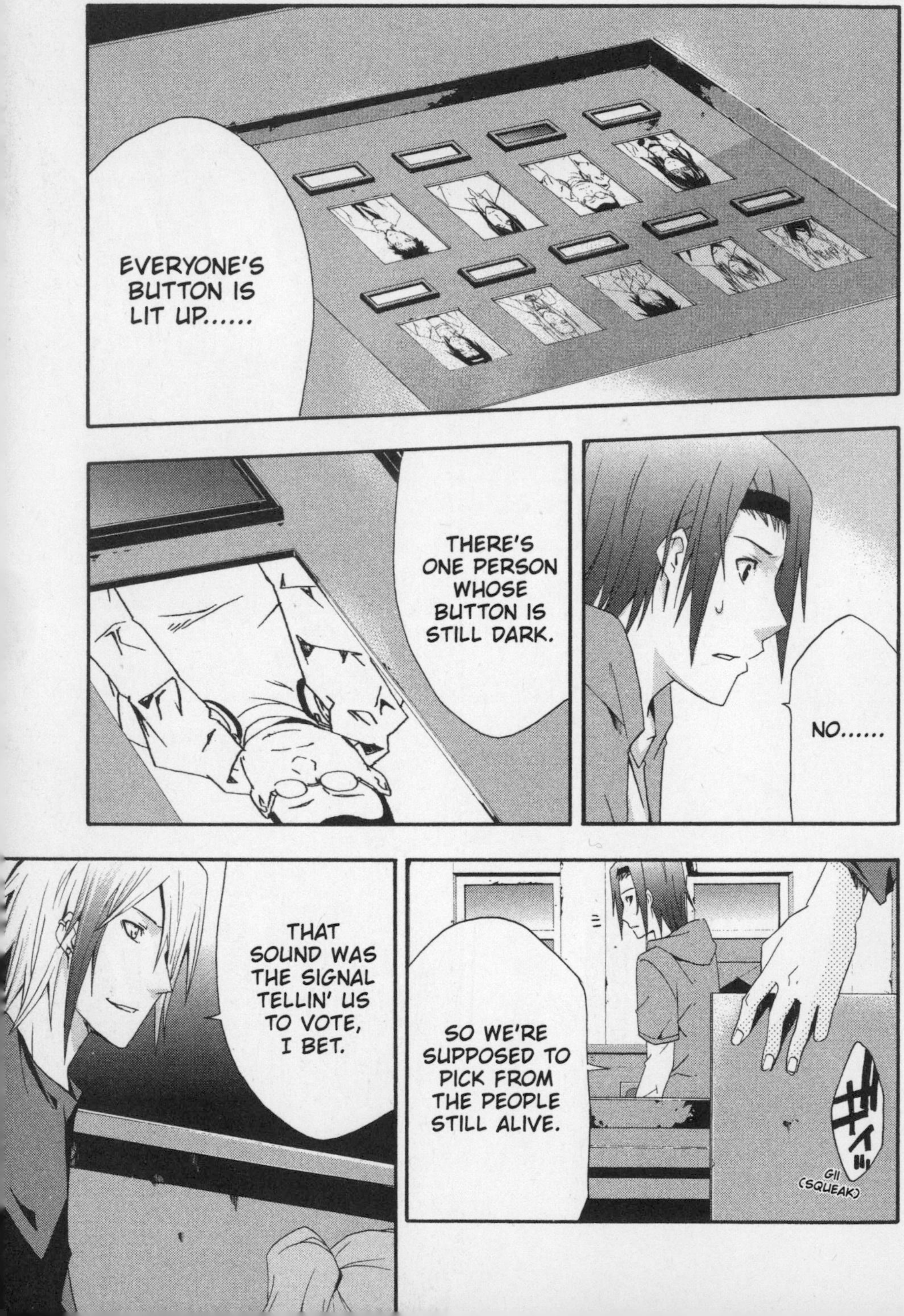
EVERYONE'S BUTTON IS LIT UP......
NO......
THERE'S ONE PERSON WHOSE BUTTON IS STILL DARK.
SO WE'RE SUPPOSED TO PICK FROM THE PEOPLE STILL ALIVE.
GII (SQUEAK)
THAT SOUND WAS THE SIGNAL TELLIN' US TO VOTE, I BET.

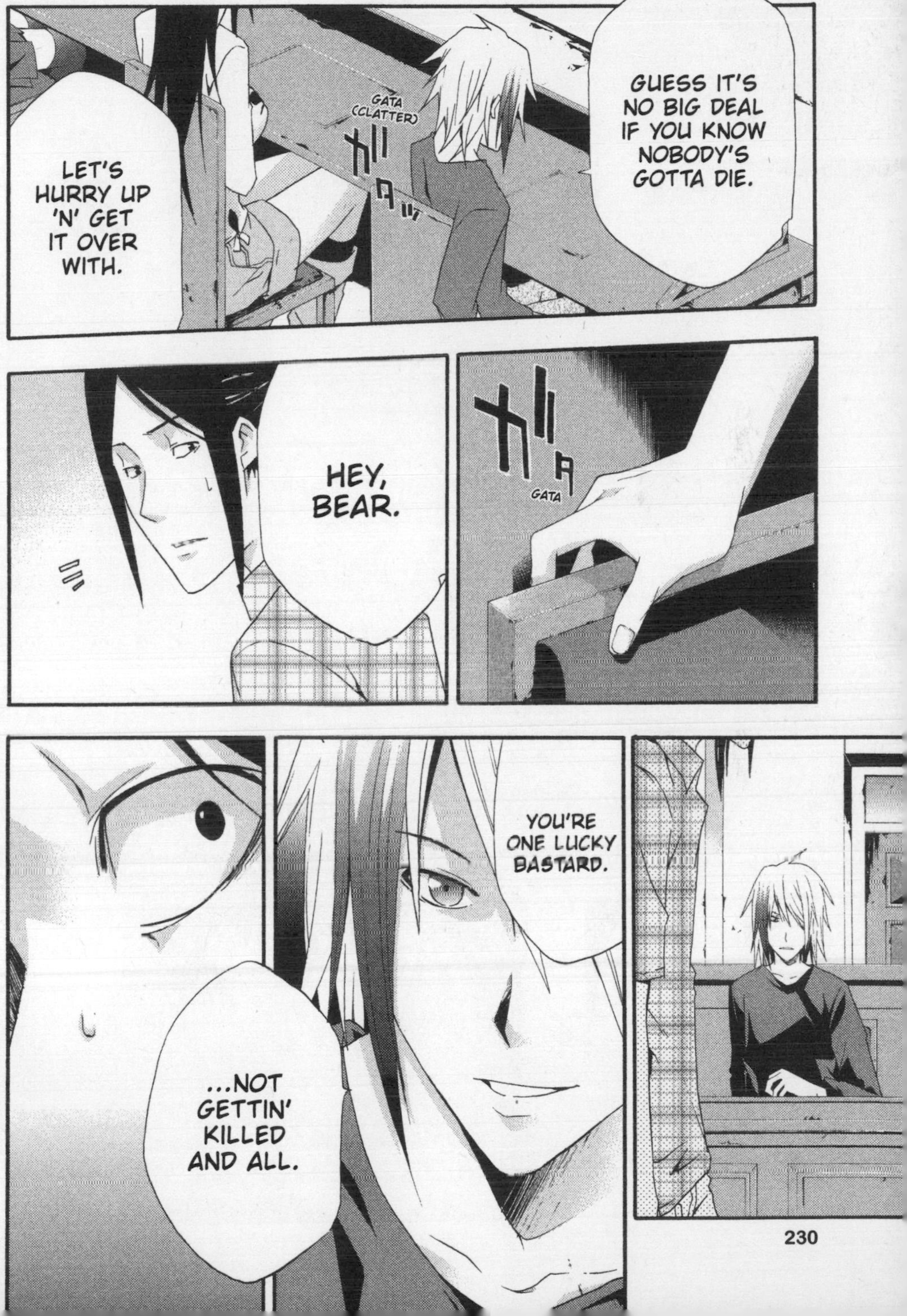
GUESS IT'S NO BIG DEAL IF YOU KNOW NOBODY'S GOTTA DIE.
GATA (CLATTER)
ガタッ
LET'S HURRY UP 'N' GET IT OVER WITH.
ガタ
GATA
HEY, BEAR.
YOU'RE ONE LUCKY BASTARD.
...NOT GETTIN' KILLED AND ALL.

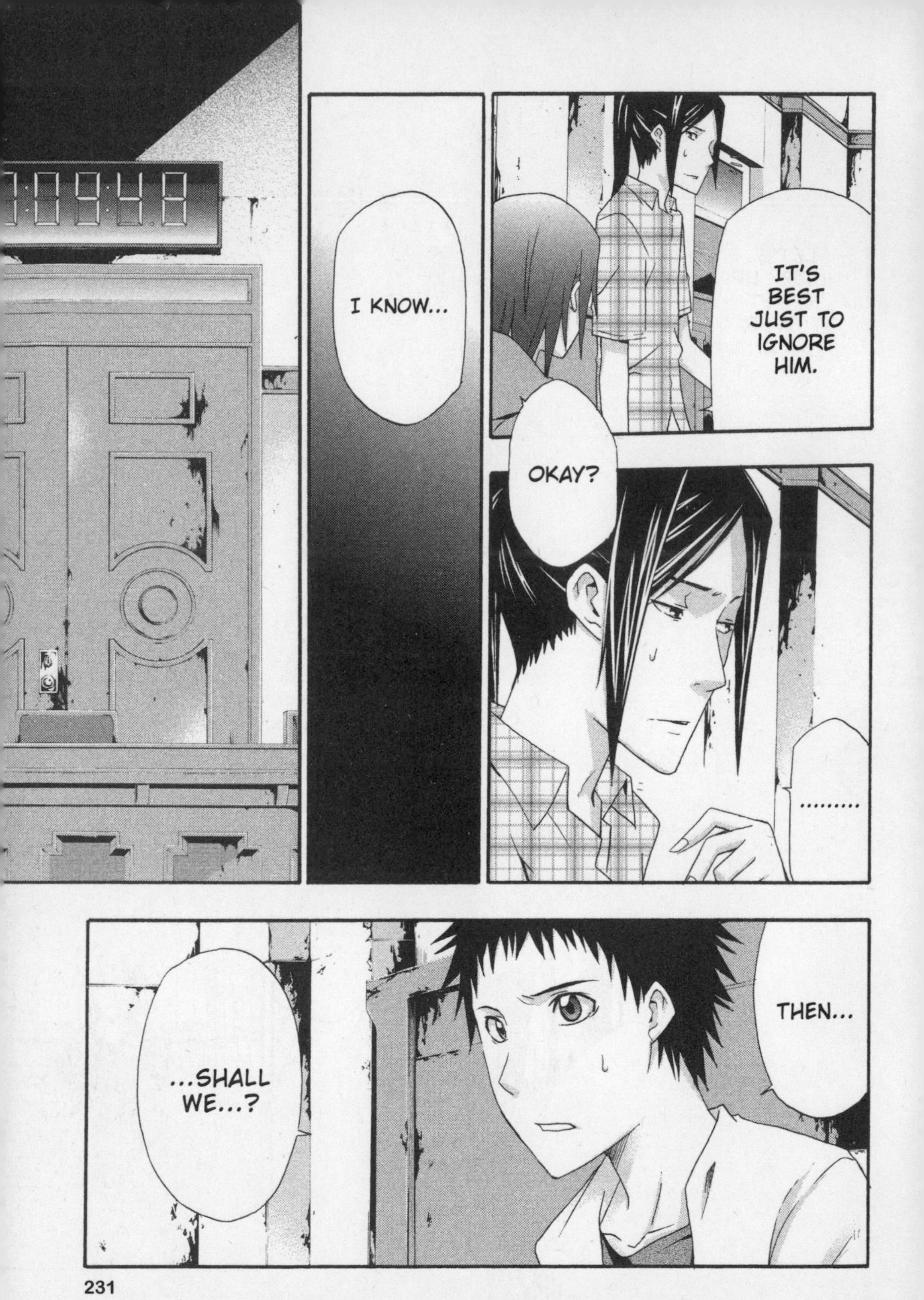
IT'S BEST JUST TO IGNORE HIM.
OKAY?
....
I KNOW...
THEN...
...SHALL WE...?

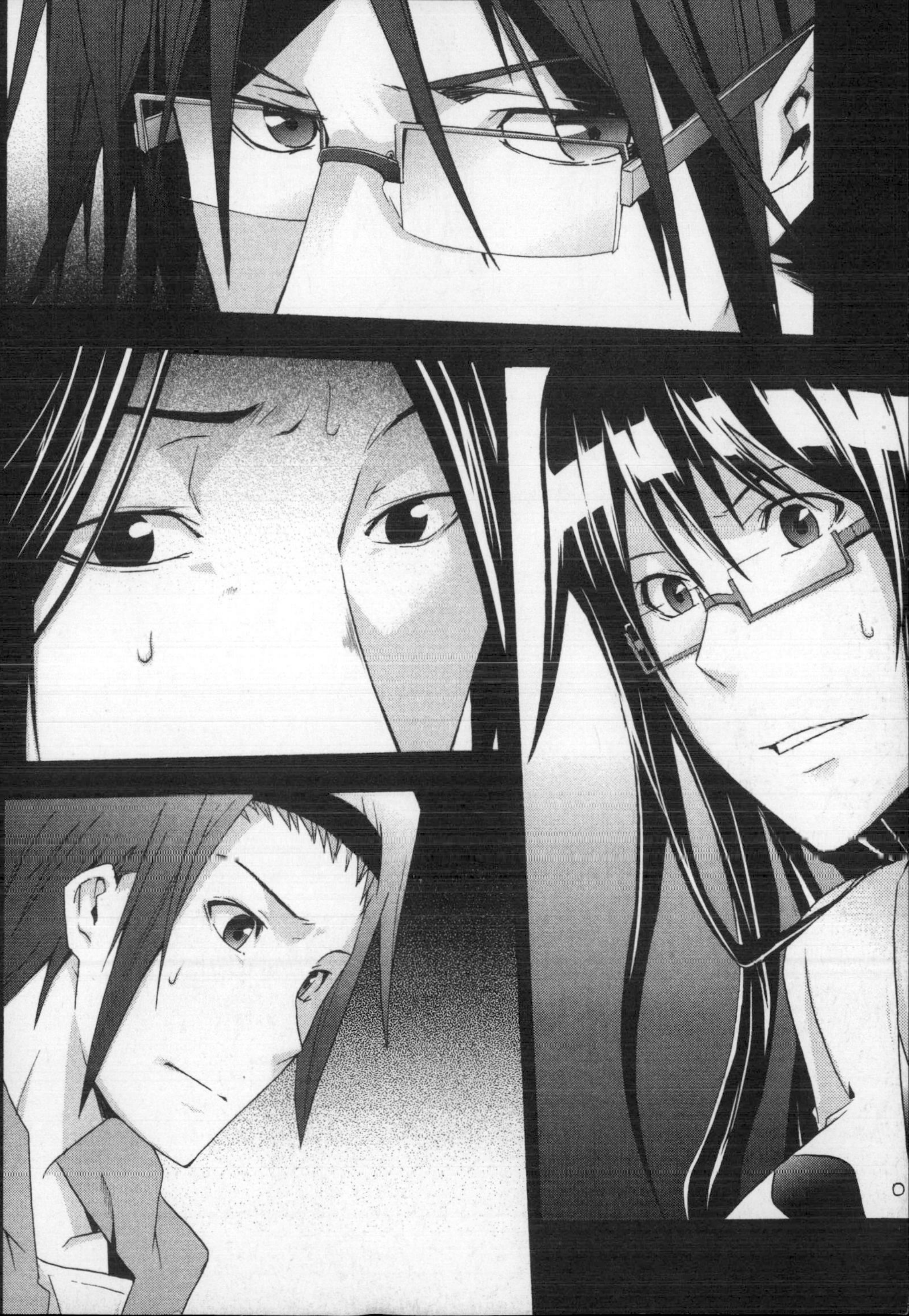

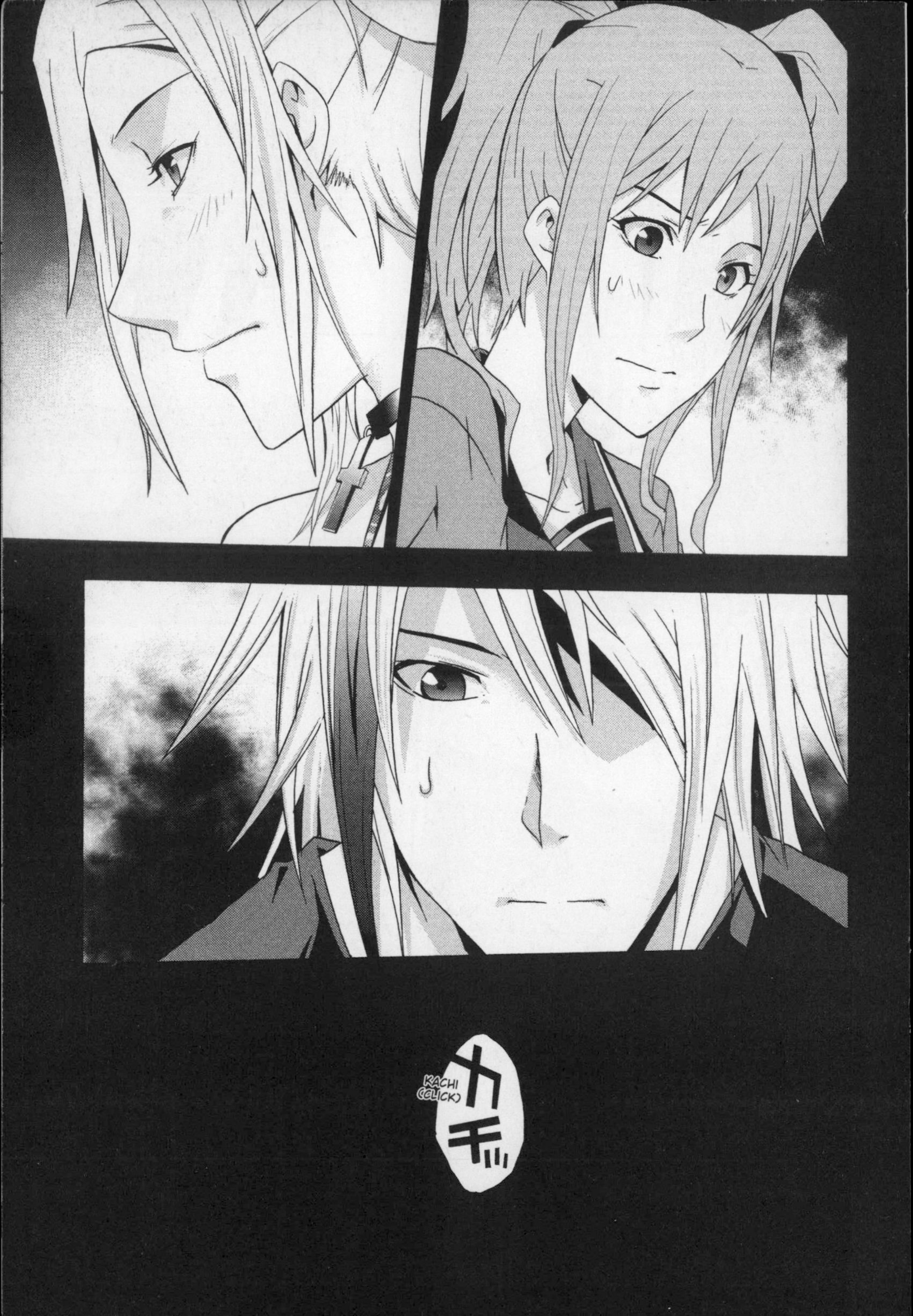
カチッ
KACHI (CLICK)

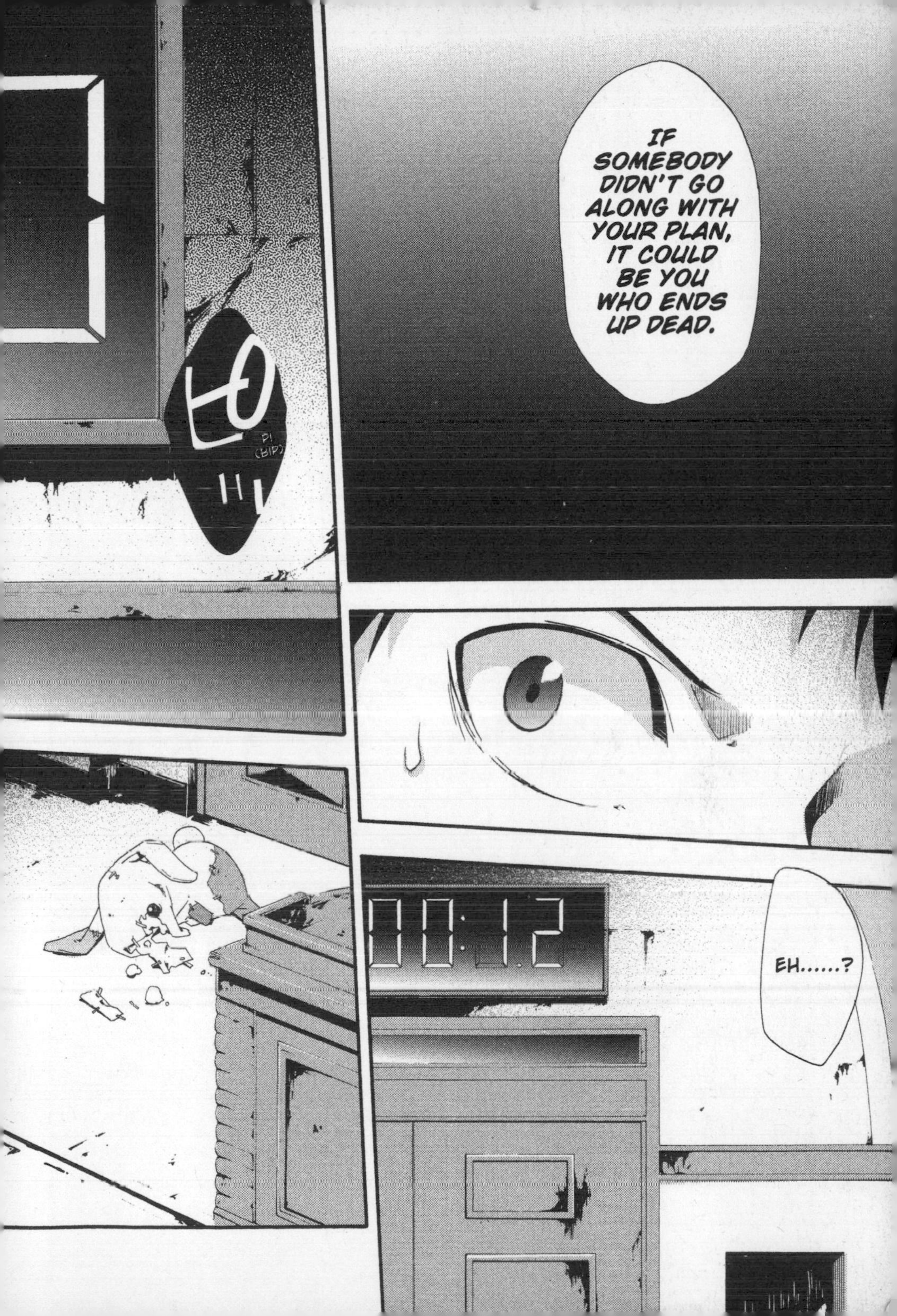
IF SOMEBODY DIDN'T GO ALONG WITH YOUR PLAN, IT COULD BE YOU WHO ENDS UP DEAD.
PI (BIP)
00:12
EH......?

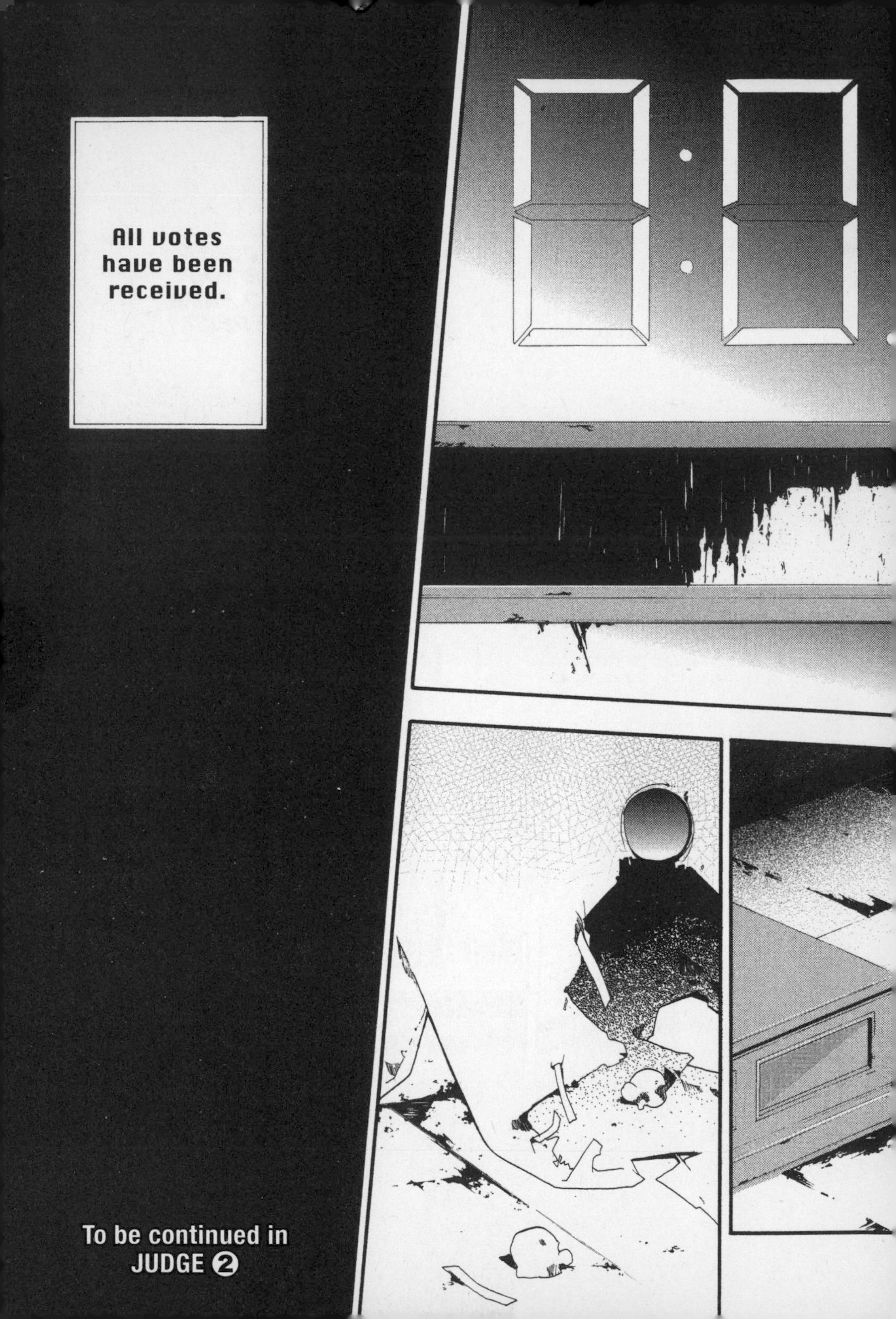
All votes have been received.
To be continued in JUDGE 2

STAFF

[MANGA]

TONOGAI

NOMURA

OIKAWA

TAKAHASHI

[THANKS]

IZUMI

MIZOE

NAGASAWA

SHINOMIYA

[EDITOR]

NOZAKI

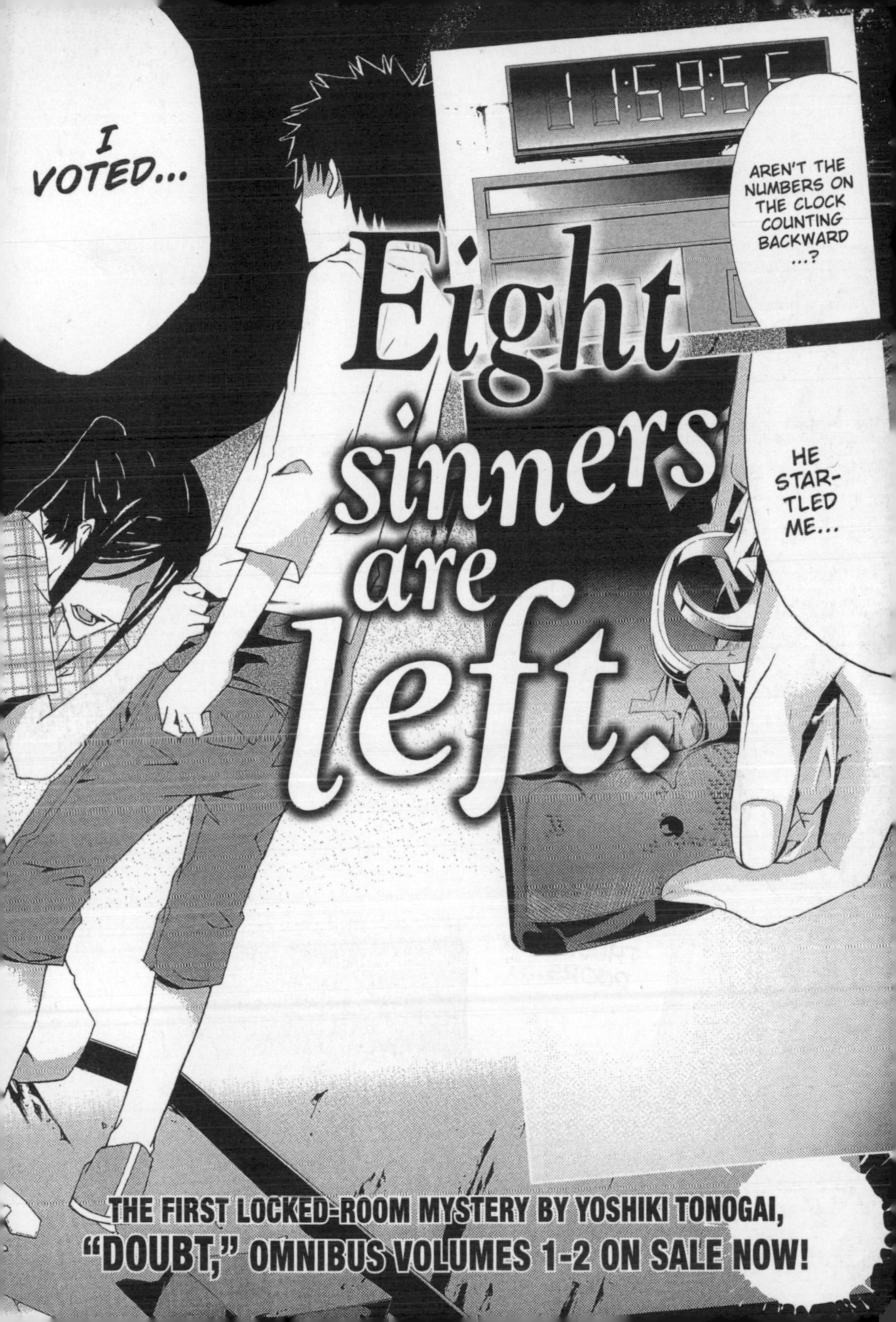

ARE'T THE NUMBERS ON THE CLOCK COUNTING BACKWARD ...?
I VOTED...
Eight sinners are left.
HE STAR-TLED ME...
THE FIRST LOCKED-ROOM MYSTERY BY YOSHIKI TONOGAI,
"DOUBT," OMNIBUS VOLUMES 1-2 ON SALE NOW!

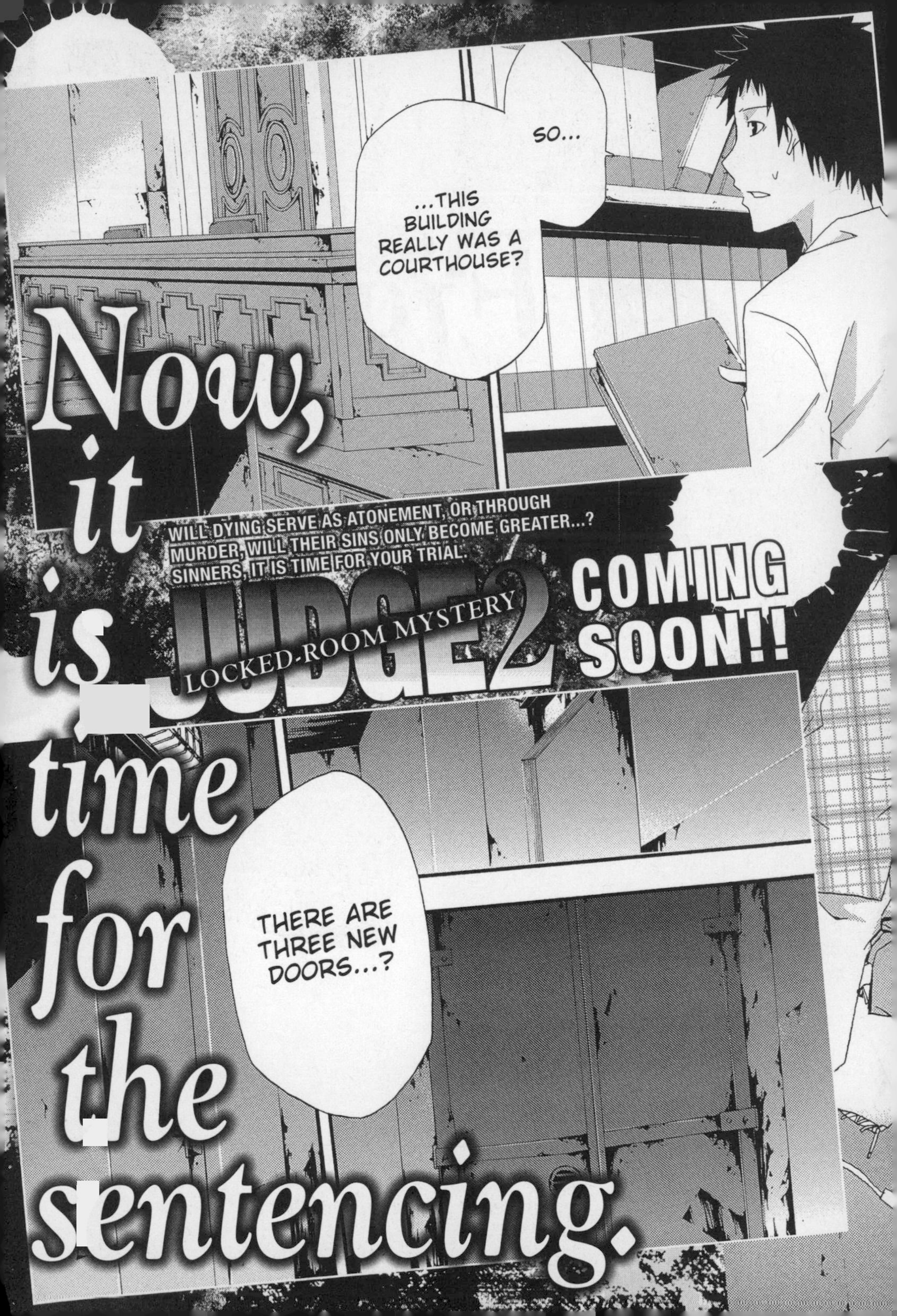
SO...
...THIS BUILDING REALLY WAS A COURTHOUSE?
Now, it is time for the sentencing.
WILL DYING SERVE AS ATONEMENT, OR THROUGH MURDER, WILL THEIR SINS ONLY BECOME GREATER...? SINNERS, IT IS TIME FOR YOUR TRIAL.
JUDGE 2
LOCKED-ROOM MYSTERY
COMING SOON!!
THERE ARE THREE NEW DOORS...?

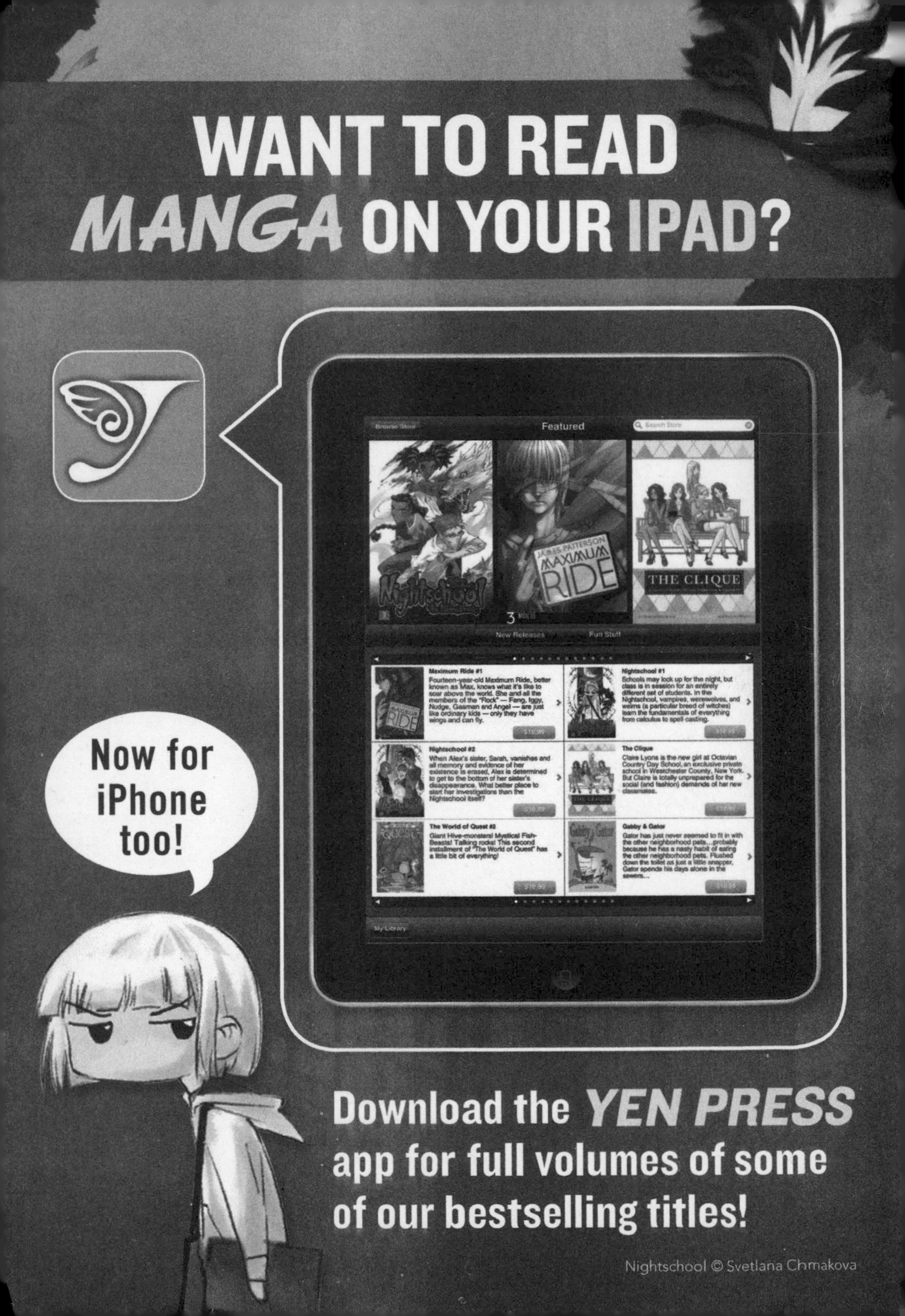
WANT TO READ
MANGA ON YOUR IPAD?
Featured
THE CLIQUE
Now for iPhone too!
Download the YEN PRESS
app for full volumes of some
of our bestselling titles!
Nightschool © Svetlana Chmakova

JUDGE 1

YOSHIKI TONOGAI

Translation and Lettering: Alexis Eckerman

JUDGE Vol. 1 © 2010 Yoshiki Tonogai / SQUARE ENIX CO., LTD. All rights reserved. First published in Japan in 2010 by SQUARE ENIX CO., LTD. English translation rights arranged with SQUARE ENIX CO., LTD. and Yen Press, LLC through Tuttle-Mori Agency, Inc.

English translation © 2013 by SQUARE ENIX CO., LTD.

Yen Press
1290 Avenue of the Americas
New York, NY 10104

Visit us at yenpress.com
facebook.com/yenpress
twitter.com/yenpress
yenpress.tumblr.com
instagram.com/yenpress

First Yen Press Edition: August 2013

Yen Press is an imprint of Yen Press, LLC.
The Yen Press name and logo are trademarks of Yen Press, LLC.

The publisher is not responsible for websites (or their content) that are not owned by the publisher.

ISBN: 978-0-316-25266-9

10 9

BVG

Printed in the United States of America